"I hope, pray, and believe that hundreds of years from now, theologians and church historians will point back to Dallas Willard's radiant light as a key inflection point in the Western church's renewal, the same way we do to Wesley and others today. Here's my opinion: Keas Keasler is an early adopter and pioneer, one of the first academics to realize not just the importance of Willard's work more broadly but to take him seriously as a theologian. No other contemporary thinker has imprinted more deeply on how I see Jesus, formation, and life in the Father's world than Willard. Keasler's book does more than synthesize Willard; it gives us a map for the next chapter in our story. It is a book worthy of your consideration. It's expertly written, adroitly argued, and profound in its clarity and conviction. I could not put it down."

John Mark Comer, author of *Practicing the Way*

"Through Dallas Willard, Keas Keasler has brought us a theologically sophisticated program to address the challenges facing Christian leaders tempted by the craving for personal power or the lure of Christian nationalism. Keasler offers Willard's framing of the Christian life as co-reigning with Christ to enable personal Christoformation through friendship with the naked Christ, leading to deep character transformation. It will strengthen the witness of the church."

Ellen T. Charry, professor emerita of theology at Princeton Theological Seminary

"This book is a tour de force. Not only will it put its author on the map as being one of the leading interpreters of the tradition of Dallas Willard, but it will also have the splendid consequences of applying Willard's thought to the realm of missiology. Though academic, this volume has so many practical implications for the church that it is difficult to fully appreciate it. Keas Keasler has shown us what Willard's thought looks like on the ground of the mission of God in the world today. Simply delightful."

A. J. Swoboda, associate professor of Bible and theology at Bushnell University and author of *A Teachable Spirit*

"We live in a time when Christians are trying to understand afresh what Christian mission involves. Keas Keasler's book is incredibly timely in providing a theological vision of formational-missional discipleship to Jesus that constructively draws on the work of Dallas Willard. In contrast with many, Willard taught that the church is not for mission in the world. Rather, the church is for training disciples of Jesus, and disciples of Jesus incarnate God's mission in the world. There is no other book that draws this point out and drives it home better than *Kingdom Apprenticeship*. This book is a breath of fresh air for anyone looking to be an effective witness in the world today."

Steve L. Porter, senior research fellow and executive director of the Martin Institute for Christianity and Culture and the Dallas Willard Research Center at Westmont College

"This winsomely written and impeccably researched book is for all who care about what it means to live the Christian life. Combing through unpublished papers, manuscripts, and letters, and engaging with Dallas Willard's philosophical works alongside his more popular writings, this book offers the most nuanced and comprehensive view of Willard's formational theology yet published, helping us see even more fully the invaluable contribution Willard has made to the understanding and practice of Christian formation. Through the lens of Willard's work, it invites us to put to rest false dichotomies between discipleship and mission to consider how God forms us into Christlikeness so that we can embody our calling as Christians in this world. In the midst of today's crisis in Christian formation, this book could not be more timely or important."

Kristen Deede Johnson, principal and Helliwell Professor of Theology, Ministry, and Culture at Wycliffe College at the University of Toronto

"A large part of the enduring appeal of Dallas Willard's work is its combination of systematicity and its recurring appeal to experientially discoverable features, both essential and contingent, of human persons and our condition. In this powerfully written work, informed by exhaustive research of Willard's vast body of written and recorded material, Keas Keasler skillfully and critically guides us through the core commitments and the fine details of Willard's theology of discipleship and its connections with his distinctive brand of realist phenomenological personalism. It is a monumental contribution to the growing body of literature on Willard's theological and philosophical work."

Walter Hopp, department chair and professor of philosophy at Boston University

"Keas Keasler's carefully researched work is the first comprehensive study of Dallas Willard's theology of the Christian life. Keasler's analyses are thorough and nuanced, his conclusions guarded and judicious. For anyone looking for a reliable guide to Willard's thought, this is a book I highly recommend."

Simon Chan, former professor of systematic theology at Trinity Theological College in Singapore and author of *Spiritual Theology*

"A broken and struggling evangelical church needs the wisdom of Dallas Willard, and Keas Keasler brings it for a new generation, in all its beauty and challenge."

Beth Felker Jones, professor of theology at Northern Seminary and author of *Practicing Christian Doctrine*

"Keas Keasler has accomplished a rare feat. For Dallas Willard fans, he has provided years of scholarship, artfully expressing Willard's constructive theology of the kingdom and its missional extension with clarity and precision. If you are hungry to take a deeper dive into Willard's heart and mind and come away with hope and insight, then here's your opportunity. I am delighted to recommend this important work to all who believe in Christlike change."

Keith J. Matthews, professor emeritus of Christian formation and leadership at Azusa Pacific University

"Organized thematically, Keas Keasler's synoptic study of Dallas Willard's teaching helpfully elucidates in detail Willard's prophetic insistence that real spiritual knowledge and real spiritual transformation is not only possible but necessary for the Christian who follows Jesus Christ and apprentices to him. More than this, however, Keasler highlights the sometimes overlooked insight in Willard that mission (vocation) and formation (character) are inseparable. This carefully researched book helpfully lays to rest the false idea that spirituality can ever be a matter of merely private piety."

Bruce Hindmarsh, James M. Houston Professor of Spiritual Theology and professor of the history of Christianity at Regent College

"Whether you're inquiring about Dallas Willard's work or already riveted by it, Keas Keasler's investigation of it is an insightful guide and companion. He explains not only what he has discerned as Willard's eight themes of spiritual formation, but also puts in plain words how these themes connect with our own transformation and that of the church."

Jan Johnson, coauthor with Dallas Willard of *Renovation of the Heart in Daily Practice* and *Study Guide to the Divine Conspiracy*

KINGDOM
APPRENTICESHIP

KINGDOM APPRENTICESHIP

Dallas Willard's Formational Theology and Missional Vision

KEAS KEASLER

An imprint of InterVarsity Press
Downers Grove, Illinois

InterVarsity Press
P.O. Box 1400 | Downers Grove, IL 60515-1426
ivpress.com | email@ivpress.com

©2026 by David Johnston Keasler

All rights reserved. No part of this book may be reproduced in any form without written permission from InterVarsity Press.

No part of this book may be used in any manner for purposes of training artificial intelligence technologies without prior written authorization. The rights holder expressly reserves all rights related to the reproduction and extraction of this work for the purposes of text and data mining (TDM).

InterVarsity Press® is the publishing division of InterVarsity Christian Fellowship/USA®. For more information, visit intervarsity.org.

All Scripture quotations, unless otherwise indicated, are taken from The Holy Bible, New International Version®, NIV®. Copyright © 1973, 1978, 1984, 2011 by Biblica, Inc.™ Used by permission of Zondervan. All rights reserved worldwide. www.zondervan.com. The "NIV" and "New International Version" are trademarks registered in the United States Patent and Trademark Office by Biblica, Inc.™

The publisher cannot verify the accuracy or functionality of website URLs used in this book beyond the date of publication.

Cover design: Gearbox with Faceout Studio
Interior design: Daniel van Loon
Image: Cover photo by Greg Schneider. Photo was taken at Dallas Willard's office at the University of Southern California, Los Angeles, on April 22, 2005.
Back cover author photo by Jenny Myers.

ISBN 978-1-5140-1284-0 (print) | ISBN 978-1-5140-1285-7 (digital)

Printed in the United States of America ∞

Library of Congress Cataloging-in-Publication Data
Names: Keasler, Keas author
Title: Kingdom apprenticeship : Dallas Willard's formational theology and missional vision / Keas Keasler.
Description: Downers Grove, IL : IVP Academic, [2026] | Includes bibliographical references and index.
Identifiers: LCCN 2025041642 (print) | LCCN 2025041643 (ebook) | ISBN 9781514012840 paperback | ISBN 9781514012857 ebook
Subjects: LCSH: Willard, Dallas, 1935-2013 | Spiritual formation
Classification: LCC BX4827.W47 K43 2026 (print) | LCC BX4827.W47 (ebook)
LC record available at https://lccn.loc.gov/2025041642
LC ebook record available at https://lccn.loc.gov/2025041643

Syd Keasler
Kathy Keasler
Darrell L. Guder
C. W. Williams
Johnny M. Williams

"They were the heroes of old, men of renown."

CONTENTS

INTRODUCTION

  1 Rediscovering Willard   *1*

  2 A Theologian of the Christian Life   *14*

PART 1: THE LARGER FRAMEWORK AND FOUNDATION OF FORMATION

  3 Training for Reigning   *47*

  4 Intelligent Mysticism   *78*

PART 2: THEOLOGY OF FORMATION PROPER

  5 The Heart of the Human Problem   *107*

  6 The Metaphysics of Grace   *140*

  7 Heuristics for Spiritual Transformation   *161*

PART 3: THE CONSEQUENCES OF FORMATION

  8 Rectification of the Social Order   *189*

  9 The Church as a Divine Sociality and School of Life   *227*

  10 Restoring Evangelism (and the Gospel) Through Discipleship   *247*

CONCLUSION

  11 Exercise unto Godliness . . . and Godlikeness   *267*

Acknowledgments   *285*

Bibliography of Works by Dallas Willard   *288*

Bibliography of Other Works   *299*

General Index   *306*

Scripture Index   *310*

ONE

REDISCOVERING WILLARD

I HAVE FOUR MAJOR claims about Dallas Willard, which gave rise to this book. First, he should be understood as a theologian of the Christian life, putting him in good company with ancient theologians but in a minority among contemporaries. Although a remarkable thinker and competent in multiple domains of knowledge, in the final analysis Willard is essentially practice-oriented rather than theory-oriented. Yet that is not to say his work belongs solely in the field of "practical theology," as it is understood today. Rather, it is to say that he is first and foremost interested in how we live as Christians, and he uses all theoretical resources available to get to this question—which means he does not belong with the systematicians either. Modern theology has increasingly become an intellectual exercise confined to academic institutions, detached from the practical realities of life. Though promising efforts to integrate theology and real living exist, they remain exceptions rather than the rule. In much of the academy, theology is treated primarily as an object of study rather than a way of life. But for Willard, all theology should be *clinical* theology, aimed at helping people flourish by knowing and growing in Christ. In this, he has much in common with the patristics and other "doctors" of the church who viewed theology as therapeutic and as medicine for the soul.

Second, Willard's theory of spiritual formation represents a lifetime of thinking deeply on the theological and phenomenological dynamics of personal transformation, with much to offer today. It deserves careful study and analysis, as well as comparison with the work of other theologians to identify what is unique and significant about his approach. There is a critical need for the American church to devote more attention to the doctrine of sanctification, especially given the crisis of character currently experienced in the church and society. Willard's formational theology can greatly contribute to this task.

Third, Willard's approach to formation reflects a profound understanding of the relationship between divine grace and human action that is participatory yet not Pelagian.[1] The extreme anxiety over works righteousness shared by many modern Protestant thinkers has significantly contributed to the development of a reductionistic soteriology and corresponding intellectualist approach to spirituality prevalent in Western Christianity. Willard's paradigm of formation, with its interplay of heart and habits, virtue and action, and emphasis on active apprenticeship to Jesus, serves as an important corrective. Moreover, this relationship between grace and human effort extends to his understanding of vocation and ministry. Participation in God's divine conspiracy—his master plan to overcome evil with goodness—is surely an effort, but it is an effort that opens us to God's grace. It is not about merit but rather a spiritual discipline of increasing dependence on God.

Fourth, Willard's theory of formation is inherently missional—an aspect that has not been recognized or appreciated even by those who most admire his work. By *missional*, I mean participation in the triune God's ongoing work to redeem and renew the world. Much of the spiritual formation literature within Protestantism over the past fifty years has lacked a missional framework for spirituality and sanctification. Considering Willard was a major figure in what has come to be known as the spiritual formation movement, it may come as a surprise to learn there is a missional thread that runs throughout his

---

[1]Pelagianism is the belief that salvation or moral transformation can be achieved without God's enabling grace.

theory. He sees spiritual formation as part of God's mission but also as necessary for God's mission. Thus, when truly understood, Willard's formational theology is both a practical curriculum for Christlikeness and a crucial strategy for the church's mission.

DISCOVERING AND REDISCOVERING

This last claim was my initial impetus for researching Willard's work. But that came later in my story. First, let me describe how I discovered Willard—and then, years later, rediscovered him.

As a sophomore in college I was given a copy of Richard Foster's *The Celebration of Discipline*. The book did wonders for my faith, as it introduced me to a host of past luminaries and guided me into the practice of ancient spiritual disciplines. But another consequence was that it piqued my interest in this philosopher "Dr. Dallas Willard," whom Foster describes in his introduction.[2] So the next time I was at the bookstore, I went looking for a book by Willard and found *The Spirit of the Disciplines*. The year was 2002, and looking back on my copy now, I see that I initially only made it through a couple of chapters before skipping to one near the end that surveys the classical spiritual disciplines. (The dead giveaway is the pink highlighter, a relic from an era when I thought marking up a book meant attacking it with neon.) If I'm being perfectly honest, most of the book went over my head, which is why I didn't read it cover to cover. I wasn't yet ready for all Willard had to offer. At some point, after hearing much ado about Willard's *The Divine Conspiracy*, I added it to my library as well, but it remained unread—a grievous but all-too-common sin of many book lovers.

Fast-forward a decade to when I was pastoring a small church in Miami. A spiritual rhythm of mine then and still now is to go every few months on what I call a "desert day," an entire day outside my zip

---

[2]Luckily for me, my copy of *Celebration of Discipline* was the 20th anniversary edition (1998), which includes a new introduction wherein Foster explicitly names Willard as a major influence for the book.

code for prayer, reading Scripture, and simply being in the presence of God. Now, you should know that I love theology—which will become apparent in this book—and I can happily disappear down a rabbit hole of doctrine with the best of them. But desert days are for knowing God, not merely knowing about God (a vital distinction), so I often bring along a book that deepens my friendship with God or invites deeper attentiveness to his presence and voice. A friend had suggested Willard's book *Hearing God*, which I brought with me on my next desert day.

I did not expect to find such profundity in the book—and with a quietly winsome touch. Willard explained how divine knowing is possible, even in a skeptical and secular age such as ours, and he seamlessly wove—so it seemed to me—the biblical account of those who walked with God into practical guidance for us today. This motivated me to pull *Divine Conspiracy* off my shelf, which I quickly devoured—or, considering its weight, both literal and theological, as "quickly" as one can. I was amazed and quite moved by, among other things, Willard's commonsense Christology. He described Jesus as not only Lord but brilliant. Reading about how this first-century Palestinian Jew is the smartest person who has ever lived—about how Jesus is Master because he is Maestro—made me fall in love with Jesus all over again.

Soon I was working through Willard's *Renovation of the Heart*, struck by the clarity with which he describes human personhood and how, by God's grace, it might be transformed through what I've come to call kingdom apprenticeship—learning to live as a student of Jesus under the reign of God. Coming full circle, I now returned to *Spirit of the Disciplines*—but this time I was prepared for its depth. In these writings on spirituality, Willard clearly has scholarly chops. Yet he labors to translate his ideas for people in the pews, not theologians in the towers.

Somewhere along the way, I discovered his short essay "A Cup Running Over" in, of all places, a volume on preaching.[3] Dynamite comes in small packages, and I still return to this small gem—perhaps my single favorite piece by Willard—every six months or so for my own edification. That essay is a fitting example of how Willard's work has shaped me both personally and pastorally. Differentiating between the two is difficult. Furthermore, it is unnecessary—at least from Willard's perspective. A key conviction of his is that the most important thing we get out of life, far surpassing any work or leadership roles we might have, is the person we become. (This is also, he believes, the most important thing God gets out of our life.)

Now, as a pastor striving to form mature disciples engaged in God's work in the world, I constantly encountered a tension in the church between the inner and outer life, a tendency to favor either personal spiritual growth or missional activity at the expense of the other. Should we focus on contemplative practices that foster connection with God and growth in Christlikeness or on missional living that extends God's love and invitation to others? For the former, I read literature from the spiritual formation movement; for the latter, I explored works by those associated with missional Christianity. But there was little to no overlap between the two—a gap I observed not only in our local congregation but also more broadly in the American church.

Through reading Willard, however, I sensed that he somehow bridged this divide. Although at the time I did not yet fully comprehend how this was worked out in his theology, I found a companion in my desire to combine discipleship and spiritual formation with vocation and missional consciousness.

---

[3]Dallas Willard, "A Cup Running Over," in *The Art and Craft of Biblical Preaching*, ed. Haddon Robinson and Craig Brian Larson (Zondervan, 2005), 71-73.

THE JOURNEY BEHIND THIS BOOK

In 2016 I became, quite unexpectedly, a full-time theology professor. Even though I did not seek out this change (my journey to the academy was quite unorthodox), I had for some time felt called to both pastoral and academic work. Yet transitioning from the church to the classroom did not diminish my engagement with Willard's work. In fact, it only increased it, as I found a companion once again—this time in terms of a pastor becoming a professor, a path Willard took in the 1960s. As a newly minted professor, I immersed myself in his reflections on the current state of higher education, the disappearance of moral knowledge, the need for a renewal of the Christian mind, and the philosophical texture underneath his spiritual writings, as well as the vision behind his calling as both a university teacher and a minister of the gospel—a vocational understanding that continues to inform my own.

As mentioned, when I was pastoring I had an intuitive sense that Willard somehow resolved the tension between spiritual formation and missional living. Following that hunch, I embarked on a research project in which I systematically worked through his entire body of work. In the process, I came to see just how valuable his formational theology is for the church today. His account of spiritual growth in Christlikeness is not only cohesive and comprehensive but also permeated with missionary logic. The aim of God in human history, says Willard, is the formation of an all-inclusive community of loving persons who will one day share in God's governance of the cosmos. Our present life, then, is the training ground for becoming the kind of people—characterized above all by *agapē* love—whom God can entrust with that responsibility. This is the missional vision that sits firmly behind his formational theology.

The intimate connection between formation and mission may have been what first drew me to engage more deeply with Willard, but once the keg was tapped, a continuous flow of insights from his thought followed. For instance, his metaphysic of grace is unlike anything I had encountered in my study of modern theology. This metaphysic, however, is predicated on a profound doctrine of God, which seamlessly connects to a relational epistemology that makes intimate knowing of God possible—a knowing that is inherently transformative. Further, Willard's ecclesiology and theory of societal transformation, both largely unexplored until now, proved more robust than I had imagined. They emerge naturally from his understanding of personal transformation and align closely with his vision of salvation history and God's ultimate purposes for humanity.

The book you are holding represents seven years of research. To truly comprehend Willard's thought, I read everything he published in theology and spirituality and all his major philosophical writings, listened to hundreds of his recorded lectures and sermons, and spent multiple weeks in the basement of Westmont College's library studying his unpublished papers and notes.[4] I want to take you on a journey through what I discovered. That may sound like an odd way to introduce a scholarly book of theology, but this truly is a journey. It traverses his philosophical and churchly concerns, pinpoints the areas he identified as most crucial for human transformation in the Spirit, reveals the biblical and theological underpinnings of his paradigm, and brings together those findings to reflect on the relevance of his approach to formation for the church today.

Along the way, I also explore potential weaknesses in his formation theory and how they might be overcome. For Willard to be engaged

---

[4]I reference many of these unpublished works throughout this study, all of which are available in the Dallas Willard Collection at Westmont College, Santa Barbara, California. In footnotes, I provide abbreviated citations (typically title and date); full details are listed in the bibliography. A note about how audio and video recordings of Willard are cited in this study: Because the full bibliographic information of these recordings is usually much lengthier than that of books or articles, in footnotes I provide the recording's title, date, and format (MP3 or video) the first time it is cited in each chapter. I also provide a time mark when quoting or referencing a particular discussion in a talk. In the rare case that multiple talks have the same title, I provide the talk's date each time it is cited. Full details of the recordings are provided in the bibliography.

constructively by theologians moving forward, the study of his thought must also include critical analysis. That said, I will go ahead and lay my cards on the table. Although certain areas of his model may need further development, I believe you will find that Willard's formational theology presents a sophisticated account of personal transformation in the Spirit with a rather sharp missional edge, one that is incredibly important in our cultural moment. And it is a theology that, as my own story shows, warms the heart while informing the mind.[5]

WHAT WE'RE TALKING ABOUT

Since this is a study of Willard's theology of spiritual formation, it is helpful to explain as briefly as possible what we are talking about when we talk about spiritual formation in Christ—at least in this book. Let me first delineate between a Christian understanding of spirituality and spiritual formation, since the two are intimately connected but different in critical ways. While Christian spirituality has a broad designation, encompassing all of one's relationship with the triune God, *Christian spiritual formation* is a more refined term referring to a particular dynamic within Christian spirituality.[6] Willard describes it as "the Spirit-driven process of forming the inner world

---

[5] I say this at the risk of sounding sentimental. But it is a risk worth taking, since the gap between serious theological inquiry and heartfelt adoration of God is one more divide I hope to bridge—as did Willard. In this, he certainly is not alone. For instance, Jonathan Edwards argued that a truth is not fully known until one experiences the affections appropriate for such truth, while John Wesley believed Christian scholarship must seek not only *light* but also *heat* if it is to be true to its design.

[6] See Tom Schwanda, "Formation, Spiritual," in *Dictionary of Christian Spirituality*, ed. Glen G. Scorgie (Zondervan, 2011), 452. Historically, the language of *spiritual formation* was primarily used in the Roman Catholic tradition, where it referred to one of the four core areas of training for priests prior to ordination, alongside human, intellectual, and pastoral formation. Protestant seminaries later adopted this language to emphasize character development and the nurturing of spiritual and emotional life, in addition to theological education. Only in recent times has the term come to be widely understood as an essential aspect of maturing in the Christian life, applicable to all believers, rather than merely a teaching tool for preparing individuals for church ministry. As a case in point, "spiritual formation" does not appear as an entry in the original *Westminster Dictionary of Christian Spirituality* (1983) but was added in the *New Westminster Dictionary of Christian Spirituality* (2005).

of the human self in such a way that it becomes like the inner being of Christ himself."[7]

Of course, spiritual formation is hardly exclusive to Christians. As spiritual beings, our interiority is continually being shaped in one direction or another, whether we are intentional about it or even aware of it.[8] Yet Christian spiritual formation is laser-focused on the process of *becoming like the person of Christ*—which requires nothing less than transformation of the human spirit. As a domain of theological reflection, it includes all attempts, means, instructions, and disciplines intended to foster spiritual growth and further Christian maturity. So, while Christian spirituality is a broader subject dealing with our relationship with God in general, it embraces Christian spiritual formation, with its sharp focus on character transformation in Christlikeness, as a cornerstone of its vision.[9]

Christian spiritual formation is thus sometimes described as character transformation. *Character* has been defined in a variety of ways in theological-ethical literature, but it generally refers to the settled dispositions that a person possesses or, perhaps more accurately, is possessed by, since they largely dictate a person's choices and behaviors. For Willard, "spiritual formation is character formation" since, in the Christian tradition, "it is the process of establishing the character of Christ in the person."[10] Yet some scholars distinguish between spiritual, characterological, and moral formation while maintaining that these different dimensions of growth are

---

[7]Dallas Willard, *Renovation of the Heart: Putting On the Character of Christ* (NavPress, 2002), 22. Willard was fond of italics, but to streamline the reading and avoid unintended overemphasis, I occasionally omit them. Any italics that remain are his, and those I have added are noted accordingly.

[8]Adrian van Kaam insists that all human formation is spiritual formation since the spiritual dimension, as a gift from God, is the unique, defining characteristic of being human. See van Kaam, *Fundamental Formation* (Crossroad, 1989), 13-14, 243.

[9]See Evan B. Howard, *The Brazos Introduction to Christian Spirituality* (Brazos, 2008), 23-24.

[10]Dallas Willard, interview by Agnieszka Tennant, "The Making of the Christian: Richard J. Foster and Dallas Willard on the Difference Between Discipleship and Spiritual Formation," *Christianity Today* 49, no. 10 (2005): 42.

interconnected.[11] While acknowledging the usefulness of making these conceptual distinctions when describing the comprehensive and diverse nature of Christian spiritual formation, in this book a singular and synthetic understanding of spiritual formation is assumed that encompasses all three notions of formation. Thus, throughout this study it is taken for granted that genuine spiritual change also brings about genuine character and moral change, and Christian spiritual formation is concerned with all of these changes.

It is also important to delineate between Christian spiritual formation and *discipleship*, another set of interrelated terms. Historically, both refer to the process of becoming conformed to Christ's image through obedience to Jesus and imitating his way of life, by means of being with him and learning under his care and direction. In modern usage, *Christian spiritual formation* commonly designates the academic study of this process, whereas *discipleship* signifies the actual, on-the-ground practice of it. For the purposes of this study, then, discipleship will be defined simply as the act of following Jesus by obeying his teachings and patterning one's life after him. Christian spiritual formation explains what happens to a person's character through discipleship, the process one undergoes when apprenticing oneself to Jesus. Discipleship is a *status* of relational activity, while spiritual formation is the *process* experienced in that status.[12]

In the spiritual formation literature, the terminology *apprenticeship to Jesus* is often used interchangeably with *discipleship to Jesus*, largely due to Willard's influence. Indeed, *apprentice* is a primary term for Willard, and in *Renovation of the Heart* alone the word appears

---

[11] Steven L. Porter et al., "Measuring the Spiritual, Character, and Moral Formation of Seminarians: In Search of a Meta-Theory of Spiritual Change," *Journal of Spiritual Formation & Soul Care* 12, no. 1 (2019): 5-24. See also Joanna Collicutt, *The Psychology of Christian Character Formation* (SCM Press, 2014), 3-42.

[12] Dallas Willard, "Christian Discipleship and the Mission to the World: Churches and World Leadership" (January 8, 2010), video, 40:45. See also Willard, "Spiritual Formation as a Natural Part of Salvation," in *Life in the Spirit: Spiritual Formation in Theological Perspective*, ed. Jeffrey P. Greenman and George Kalantzis (IVP Academic, 2010), 54, 58.

fifty-nine times, though he is not the first to emphasize the medieval apprentice model for understanding the disciple-rabbi relationship Jesus had with the Twelve.[13]

Lastly, a word should be said about the correlation between Christian spiritual formation and *sanctification*, the doctrine of growth in Christian holiness. Although there are subtle conceptual nuances between the two terms, some of which will surface later in my treatment of Willard's theology, they have the same fundamental referent since we are talking about *Christian* spiritual formation. In this book, then, the terms are treated as synonymous. One important difference, though, which I have mentioned, is that spiritual formation per se is not uniquely Christian; it is a human phenomenon. Regardless of a person's faith or lack thereof, spiritual formation is always taking place. Sanctification, by contrast, more narrowly refers to the nature of spiritual growth in a Christian's life from the time of regeneration until the time of glorification.[14] The language of Christian spiritual formation thus reminds us this is one particular direction in which the human spirit can be formed—and if not in this direction, it will certainly be formed in another direction. There are many lords and spirits and powers, after all. Sanctification simply does not convey this same universal scope; however, it bears repeating that Christian spiritual formation and sanctification refer to the same reality but from different vantage points. Therefore, to stress the ubiquitous experience of spiritual formation—and because I am

---

[13]For an earlier example, see Aaron Milavec, *To Empower as Jesus Did: Acquiring Spiritual Power Through Apprenticeship* (Edwin Mellen, 1982). Willard also uses the more common nomenclature of *disciple* but prefers *apprentice* since (in his view) the contemporary meaning of *disciple* often denotes merely an assent to particular doctrines about Jesus—roughly the equivalent of *believer*—rather than an intentional and persistent learning to live like Jesus through being with Jesus. As he explains, "I like the word *apprentice* because of the connotation of *applied knowledge*. So we have apprentices in practical fields because we all know that it's one thing to have it in your head and another thing to have it in your hands." Dallas Willard, "The Good Life and the Good Person Made Real by Jesus: Rethinking the 'Sermon on the Mount'" (October 10, 2008), MP3, 20:45.

[14]Steven L. Porter, "On the Renewal of Interest in the Doctrine of Sanctification: A Methodological Reminder," *Journal of the Evangelical Theological Society* 45, no. 3 (2002): 416.

chiefly concerned with its Christian expression—*spiritual formation* and *formation* in this book imply Christian spiritual formation, unless otherwise specified.

In summary, *spirituality* refers to how a person or community relates to and interacts with transcendent reality. For Christians, this transcendent reality is understood as the triune God. *Spiritual formation*, a narrower term, pertains to how a person's or community's spiritual core (inner life) and character are being shaped. And *Christian spiritual formation* pertains to how this spiritual core and character are being shaped in the image of Christ, by the power of the Spirit, for the glory of God, which takes place through discipleship to Jesus.

CHARTING THE COURSE

Since I have described this book as a journey, allow me to guide you through what lies ahead. To begin, I provide a brief biographical sketch of Willard (chap. 2) to shed light on the unique shape of his vocation, the distinctive character of his theological writings, and his impact on the church. Given the rather unusual source materials we have at our disposal for researching his thought, I also describe and categorize his corpus to help the reader comprehend its diverse parts.

The heart of this book (chaps. 3–10) delves into the core themes within Willard's formational theology and missional vision. More specifically, I critically examine eight themes of his theory of spiritual formation, teasing out its latent missional logic. These themes are not isolated but interwoven, reflecting the holistic nature of his thought and its implications for personal transformation and the church's mission; they are thus clustered together in three parts.

Part one lays the groundwork with the teleological and epistemic convictions that anchor Willard's theory. Central to his approach, and running throughout, is the eschatological concept of training for reigning (chap. 3), which suggests the ultimate purpose of Christian formation. From there, we turn to the deeply relational and epistemic foundations of his theory (chap. 4), which might be described as "intelligent mysticism."

Part two focuses on Willard's view of formation proper—the theological and phenomenological dynamics at the core of spiritual transformation. We open with his theological anthropology (chap. 5) and its significance for his approach to formation. This sets the stage for us to explore the dynamic relation between God's sovereign work and the disciple's obedient participation in the sanctifying process (chap. 6)—a theologically complex area where Willard's insights shine. Finally, we consider the pedagogical tools and strategies he developed to help people actively engage in this transformative process (chap. 7).

Part three addresses the broader consequences of spiritual formation, including Willard's views on the direction and flow of social redemption (chap. 8), the nature and calling of the church (chap. 9), and the logic of evangelism when recast as an invitation to active discipleship (chap. 10).

This journey concludes (in chap. 11) with reflections on how Willard's formational theology speaks with urgency and clarity to the challenges facing the church in our cultural moment. By the end, I hope you will see not only the depth of his insights but also the transformative potential they hold for both individuals and communities seeking to follow Christ faithfully.

At times in my descriptive treatment of his paradigm, I reference historical theology or contemporary philosophical or theological works for the purpose of comparison or to situate his views within the larger intellectual landscape. But on the whole, I try to keep this to a minimum as my main goal is to describe his theology from the inside out, allowing him to speak for himself before analyzing it by means of others' views. The bulk of chapters three through ten is devoted to this task. Yet before we approach Willard's formational theology head-on, we should know more about the man himself and what formed him.

TWO

A THEOLOGIAN OF THE CHRISTIAN LIFE

Young Dallas Willard wanted to be a preacher. At eighteen years old, he cut his ministerial teeth preaching from the back of pickup trucks and in local jails. As college students and newlyweds, he and his bride, Jane, dreamt of becoming overseas missionaries. With a heart for evangelism and proclaiming God's word, Dallas was ordained to the ministry and began pastoring a local church. But he "left the ministry," as some have said, to study philosophy in the early 1960s and chose to stay in that field. Yet I contend he never really left the ministry—and that his unique vocational path and intellectual eclecticism prepared him well to speak into some of the deepest issues concerning the human condition.

PHILOSOPHER BY DAY, PREACHER BY NIGHT

Willard was ordained as a Southern Baptist minister in the mid-1950s, a time when many conservative American churches were intent on soul winning while resisting what they perceived as modernist influences and a growing secularism. Since Willard did not keep a journal, and we have no recordings of his sermons from this period, we are left to imagine how he, as a young man, made sense of his calling and the challenges of this particular time. We do know that at a certain point he decided that to pastor people well, more schooling was needed since he felt woefully ignorant of God and the human soul and was sure he would be a "public hazard" in the pulpit.[1] So he enrolled in graduate school at the University of Wisconsin to study philosophy for a couple of years, although he never intended to take a degree. To others it may have seemed odd that an ordained minister would choose to study philosophy at a secular university rather than pursue more biblical and theological studies at a seminary. But by this point he was convinced that philosophers spent more time than anyone else talking about the topics that matter most to life.

While in graduate school, Willard pored over the writings of ancient and contemporary philosophers. Although several influenced his intellectual development, it was Edmund Husserl's work that left the deepest impression on him.[2] Willard excelled in his studies and did end up completing a PhD, whereby he was invited to teach courses in the school's philosophy department while continuing to pastor a local church. At this time he faced a vocational crisis: Should he remain in the church or in the university? He was convinced God spoke to him, saying, "If you stay in the universities, the churches will be open to you. If you stay in the church, the universities will be closed to you."[3] Soon after, he accepted a faculty position in the philosophy department at the University of Southern California (USC), where he taught for forty-seven years.

A prodigious learner, Willard was literate in a wide variety of subjects, including psychology, theology, church history, and the history of science. His admiration for philosophy in particular stemmed from his belief that the four foundational questions asked in the field are the same basic questions addressed in Scripture: (1) What is real? (2) What is the good life? (3) Who is a good person? and, (4) How does one become a good person?[4] During his long teaching tenure at

---

[1] Dallas Willard, interview by Hope McPherson, "Going Deeper," *Response* (Winter 2000): 10. See also Willard, "Introduction to Spirituality" (July 28, 2008), MP3, 7:45.

[2] Husserl's impact on his thinking, as well as Willard's appropriation of Husserl's key insights, will be further examined in chap. 4.

[3] Dallas Willard, "Dialogue with Dallas Willard" (October 26, 2010), MP3, 3:30.

[4] For his explication of these four questions, see Dallas Willard, "Our Current Situation and the Four Great Questions of Life" (July 25, 2000), MP3; Willard, *Knowing Christ Today: Why We Can*

USC, he taught courses on all philosophical subjects, but his favorites were metaphysics and epistemology. He believed that a proper epistemology built upon a proper metaphysics was indispensable for attaining the spiritual knowledge necessary for the Christian life. This insight leads us to what we might call Willard's second vocation.

In addition to his day job at the university, Willard moonlighted as a preacher and spiritual writer. In the years after the Willard family moved to Southern California, he focused on settling into his new role at USC but also gradually took on an increasingly busy speaking schedule. The invitations kept coming, and he kept accepting them. This was just as true by the late 1970s, when he was still relatively unknown except among local pastors and parishioners, as it was after he became widely known for his writings in spirituality in the late 1980s and 1990s. If he could fit it into his schedule—that is, if he did not already have something penciled in on his calendar—he would accept the invitation. Church basements, Sunday school classrooms, retreat centers, living rooms—he delivered sermons and lecture series wherever he was asked to, no matter the size of the group. At one point, his friend Richard Foster intervened. He would literally take Dallas's calendar and cross things off, then have his own secretary make the phone calls to cancel. Later, his wife Jane organized a small discernment group—a supervisory council of sorts—which included their pastor and a couple of close friends, to help Dallas decide which invitations to accept. Even then, she reflects, he struggled with saying no to any invitation to preach or teach right up until the end of his life.[5] This reluctance came from a deep-seated conviction he held, a conviction that God had called him to be a minister of the gospel and that this ministry required embodiment.

I stress this point because it helps explain how the Willardian corpus took shape, and something of its distinctive character, as well

---

Trust Spiritual Knowledge (HarperOne, 2009), 45-56. In the latter, he adds a fifth question: How do we know which answers to the four questions are true?

[5]Jane Willard, personal communication, March 8, 2018.

as its limitations. Other than with his academic writing in philosophy and one particular theological work,[6] Willard never solicited a book to be published. Instead, all his books came about by the request and prodding of others. He had preached or taught the content of these books prior to their being published, with the exception of *Renovation of the Heart*, which he wrote at the urging of a publisher. This explains the practical nature of his spiritual writings. They deal with weighty subjects and are not light reading, yet they were not written as academic monographs. Behind the pulpit and in other teaching settings, Willard was trying to help ordinary people comprehend the spiritual realities of God and his kingdom and develop Christlike character through interaction with them. His books and articles are a reflection of that. This is a main reason he does not show more of his homework in his theological writing, in footnotes and with citations, as he does in his philosophical writing.[7] It also explains why he never lays out his theology in a systematic manner. Although he did leave behind a sizable number of articles in addition to the books, it seems undeniable that he would have produced more literature, in more subjects, and in more depth had he curtailed his preaching and speaking ministry as many of his close friends encouraged him to do.[8]

---

[6] Willard had a special relationship with what was eventually published as *The Divine Conspiracy* (1998). He felt compelled, even convicted, that its message be heard. This urgency comes across in a personal letter to Richard Foster, dated June 24, 1992 (Dallas Willard Collection), in which Willard seeks his friend's help in finding a publisher for the book.

[7] Another reason is his realist approach in discussing subjects. Rather than citing multiple sources to prove a point or referencing other possibly relevant discussions, Willard wanted his readers to compare what he was saying to reality itself. If the goal is knowledge—and it always is for Willard—then he felt it imperative that persons "go to the things themselves" (the rallying cry of phenomenology), or as close as possible, to attain knowledge for themselves. There is, in his view, no replacement for *firsthand* knowledge. Nevertheless, it would have been beneficial, not least for those of us trying to trace his influences or reconstruct his thought, had he left a few more breadcrumbs in footnotes.

[8] A case in point is found in a personal letter from Richard Foster, dated October 2, 1996 (Dallas Willard Collection), in which he lists six detailed reasons Willard should greatly reduce the number of speaking requests he accepts in order to concentrate on his writing. Foster writes, "I urge you to value the periods of sustained concentration as priceless pearls and refuse to break them up by the demands of an adoring public."

Though Willard did receive moderate recognition in his chosen field of philosophy, he became more well-known for his work in Christian spirituality and, more specifically, Christian spiritual formation. Consequently, he unintentionally became a decisive figure in the spiritual formation movement. While spiritual formation is certainly not a new phenomenon in the Christian church, the "spiritual formation movement" refers specifically to the reception of and emphasis on spiritual formation among Protestants over the past half century.[9] That his teaching and writing increasingly moved in the direction of this movement is more a historical accident than a planned trajectory.

His relationship with Quaker author Richard J. Foster is highly significant in this regard. The two met first in 1970 when Foster became pastor of a small Friends congregation in Southern California where Willard was already a member. They became close friends and remained so until Willard's death. Whenever Willard would teach Sunday school, Foster would cancel the other classes. Some people, including Foster, would bring tape recorders. This would prove to be fortunate, for one particular series Willard taught on the spiritual disciplines became a catalyst for Foster's writing *Celebration of Discipline* a few years later.[10] The publication of this book is seen as the symbolic beginning point of the contemporary spiritual formation movement, as it introduced Protestants to historic spiritual disciplines[11] beyond the standard practices of prayer and Bible study, as well as to classic spiritual writers such as Thomas à Kempis and Madame Guyon.

The book quickly became a bestseller and brought national attention to Foster. In turn, he used his commercial success to elevate

---

[9] An article tracing the development of the Protestant spiritual formation movement, coauthored by Steve Porter and myself, is forthcoming in a special issue of the *Journal of Spiritual Formation & Soul Care*. The entire special issue will be devoted to examining the spiritual formation movement in North America.

[10] Richard J. Foster, *Celebration of Discipline: The Path to Spiritual Growth* (Harper & Row, 1978).

[11] At the time, many Protestants did not know the term "spiritual disciplines," and those who did generally associated it negatively with a form of works righteousness.

Willard's voice. Willard thus significantly shaped the spiritual formation movement, and the movement also shaped Willard by influencing what topics and questions he devoted his attention to. If one listens to early audio recordings of his sermons and Bible studies from the 1970s, he covered a much larger array of topics than just the three D's he would later become famous for: disciples, discipleship, and disciplines.[12] That his niche became Christian spirituality, rather than Christian theology in general or some other area of Christian thought, is largely an accident of history.[13] This outcome owes much to how the spiritual formation movement pulled him in and looked to him as a leader.

Yet regardless of how different his career might have been apart from this movement, there seems little doubt that the doctrine and goals of sanctification would have remained dear to his heart. From the earliest days of his ministry that we have on record to his last months in 2013, Willard longed for spiritual renewal in the church.[14]

---

[12]On this, see Michael Stewart Robb, *The Kingdom Among Us: The Gospel According to Dallas Willard* (Fortress, 2022), 17-18. Robb's monograph is a landmark work in the study of Willard's theology and thus will occasionally be cited or engaged with in the coming chapters. The main distinction between my book and Robb's lies in their doctrinal focus. Borrowing phrases from Jonathan Edwards and Oswald Chambers, respectively, Willard spoke of both "the history of redemption" and "the psychology of redemption" (38). The former concerns God's salvific work in human history, while the latter focuses on God's salvific work within the individual soul. Robb's book explores Willard's view of the history of redemption while periodically foraying into the psychology of redemption. By contrast, my book, as a study of Willard's theory of spiritual formation, centers on his view of the psychology of redemption, crossing the street to the other side (the history of redemption) only tangentially when necessary. For further discussion of the importance of Robb's work for Willard scholarship, readers may consult my lengthy review: Keas Keasler, "Book Review: *The Kingdom Among Us: The Gospel According to Dallas Willard*," *Journal of Spiritual Formation & Soul Care* 16, no. 1 (2023): 167-76.

[13]Yet, is this not true of many, if not most, important Christian thinkers in history? Augustine, Aquinas, Luther, Calvin, and Wesley cannot be separated from the accidents of history that influenced the direction of their lives, what issues they took up, and how they are remembered. So perhaps the trajectory of Willard's career is not so unique in this regard.

[14]The oldest extant recording of a sermon or teaching I know of is from November 1971 ("The Kingdom Comes in Power," MP3), and his first theological essay published by a major Christian periodical was in 1980. See Dallas Willard, "Discipleship: For Super-Christians Only?," *Christianity Today* 24, no. 17 (1980): 24-27. His last contributions were a set of talks he gave in February 2013 at a conference centered on equipping pastors to be "teachers of the nations" (released as

He was burdened by the lack of true discipleship he saw happening there. The elephant in the church, he often said, is that so many "undiscipled disciples" fill its pews. In the introduction to *The Great Omission* he states,

> The greatest issue facing the world today, with all its heartbreaking needs, is whether those who . . . are identified as "Christians" will become *disciples*—students, apprentices, practitioners—*of Jesus Christ*, steadily learning from him how to live the life of the Kingdom of the Heavens into every corner of human existence. Will they break out of the churches to be his Church—to be, without human force or violence, his mighty force for good on earth, drawing the churches after them toward the eternal purposes of God? . . . There is no greater issue facing the individual human being, Christian or not.[15]

Willard believed the way to change the world was to change the church. Christians must first undergo the character transformation that happens through lifelong, serious apprenticeship to Jesus if they are to make a real difference in the world. Yet the main hurdle to serious apprenticeship is that "we don't preach life in the kingdom of God through faith in Jesus as an existential reality that leads to discipleship and then character transformation."[16] In his mind, there is a clear line from (1) a faulty view of the gospel and the kingdom, to (2) a lack of discipleship and character transformation, to (3) an impotent church that has lost the plot. The spiritual formation movement has been centrally concerned about the middle part of this equation: discipleship and character transformation. Yet Willard stated on numerous occasions his concern that the movement would grow without a solid biblical, theological, and anthropological foundation and

---

a DVD titled *Living in Christ's Presence*) and a set of talks given in mid-March 2013 at a residency for the Renovaré Institute that were not recorded. He died on May 8, 2013.

[15]Dallas Willard, *The Great Omission: Reclaiming Jesus' Essential Teachings on Discipleship* (HarperSanFrancisco, 2006), xv.

[16]Dallas Willard, quoted in Christine A. Scheller, "A Divine Conspirator," *Christianity Today* 50, no. 9 (2006): 47.

would degenerate into technique and legalism.[17] As we will see, much of his work was aimed at providing this foundation.

WILLARD'S INTELLECTUAL ECLECTICISM

As I have noted, Willard was a professional philosopher who moonlighted as a preacher and author of theological books, becoming much more known for this side job than his nine-to-five work in the academy. In this respect, he is comparable to a British figure from a generation earlier. A scholar of medieval literature, C. S. Lewis taught across the humanities but is best known for his Christian nonfiction and novels.[18] Eclectic and incredibly well-read, both men defy easy categorization and were deeply committed to the practical implications of ideas. Even a brief comparative glance further illuminates the nuances of Willard's intellectual approach.

To begin, both were remarkable thinkers whose enduring influence extends beyond their academic fields. More important, though, is the idiosyncratic way they went about their work. In the mind of an eclectic thinker, philosophy and theology (as well as other domains of knowledge) are not sharply distinguished but often overlap. Willard's thoughts are not necessarily unique in content, but they are distinctive in the cross-disciplinary way they are formed and expressed. Although quite competent in theology, he was not a standard theologian; and while he was both a Christian and a philosopher, it is

---

[17]"Unless the interest in spirituality, as it is now sometimes called, finds a foundation in the nature of human personality and in God's redemptive interactions therewith, it will be at most a passing fad. Moreover, it is possible for people not only to be disappointed in this area, but seriously harmed." Dallas Willard, "Spiritual Disciplines, Spiritual Formation, and the Restoration of the Soul," *Journal of Psychology and Theology* 26, no. 1 (Spring 1998): 101.

[18]I am not the first to make this comparison. See Gary W. Moon, "Getting the Elephant Out of the Sanctuary: An Interview with Dallas Willard," *Conversations Journal* 8, no. 1 (2010): 12; Gary Black Jr., *The Theology of Dallas Willard: Discovering Protoevangelical Faith* (Pickwick, 2013), 183. However, those comparisons are passing and seem to be in terms of (1) the influence of Lewis's and Willard's writings on Christian leaders and (2) their intelligent and winsome articulation of the faith. While affirming both points—though the first may be overblown, since Willard's reach is still nowhere near Lewis's—my comparison focuses on their vocational self-understanding and idiosyncratic modes of thought.

not entirely accurate to classify him as a "Christian philosopher" in the same mold of Alvin Plantinga, James K. A. Smith, and Rebecca DeYoung. His intellectual eclecticism meant that he, like Lewis, was a bit of everything—theologian, philosopher, psychologist, and so on—and able to lecture at the drop of a hat on a wide range of topics.[19] Yet the ultimate interest of both men lay in the practicality of theories and ideas, which in turn sparked their intellectual pursuits, guided by the question of what makes human life go well.[20]

The vocational parallels go further. Each was a kind of contextual evangelist within secular higher education, Lewis in Britain and Willard in America, laboring to communicate the gospel in the rare, intellectual atmosphere of their respective settings. And both were deeply concerned about how prevailing epistemologies obscure the nature of truth.[21] Less positively, there is a certain unreflective assumption, even prejudice, that some in the guild have about the work

---

[19]Although a minor detail, Michael Stewart Robb also references Lewis, but by way of *contrast*. He states, "It is not accurate to regard Willard as a lay theologian—as, for example, we often rightly regard C. S. Lewis." Willard should instead be regarded, particularly in his churchly and theological work, as akin to Dietrich Bonhoeffer, "who combined trust in the gospel and a pursuit of the best knowledge with an active and time-consuming concern for the welfare of the church and individuals in his time" (Robb, *Kingdom Among Us*, 507). While I affirm this resemblance between Willard and Bonhoeffer (and one should note Robb has other rhetorical reasons for drawing the comparison, which are quite suggestive; see the last paragraph of his book), my comparison of Willard and Lewis is less about them as theologians and more about their intellectual eclecticism. That said, I wouldn't be as prudish as Robb about a straightforward comparison of them as theologians, for I believe a compelling case can be made for Lewis as a theologian of the highest order. Of course, my study is not on Lewis, so I leave that argument to others. For those interested, see Alister McGrath's "Outside the 'Inner Ring': Lewis as a Theologian," in *The Intellectual World of C. S. Lewis* (Wiley-Blackwell, 2014), 163-83.

[20]Toward the beginning of a weeklong intensive on spiritual formation he taught at Denver Seminary, Willard remarks that the lectures would get more practical as the week progressed but that students must first work on theory, for if "you don't [get the concepts right], it won't work," adding, "there's nothing more practical than a good idea." Dallas Willard, "Taking 1 Corinthians Seriously: Intending to Do It 1" (January 5, 2010), video, 5:30. This practical theological approach should not be confused with *pragmatism* in the technical sense. For Willard's explicit distancing of his theory of knowledge from the school of pragmatism, see Willard, "Faculty Q & A" (October 9, 2008), MP3, 12:45.

[21]See Dallas Willard, "C. S. Lewis and the Pursuit of Truth Today," *Sacred History* (December 2005): 69-73, 111-15.

of both. Due to the practical character of Willard's spiritual writings, some theologians and biblical exegetes have dismissed him as a theological lightweight. This accounts for why, despite his significant influence on the North American spiritual formation movement and his broad readership among Protestant Christians, his work has received little scholarly engagement from the academy.[22]

Likewise, some of Lewis's peers never considered him a true academic because of his popular writings, works in fiction, and evangelistic endeavors. It is well documented that this was why he was never appointed as professor at Oxford, only lecturer, and thus eventually switched to Cambridge since it offered him a professorship. All this to say, both Lewis and Willard were serious thinkers but had peers who saw them as second-class academics because of their popular writings and practical approaches.

A key difference, however, is in their sense of calling. Lewis, for all his pastoral impact, was uneasy offering personal spiritual counsel and hesitant to adopt the mantle of pastor or spiritual director, leading one biographer to describe him as a "reluctant guide."[23] Willard, by contrast, readily embraced these roles, seeing himself above all as a minister of the gospel. His willingness to give spiritual counsel was well known, and this same pastoral spirit permeates his theology—a point to which I now turn.

THE PASTORAL RESPONSIBILITY OF A THEOLOGIAN

In a 2006 seminar held in Europe, Willard defined the domain of theology as "inquiry into the existence and nature of God and of his relations to creation, with special reference to the purposes of human

---

[22]The dearth of secondary literature on Willard serves as empirical evidence of this bias. On a more anecdotal note, I had a conversation with N. T. Wright some years ago in which he shared his experience of trying to read Willard. Wright admitted he found it frustrating and "just couldn't make it through the book." Little did he know that later that evening he would be honored on stage with the Dallas Willard Lifetime Achievement Award (!) at the conference we were attending.

[23]Lyle W. Dorsett, *Seeking the Secret Place: The Spiritual Formation of C. S. Lewis* (Brazos, 2004), chap. 6.

life and salvation." The theological task, he added, "could be pursued simply as an intellectual exercise, driven by the will to know, or as an exercise in being right, driven by the need to control." But over against such approaches, his understanding of said task "emphasizes the primary need of human beings to know how to live. The general human problem is practical: to find an adequate knowledge-base for practice."[24]

Let us examine this a bit more closely. His initial description of theology—"inquiry into the existence and nature of God and of his relations to creation"—resembles that of Thomas Aquinas's in the thirteenth century and is given a specific telos in "the purposes of human life and salvation." The Greek word for "salvation" (*sōtēria*) can also be translated as "healing," which may explain Willard's next move: distancing his understanding of theology from those who view it mainly as an intellectual endeavor without concern for its therapeutic use and real-life consequences. Hence, he stresses that theology is meant to provide "an adequate knowledge-base for practice," for "how to live." The title he assigned the seminar says it all: "The Pastoral Responsibility of a Theologian."

Further down in the lecture handout, Willard states, "Christian theology has its point in the furthering of discipleship to Jesus Christ in the present Kingdom of God. From such discipleship all else follows, and within such discipleship every human ability and resource is welcome."[25] Willard's theology could be appropriately called *therapeutic theology*, but it can also be termed *apprenticeship theology*. Theology, for Willard, is ultimately concerned with fostering divine friendship through apprenticeship to Jesus that leads to the transformation and flourishing of human persons in all aspects of their lives. Theology done well enables humans to live deeply in God's kingdom. This aligns with a lecture given a decade earlier, in which Willard

---

[24]Dallas Willard, "The Pastoral Responsibility of a Theologian" (handout, May 24, 2006), Dallas Willard Collection, 15.

[25]Willard, "Pastoral Responsibility," 15.

suggests that all forms of theology other than clinical theology should be outlawed.[26]

Here it may be advantageous to distinguish Willard's theological method from what we might call "higher thought" theology. The latter is promulgated by those who believe real theology is conducted only in the academy among trained specialists. One must read relevant monographs in the field, understand the sociohistorical background of the first-century Greco-Roman world, and possess other specialized knowledge in order to "do" theology. Complex theoretical constructs are valued over practical concerns. Theology is treated as an intellectual exercise, largely removed from the realities of everyday life and with little interest in whether the grammar of Christian belief actually corresponds to what is spiritually real. I should add that some notable thinkers have recently argued that modern theology has in large part been colonized by these higher thought sensibilities.[27] For it was within modernity that theology came to be seen as the intellectual justification of the faith, apart from the worship of God and the practice of the Christian life.

This is in stark contrast with Willard's theological approach, which holds that ordinary people can do good theology and thereby interact with the living God. That is not to say that good theology doesn't require one to think deeply and carefully, for Willard insists it does.[28] But theology is an exercise or inquiry open to all, not just some elite group who have so-called higher thought. This is where his theological method corresponds with his commonsense philosophy, namely that our everyday experiences and intuitions provide a

---

[26]Dallas Willard, "Jesus' Gospel and Ours" (May 29, 1992), MP3, 6:00.

[27]See Ellen T. Charry, *By the Renewing of Your Minds: The Pastoral Function of Christian Doctrine* (Oxford University Press, 1997); Miroslav Volf and Matthew Croasmun, *For the Life of the World: Theology That Makes a Difference* (Brazos, 2019). As the latter authors pointedly state, "Academic theology today is composed of specialists in an unrespected discipline who write for fellow specialists about topics that interest hardly anyone else" (44-45).

[28]To hear him argue this point, using C. S. Lewis as his spokesperson, see Willard, *Knowing Christ Today*, 10-11.

trustworthy basis for knowledge, and such knowledge is accessible to everyone. Willard would likely detect more than a hint of gnosticism in much contemporary academic theology.

The purpose of theology, from this perspective, is deeply pastoral and therapeutic. It aims at human healing and human flourishing through knowing and loving God. Such flourishing implies growth in character and wisdom; thus the development of virtue is a central concern of the theological task. This perspective is also why, I suggest, Willard concentrated much of his teaching on the book of Acts in the 1970s—a time before his fame rose, when he likely had more freedom in choosing his subjects, rather than being asked to address specific topics such as discipleship and spiritual disciplines. From the surviving recordings of that decade, we know he taught at least four separate series on Acts. Acts possesses a realism unique in the New Testament—save for the Gospels themselves—as it narrates the power of God unleashed in the early Christian community. Its doctrines and theological principles arise from real historical experiences, making it an ideal foundation for a theologian of the Christian life like Willard, who sought to understand and apply spiritual truths in the practical realities of everyday life. I could say more here about Willard's theological method, but the proof is in the pudding, so I prefer to show this in the chapters to come.

COMMONSENSE HERMENEUTICS

Before turning to Willard's corpus, one final observation about his theological method. It is important to note how his particular philosophy of mind, language, and reality lends itself to a commonsense approach to reading Scripture. On this, he believes he is part of a well-established tradition, citing other Christian thinkers from the past who took a similar approach, such as Augustine, Luther, Calvin, Wesley, and of course, Lewis.[29] The implications of his metaphysical

---

[29]Dallas Willard, "On Philosophy and Christianity" (June 2010), MP3, 2:00; Willard, "C. S. Lewis and the Pursuit."

and epistemological realism (offshoots of his commonsense philosophy) for particular areas of Christian experience and doctrine, such as communication with God and Christology, are discussed in later chapters. Here I will briefly note what this commitment to commonsense philosophy means for his interpretation of Scripture.[30]

First, ideas and the realities they point to are not bound by words. Against some modern and postmodern views that thoughts and concepts are determined by their linguistic expression within finite social groups, Willard contends that "thoughts and their concepts do not modify the objects which make up reality. They merely 'match up' or fail to match up with them in a certain way."[31] Hence, he reads Scripture with an eye to where concepts are present even when their corresponding terms are not, especially overarching concepts that are key to grasping the biblical narrative and God's purposes in history. For instance, he contends there is sufficient evidence for *the kingdom of God* throughout the Old Testament despite the terminology not being used. In this, his approach differs from modern exegetes who restrict their interpretation of the kingdom to its linguistic use in one phase of biblical history (Second Temple Judaism), or at least see its use during that period as *the* determinative key for understanding the biblical concept.[32]

Second, he is concerned with the meaning in the text, as opposed to a reader-centered approach. But this goes beyond even a standard author-centered approach, as he is primarily concerned with the larger question of "What is real?" as opposed to "What did the author intend?"

---

[30]For a more comprehensive treatment of the philosophical nature of his biblical hermeneutics, see Robb, *Kingdom Among Us*, chap. 3. The most illuminating primary resource I have found on this is Dallas Willard, "The Bible as Indispensable Source of Knowledge: The Best Knowledge on the Most Important Topics . . . on Earth" (June 27, 2003), MP3.

[31]Dallas Willard, "How Concepts Relate the Mind to Its Objects: The 'God's Eye View' Vindicated?," *Philosophia Christi* 1, no. 2 (1999): 20. For discussion of the "total linguisticization of human consciousness" as a major component of postmodernism or poststructuralism, see Willard, "Postmodernism: Philosophical & Historical Roots I" (August 19, 1992), MP3, 5:00.

[32]To hear Willard subtly distance himself from N. T. Wright in this respect, see Dallas Willard, "Q & A: Prayer" (July 15, 2004), MP3, 43:30; cf. Robb, *Kingdom Among Us*, 153-58.

in his exegesis. For example, in discussion of Paul's psychology of redemption, Willard argues, contra overly "spiritual" interpretations, that the apostle's language of dying daily (1 Cor 15:31) and of crucifying the flesh with its passions and desires (Gal 5:24) corresponds to the same existential reality Jesus speaks of as denying oneself and taking up the cross (Mt 16:24). He writes, "These events then are real events that have certain constant and definite properties that a believer can discover by living through them. They *can* be made a part of our plan for life in Christ."[33] In other words, Paul's "stern realism," as Willard calls it, depicts something real (in this case, mortification of the flesh as part of sanctification) that can be known experientially today.

Third, and closely related, the meaning of Scripture will present itself to those who attend closely to it and do so with intellectual responsibility. In his view, God has arranged for the Bible to be recorded in such a way that humans from very different places and in very different eras might comprehend its message through the act of *intentionality* (of consciousness). This mental act makes it possible for a person to grasp something in her mind that is beyond her mind, and for other people to also grasp this "something" in their minds at the same time or at another time.[34] This is the classic doctrine of biblical inspiration topped off with Husserlian phenomenology.

Willard holds there is an important place for higher and lower biblical criticism in the life of the church,[35] yet he is adamant that biblical interpretation is not the domain solely of historical, exegetical scholarship but belongs to all persons who desire to know for themselves the truths God has revealed in Holy Writ and passed down through Israel and the church. We find a plain summary of this in the introduction to *Divine Conspiracy*:

---

[33] Dallas Willard, *The Spirit of the Disciplines: Understanding How God Changes Lives* (Harper & Row, 1988), 109.

[34] I must ask the reader's patience, since I will unpack the relevance of Willard's phenomenology and ontology of knowledge for his theology in greater detail in a future chapter.

[35] Willard, "Faculty Q & A," 42:00.

> The Bible is, after all, God's gift to the world through his Church, not to the scholars. It comes through the life of his people and nourishes that life. Its purpose is practical, not academic. An intelligent, careful, intensive but straightforward reading—that is, one not governed by obscure and faddish theories or by a mindless orthodoxy—is what it requires to direct us into life in God's kingdom.

Willard then adds, "To what extent this belief of mine is or is not harmfully circular, I leave the philosophically minded reader to ponder."[36] He expresses this more bluntly in a public talk:

> One of the things which we must believe is that good common sense should never leave us when we read the Bible. Now, I hope you don't think that's blasphemous—some people think that it is. They believe that when you read the Bible your wits should leave you utterly. And that's why we see so much harm done and so much disgrace brought upon the Scriptures.[37]

This plainspoken (and somewhat cheeky) remark encapsulates his rejection of both fideistic literalism and obscurantist academic methods, both of which he sees as out of step with the rational and accessible nature of divine revelation.

It is beyond the limits of this book to argue for or against Willard's commonsense hermeneutics in its application to Scripture. But regardless of how one judges his hermeneutics, his position is far from the literalism or biblicism of Christian fundamentalism. Willard, as an eclectic Christian thinker, had a well-hewn epistemology of the Bible, informed by his study of Husserl and deep-seated convictions about the ontology of knowledge.

---

[36] Dallas Willard, *The Divine Conspiracy: Rediscovering Our Hidden Life in God* (HarperSanFrancisco, 1998), xvi-xvii.

[37] Dallas Willard, "The Last Shall Be First" (May 15, 1984), MP3, 20:45.

THE WILLARDIAN CORPUS

If Willard's formational theology is to be studied seriously, one must first know the lay of the land—the source materials available for researching his thought—especially since his corpus is somewhat unusual. Its main categories are his (1) philosophical works, (2) recordings of sermons and public lectures, (3) pentalogy (five major theological books) and related articles, and (4) popular and posthumous writings in spirituality. A helpful analogy for this body of work, which illustrates the place and role of its diverse parts, is the layering of the earth's structure, typically divided into four major layers: inner core, outer core, mantle, and crust. Using this image, I begin at the center—the deepest point of the Willardian corpus—and work outward toward the surface and most accessible level. Since the study of his theology is still in its infancy, it is necessary to lay things out carefully and concretely.

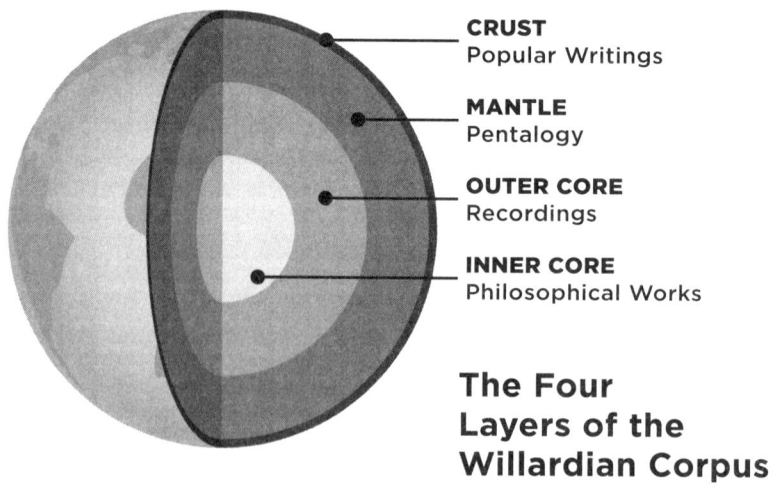

Figure 2.1. The four layers of the Willardian corpus

Inner core: Philosophical works. Had Willard left us his philosophical writings but never produced his theological work, it is conceivable we could build on the former to eventually arrive at many of the latter's conclusions. Conversely, this would be much more difficult, if possible at all, to do moving in the opposite direction—using his theology to arrive at his philosophy—for the simple reason that nearly all of his theological writings assume his philosophical positions but do not argue straightforwardly for them. For those who have read both his philosophy and theology, it is clear that Willard's philosophy exerts a gravitational pull over the rest of his work.[38]

Although Willard commented on nearly every philosophical subject, his first love within the field was *perceptual realism*, what he also called, in his USC lectures, "super-sophisticated realism" (or, more crassly, "pig-headed realism"), which he arrived at via phenomenology and more specifically through studying his intellectual mentor, Edmund Husserl.[39] Two of his three major works of philosophy deal extensively with and defend Husserl's epistemology: his PhD dissertation, "Meaning and Universals" (1964), and first book, *Logic and the Objectivity of Knowledge* (1984).[40] Willard's second book, *The Disappearance of Moral Knowledge* (2018), published posthumously, also keeps epistemology front and center while traversing into a wider terrain of intellectual history and ethical theory.[41]

While Willard's philosophical oeuvre received modest attention in the field of philosophy,[42] it has, unsurprisingly, garnered even less attention among his many readers in the church and seminary. Yet

---

[38]See, e.g., Greg Jesson, "The Husserlian Roots of Dallas Willard's Philosophical and Religious Works: Knowledge of the Temporal and the Eternal," *Philosophia Christi* 16, no. 1 (2014): 7-36.

[39]Dallas Willard, "Metaphysics," PHIL 460 (transcript, University of Southern California, fall 1993), Dallas Willard Collection, 409; Willard, "Realism" (January 15, 2003), MP3, 1:45.

[40]Dallas Willard, "Meaning and Universals in Husserl's Logische Untersuchungen" (PhD diss., University of Wisconsin, 1964); Willard, *Logic and the Objectivity of Knowledge: Studies in Husserl's Early Philosophy* (Ohio University Press, 1984).

[41]Dallas Willard, *The Disappearance of Moral Knowledge*, ed. Aaron Preston, Gregg Ten Elshof, and Steven L. Porter (Routledge, 2018).

[42]See Burt C. Hopkins, "Dallas Willard's Contribution to Phenomenology," *Husserl Studies* 35 (2019): 117-30; Micah D. Tillman, "Dallas Willard: Reviving Realism on the West Coast," in *The Reception of Husserlian Phenomenology in North America*, ed. Michela Beatrice Ferri (Springer, 2019), 389-407.

he cannot be fully understood apart from his philosophical writings, especially those on early Husserlian realism, on which Willard pitched his philosophical tent. In contrast to perceptual relativity or representationalism, which defines much of contemporary philosophy, Husserl held that we are not limited to knowing only the contents of our minds (our representations) but can have direct perceptual contact with the world; thus it is possible for knowledge to grasp realities (the things themselves) beyond one's own mind. Willard's own theological epistemology begins with this basic premise, as we will see.

It deserves mention again that Willard never intended to become a university professor, nor did he plan to write books in philosophy. As a young man he aspired to be a minister—in particular an evangelist. Although he stepped away from formal ministry in the 1960s to teach within the field of philosophy, I maintain he continued to live out his ministerial calling through and through.[43] He became and remained a professional philosopher due to his conviction that philosophical matters must be at the heart of any faithful missionary encounter with Western culture. When read within the larger body of his work, his writings in philosophy reveal that Willard was a subversive apologist laboring for gospel plausibility in a pluralistic, secular age; his thinking was missionary all the way up from this deep core.

Outer core: Recordings of sermons and public lectures. The second layer of the Willardian corpus is composed of audio and video recordings of talks and teachings he gave spanning over four decades. As mentioned, Willard kept a relentless speaking schedule outside and in addition to his professorial duties at the university. Although

---

[43]In the late 1970s, he remarks, "The fact that I teach at a university does not mean that I don't think of myself as a minister of the gospel. I'm there because of that." Dallas Willard, "The Great Inversion of the Kingdom of God: Blessedness" (April 9, 1978), MP3, 7:30. Much later, in the late 1990s: "I pastored for a number of years, and I feel like I never left the pastorate but rather just simply took a different role. The work of the ministry of the word and evangelism and teaching is really the heart of all that I do." Willard, "Kingdom Living" (February 21, 1997), MP3, 2:00.

there is no indication Willard ever brought a tape recorder with him—and only occasionally requested his presentations be recorded—many others felt compelled to preserve what he shared. There exists over twelve hundred hours of audio and video recordings of his sermons, Sunday school lessons, conference talks, seminary teachings, and invited lectures. Following his death, the Dallas Willard Center at Westmont College began gathering and cataloging these recordings for their permanent collection.

Situated with his philosophical works on one side and major theological writings on the other, this layer of his corpus acts as a floating bridge between the two. In other words, these speaking occasions gave him the opportunity to explicitly flesh out the theological content of his philosophical ideas and translate them for the life of the church. His day job as a philosopher saw him produce some sixty articles and twenty critical reviews for books and journals, in addition to his major writings in the field previously noted, not to mention class lectures, grading students' work, and overseeing PhD candidates. So the floating-bridge metaphor is apt when we think about what he was doing away from campus and on weekends and evenings when giving these sermons and talks. Willard was not simply shifting from philosophy to biblical studies or theology but offering implicit connections between the two. The subjects were not compartmentalized in his mind as such, and besides, Willard made it a point to study the Bible and the Christian tradition *philosophically*, something he saw no need to apologize for.[44]

The recordings are admittedly a more cumbersome resource for research than those in printed form. (This will hopefully become less so as more talks are transcribed.) But in comparison to the other source materials of his corpus, such as his theological writings, in

---

[44]To hear Willard describe the congruity between his work as a philosopher and his work as a "minister of the gospel," as well as how Scripture addresses deep philosophical questions, see Dallas Willard, "The Biblical Understanding of the Reality of God" (April 24, 1990), MP3, starting at 00:15.

these recordings he addresses a wider range of subjects and many subjects in more detail. This is bound to be the case from the sheer number of extant recordings that exist. The recordings also provide a better sense of how his thought developed over time, especially since he was never in the habit of journaling and thus did not leave behind the type of personal documentation that can be consulted for understanding his early thought. Lastly, the recordings provide clues as to the organic connection between related subjects in his thinking and how he connected the dots and logically arrived at certain conclusions. These clues are helpful as he generally does not spell these connections out in his theology books (except occasionally in footnotes), and since in his speaking (as opposed to his writing) he often felt the need to back up one or two more steps when explaining a concept or interpreting a scriptural passage for an audience.

Whether using detailed notes or a rough outline, Willard usually improvised certain bits on the spot and went off script. Yet again, and this cannot be overstated, these recorded talks serve as the middle, mediating ground between his philosophical works and his theological writings. Especially before 2000, Willard's preparation for speaking engagements was meticulous and time consuming. He thought deeply about the concepts he was communicating behind the pulpit, on stages, and in other public venues, often spending days in preparation for a single talk.[45] For this reason and the others mentioned, these recordings are incredibly valuable for studying Willard, though few scholars have recognized this even within the spiritual formation movement.

Mantle: Pentalogy and related articles. The third layer of the Willardian corpus is his pentalogy and related articles. These five major

---

[45]Willard's speaking schedule became its busiest around 2000 onward, as local, national, and international requests steadily poured in after the publication of *The Divine Conspiracy* (1998). Consequently, he did not give near as much time to preparing for talks and also repeated a lot of the content. Even so, he never gave the same talk twice but always prepared a fresh outline to work from.

theological monographs, written over a span of twenty-five years, are what put Willard on the church's map and led to his rise as a public Christian thought leader. Along with the recordings, this series of books continues to be the most important resource for scholarly reflection on Willard's view of spiritual formation and on his theology as a whole.[46]

The first in the set is *In Search of Guidance* (1984), which did not receive a wide audience until it reached its third edition and was released with a new title, *Hearing God*.[47] This text eventually found a place among evangelical manuals on how to discern God's will,[48] but

---

[46] My position here mitigates that of Michael Stewart Robb, who asserts that, for the study of Willard's thought, the "vast sea of recordings" of his speaking over the decades is the single most valuable resource (*Kingdom Among Us*, 27). Robb's published work on this subject is to be commended above all for arguing the recorded talks are crucial for the scholarly study of Willard. However, in correcting the situation Robb tilts things too far in the opposite direction. About these recordings he states, "They, not the books, are where Willard is Willard" (27). I cannot imagine Willard agreeing; he thought these books offered the best of his biblical and theological reflections. And, as relayed to me by Rebecca Willard Heatley (Dallas Willard's daughter), he sometimes remarked that one of the best things about writing books is that they're out there working while you're taking a nap (personal communication, June 4, 2021). He is not known to have said anything similar about his recorded speeches even though the same logic could be applied. Heatley further clarified that her father was selective about what recordings were made public: "He wouldn't let me just load everything up on the website. . . . He wanted us to filter out the best of each topic and just use those" (personal communication, May 15, 2025). For reasons already mentioned, the recordings are an extremely valuable resource for researchers, on par with only the pentalogy and related articles, even if they are not as convenient a resource as those in printed form. Yet they should not be elevated above the pentalogy. Willard's five theological monographs constitute what "rose to the top" and "made the cut" from his talks. Thus, in the approach taken here, the recordings and pentalogy are to be studied in tandem and treated as supplementary to each other in understanding Willard's theology.

[47] Dallas Willard, *In Search of Guidance: Developing a Conversational Relationship with God* (Regal, 1984). Other than adding an epilogue, few changes were made in the second edition (HarperSanFrancisco, 1993). However, strategic cuts were made in the third edition, *Hearing God: Developing a Conversational Relationship with God* (InterVarsity Press, 1999), to remove some of the denser philosophical material. A lightly updated fourth edition followed (InterVarsity Press, 2012), adding lectio divina exercises by Jan Johnson. While later edits did not alter the substance of Willard's arguments and in some cases improved readability—especially edits in the fourth edition—Robb argues convincingly that scholarship should rely primarily on the second edition (*Kingdom Among Us*, 24n38). It is not only the most complete edition but also best preserves Willard's original intent, as he seemed not all that pleased with having some of his original argument shortened or removed. Henceforth, throughout this work, I will cite the second edition (1993) unless otherwise indicated.

[48] See T. M. Luhrmann, *When God Talks Back: Understanding the American Relationship with God* (Knopf, 2012), 373. See also the revised and expanded version of Gary Friesen's bestselling *Decision Making and the Will of God: A Biblical Alternative to the Traditional View* (Multnomah,

it stands out in the genre for two reasons. First, divine guidance is a focal point but is framed as a consequence (rather than the cornerstone) of an ongoing, interactive relationship with God, which is the real thrust of the work. Willard attempts to articulate, in layperson's terms, a profound phenomenological understanding of the relational knowing at the heart of the Christian faith. Second, Willard's serious philosophical metaphysic is never far from view, even in sections that deal with the more practical matters of seeking God's leading in making decisions. This is probably why his book remains one of the more serious reads on the subject, even forty years later.

In 1988 Willard published his breakout book that garnered him national attention, *The Spirit of the Disciplines*. His two original working titles for the work, neither of which the editor finally chose— *The Theology of the Spiritual Disciplines* and *Exercise unto Godliness*— communicate more clearly what he hoped to accomplish in its pages: a psychologically sound theological understanding of the spiritual life and of its disciplines.[49] Written partly to supplement Foster's *Celebration of Discipline*, published a decade earlier, Willard's work sought to provide a solid biblical-theological foundation for the growing interest in spiritual practices that ensued in the wake of Foster's bestseller. While *In Search of Guidance* is a primer on Willard's realist philosophy applied to the divine-human relationship and his understanding of how interaction with spiritual reality is transformative, *Spirit of the Disciplines* introduces nearly all the other major themes of his theological project, at least in outline, such as salvation as a life and its key ingredients, the crux of theological anthropology, the

---

2004), where Willard's book is included in the appendix, titled "Review of Books on Finding God's Will." That Friesen's review of Willard's book (444-46) is critical comes as little surprise, given that Willard subtly but strongly critiques Friesen in *In Search of Guidance*, 106-7. This section was omitted in later editions. Further, Willard once told an audience he was prompted to write his book to refute Friesen's view, "which in effect says God does not communicate to you personally." Dallas Willard, "Spiritual Direction and How It Relates to Psychological Counseling" (August 20, 1987), MP3, 14:15.

[49]Willard, *Spirit of the Disciplines*, xi.

availability of God's kingdom, the human side of holiness, the eschatology of spiritual formation, and Christian discipleship as the means of sociopolitical change. Willard would have much more to say over the next two decades. But it is important to see that his first two monographs contain practically all his major theological claims, even if they are not yet articulated in their most sophisticated form. He would continue to develop these key ideas—in some cases, devoting an entire book to unpacking one or two of them—yet this was always an instance of him returning to stakes he had already placed in the ground.

Many consider *The Divine Conspiracy* (1998) to be Willard's magnum opus. It is his longest work—some four hundred pages—and was a long time in the making. He reworked the manuscript numerous times in the 1990s, though he had been teaching its main concepts in sermon series and Sunday school lessons dating back to the early 1970s and then with increasing frequency from the mid-1980s onward. Ambitious in scope, the book has a more polemical tone than the others: He critiques modern evangelical versions of the gospel on both the right and left as reductionistic messages of "sin management," contending that the good news that Jesus himself preached was the announcement that anyone can live within the present reality of God's kingdom through apprenticeship to and reliance upon Jesus. Willard argues this is the secret to true personal, social, and political transformation, for it is, in sum, God's master plan and methodology for overcoming evil with good in human history. At some point while working on the book, he came to see it in relation to his two earlier books as the completion of a trilogy.[50] Yet two more books would follow that further expanded the series.

In the 1990s Willard agreed to write a short manual-type book as part of a series of spiritual formation books for NavPress. This "short" book, which ended up taking two years to write, became *Renovation*

---

[50]Willard, *Divine Conspiracy*, xvii.

of the Heart (2002). If *Divine Conspiracy* is the zenith of Willard's work in biblical and theological studies, then *Renovation of the Heart* is the equivalent in the realm of Christian psychology. Yet woven through the pentalogy, regardless of what domain of thought he ventures into, is the question of how the human spirit is formed under the grace and guidance of the Holy Spirit. Here the question is explored through a complex theological anthropology. He examines the different dimensions of the human person, depicted in five concentric circles, and what role they play in character transformation. His thesis is that by default, the whole self—the will (heart or spirit), mind, body, social environment, and soul—is integrated and works together; thus all the parts of personhood need to be transformed by God's Spirit, and every part suffers when one part is not surrendered to this process.

The last in the pentalogy, *Knowing Christ Today* (2009), was intended as an abbreviated and pastoral version of a much fuller and more philosophical volume on moral knowledge that Willard was intermittently working on for nearly two decades and which remained unfinished at the time of his death.[51] His epistemology is latent in one form or another in all his theological writings, but here he explicitly spells out his account of knowledge and its (friendly) relation to faith and makes a case for taking Jesus seriously as a logician and moral authority.[52] Because of the book's complex subject matter and Willard's somewhat technical prose,[53] some readers may find this volume

---

[51] Three scholars and former students of Willard (Aaron Preston, Gregg Ten Elshof, Steven L. Porter) completed his manuscript, which was published posthumously as *The Disappearance of Moral Knowledge*.

[52] It should be said that *Knowing Christ Today* is an odd and perhaps even misleading title for this book. It gives the impression that it is a devotional work. While that might be true in a roundabout way—in the sense that its contents, if comprehended, have important implications for the devotional life—this text is in the end a primer on *spiritual perceptual realism*. Thus the book's subtitle, *Why We Can Trust Spiritual Knowledge*, is more appropriate, as is the title of the British edition, especially its subtitle: *Personal Religion, Public Reality? Toward a Knowledge of Faith* (Hodder & Stoughton, 2009).

[53] Likely due to his busy schedule during this late period of his life and work, Willard does not appear to have given as much time to preparing and editing this book as the previous four books.

to be the odd one out in the pentalogy.⁵⁴ Yet in many ways, Willard has ended the series where he began in *In Search of Guidance*: with a phenomenological rendering of the divine-human relationship that makes knowledge of the spiritual life—and, moreover, of Christ himself—possible. The main differences between his first and fifth books may be that here he is writing expressly for pastors and thus is more forthcoming with his argument and more instructive. But the vision behind the bookend volumes is quite similar.

Along with the pentalogy, included in this category are a number of other articles that elucidate or expand his theory of spiritual formation rather than merely repeat what is said in the five books. More scholarly in nature than Willard's other occasional essays, most of these were published in academic journals or volumes.⁵⁵ This layer of his corpus also includes his footnotes and references to relevant material (books, articles, etc.), most of which are supplied in his pentalogy. As a phenomenologist, Willard was more interested in presenting an idea or argument in a manner it could be best comprehended—and hopefully even tested—by the reader or listener than in quoting an authority to support his case or naming those who agreed with him, including from whom he learned a particular concept. Thus when Willard does cite an author or book, he hoped his readers would get their hands on these works and further investigate the matter for

---

⁵⁴Professor Klaus Issler of Biola University excludes *Knowing Christ Today* in his otherwise excellent summary of the pervasive themes in Willard's writings on spiritual formation, since he takes for granted that Willard wrote "four key books on the subject." See Issler, "An Orientation to Four Pervading Themes of the Christian Life from Dallas Willard," *Talbot School of Theology Faculty Blog*, March 9, 2015, www.biola.edu/blogs/good-book-blog/2015/an-orientation-to-four-pervading-themes-of-the-christian-life-from-dallas-willard.

⁵⁵Some noteworthy, which I engage in this book, are Dallas Willard, "Spiritual Formation and the Warfare Between the Flesh and the Human Spirit," *Journal of Spiritual Formation & Soul Care* 1, no. 1 (2008): 79-87; Willard, "Discipleship," in *The Oxford Handbook of Evangelical Theology*, ed. Gerald R. McDermott (Oxford University Press, 2010), 236-46; Willard, "Jesus," in *Dictionary of Christian Spirituality*, ed. Glen G. Scorgie (Zondervan, 2011), 58-63; and his five essays in *The Renovaré Spiritual Formation Bible*, ed. Richard J. Foster et al. (HarperSanFrancisco, 2005), such as "The People of God in Individual Communion with God," 1-5. Willard served as a general editor for this last work, which was later renamed *The Life with God Bible*, and was responsible for drafting a key section of its introductory essay.

themselves. For the study of Willard's thought, careful exploration of footnotes and references may yield important insights.

These five works and related articles, taken together, allow for the reconstruction of a unified theory of spiritual formation. Also, if the philosophical writings are the most *fundamental* and the recordings the most *voluminous* of the Willardian corpus, the pentalogy is (or at least has been) the most *consequential*, in terms of influence. For those who have been deeply impacted by Willard's ideas, these five books were often the catalyst. For that reason, I have included a summary of the pentalogy in table 2.1 as a reference point for what follows.

Crust: Popular and posthumous writings in spirituality. This brings us to the outermost layer of the Willardian corpus: his popular and posthumous writings in spirituality. Over the years, Willard wrote various short pieces and gave interviews for popular books and magazines. One of his bestselling books, in fact, is a collection of these essays and interviews, most of which were previously published: *The Great Omission* (2006). While this book and others like it make his ideas accessible and are an entry point for those not familiar with his work, they should not be counted in the same category as his pentalogy and related articles for a few reasons.

First, by design, they do not exhibit the same depth, and what insight they do offer can be found in the five main books with more substance. Willard's name appears as coauthor on a few books translated and adapted by colleagues or friends who sought to bring his ideas to a wider audience.[56] These writings do not evidence the same complexity of thought as the pentalogy.[57] I would also include in

---

[56]E.g., Dallas Willard and Donald Simpson, *Revolution of Character: Discovering Christ's Pattern for Spiritual Transformation* (NavPress, 2005); Willard and Jan Johnson, *Renovation of the Heart in Daily Practice: Experiments in Spiritual Transformation* (NavPress, 2006). Both books were produced entirely by the coauthor, and by all accounts Willard would have preferred that they receive full credit.

[57]One exception may be *The Divine Conspiracy Continued: Fulfilling God's Kingdom on Earth* (HarperOne, 2014), which Willard coauthored with Gary Black Jr. and was published posthumously.

Table 2.1. Summary of Willard's pentalogy

In Search of Guidance (1984, 1993), retitled *Hearing God* (1999, 2012)	A wise and accessible introduction to Willard's realist understanding of how we interact with God, shaped by his philosophical convictions about metaphysics and knowledge. Written in layperson's terms, it presents divine guidance not as the centerpiece but as a natural consequence of an ongoing, conversational relationship with the triune God.
The Spirit of the Disciplines (1988)	Willard's biblical and theological foundation for spiritual transformation, this work presents salvation as a life lived with God, not merely the forgiveness of sins. It makes a compelling case for the disciplines as means of grace and sketches the central themes of his holistic theory of formation, including its societal and cultural implications.
The Divine Conspiracy (1998)	Often regarded as Willard's magnum opus, this book reframes the gospel as the present availability of life under God's reign through apprenticeship to Jesus. It offers a penetrating critique of "sin management" versions of Christianity and recasts the Sermon on the Mount as a manifesto for living deeply in the kingdom and participating in God's redemptive work.
Renovation of the Heart (2002)	Willard's most psychological work and his mature theological anthropology, this book explores the nature of the human person through a model of formation from the inside out. It shows how each dimension of the self—spirit, mind, body, social context, and soul—can be renewed by God's Spirit through kingdom apprenticeship, that is, a process of transformation grounded in living as a student of Jesus.
Knowing Christ Today (2009)	A pastoral distillation of Willard's epistemology for the with-God life, this work retains its philosophical depth while arguing that moral and spiritual knowledge belong in the public domain. It calls for Jesus to be taken seriously not only as Savior but as the supreme intellectual and moral authority.

this category the many forewords Willard wrote to books, which tend to be short and laudatory, as one would expect, but also indicate some of his interactions with the thoughts and theologies of other contemporary authors.[58]

Included in the crust layer are also transcribed books published posthumously and based on sermon series or talks Willard gave, such as *Living in Christ's Presence* (2013), *The Allure of Gentleness* (2015), *Life Without Lack* (2018), and *The Scandal of the Kingdom* (2024).[59] Considering the number of recorded sermons and other lectures out there, more of these types of books are likely to come. Willard customarily heavily edited his books before their final draft, so those studying his thought may reference these transcribed books, but they should not be treated as on the same level as the pentalogy or even the extant recordings they are based on.[60]

Yet, as others have pointed out, it is not always clear whether the arguments there are primarily Willard's or Black's. On this, see Michael Stewart Robb, "The Kingdom Among Us: Jesus, the Kingdom of God and the Gospel According to Dallas Willard" (PhD diss., University of Aberdeen, 2016), 18. However, as strictly an editor, Black produced a thick volume of Willard's articles and interviews titled *Renewing the Christian Mind: Essays, Interviews, and Talks* (HarperOne, 2016), which also contains fourteen unpublished writings previously only accessible in the Dallas Willard Collection. This volume invites a deeper engagement with Willard among his general readership; however, those interested in primary research should consult the original, unedited documents.

[58]E.g., Dallas Willard, foreword to *Christianity in the Academy: Teaching at the Intersection of Faith and Learning*, by Harry Lee Poe (Baker Academic, 2004); Willard, foreword to *How I Changed My Mind About Women in Leadership: Compelling Stories from Prominent Evangelicals*, by Alan F. Johnson (Zondervan, 2010).

[59]Dallas Willard, John Ortberg, and Gary W. Moon, *Living in Christ's Presence: Final Words on Heaven and the Kingdom of God* (InterVarsity Press, 2013); Willard, *The Allure of Gentleness: Defending the Faith in the Manner of Jesus*, ed. Rebecca Willard Heatley (HarperOne, 2015); Willard, *Life Without Lack: Living in the Fullness of Psalm 23*, ed. Larry Burtoft and Rebecca Willard Heatley (Thomas Nelson, 2018); Willard, *The Scandal of the Kingdom: How the Parables of Jesus Revolutionize Life with God*, ed. Rebecca Willard Heatley and Jan Johnson (Zondervan, 2024). A set of Willard's speeches transcribed also appears in Jim Wilder, *Renovated: God, Dallas Willard and the Church That Transforms* (NavPress, 2020).

[60]See, e.g., the preface by Rebecca Willard Heatley in *Allure of Gentleness*, where she describes Willard's view on having his talks transcribed into books. After listening to old cassette tapes of a four-part series of talks he gave at a church in 1990, she asked her father whether he would consider letting her transcribe the talks so they might be published as a short book. He agreed, but with the stipulation that he would add additional topics and edit the final manuscript. She goes on to explain, "Before we were able to work on those additional topics, my father began struggling with health issues and was eventually diagnosed with cancer. For many months he

Since this study of Willard focuses on his formational theology, my primary sources are his pentalogy and audio/video recordings. Over the course of my research, I also read his major philosophical writings to better understand the foundations of his thought. Yet, when reconstructing his theory of formation, I prioritize his theological writings, drawing on his philosophical work only when a deeper level of logic or argumentation is needed. And in this book, I rarely engage with his popular/posthumous writings in spirituality, as Willard articulated nearly all his ideas with greater sophistication elsewhere.

THE DNA OF WILLARD'S FORMATION THEORY

Considering earlier observations about Willard's eclecticism of mind, analyzing his theory of formation in a strictly systematic theological fashion risks misrepresenting or stifling his paradigm and the unique manner in which he develops it. Furthermore, given my discovery that Willard's formational theology has a rather sharp missional edge, its presentation should reveal this implicit dimension. Thus, in the following chapters I will describe his theory in terms of its foundational themes while also drawing out its latent missional logic.

These foundational themes are the DNA, so to speak, of Willard's approach to spiritual formation—they act as basic doctrinal rules that hold together his theory. That said, I should note the limitations of my approach from the onset. These themes are not readily available in Willard's corpus (i.e., he does not set them forth in any systematic manner) but need to be reconstructed by an analysis of his work. Interpretive decision-making is inevitable.

I arranged the chapters to show how certain themes build on one another and how, in Willard's view, discipleship to Jesus in the

---

told me, 'Don't do anything with the book yet. We'll work on it when I'm feeling better'" (xii). Willard never recovered, so Heatley was left with his papers and other recordings to use to fill in gaps and expand the material. We should be thankful for the hard work Heatley and others are doing to bring to light some of Willard's teachings that have remained obscure because they exist only in recorded talks. Yet this shows why these transcribed books should not be treated with the same authority as the pentalogy and related articles, and why the recordings themselves cannot be placed above the pentalogy.

kingdom naturally leads to outward, externalized engagement with the world. However, apart from this structure, the themes should be understood as nonlinear. While Willard did give more attention to certain topics in his writing and teaching, this was not necessarily because he deemed them more important. He may have elevated some themes due to their significance, or perhaps felt they needed emphasis because the church has neglected them or our cultural situation demands it. While I do not presume to know which is which, I contend Willard would say all of the themes covered here are crucial for persons to be formed in the image of Christ as an integral part of God's redemptive work in the world.

The following eight chapters systematically analyze the foundational themes that underlie Willard's theology of spiritual formation and missional vision. The central issue these chapters seek to explain is: How can people be transformed in Christlikeness, and how does this formation relate to God's ongoing redemptive work in the present age and the one to come?

PART 1

THE LARGER FRAMEWORK AND FOUNDATION OF FORMATION

THREE

TRAINING FOR REIGNING

BURIED IN A FOOTNOTE in *Spirit of the Disciplines*, Willard takes a subtle yet strong shot at two cherished pieces of historical theology, spanning the Protestant and Catholic worlds: the opening line from the Westminster Catechism and the "First Principle and Foundation" of Ignatius's *Spiritual Exercises*.[1] Not known for having a polemical style, why do the gloves come off for Willard here? Because as helpful and eloquent as these statements are otherwise, they have, in his estimation, defined spirituality without reference to vocation, thus severing the eschatological dimension from formation in Christlikeness.

What is the telos or end state of our formation in Christ? This question addresses the divine purposes of God—why the Father intends we be formed in the image of the Son through the agency of the Spirit—and is perhaps the crux of any treatment of spiritual formation, since the stated goal will serve as the organizing framework, determining toward what end all other elements are oriented.[2] Some accounts of sanctification delineate between the penultimate and ultimate goals, between the ancillary and the telos.[3] If we follow this

---

[1] Dallas Willard, *The Spirit of the Disciplines: Understanding How God Changes Lives* (Harper & Row, 1988), 55n2.

[2] For further discussion of this point, see Steven L. Porter, "On the Renewal of Interest in the Doctrine of Sanctification: A Methodological Reminder," *Journal of the Evangelical Theological Society* 45, no. 3 (2002): 416-20.

[3] E.g., Frederick D. Aquino, "Spiritual Formation, Authority, and Discernment," in *The Oxford Handbook of the Epistemology of Theology*, ed. William J. Abraham and Frederick D. Aquino (Oxford University Press, 2017), 157-72. It could also be argued that eighteenth-century American

course with Willard, we might name these as union with God and reigning with God, respectively. However, these aims are inextricably connected in his theology, so ultimately such a neat distinction breaks down.

In short, Willard's view of the telos of spiritual formation is a complex one involving several essential parts, but *reigning* is the most summative of the whole.[4] In his view, the fullness of our reigning will be realized only after Christ's second coming, hence this present life (and the present age until the parousia) is understood as one of *training* for reigning.[5] This should be kept in mind (and tested) for the remainder of our treatment of this theme.

When it comes to training for reigning, or the eschatology of formation,[6] Willard employs a few particular biblical concepts to explain its rationale. These are the *imago Dei* in the human creature, the spiritual nature of kingdom, and the paradigmatic system of judges in the Old Testament.

---

theologian Jonathan Edwards follows this structure or hierarchy by sharply delineating between the *chief* and *ultimate* ends of human life and virtue. I shall have more to say about Edwards's view later.

[4]Willard also occasionally states that the aim of God in history is the formation of an all-inclusive community of loving persons with God at its center. I will discuss this later in the chapter and explain its connection—and, ultimately, subordination—to the theme of reigning with God in Willard's theology.

[5]One place this is parsed out is Dallas Willard, *The Divine Conspiracy: Rediscovering Our Hidden Life in God* (HarperSanFrancisco, 1998), 396-99, where he describes three progressive stages of the with-God life we are invited to experience, beginning here and continuing into eternity. The first ("the time of growing steadily") concerns the gradual transformation our character should undergo through friendship with the Trinity in *this life*. The second ("the time of passage") is our transition *through death* into a new phase of existence in God's full world. And the third ("the time of reigning with Jesus") marks our *eternal destiny* in the creative governance of God over the cosmos. Of its timing, Willard writes, "I can only imagine it will be some while after our passage into God's full world [that] we will begin to assume new responsibilities" (398). Notably, Willard reserves "reigning with God" for the third stage, while our present life is described as one of "co-laboring with God." This distinction is crucial to his understanding of the different roles in each stage.

[6]My approach to the doctrine of last things concerns not only the end of history, what comes last in a temporal and sequential sense, but also the divine telos and intention behind God's activity in history. Thus, eschatology here is understood as inclusive of teleology.

THE *IMAGO DEI* IN THE HUMAN CREATURE

To understand the meaning of the image of God in humans, Willard turns to the "human job description" spelled out in Genesis 1.[7] The mandate given to the first humans was "to exercise lordship, care, and supervision over the zoological creation" and the rest of the created order on earth.[8] God created humanity to rule over an appropriate domain of reality under his lordship, and we are each given a measure of independent power to accomplish this. Willard's view might be said to draw from or integrate the three main perspectives on how humanity bears the image of God—the structural, functional, and relational—without landing squarely on one.[9] The *imago Dei* is structural in that it involves a human ability, but unlike other structural accounts, especially those of the early church and medieval scholastics, this ability is not rationality or moral consciousness but

---

[7]Willard, *Divine Conspiracy*, 22.

[8]Willard, *Spirit of the Disciplines*, 48. Feminist and postcolonial theologians, such as Ada María Isasi-Díaz, have challenged the patriarchal and imperial connotations of biblical terms such as *dominion*, *subdue*, and *kingdom*, proposing, for instance, alternatives such as *kin-dom* to emphasize mutuality and shared participation across the created order. Other biblical theologians, such as Old Testament scholars Ellen Davis and J. Richard Middleton, do not adopt this revised terminology but share many of the same concerns, especially regarding the misuse of *rule* (Hebrew *rādâ*) in Gen 1. Davis, in *Scripture, Culture, and Agriculture: An Agrarian Reading of the Bible* (Cambridge University Press, 2008), reclaims the language of dominion by reading it through an agrarian and covenantal lens: Humans are to exercise skilled, relational stewardship that reflects God's own life-giving governance. Middleton, in *The Liberating Image: The Imago Dei in Genesis 1* (Brazos, 2005), portrays the Genesis account as drawing upon and subverting ancient Near Eastern kingship: Rule is not control but care, the royal task of representing the divine presence by ordering and stewarding life. As we will see, these interpretations closely align with Willard's understanding of dominion/rule as participation in God's redemptive and loving care for creation, a vocation fulfilled only through union with the Trinity and the cultivation of agapeic character.

[9]To what extent Willard was aware of these three positions or of the long historical discourse in theology surrounding them is unclear since he does not wade into the debates or use the technical terminology to describe his own position. He does make a point to distance himself from the classic structural view, but what he proposes in its place appears to be a cross between the structural and functional, and it is also deeply relational. Hence, he often connects all three dimensions in short order when commenting on the creation covenant or the *imago Dei*. For example: "Creative will is the image of God in man. And we're meant to live and work with God, act with God. And that's how Adam and Eve were supposed to do what they did, [by] acting with God." Dallas Willard, "Session 1—Part 2" (March 9, 2004), MP3, 40:30.

creative will.[10] Yet it is also functional since creative will is not a static attribute of human persons but one that does something: it moves to create, thus it consists of *creative action*.[11] Willard most often emphasizes the functional view, yet on closer inspection we see that the structural and the functional (and the relational, to a lesser degree) interpenetrate each other in his thought; one does not come without the other.[12] Lastly, the *imago Dei* is also relational in that it entails *shared responsibility*—with other humans and creation, but above all with God himself. We are to exercise dominion (through the use of creative will) with God over the earth. As Willard explains:

> However unlikely it may seem from our current viewpoint, God equipped us for this task by framing our nature to function in a conscious, personal relationship of interactive responsibility *with* him. We are meant to exercise our "rule" only in union with God, as he acts with us. He intended to be our constant companion or co-worker in the creative enterprise of life on earth. That is what his love for us means in practical terms.[13]

The first book in Scripture tells how, when humanity distanced itself from God, fumbling its high calling, God did not abandon his original intention and dream for human life. Instead, he launched a redemptive project—a "divine conspiracy"—that would adequately address our sin and rebellion to bring about our renewal, so that we might eventually become the sort of people who could fulfill that original calling and vocation. According to Willard, God's divine conspiracy is nothing less than the "redemption of *our* rule."[14]

---

[10]Dallas Willard, "Leadership as Love of God and Neighbor" (May 15, 2000), MP3, 20:15.

[11]Dallas Willard, "The Biblical Understanding of the Reality of God" (April 24, 1990), MP3, 59:15.

[12]For an example of the interpenetration between the structural and functional, see his discussion in *Spirit of the Disciplines*, 52-53, of how the human body is a part of the *imago Dei*, since the body "is the vehicle through which we can effectively acquire the limited self-subsistent power we must have to be truly in the image and likeness of God," and thus "is our primary area of power, freedom, and—therefore—responsibility" (53).

[13]Willard, *Divine Conspiracy*, 22.

[14]Willard, *Divine Conspiracy*, 23.

The last book in Scripture points toward a future in which God's people, under God's loving rulership and leadership, will govern the earth (Rev 5:10), and these saints will reign with him forever over the cosmos (Rev 22:5).[15] Echoes of this same reality are heard in the epistles, with Paul asking the church in Corinth, "Do you not know that the Lord's people will judge the world?" (1 Cor 6:2). For Willard, the burden of the whole of God's revelation points to the fact that in the life to come God's people will be given great responsibility as they reign with Christ. Our present life, then, is the training ground for growing into the type of people God can entrust with that responsibility.[16] Thus the eschatological logic of spiritual formation moves backward: Reigning with Christ—the fulfillment of the original vocation given to humanity—requires we first have the agapeic character that can handle such power.

THE SPIRITUAL NATURE OF KINGDOM

There is an organic connection in Willard's thought between the *imago Dei* and the biblical notion of kingdom. Since humans were made to rule, every person has, to some extent, a kingdom or queendom—the range of reality they genuinely have say over. This is as true for those who have no interest in God's purposes as it is for those who are in lockstep with God's will, who walk by the Spirit, since the capacity to "say so," even if only over a small and limited sphere, is an essential dimension of personhood. The image of God

---

[15]This is one of the ways Rev 21–22 is the fulfillment of Gen 1–2.

[16]Willard, as an editor for *The Renovaré Spiritual Formation Bible*, suggests this would be the case even if the fall had never occurred and Adam and Eve were without sin. Yet given the indispensability of character and virtue for right living, it was inevitable that our primordial parents would fall. As the editors note, "Adam and Eve 'fell' because, though innocent, they lacked character. Innocence is not virtue. Innocence, for all its beauty, is a form of ignorance and lack of character." See the editors' essay, "A Panoramic View of God's Purpose in History," in *The Renovaré Spiritual Formation Bible*, ed. Richard J. Foster et al. (HarperSanFrancisco, 2005), xxxvii. Cf. Dallas Willard, "The Moral Significance of the Academic Life" (November 29, 1990), video, starting at 28:30. The vocation God has given to humanity requires that they partner with him and partake of his power (empowerment) to be more fully formed in his likeness and therefore capable of co-reigning with him.

(as creative will) can become corrupted and grossly distorted in a human being, but it cannot be completely lost, for, as Willard states, "Any being that has say over nothing at all is no person."[17]

Likewise, for Willard, the kingdom of God is fundamentally a *spiritual* kingdom in contrast to a social/political one. It is the range of God's effective will, the realm of reality over which God has the deciding voice and what he wants done is done. This is not to say God's kingdom does not relate to the social and political or cannot be expressed in the social/political order, for it does and can. But to start there—or to place our primary concern there—is to radically misapprehend the fundamental nature of God's kingdom.[18] The kingdom of God is an *eternal* reality, says Willard. It is all that God rules over, beginning with the spiritual order that derives from God's personality and action.[19] This means Jesus did not bring or inaugurate God's kingdom; it has existed since before creation and is older than time. What was new in Jesus' ministry was the *availability* of that kingdom, the good news that *all* may now enter and experience life under the reign of God through the person of Jesus.[20] Part and parcel of this *euangelion* is that as we grow in confident reliance on Jesus, we learn

---

[17] Willard, *Divine Conspiracy*, 22. This statement raises important questions about persons with profound intellectual disabilities or those in a coma. In fact, some parents of children with significant disabilities contacted Willard about this very issue. His daughter, Rebecca Willard Heatley, recalls discussing at least one such case with him and said it was clear he was grieved by how his words were being received, for that was never his intention (personal communication, May 19, 2025). He may have preferred the more careful phrasing used above: "an essential dimension."

[18] According to Willard, this was the *main* misunderstanding among late Second Temple Jews that Jesus came to set right: "In first-century Judaism, it was clear that the kingdom of God was supposed to be something political that appeared and led the Jews to triumph.... But the primary task that Jesus had was *correcting the view* that people of his day imposed on the kingdom of God." Dallas Willard, "Q & A: Prayer" (July 15, 2004), MP3, 45:15, 48:00.

[19] See Willard, *Spirit of the Disciplines*, 67; Willard, *Divine Conspiracy*, 25-26. In terms of doctrinal placement in systematic theology, Michael Stewart Robb argues convincingly that Willard would place the kingdom under theology proper. See Robb, *The Kingdom Among Us: The Gospel According to Dallas Willard* (Fortress, 2022), 58, 175-76.

[20] There is also a sense, for Willard, in which Jesus himself is the kingdom, but he invokes this formula (or rather, he quotes those who invoke it) in a reserved fashion. For discussion, I again refer the reader to Robb's detailed study of the subject; see *Kingdom Among Us*, 366-67.

to govern our small affairs—our kingdom or queendom—as he would. This is how our rule becomes integrated with God's rule, and in time we are given a bigger share in the governance of God.

Although Willard's emphasis on the here-and-now-ness of the kingdom is an alternative to the "already and not yet" view of God's present rule on earth, he does reach a similar conclusion but in a roundabout way. There is still a future degree of the kingdom to be realized, a fullness to God's reign that we await, but the human condition is the sole reason why the "not yet" has, well, not yet come. Again, Willard holds that we are not waiting for the kingdom to come into existence, for it has always existed. If one were to summarize his position in a phrase comparable to Oscar Cullmann's and George Eldon Ladd's well-known "already and not yet" formula for God's kingdom, I suggest it would be "always, already, and not yet." It is the *always* dimension of the kingdom—in short, its eternality—that Willard feels modern theology neglects.[21] But he recognizes there is also more kingdom to come, more of the domain of God's effective will to be in effect. He expounds on this in discussion of the phrase "Thy kingdom come" in the Lord's Prayer:

> The kingdom of God is from everlastingly earlier to everlastingly later. It does not come into existence, nor does it cease. But in human affairs other "kingdoms" may for a time be in power, and often are. This second request [of the Lord's Prayer] asks for those kingdoms to be displaced, wherever they are, or brought under God's rule. . . . And we are especially praying about the structural or institutionalized evils that rule so much of the earth. . . . We therefore pray for our Father to

---

[21]Now, it should be noted that modern scholars advocating an already-and-not-yet view (Ladd, N. T. Wright, Richard Bauckham, etc.) also grant that God's kingdom has always existed. What they mean by "not yet" is that it is "not yet fully realized *on earth*" due to sin and the fallenness of creation. But Willard thinks this theological "already/not yet" balancing act has the practical result of leading most people to delay life in the kingdom until the "not yet." He goes so far as to say on one occasion that such talk is "really dangerous." Dallas Willard, "The Self/Spiritual Transformation and Discipline" (May 17, 2000), MP3, 19:00. Willard's view may also bear some semblance to contemporary Pentecostal views of the kingdom being "hidden" and becoming "manifest" (which is quite different from "already" and "not yet"), but I cannot explore this here.

break up these higher-level patterns of evil. And, among other things, we ask him to help us see the patterns *we* are involved in. We ask him to help us not cooperate with them, to cast light on them and act effectively to remove them.[22]

We are waiting not for a future act of God so much as for humanity to get its act together. This is the plain meaning, for Willard, of Paul's words that creation is eagerly awaiting the "manifestation of the children of God" (Rom 8:19).[23] As long as the little kingdoms of many individuals stand in contradiction to the plan and purposes of God's reign, there will remain a clash of kingdoms, and the presence of evil will persist in social structures and human life.

What is needed, then, is a complete overhaul of life as we know it and, in its place, a comprehensive and ordered system of discipleship to Jesus that is capable of thoroughly transforming the inner life and overall character of human beings so the vision and values of God's loving reign become embedded in human life and, eventually, throughout society. Willard contends the contours of this type of full-scale discipleship project can be found in the Sermon on the Mount and other New Testament writings but that it remains an open question whether the church will commit itself to actually implementing such a curriculum in the lives of its members. As he often stated, "Discipleship is for the world; the church is for discipleship."[24]

Excursus: The Sources of Willard's Kingdom Theology

Considering the relative uniqueness of Willard's view of God's kingdom and its formidable place in his work, it is worth briefly commenting on

---

[22] Willard, *Divine Conspiracy*, 260.
[23] Dallas Willard, "Last Things" (August 20, 1987), MP3, 6:45, 7:45, 8:45.
[24] Dallas Willard, "What Does Holiness Look Like Shorn of Its Legalistic Expressions? 1" (January 4, 2010), video, 10:45. See also Willard, *Knowing Christ Today: Why We Can Trust Spiritual Knowledge* (HarperOne, 2009), 209.

its possible sources in modern theology. We know from footnotes, comments made in sermons and interviews, and occasional direct endorsements that Willard was influenced by John Bright's *The Kingdom of God* (1953), E. Stanley Jones's *Is the Kingdom of God Realism?* (1940), Ladd's kingdom theology, and to a lesser extent C. H. Dodd's realized eschatology. Yet it is far from clear to what degree one can say his view is derivative of these.

For instance, he first read Bright's study for a college course at Baylor in 1958, later describing the experience as "really a turning point."[25] Yet if this text had as much of an impact on his thinking as he indicated toward the end of his life, listing it among his top five all-time books,[26] it seems odd he waited five decades to publicly mention the book. And it is especially curious that he does not engage it in *Divine Conspiracy*, his most substantive reflection on the kingdom. As for Jones's book, Willard had a certain affinity for it and its author. He quotes from it in his earliest teachings on the kingdom we have on record and later cites Jones among the great writers "of the quite recent past" promulgating a life-changing gospel.[27] The famous missionary was also one of the few popular spokespersons stressing the kingdom of God as the central message of the Bible at a time when the young Willard was training for ministry.[28] One might be able to trace certain ideas Willard intimated from Jones and then further

---

[25] Dallas Willard, "Q & A with Keith Matthews" (March 16, 2012), MP3, 18:00.

[26] Dallas Willard, "My Personal Top 5," in *25 Books Every Christian Should Read*, ed. Julia L. Roller (HarperOne, 2011), 155. For his only other mention of the book in written form, see Willard, "The Gospel of the Kingdom and Spiritual Formation," in *The Kingdom Life*, ed. Alan Andrews (NavPress, 2010), 59.

[27] Dallas Willard, "Jesus' Good News of God's Kingdom" (handout, June 18–September 10, 1972), Dallas Willard Collection, 6; Willard, *Divine Conspiracy*, xviii.

[28] Since realism is a main theme in Jones's writings on the kingdom (as the title of his book implies) and in the next chapter we will examine Willard's phenomenological realism, I should mention that Jones uses the terms *realism* and *idealism* in a straightforward manner, different from their technical meaning in philosophical discourse. For Jones, realism essentially means *realistic* or "pre-occupation with and devotion to fact," and idealism means *idealistic* or "pre-occupation with and devotion to idea." E. Stanley Jones, *Is the Kingdom of God Realism?* (Abingdon-Cokesbury, 1940), 14.

developed,[29] but he does not himself suggest a direct connection in any writings or recordings I am aware of.

Although appreciative of Ladd's work, at one point stating, "the best writings I know on the kingdom of God are by a man named John Ladd [sic]," Willard pushes back against, or at least significantly reconfigures, the "already and not yet" view of the kingdom formulated by Cullmann and later popularized by Ladd.[30] I have already indicated how the Cullmann-Ladd kingdom timeline might be rendered with a Willardian twist. Lastly, Willard twice quotes Dodd's *The Parables of the Kingdom* (1935) in *Divine Conspiracy*—once approvingly, the other disparagingly—and briefly mentions him affirmatively in a coauthored article.[31] To my knowledge, these are his only references to Dodd. I find this the most surprising, considering Dodd's realized eschatology (with its emphasis clearly on the "already" rather than the "not yet") is perhaps the closest comparison in modern exegetical scholarship to Willard's view of the kingdom, albeit Dodd does not emphasize the kingdom's *availability* as Willard does.

I should mention that while researching at the Dallas Willard Collection, I perused all books by these authors in what remains of Willard's personal library (the archivists estimate that 65 percent of his approximately 10,730 personal books was not retained). We can assume he owned the above work by Dodd, but it no longer remains,

---

[29] E.g., compare Willard's view, which I have phrased as "always, already, and not yet," with Jones's discussion of the three phases of the coming of the kingdom, based on his exegesis of the threefold designation of God in Rev 1:4, "He who *is* and *was* and is *coming*" (Moffatt translation). Allow me to piece together a summary of the latter in Jones, *Is the Kingdom of God Realism?*, 59-60. Jones argues the kingdom *was*, in that "it was prepared from the foundation of the world, built into its very structure, the method of its working, the laws of it being," yet it is also *coming*, in that "it is coming all the time as men receive it" and "it is the Great Consummation to which the whole universe moves." Nevertheless, "primarily and fundamentally the Kingdom *is*. These emphases on the past and the future are essential, but not *the* essential. The essential thing to be burned into our thinking is the fact that the Kingdom *is*."

[30] For this appreciative comment, see Dallas Willard, "What Is the Kingdom of God?" (January 13, 1985), MP3, 22:30; for his subtle polemic, see *Divine Conspiracy*, 402n19; for his reconfiguration of this view, see *Divine Conspiracy*, 29.

[31] Willard, *Divine Conspiracy*, 29, 73; Robert F. Cochran Jr. and Dallas Willard, "The Kingdom of God, Law, and the Heart: Jesus and the Civil Law," in *Law and the Bible: Justice, Mercy, and Legal Institutions*, ed. Robert F. Cochran Jr. and David VanDrunen (IVP Academic, 2013), 156.

which means it likely was absent of significant marginalia since this was a criterion for determining what volumes were kept. I did locate Bright's book, Jones's book, and four of Ladd's books, all of which showed heavy engagement from Willard, with lots of markings and some notes. It is clear he agreed with much that he read, but there are plenty of critical notes of Ladd. For example, next to certain passages Willard penned, "just wrong," "NO!" or "nuts."

To reiterate, these are the prominent kingdom theologies Willard commends, but it is hard to definitively say they are the sources of his own view.[32] And apart from Bright and Jones, his commendation of these authors and works is enigmatic at best.

THE PARADIGMATIC SYSTEM OF JUDGES IN THE OLD TESTAMENT

A third aspect of Willard's eschatology of formation deals with Israel's system of judges as paradigmatic of godly human leadership and governance. (Please note: this is a reference to the *system of judges* implemented by Moses, not the *book of Judges* in the biblical canon, though we will see Willard has something to say about the tragic tale of the latter.) The connection between the *imago Dei* and kingdom further extends as a bridge to this particular model of social organization in the Old Testament. The line of thinking is as follows: Humans were created to rule with God—to mesh their little kingdoms with his great kingdom and so share in the governance of the heavens and of earth through their creative will. This vocation requires virtue, and God designed personhood in such a way that virtue must be developed through volition and habituation. Yet sin has so greatly mired the creative will in humans that we have come to accept the fallen, sad state of humanity as normal. What is required, then, is not merely the formation of human character but its radical transformation. The

---

[32]For a more extensive examination of the possible sources of Willard's view, including a comparison with N. T. Wright's position, see Robb, *Kingdom Among Us*.

church must commit itself to a program of "full-throttle discipleship to Jesus Christ," for there is no way except through the path of genuine spiritual transformation for God's people to become those who can lovingly govern the world with the wisdom and power of Jesus.[33] So, if this is to become a reality, what might shared governance with God look like in human society?

Willard suggests it has been foreshadowed in very practical ways by the nation of Israel from the time of its sojourn in the wilderness up to the institution of the monarchy. Before the Sinai lawgiving material appears in the book of Exodus, Moses' father-in-law, Jethro, advises Moses on the art of delegation and specifically on how to decentralize authority for a more tribal structure. We are told that Moses "did everything [Jethro] said" (Ex 18:24) and thus initiated a system of "judges" or "officials" appointed to guide, counsel, and lead the nation in all aspects of its societal life (cf. Deut 1:9-18; Num 11:16-17). "There is every reason to believe, when we penetrate into the life context of Old Testament events," says Willard,

> that the attitude in which this system was to be carried out was that of thoughtful, compassionate neighbors who were living entirely within the letter and the spirit of the Ten Commandments and with the help of other counsels of God to the Jewish people. . . . Legitimate needs of the individual would be known and would be cared for from the resources of the community, wherein all lived with a consciousness of provision by God. To "judge" was to have the responsibility for making sure that justice was being done in the community, that things were going as they should.[34]

---

[33] Dallas Willard, *Renovation of the Heart: Putting On the Character of Christ* (NavPress, 2002), 239.

[34] Willard, *Spirit of the Disciplines*, 240. Nearly two decades later, Willard's editorial hand is evident in an introductory essay on the last four books of the Torah, which presents the judiciary system established in Ex 18 as one of the "blessings and benefits" derived from this period of Israel's history: "The judge is the first level of an administrative or political structure that is also composed of priests and, ultimately, God. We call this kind of political system a 'theocracy.' The person of the judge becomes a primary way for God's presence to be mediated even in the everyday disputes between members of the community." The editors' essay, "The People of God in Exodus," in Foster et al., *Renovaré Spiritual Formation Bible*, 90.

A tiered network of qualified leaders adequately distributed and positioned throughout society acting in concert with God and in service to God's people is, for Willard, the model of what the rule of God looks like in human affairs.[35]

Sadly, this system of judges ultimately failed in Israel's day strictly on account of the leaders who occupied the places of authority and power. With the exception of a precious few, these leaders lacked the maturity and moral strength needed to exercise Yahweh's power responsibly throughout the social order. Yet Willard maintains that the system still stands as a valid model of leadership and governance and that God intends for it to become a functional social reality one day.[36] However, such an arrangement will forever remain a frightening prospect unless those judges or leaders put in charge have developed the character and wisdom required for this human structure to be a mass social blessing rather than a menace to society. I cannot overstate how crucial this is for Willard. "God is greatly concerned with the quality of character we are building," he writes. "The future

---

[35] In *Spirit of the Disciplines*, Willard focuses more on the system of judges instituted by Moses in the newly formed nation of Israel than on the way this system was appropriated per se in the book of Judges. He does comment on the latter sparingly, also offering a rather unusual interpretation of the book's closing line: "every man did that which was right in his own eyes" (Judg 21:25); see *Spirit of the Disciplines*, 242. However, in public talks given in the mid-1980s while he was presumably working on *Spirit of the Disciplines*, he is more forthcoming about the book of Judges, calling it "perhaps the single most misunderstood and important book in the Old Testament" and "a pivotal book in the whole story of redemption . . . because it has to do with how God intends to govern and rule and judge the world through human beings." Willard, "What Is the Kingdom of God?" (January 13, 1985), 15:45; Dallas Willard with A. Grace Wenger, "The Saints Shall Judge the World" (January 16, 1985), MP3, 1:18:45. Willard clearly viewed the book of Judges as exemplifying the Mosaic system of judges and thus God's desire to reign through transformed individuals who carry his character, while acknowledging that the experimental run it was given in this period of Israel's history was grossly marred by those who held the position of "judge."

[36] In fact, Willard likens the role of Old Testament judges to that of pastors today, since both are primarily responsible for providing guidance and wise counsel. See Dallas Willard, "The Pastor" (August 5, 1987), MP3, 44:00; see also Willard, "Last Things," starting at 35:00, where he comments that when God's people judge the nations in the future, it will be "in the sense of the Old Testament, of guiding them and helping them know how to live—not in the sense of passing judgment on their sins or anything like that." He thus recommends that when studying the concept of judges in the Old Testament, we think of it as "*leading* instead of *judging*," which better reflects "what we're going to actually be doing" in the future.

He has planned for us will be built on the strength of character we forge by His grace. Intelligent, loving devotion to Christ will grow in importance through eternity and will never become obsolete," and conversely, "Power without Christ's character gives us our modern-day Sampsons and Sauls."[37]

From Willard's perspective, the process of individuals progressing characterologically into mature, godly leaders who can handle great responsibility is the telos of Christian spiritual formation. And just as there was a "fullness of time" at which Christ first entered the world (Gal 4:4), Willard contends there will be another fullness of time in which God's people finally fulfill their divinely ordained role, anticipated in part by the Mosaic system of judges, to lovingly govern the world under their Lord's leadership.[38] In his words:

> What we are suggesting is that the details of Christ's coming reign consist in the reorganization of society on the model of the "judges," around those who assume loving responsibility for their neighbors with that fully developed character and power of Jesus Christ to which the ministry of the Kingdom of God has brought them, under the real, personal presence of Christ on earth.[39]

The holy process of forming people in Christlikeness is in the end how the world's evil power structures will be dissolved and replaced by structures of governance and a social life congruent with the reign of Christ. Thus it will come to pass, says Willard, that the saints shall judge the world.

ON MILLENNIALISM AND POLITICAL THEOLOGY

It is necessary at this point to say something evaluative about Willard's suggestion that by creating godly societal structures and government systems, we might somehow "prepare" Christ's coming, as

---

[37] Dallas Willard, "Personal Soul Care," in *The Pastor's Guide to Effective Ministry*, ed. William H. Willimon (Beacon Hill, 2002), 12, 17.
[38] Willard, *Spirit of the Disciplines*, 243.
[39] Willard, *Spirit of the Disciplines*, 248; cf. 127.

well as his particular view of what it means that the saints will rule the world. The first of these concerns the doctrine of millennialism, the second whether such a view sanctions a theocratic vision and Christian triumphalism.

While Willard seems to indicate that the church has been given everything it needs to usher in the fullness of God's reign here and now, he also asserts that the consummation of the kingdom requires the return of Christ: "A distinct reentry of the person of Christ into world history is required to complete the work."[40] On the other hand, he suggests that what must necessarily precede this future parousia is the transformation of character in God's people in such a way that they are able to mediate God's agapeic leadership through the social order: "They will then prove capable of assuming positions of leadership or 'pastoring' in all levels of society so that the whole of humankind can, at the appropriate moment in history, receive the risen and ascended Christ as its effectively reigning Lord."[41] The section that follows this passage in *Spirit of the Disciplines* is fittingly titled "Restructuring for Christ's Reign."

To further elucidate his position, let us consider a 1987 lecture given in South Africa on the topic "Last Things" and more specifically the parousia, presumably during the same time period he was working on *Spirit of the Disciplines*. These passages deserve to be quoted in full since at the time of my writing they exist only in audio form. After posing the question, "What is the fullness of time that this event awaits on?" he replies, "I'm not going to draw you a diagram tonight and tell you when it's going to happen because I don't know when it's going to happen in that [temporal] sense, but I do know when it will happen . . . *in the conditions of its occurrence.*"[42] Willard intimates

---

[40] Willard, *Spirit of the Disciplines*, 238.

[41] Willard, *Spirit of the Disciplines*, 237-38. A lot seems to hinge on what Willard means by "the real presence of Christ," a phrase he uses twice in the larger passage. The most straightforward interpretation, I submit, is that Christ's real presence is mediated through his people living in the world, what he elsewhere calls the "continuing incarnation."

[42] Willard, "Last Things," 16:00, emphasis added.

what these conditions are and how they relate to the preaching and reception of the gospel in his exegesis of Matthew 24:14, "And this gospel of the kingdom shall be preached in all the world for a witness unto all nations; and then shall the end come" (KJV).

> When that has been preached in word and in deed and certainly in power throughout all of the earth, *so that from all nations there is called out a people who are living in that kingdom*, then Jesus will return. This is not just a matter of preaching the gospel of forgiveness of sins to every nation. This is the full gospel of the kingdom of God. And when that is preached in power *and in demonstration of its reality throughout the earth*, then we will come to the point to where Jesus can return and claim his people and finish his work on earth.[43]

It is not the *mere proclamation* of the kingdom gospel that must occur but the *personal transformation* of those who receive that gospel proclamation around the world. It is Christ via the Spirit working in and through them to create a people in his image that must precipitate Christ's physical return.[44]

> You see, the only realistic hope that this world has for dealing with its problems is the person and gospel of Jesus Christ, living in the flesh-and-blood, here-and-now people who are his by total identification achieved through the appropriate exercise of the disciplines of the spiritual life, under the ministry of the word of the kingdom of heaven. This kind of faith and discipline yields a new humanity.[45]

After going on to describe the generative qualities of this "new humanity" with various scriptural passages (Mt 6:25; Phil 4:6-7; Ps 46:2; etc.), he adds: "When people of this type stand forward throughout all nations of the earth, distributed throughout the population, so that in all of the places that there is a need of leadership there are people

---

[43] Willard, "Last Things," 17:15, emphasis added.
[44] To hear Willard differentiate between being made in the *imago Dei* and being conformed to the *imago Christi*, see "Biblical Understanding of the Reality," 1:01:00.
[45] Willard, "Last Things," 18:00.

of this type standing ready to lead under Christ, *then* Christ will return. Christ will return. And that's what he's [Jesus] talking about in Matthew 24."[46]

Lastly, Willard describes the true nature of Christ's return and "last things," in contrast to what he considers a common (premillennial) misconstrual:

> Sometimes a lot of my friends in the United States present the coming of Christ as if he were going to come down with a very big stick and beat everyone into submission, as if the coming of Christ were to be the greatest act of violence in human history. I can't buy that. Jesus is not going to come back and beat everyone into submission. He's going to come back and inhabit *a prepared people* who can show the world how to live by grace and truth, who can show that mercy is the last word in human affairs as well as in the divine character.[47]

Willard therefore teaches that the conditions of Christ's second coming have to do with God's people on earth and that these conditions are both spiritual and social, in the sense that they concern the spiritual maturity of "a prepared people" and their social presence in the world.

Suffice it to say, Willard's view does not fit neatly into any of the standard categories of millennialism.[48] The fullness of the kingdom on earth is not possible without the return of Christ, yet Christ's second coming depends, to a large extent, on the maturation of

---

[46] Willard, "Last Things," 19:45, emphasis added.

[47] Willard, "Last Things," 23:45, emphasis added. Cf. Dallas Willard, "The Desire of All Nations" (May 1985), MP3, 34:15, where he states, "Now we have these excessively militaristic visions of what it's going to be like when Jesus comes back, and if there's anything that should make you uneasy about them, it is the fact that that's exactly how they thought he was going to come the first time."

[48] As further proof, consider these comments made in a 1979 Sunday school lesson. Willard states, somewhat provocatively, "I'm inclined to believe that the church of Jesus Christ, the body of Christ, is actually going to come to the place to where it governs the world." Someone then jokingly asks, "Next week?" to which he replies, "Not next week. It isn't necessarily postmil. And I think, yes, it will be during the millennium, as far as we can give precise significance to that term." Dallas Willard, "What Christ Did to Save Mankind" (1979), MP3, 47:00.

Christ's followers. When preaching on the topic of last things or heaven, he generally sidesteps the issue of millennialism, but there are at least two places in the late 1980s where he clearly espouses a premillennialist timetable.[49] In both instances, he moves on rather quickly from this, apparently because it does not mean much for him practically. Further, in a contributed essay to the Renovaré study Bible that deals with the book of Revelation, he writes, "We will never escape our finitude in this life or find complete freedom from the presence of evil around us. Therefore we must not expect to escape some measure of suffering and failure."[50] Yet apart from these examples and his straightforward statements about Christ returning to complete the work cited above, most of his teaching on the future of redemptive history can be interpreted as postmillennial, as the emphasis is on the need for mature persons in Christ to exercise godly leadership throughout the land, not least in the public sphere, to precipitate the Lord's return. What are we to make of this?

This sheds further light on his practical theological approach, which we explored in the previous chapter. Moreover, we find this same general principle at work in his position on the doctrine of complete sanctification or Christian perfectionism. His practical position on Christian perfectionism can be described as this: Whether one believes becoming perfect this side of heaven (i.e., within this lifetime) is possible or not, the only sensible thing to do is to intend to be perfect since the only other option is to intend to sin.[51] So, when it

---

[49]Dallas Willard, "The Blessed Hope" (October 19, 1986), MP3, 53:30; Willard, "Last Things," 32:15. In these talks, he gives an interesting interpretation of what the rapture is—or rather, why it will occur—which logically follows from his eschatology of formation and is thoroughly different from the doomsday interpretations common during this time. I should also note that we do not find this in his mature work, roughly 1990 onward.

[50]Dallas Willard, "The People of God into Eternity," in Foster et al., *Renovaré Spiritual Formation Bible*, 2263.

[51]E.g., "You may think: Oh, he's talking about sinless perfection, this can't be. Well, you know when we get to talking about sinless perfection I always want to ask people, 'Are you planning to continue on sinning?' You see, the issue need not be perfection. The issue is a very simple one of how we plan to live"; and "Now, I don't know that you are going to have to worry about perfection in any sense for some time, but the intent is to come to be the kind of person who sees

comes to society, his view is quite similar: Whether one believes the perfection of society this side of heaven is possible or not, the only sensible thing to do is to strive for a perfect society since the only other option is to strive (or settle) for an imperfect society.[52] Of course, this dodges the question of whether the entire transformation of self or society this side of heaven is possible, but it dodges it by pointing out that for all practical purposes, the answer does not matter. This is a case of Willard's utter practicality in theological reflection. If competing theoretical views do not make a substantive practical difference, then (he would say) we can right-size the significance of the debate.[53] The fact that we have, in addition to his writings, recordings of over a thousand hours of his preaching and teaching on all matters of theological topics, many of which include question-and-answer sessions, and he essentially eschews being pigeonholed into one particular end-times position is notable.

As for his view that the saints will share in God's governance in history, it is an open question whether he goes too far in interpreting Israel's system of judges in the Old Testament as the prototype for, or even foreshadowing of, God's rule in human affairs, and whether it is reasonable (and prudent) to promote this as an ideal for contemporary society. (There is also a concern about overspeculation, as his account of co-governance and power distribution in the eschaton is

---

the goodness of the law and learns to live there." Dallas Willard, "Spirituality and Mission" (May 1985), MP3, 23:45; Willard, "Biblical and Theological Foundations for Spiritual Formation in Christ 3" (October 11, 2011), 39:30.

[52]Willard's view of the social order and of societal transformation will receive sustained attention in chap. 8. I will note here, however, that his view of Christian perfectionism has similarities to the sociopolitical concept of "hopeful realism" or "aspirational imperfectionism" recently advanced by some Christian political theorists, which is grounded in natural law theory and Augustine's political thought. For instance, the hopeful-realism approach argues that even if ultimate perfection is unattainable, we should still engage in the pursuit of societal good and justice as a meaningful endeavor; this resonates with Willard's emphasis on striving for transformation despite practical limitations. On this, see Jesse Covington et al., *Hopeful Realism: Evangelical Natural Law and Democratic Politics* (IVP Academic, 2025).

[53]To hear him respond to the question of millennialism in precisely this vein, see Dallas Willard, "What to Do 'in Church': Eternal Living Fostered by Church Activities" (August 5, 2010), MP3, 00:15.

quite specific.) This will surely raise some hermeneutical eyebrows, so some scholars will want to interrogate his interpretation. But it is not without theological precedent, as similar views can be found among Catholic, Reformed, and even Anabaptist thinkers. Aquinas taught that the Mosaic structure of governance represented the ideal blend of aristocracy (virtuous leaders) and democracy (rulers chosen by the people) under God.[54] Calvin saw Jethro's proposed republican-type polity of "rulers over thousands, hundreds, fifties and tens" in Exodus 18:21 as divinely ordained, praising it as the most desirable kind of liberty—one that could not have originated from human ingenuity.[55] John Howard Yoder viewed Israel's premonarchic, bottom-up leadership system, wherein judges and elders led in mutuality, as a precursor to the church as an alternative polis under Christ's lordship.[56] Still, these precedents do not exempt Willard's reading from critical scrutiny.

We must be cautious in how we approach the biblical concepts of *dominion* and *rule*, as the church has a history of using these to justify its right to institutional power and an authoritative position in society. Certain presentations of the creation covenant in Genesis and the kingdom of God in the Gospels have fed various forms of radical politics and Christian triumphalism. For instance, the English Puritans in the sixteenth century dreamt of a godly empire led by saints, a vision historians later described as a utopian theology of revolution.[57] More recent examples include the Dutch Reformed Church in South Africa in the twentieth century and the increasing politicization of the evangelical church in America since the 1960s, including

---

[54]Thomas Aquinas, *Summa Theologiae* 1-2.105.1, trans. Fathers of the English Dominican Province (Ave Maria Press, 1948), 1092.

[55]John Calvin, *Institutes of the Christian Religion* 4.20.8, ed. John T. McNeill, trans. Ford Lewis Battles (Westminster John Knox, 1960), 1493-94; Calvin, *Commentaries on the Four Last Books of Moses*, trans. Charles William Bingham (Baker, 1989), 1:302-10.

[56]John Howard Yoder, *Preface to Theology: Christology and Theological Method*, ed. Stanley Hauerwas and Alex Sider (Brazos, 2002), 242-43.

[57]Michael Walzer, *The Revolution of the Saints: A Study in the Origins of Radical Politics* (Harvard University Press, 1965).

the rise of Christian nationalism within certain segments over the past few decades.[58]

However, there is a counterweight and safety valve, so to speak, built into Willard's theology. The theme of reigning with God does not appear in a vacuum but is always coupled with the double theme of character transformation and virtuous, Christlike leadership.[59] His focus is on not simply reigning, but *training* for reigning, and this point should not be lost. We desperately need now, as ever, people of virtue and communities of character. In his book on the history of the Quakers, Elton Trueblood reflects on preacher and early abolitionist John Woolman, noting, "All who read Woolman have a chance to realize that the best thing in the world is a really good person."[60] How one becomes "a really good person" within Willard's model, and whether such an approach actually produces this sort of characterological change, are questions to be explored in the chapters to come.

In a public lecture Willard stated that he rejects so-called dominion theology, deeming it to be an erroneous politicizing of a biblical concept, and in another he explicitly distanced himself from R. J. Rushdoony's reconstructionism.[61] Yet considering the popularity of dominion theology among certain conservative Christian groups in America during the 1980s and 1990s, the two decades in which he commented most extensively on the creation mandate in his writing, it seems curious that he does not directly address this, if only in

---

[58]David J. Bosch, "The Afrikaner and South Africa," *Theology Today* 43, no. 2 (1986): 203-16 (see especially his exposition of the Kuyperian neo-Calvinism used to underwrite apartheid); Frances FitzGerald, *The Evangelicals: The Struggle to Shape America* (Simon & Schuster, 2017); Tobias Cremer, *The Godless Crusade: Religion, Populism, and Right-Wing Identity Politics in the West* (Cambridge University Press, 2023).

[59]In a 1975 handout for a Sunday school series Willard taught, for which we do not have recordings, he describes his final lesson with the following lines: "The triumph of Christ in the life of mankind is not one of *force*. . . . The 'bloody' eschatology current today is not in the spirit of Christ." Dallas Willard, "Studies in the Gospel of Jesus Christ" (handout, 1975), Dallas Willard Collection, 9. Cf. Willard, *Spirit of the Disciplines*, 238.

[60]D. Elton Trueblood, *The People Called Quakers* (Harper & Row, 1966), 167.

[61]Willard, "Biblical Understanding of the Reality," 59:45; Dallas Willard, "Spiritual Reality: God and the Human Soul" (May 30, 1992), MP3, 20:15.

footnotes, to refute its exegesis and disavow any associations with it. He may have felt his general audience was not in much danger of succumbing to this view or, again, that his emphasis on developing Christlike character (defined largely by the servant heart of Jesus) embedded in the notion of training for reigning was sufficient to ward off its mischaracterization.

This area of Willard's thought raises intriguing questions about the sources he drew on to develop his view of the relevance of the Mosaic system of judges for God's future reign, whether such an interpretation is valid hermeneutically, how it connects with other areas of his theology, and whether the theme wanes or is just more carefully nuanced in the last two decades of his teaching ministry. Furthermore, considering how the concept of *reigning* is particularly salient in the domain of politics and thus cannot be discussed abstractly or in a historical vacuum, more critical questions might also be posed. For instance, has Willard reflected sufficiently on the sometimes very cynical takes on earthly politics we also find in the Bible? Has he given much thought to the early Christian idea (Augustine) that humans have a certain span of control and that building a perfect society is not within this span? If God intends for his people to reign, even in part, before the eschaton, then as fallen and finite Christ-followers, surely we will reign imperfectly. Does Willard's theology account for or at least acknowledge this inevitable frailty?

Some of these matters will be addressed more thoroughly in a later chapter when we examine his social theory and how it relates to individual/societal change. I therefore submit that judgment should be suspended until we have worked through the other themes of his formational theology. I leave my reader to decide at that time whether the rest of his formational theology helps illuminate, and perhaps even warrants, his focus on training for reigning.

ETERNAL COMMUNITY AND CO-REIGNING

Before delving into the broader implications of Willard's view of training for reigning, it is important to address another significant telos that emerges within his corpus. In various places he remarks that God's aim in human history is the formation of an all-inclusive community of loving persons with God himself at its center. Is this telos implicitly woven into reigning with God, or is it an altogether separate thread? A case could be made for the latter—for a distinct thread—since reigning with God appears much more frequently than the all-inclusive community in Willard's work. And when community does appear, it is often not integrated with reigning—at least not early on.

For example, in the earliest extant recording of Willard, he states, "The intention of God in history is to create an all-inclusive community of loving and happy persons dwelt in by God himself."[62] Here the emphasis is entirely on the all-inclusive community, with no mention of co-reigning; this is characteristic of his teaching in the 1970s. However, in the next decade, as Willard's missional vision developed, he increasingly focuses on reigning, rather than mere fellowship, as the dominant activity of God's people in the eschaton, and the implications of this for our present life. By the mid-1980s, he speaks of Jesus "continuing to build and work, and among the things he's building is of course the people of God—the people of God who are to live and reign with him forever."[63] Community is still mentioned ("the people of God"), but it is downplayed and now takes a backseat to the telos of reigning with God. This focus on co-reigning reaches its highest pitch—as a solo piece, rather than a duet with a strong community theme—in the 1988 publication of *The Spirit of the Disciplines*.[64] If one stops there, it is fair to say that there are two separate teloses in Willard's theology, roughly divided

---

[62]Dallas Willard, "The Kingdom Comes in Power" (November 28, 1971), MP3, 3:15.
[63]Dallas Willard, "Many Mansions" (October 25, 1986), MP3, 47:30.
[64]See especially chaps. 4, 11.

between the 1970s (all-inclusive community) and 1980s (co-reigning with God).

But of course, Willard was not finished. In the 1990s we find his maturest thought on the subject, as he weaves together these formerly loose threads into a singular teleology. He describes redemptive history in a 1992 talk as "God's project of creating a community of loving, free individual human beings who will participate in the government of the universe."[65] In the last chapter of *Divine Conspiracy* (1998) he returns to his earlier theme of the all-inclusive community as the aim of God's purposes in history, but this time gives it more weight, more substance, framing it squarely within the vocation and responsibility of that community:

> The purpose of God with human history is nothing less than to bring out of it—small and insignificant as it seems from the biological and naturalistic point of view—an eternal community of those who were once thought to be just "ordinary human beings." Because of God's purposes for it, this community will, in its way, pervade the entire created realm and share in the government of it. God's precreation intention to have that community as a special dwelling place or home will be realized. He will be its prime sustainer and most glorious inhabitant.[66]

Herein he finally merges the two teloses, bringing them into harmony.[67] This community is not just for fellowship but has responsibility; and the responsibility of reigning takes place in, and is enabled by, agapeic community. He would strive to maintain this harmony through all his teaching. That said—and without stretching the music metaphor too far—the theme of reigning still remained the main melodic line, appearing with much more frequency and vigor throughout

---

[65] Willard, "Spiritual Reality," 55:00.

[66] Willard, *Divine Conspiracy*, 385-86.

[67] To reiterate, this move represents a significant development in Willard's missional vision. In summary, the first stage (1970s) is focused on the *fellowship* of the community, the second stage (1980s) on the *responsibility* of the community, and the third stage (1990s onward) on both the *responsibility* and *fellowship* of the community.

Training for Reigning

his later work. In my view, this reflects Willard's conviction that something essential in biblical theology had been either overlooked or deeply misunderstood by the contemporary church—not to mention by much of the historical church. His corpus would evidence something different in this respect, I suspect, had the churchly landscape been otherwise. But since it was not, from the 1980s onward the biblical call for humans to co-reign remained the ultimate telos, never far from Willard's mind whenever he preached and taught on the divine purposes of God.

LET NO ONE PUT ASUNDER

What is the significance of this aspect of Willard's formational theology? To start, it means he avoids two adverse tendencies found in the contemporary spiritual formation movement. The first is the sharp distinction between the contemplative life and the active life, with clear priority given to the former, valuing *via contemplativa* over *via activa* and, correspondingly, *being* over *doing*.[68] It would be easy to see this tendency in the current discourse as a hangover from some of the more extreme medieval mystics often quoted in the literature, but it is hardly limited to contemporary spiritual formation writers and their medieval forbears.

In fact, the idea that contemplation of God is favored over the active life dates back to the time of the church fathers and extends across centuries.[69] In the third century Origen wrote, "Contemplatives are in the house of God, while those who lead an active life are only in the vestibule,"[70] while in the fifth century Augustine stated,

---

[68]On this, see Rick Langer, "Points of Unease with the Spiritual Formation Movement," *Journal of Spiritual Formation & Soul Care* 5, no. 2 (2012): 182-206.

[69]For a thorough historical analysis, see Mary Elizabeth Mason, *Active Life and Contemplative Life: A Study of the Concepts from Plato to the Present* (Marquette University Press, 1961).

[70]Origen, in his commentary on Ps 133, quoted in Auguste Saudreau, *The Life of Union with God*, trans. E. J. Strickland (Benziger Brothers, 1927), 24. Let it be noted that Origen was the first to identify Martha and Mary as biblical models of the active and contemplative lifestyles, respectively.

"Contemplation is promised to us as the end of all our labors and the eternal fullness of our joys."[71] Contemporary with Augustine, John Cassian said the ultimate stage of the spiritual journey consists of the "contemplation of divine things" so that one might "be fed on the beauty and knowledge of God alone."[72] A century later Gregory the Great taught, "The contemplative life is greater in merit than the active, which labours in the exercise of present work, whilst the other already tastes with inward savour the rest that is to come."[73] Thomas Aquinas later echoed this same sentiment: "That which belongs principally to the contemplative life is the contemplation of the divine truth, because this contemplation is the end of the whole human life," thus "the contemplative life is simply more excellent than the active."[74] Dividing sharply between the contemplative and the active lifestyle, and idealizing the former (at times even pitting it against the latter), has a long history and remains a perennial temptation in Christian spiritualities.[75]

Closely related is a second tendency in the spiritual formation discourse to view the ultimate aim of the Christian life as attaining *godliness* or *union with God*,[76] without view of the inextricable connection

---

[71] Augustine, *The Trinity* 1.8, trans. Stephen McKenna (Catholic University of America Press, 1963), 24-25.

[72] John Cassian, *The Conferences* 14.1.2; 1.8.3, trans. Boniface Ramsey, Ancient Christian Writers 57 (Paulist, 1997), 505, 47-48.

[73] Gregory, *Homilies on Ezechiel* 1.3.9, in Cuthbert Butler, *Western Mysticism: The Teaching of Saints Augustine, Gregory and Bernard on Contemplation and the Contemplative Life* (Constable, 1922), 251.

[74] Aquinas, *Summa Theologiae* 2-2.180.4; 2-2.182; pp. 1927, 1937. Cf. "Consequently the active life, which is busy with many things, has less of happiness than the contemplative life, which is busied with one thing, *i.e.*, the contemplation of truth" (1-2.3.2; p. 597).

[75] A modern version of this tendency from a Reformed perspective is that of John Piper in *Let the Nations Be Glad! The Supremacy of God in Missions* (Baker, 1993). The book opens with this memorable passage: "Missions is not the ultimate goal of the church. Worship is. Missions exist because worship doesn't. . . . When this age is over, and the countless millions of the redeemed fall on their faces before the throne of God, missions will be no more. It is a temporary necessity. But worship abides forever" (11).

[76] Though the Protestant spiritual formation movement is commonly understood as monothetic, it is more accurate to view it as two broad trajectories rather than one. The Renovaré wing of the movement names the ultimate aim as "union with God" or "mystical union," whereas the

between these ends and *reigning with God.* Certainly, godliness and union are crucial, even ultimate, goals for life in the Spirit. Paul says we are to train or discipline ourselves "for the purpose of godliness" (1 Tim 4:7 NASB), and Peter speaks of how we, through the promises of God, "may become partakers of the divine nature" (2 Pet 1:4 NASB). Yet is the development of godly character and union with God the sole end of the spiritual life; are we meant only to *become* or *be*? Or is that becoming and being meant to result in *doing* something (creating/willing good for the other) in a certain way (like God/with love)? And what are the theological implications of an ultimate aim without any missional/vocational orientation?[77] What might that mean for both the doctrine of God and ecclesiology?[78]

Reformed wing is more prone to name it as "godliness" or "holiness." For examples of the former, see Gordon T. Smith, *Called to Be Saints: An Invitation to Christian Maturity* (IVP Academic, 2014), chap. 2; and Evan B. Howard, *The Brazos Introduction to Christian Spirituality* (Brazos, 2008), 274; for examples of the latter, see Donald S. Whitney, *Spiritual Disciplines for the Christian Life* (NavPress, 1991), 4, 19; and Jerry Bridges, *The Pursuit of Holiness* (NavPress, 1978), 22, 32-39. There are of course exceptions, such as Reformed theologian J. Todd Billings's *Union with Christ: Reframing Theology and Ministry for the Church* (Baker Academic, 2011) or Julie Canlis's essay "Sonship, Identity and Transformation," in *Sanctification: Explorations in Theology and Practice*, ed. Kelly M. Kapic (IVP Academic, 2014), which traces the theme of mystical union in Calvin's thought, but on the whole these generalizations of the Renovaré and Reformed wings hold true. Other answers can be found in the literature for the end goal of the spiritual life—Christlikeness, freedom from sin, intimacy with God, etc.—but they too seem to coalesce around the two poles of godliness and union with God.

[77]The core of these issues is the link between being and doing. Willard says God is unembodied creative will (fueled by love); if we aim at godliness and union with God, then our embodied wills also become creative and governed by love—that is, we must *do* something and do it in a certain way. Hence reigning, which involves willing the good of the other (Willard's definition of love), is the outflow of becoming like God.

[78]To hear Willard connect these doctrinal dots, see Dallas Willard, "Why There Are People on Earth" (February 19, 1989), MP3, in which he responds to a question about whether humans are innately valuable by mere fact that they have *being*, saying, "People are valuable at that level, but I don't think that's why they were put here—just to sit and be valuable. And the reason I don't is because of the charge that is laid out in the first and second chapters of Genesis, and certainly the emphasis upon *action*. Again, I can only say that I don't think God just does nothing. He doesn't just sit and be valuable. We have all these traditional conceptions of God in the theologians and metaphysicians about just someone so totally immobile, [who] never changes, [and] that's it. My, that isn't an apt expression to me of the greatness of God. He's a furnace of activity, spewing forth worlds of spirit and matter and going so far beyond that that we can't even imagine what it's like. We're not going to be that productive, but thank God we're put here to make a difference" (01:11:15).

These questions could be posed to many of our church creeds and confessions. Take, for instance, the famous statement from the Westminster Catechism, alluded to at the beginning of this chapter: "The chief end of man is to glorify God, and to enjoy him forever." There is surely room for interpreting this clause as inclusive of vocation, in the sense that God is glorified as we participate with him in his creative, ongoing work. But, as Willard points out, in Western history this statement and similar ones have often been understood in purely contemplative and mystical terms.[79] Yet if God's purpose for humankind from the beginning has been to reign and rule with him in love, and if the image of God in the human creature is creative action and engagement toward that end, then the way we come to truly know, glorify, and enjoy God "is by participating in his government."[80] That is the ultimate end toward which all other ends are oriented,[81] and it is inextricably tied to *agapē* love. In other words, a trinitarian God of love created persons to be sharers in and of his love, which requires a will and a body, both of which result in activity. As Willard emphatically states: "We were *not* designed just to live in mystic communion with our Maker, as so often suggested. Rather, we were created to *govern the earth* with all its living things—and to that specific end we were made in the divine likeness."[82] And let it not be lost that he ends *Divine Conspiracy* with a sharp critique of Augustine on this very point.[83]

---

[79]Willard, "Biblical Understanding of the Reality," 59:45; cf. Willard, *Spirit of the Disciplines*, 55n2.

[80]Willard, "Biblical Understanding of the Reality," 1:00:00.

[81]In his two dissertations *Concerning the End for Which God Created the World* and *The Nature of True Virtue* (1765), Jonathan Edwards distinguishes between the *chief* end and the *ultimate* end of an action or endeavor. An ultimate end, in his view, is merely the last in a series or chain of ends, those occurring before it being subordinate ends, whereas a chief end is the highest and most valued end. There may be a plurality of ultimate ends if those ends are not subordinate to one another, i.e., if they do not belong to another series or chain of ends. Yet there can be only one chief end since it is chief not in terms of sequence but esteem. Edwards contends that "the glory of God" is the chief end of all creation and human existence as well as the momentum behind true virtue. See Edwards, *Ethical Writings*, ed. Paul Ramsey, The Works of Jonathan Edwards 8 (Yale University Press, 1989), 399-627. Even if we agree with Edwards that the chief end of human life and virtue is to glorify God, it still raises the question of what ultimate end most glorifies God.

[82]Willard, *Spirit of the Disciplines*, 48.

[83]Willard, *Divine Conspiracy*, 399-400.

And yet, Willard never places a wedge between the *product* and *process* of formation. Mature persons capable of mediating the wisdom and power of Jesus through the social order in loving submission to God is what formation by the Spirit aims to ultimately produce, but the process by which this formation happens is relational and interpersonal through and through. Interactive relationship with God/Jesus/the Spirit is at the heart of how one trains to reign with Christ. So, it cannot be that union with God is *merely* a penultimate end if union with God is essential to the ultimate end of ruling with God. The ultimate telos is, for Willard, more complex than that. It is complex in that we are made to rule in a certain kind of way: in loving relationship to God and others. This is similar to what we saw with his view of the *imago Dei*, in which the functional (creative action) is emphasized over the structural (creative will) and relational (shared responsibility), yet these three dimensions of the image of God in the human person interpenetrate and merge with one another. Similarly, here the structural (godliness) and relational (union with God) ends of formation are understood as subsidiary to the functional and ultimate end (ruling with God), yet the three aims interpenetrate one another.

Let me state this differently. In Willard's view, it is the very nature of God to rule, to reign. God, by virtue of his being God with a creative will and ability to act creatively, rules and reigns over everything—and does so in the most loving manner conceivable. Thus the creation mandate for humans to rule is not necessarily (just) a command to perform but a declaration of purposeful design. In other words, it is built into us *qualitatively* to exercise our will over that part of reality to which we have access and influence by virtue of the *imago Dei*; however, spiritual formation determines the manner in which we do it—either like God or not like God. Willard maintains we each have a kingdom or a queendom, so in a sense we already rule. The issue is whether we rule *like/with God* or not.[84] Spiritual formation

---

[84] Herein the inescapable connection again, for Willard, between reigning like/with God and *agapē* love: "God himself doesn't just love me or you, he *is* love. He is creative will for all that is good.

into Christlikeness is not an end in itself, but that spiritual formation serves, and is intricately bound with, the activity of ruling with and like God. And let us not forget that Willard eventually found a way to combine the aims of God to create an all-inclusive community and to have humans co-reign with him. Therefore, in the final analysis we must say that the telos in Willard's formational theology is a complex one involving several essential elements.

The eschatological dynamic in Willard's theory shows how he refuses to separate vocation from spiritual formation. He recognizes that spiritual formation shorn of its teleological dimension is formation for its own sake—and formation turned in on itself, lacking an orientation toward action and others, is not formation in the image of Christ. Not to put too fine a point on it, but this is where Willard parts ways with many peers in the field. His framing of character formation as *training for reigning* means there is a vocational impulse kneaded into the whole of his theory, dating back to his early teachings and writings, even though his missional logic was not influential on other formational literature.[85] In addition to what we find in his early recorded talks, Willard's second theological book, *Spirit of the Disciplines*, devotes a considerable amount of attention to the "why" of spiritual formation. He argues that discipleship unto Christlikeness is how Christ's coming reign and the subsequent "healing of the nations" (Rev 22:2) will be realized—in fact, it is the means by which it will be ushered in. Future works by Willard, not least *Divine Conspiracy*, only deepened this connection between formation and vocation,[86] a

---

That is his identity, and explains why he loves individuals, even when he is not pleased with them. We are directed by Paul to 'be imitators of God, as beloved children; and walk in love, just as Christ also loved you and gave himself up for us.' (Eph. 5:1-2) We are called and enabled to love as God loves." Dallas Willard, "Getting Love Right" (presented paper, September 15, 2007), Dallas Willard Collection, 4-5.

[85] Although some later developed a missional edge to their approaches to spiritual formation (M. Robert Mulholland Jr., Diane Chandler, Evan Howard), they did so quite differently from Willard.

[86] Gary Black Jr. and Dallas Willard, *The Divine Conspiracy Continued: Fulfilling God's Kingdom on Earth* (HarperOne, 2014), also addresses this connection, focusing on a variety of specific vocations subsumed under the general call of the Christian. However, due to the reasons stated in chap. 2, I have chosen not to include it as part of my argument.

vocation that entails reigning with God. It must be reiterated, however, that for him this (eschatological) reigning is always defined in terms of the character of Christ, thus training is always aimed at developing above all the servant heart and *agapē* love of Jesus. How this actually happens—how persons grow in Christlikeness—well, Willard has much more to say about that.

FOUR

INTELLIGENT MYSTICISM

One of the major concerns, not just of Willard's work in spiritual formation but of his project as a whole, has to do with the nature of reality and to what extent it can be accessed by the mind, terrain normally covered in the philosophical fields of metaphysics and epistemology. In a certain way, this is *the* foundational theme of his formation theory: God and his kingdom are reality at its deepest level; this reality can be known in thought and experience; such knowing is not a "making" but a "finding"; it has the potential to change the knower, and human knowers are changed as they integrate themselves with this reality. Willard saw an ontology of knowing—wherein knowledge of mind-independent reality is possible—as essential to his account of spiritual formation, arriving at this position through a matrix of philosophical moves and biblical exegesis, which I attempt to clarify below.[1] What results is a deeply relational approach to spiritual and moral growth.

Moreover, in addition to what makes direct, intimate relationship with God possible, Willard believed knowledge was crucial for

---

[1] Ontology of knowledge concerns fundamental questions about what it means for knowledge to "be" and how it fits into the broader structure of reality. Willard understood epistemology more broadly than is common in contemporary analytic philosophy, where epistemology often focuses narrowly on how knowledge is acquired, justified, and warranted (what he called "criteriology"). For Willard, epistemology encompassed both the ontology of knowledge and criteriology, reflecting—he would say—a historically fuller understanding of the field. In discussing these matters, I follow his lead, but, to be clear, I will not attempt a full exploration of Willard's epistemology but rather will focus on particular theological implications thereof, specifically how human beings can know God directly and the transformative power of that knowing. For a more comprehensive treatment of Willard's epistemology, readers may consult Walter Hopp, *Phenomenology: A Contemporary Introduction* (Routledge, 2020), by a former doctoral student of Willard. Hopp's book is not primarily about Willard; however, he engages extensively with his mentor's work, making it, to date, the most insightful commentary on Willard's epistemic commitments.

formation for at least two other reasons. First, understanding is the basis of care, and knowledge is the surest way to accurate understanding. So, if a person wants to care for her spiritual core—what Willard refers to as the human spirit/will/heart—then she must come to adequately understand what it is and what it does. Second, knowledge confers the right or authority to act, teach, supervise, propose policy, and so on, such that without knowledge of spiritual formation there will not be the sort of cultural and institutional affects that are needed. Both reasons are relevant to themes discussed later, so they receive only brief attention here.

A final note: The first few sections of this chapter may be more challenging for those without a background in philosophy. In stark contrast to his theology books, Willard wrote philosophy mainly for other professional philosophers. Engaging his philosophical writings is not an easy task, but they cannot be bypassed if his work, including his theology, is to be fully understood. I would therefore encourage the weary reader to hug the cactus, so to speak, and for my part I will strive to make the concepts as understandable as possible.

REALISM(S), PERSONALISM, AND PHENOMENOLOGY

In light of this, allow me to define a few philosophical terms. For our purposes, we can think of *metaphysical realism* as positing that certain objects exist, and their existence does not depend on their being the actual or possible object of thought or discourse by finite minds.[2] For our purposes, we can think of *epistemic realism* as positing that objects as they truly are, as well as the characteristics they have when perceived, can be known and comprehended by minds without the object or its characteristics changing by the act of being perceived.[3] Thus epistemic realism presupposes metaphysical realism: certain

---

[2]Dallas Willard, "The Theory of Wholes and Parts and Husserl's Explication of the Possibility of Knowledge in the Logical Investigations," in *Husserl's Logical Investigations Reconsidered*, ed. Denis Fisette (Kluwer Academic, 2003), 163-64.

[3]Dallas Willard, "The World Well Won: Husserl's Epistemic Realism One Hundred Years Later," in *One Hundred Years of Phenomenology*, ed. D. Zahavi and F. Stjernfelt (Kluwer Academic, 2002), 69.

objects are real and can be known.⁴ Yet metaphysical realism does not entail epistemic realism. For example, Immanuel Kant is often interpreted as a metaphysical realist about certain entities but an epistemic antirealist about phenomena. In other words, he believed that things exist in a manner intrinsic to themselves yet remain unknowable; that is, we cannot entertain true thoughts of them.

Personalism posits that personhood is at the core of reality and therefore is the proper starting point for all philosophical and theological reflection.⁵ Although most forms of personalism take for granted that God or a supreme being is the primary instance of personhood, personalism is not limited to any particular position in metaphysics or epistemology (realism, idealism, etc.). Conversely, realism in metaphysics or epistemology does not necessitate a personalist theory of the universe, much less one with divine persons. One can be a personalist and a realist or idealist—the latter being the view that reality is fundamentally mental or mind-dependent—just as one can be a realist or idealist and have an impersonalistic view of reality.

Willard held to metaphysical and epistemic realism with a distinctly personalistic inflection,⁶ and he believed philosophical phenomenology

---

⁴I am aware that this is a rather strong version of realism, especially when compared to current notions on critical realism. But on this matter, Willard will not budge. See, e.g., his discussion in Dallas Willard, "Faculty Q & A" (October 9, 2008), MP3, after stating, "I want to go beyond 'critical realism'—just 'realism'" (38:45). However, I will later discuss the potential this area of his thought has for spiritual formation regardless of whether one accepts all the premises of his philosophical realism.

⁵Since there is no particular thinker or single doctrine to which all personalists adhere, personalism is better thought of as an approach or mode of thought rather than as a distinct school of philosophy. Most forms of personalism insist the personal nature of existence is of supreme value, affirm the dignity and worth of human personality, consider the person a social being who never exists in isolation, and contend that physical reality is better explained by personal reality than vice versa. For further definition and discussion, see Thomas D. Williams and Jan Olof Bengtsson, "Personalism," in *The Stanford Encyclopedia of Philosophy*, Summer 2022 ed., ed. Edward N. Zalta, https://plato.stanford.edu/entries/personalism/.

⁶That Willard was a personalist in the broad sense of the philosophical term is evident, though he harbored ambiguous feelings toward the American version of personalism, which arose in the late nineteenth century and flowered in the next under its primary architect and advocate, Boston University professor and Methodist minister, Borden Parker Bowne. One of Bowne's pupils, Ralph Tyler Flewelling, who became a professor himself, brought it to the University of Southern

(of the Husserlian variety) was a primary mode of thinking to elucidate this. *Phenomenology,* as he understood it, is concerned about the encounter with "things themselves," not merely theories about them. More specifically, it is concerned with the essential relationship among these things. In numerous places, the father of phenomenology, Edmund Husserl, boils down the phenomenological task to investigating the essential correlations between (1) mental acts or experiences, that is, consciousness, (2) their objects, and (3) their contents or meanings.[7] While there are a variety of nuanced positions persons might take on these issues, one way to understand them is that every mental act has a subjective side as well as an objective side, and the content of the objective side is always something other than the mental act itself. In other words, the objective side of a mental experience always reaches for something outside one's mind. This "reaches for" or pointing feature of consciousness is called intentionality, and it sits at the very center of all knowing ventures.

HUSSERL'S INFLUENCE

It is high time in this book that I say more about the influence of Edmund Husserl (1859–1938) on Willard's thought as well as the

---

California, which became the second important hub of American personalism with his founding of *The Personalist,* an academic journal devoted to the movement. A strong presence of personalist thought would have permeated the university's philosophy department when Willard began teaching there in 1965. Willard occasionally referred to himself as a "personalist" and frequently contributed to *The Personalist* before it changed direction and became *Pacific Philosophical Quarterly* in 1980. He also wrote, "In the language of technical philosophy, Jesus was a 'Personalist,'" so we can safely assume he also considered himself one. Dallas Willard, *Knowing Christ Today: Why We Can Trust Spiritual Knowledge* (HarperOne, 2009), 50. Yet he did not take up the causes of personalist philosophy directly in his writings—including his many essays in *The Personalist*—and made no intentional effort to associate himself with the movement, perhaps because the leading American personalists were idealists, and by this time Willard had thoroughly committed himself to realism, discerning there was more at stake in that philosophical distinction. Moreover, Willard derived his personalistic view from eclectic sources and not necessarily card-carrying "personalists," such as Bonhoeffer, William James, and above all, the biblical writers. (He also would have encountered a personalistic approach to phenomenology in the writings of Max Scheler and Edith Stein, both students of Husserl.) For a grounding of his personalism in the biblical depiction of a trinitarian universe, see the section "A Universe Responsive to Personality" in Willard, *The Divine Conspiracy: Rediscovering Our Hidden Life in God* (HarperSanFrancisco, 1998), 246-47.

[7]Hopp, *Phenomenology,* xviii.

particular way Willard interpreted Husserl. Since others have written detailed accounts of this, I need only give an overview here.[8]

The main philosophical problem that Husserl attempted to overcome concerns the *objectivity of knowledge*—the question of how we are to understand "the relationship, in particular, between the subjectivity of knowing and the objectivity of the content known."[9] Husserl's doctorate was in mathematics, and his earliest philosophical writings were on what number or numerosity is.[10] In the course of working on this issue, he found himself describing in painstaking detail the acts of cognition involved in counting things. Once he grasped the process involved in cognitively apprehending a number, he realized that the number is still there whether or not it is counted, whether or not a person goes through the process to cognitively apprehend it. This intuitive insight, as basic as it might be, led him to see that mathematical work has little or nothing to do with the essence of numerosity. A mathematician rarely ever thinks of "number" when doing arithmetic, even though that is the essence or realm of reality she is working with. As a result, Husserl began to shift his attention from objective essences to the essence of experience or consciousness in general.

Husserl would go on to formulate a sophisticated account of consciousness and of cognition, which he believed allows for knowledge of the mind-independent world. His method was predicated on three objective aspects of acts of knowledge being reconciled with the subjectivity of cognitive acts.[11] These are (1) *transcendence toward an independent object*, or the acknowledgment of an object's existence even when it is not being perceived; (2) *conformity to general order or*

---

[8]See especially Greg Jesson, "The Husserlian Roots of Dallas Willard's Philosophical and Religious Works: Knowledge of the Temporal and the Eternal," *Philosophia Christi* 16, no. 1 (2014): 7-36.

[9]Edmund Husserl, *Logical Investigations*, trans. J. N. Findlay (Routledge, 1970), 1:2.

[10]To the following, Dallas Willard, "Historical and Philosophical Foundations of Phenomenology" (unpublished paper, 1988), Dallas Willard Collection.

[11]To the following, Dallas Willard, *Logic and the Objectivity of Knowledge: Studies in Husserl's Early Philosophy* (Ohio University Press, 1984), 3.

law, or adherence to a foundation of generalities in order to interpret particularities; and (3) *a certain community of what is cognized*, or other persons' confirmation or denial, based on their perceptions, of what a person perceives is true to reality.[12] Willard summarizes these three aspects of the knowing process as transcendence, law, and community, and contends that for Husserl they are interconnected.[13]

If Willard viewed himself first and foremost as a minister of the gospel, why did he champion Husserl—a mathematician turned logician—and place so much stock in Husserl's intricate method of phenomenological thinking? In an article titled "The World Well Won: Husserl's Epistemic Realism One Hundred Years Later," he explains how Husserl saw the possibility and hope of recovering authentic knowledge of reality, and he (Husserl) viewed himself as starting, or at least stumbling on, a project aimed at this recovery—but one that others would have to pick up if it was to be completed.[14] Did Willard see himself as one of these "others" who would carry the task forward after Husserl? We have good reason to suspect so. But how he carried it forward was hardly confined to philosophical inquiry. It is not an overstatement to say that much of Willard's theological project is an appropriation of Husserl's epistemic realism in the spiritual life. He wrote much more in philosophy than in religion (*wrote* is the keyword here, not *published*), but by his own admission, his writing in philosophy helped him in everything else he did.[15]

---

[12]This third act or point shows in Willard's rephrasing of one of Paul's communal admonitions in Rom 12:9-21, "Having due regard for what everyone takes to be right." Dallas Willard, *Renovation of the Heart: Putting On the Character of Christ* (NavPress, 2002), 196.

[13]Willard, *Logic and the Objectivity*, 11.

[14]Willard, "World Well Won," 73. Yet here is where Willard's interpretation of Husserl might be seen as contentious. The standard view of Husserl is that he radically altered his philosophy later in his career, the most significant move being a shift from realism to idealism. Willard asserts, on the contrary, that Husserl developed the basis of his epistemic realism in his early work *and never later retracted his basic position* (69).

[15]Dallas Willard, "Dialogue with Dallas Willard" (October 26, 2010), MP3, 7:00; Willard, "My Journey to and Beyond Tenure in a Secular University" (transcript, June 21, 2003), Dallas Willard Collection. In this latter presentation, he mentions that his first two published philosophical papers each required "two solid years" of writing, as he rewrote them "probably sixty-five times."

This is not to suggest Willard was a one-trick pony. On the contrary, he specialized in phenomenology but was a broad philosopher. He drew from any number of philosophical thinkers and traditions and taught an exceptionally wide variety of courses in the field at USC.[16] Willard's departmental colleague, eminent philosopher of language Scott Soames, described him as "the teacher with the greatest range in the School of Philosophy," who "regularly taught courses in logic, metaphysics, ethics, aesthetics, history of ethics, philosophy of religion, and the history of philosophy from the seventeenth through the twentieth centuries, including both sides of the twentieth-century split between analytic philosophy and phenomenology."[17] Willard also differed from Husserl in numerous ways, not least because of his firm Christian convictions and all that accompanies such (doctrine of revelation, biblical inspiration, the Spirit, etc.). Nevertheless, there is a deep affinity between phenomenological thinking and Willard's religious thought, although he rarely commented about it directly.[18] Vindicating the possibility of the objectivity of knowledge, which answers how the subjective can "get hold of" that which is objective, was for him an enormously important thing for theological epistemology.[19]

---

[16]A document of course listings, provided by the philosophy department at the University of Southern California, shows that Willard taught courses on no fewer than eighty different subjects in philosophy during his tenure.

[17]Scott Soames, foreword to Dallas Willard, *The Disappearance of Moral Knowledge*, ed. Aaron Preston, Gregg Ten Elshof, and Steven L. Porter (Routledge, 2018), viii.

[18]One of the rare instances he does so is a 2009 interview published in Gordon College's magazine. Asked whether there is a connection between his work on Husserl and his work in spiritual formation, he replies that phenomenology is concerned with the life of the whole person in the world, which is why Husserl meticulously describes the mind or soul and how it works. Willard concludes, "So Husserl's focus fits right in with spiritual disciplines, spiritual growth—it's really very much the same topic." Patricia Hanlon, "The Man Behind the (Divine) Conspiracy: A Conversation with Dallas Willard," *Stillpoint* (Spring 2009): 9. Rebecca Willard Heatley shared with me a conversation she had with her father during his final days in the hospital, in which he expressed regret about not making these connections between his philosophical thinking and theological teaching more explicit (personal communication, May 19, 2025).

[19]To what extent this Husserlian influence runs through Willard's thought is another point on which I differ slightly from Michael Stewart Robb. See Robb, *The Kingdom Among Us: The Gospel According to Dallas Willard* (Fortress, 2022), 501; cf. 79-88. Robb is certainly right that Willard was an intellectual maverick in many respects and that he built his own system. But the system

THE OBJECTIVITY OF (SPIRITUAL) KNOWLEDGE

The densest philosophical ground is nearly behind us, but a few crucial points about Willard's ontology of knowledge remain to be addressed before concentrating on his account of divine knowing in spiritual transformation.

First, in his philosophical work Willard stridently defends a *correspondence* theory of truth, which posits that truth is a matter of a belief or idea matching up to reality, over against a *constructionist* view of truth—what he often called "Midas touch epistemology," since it posits we cannot know things as they really are but only as we perceive them.[20] Second, he describes *knowledge* in the dispositional sense (in which things are known that are not necessarily being thought of at the time) as the ability to represent (by thinking, speaking, dealing with) a subject matter as it really is, on an appropriate basis of thought and experience.[21] Third, he distinguishes between two types of knowing: knowledge by *description* and knowledge by *acquaintance*.[22] Only the latter entails interactive or interpersonal relationship with that which is known, and Willard insists the scriptural account of knowledge is of this kind. In the Old Testament, to know God is to know him by acquaintance: through firsthand interaction. Likewise, in the New Testament the kingdom life—a way of life reflecting the Sermon on the Mount and manifesting the fruit of the Spirit—is sustained only through firsthand interaction with the person of Jesus.

---

was not built from scratch, and quite a large portion bears the stamp of a certain Austrian-German phenomenologist. This admission is important for reasons that will become clear as we proceed.

[20]Dallas Willard, "Predication as Originary Violence: A Phenomenological Critique of Derrida's View of Intentionality," in *Working Through Derrida*, ed. Gary B. Madison (Northwestern University Press, 1993), 120-36. For his response to the charge of naiveté in holding a correspondence theory of truth, see Willard, "Knowledge and Naturalism," in *Naturalism: A Critical Analysis*, ed. William Lane Craig and J. P. Moreland (Routledge, 2000), 36-39.

[21]Willard, *Disappearance of Moral Knowledge*, 19-23. I should mention that Willard's particular conceptual framework for thinking about knowledge, especially in its relation to belief, is quite different from the majority view in contemporary analytic epistemology ("justified, true belief"). See Willard, "Knowledge and Naturalism," 32-33.

[22]Willard, *Knowing Christ Today*, 141-42.

A fuller explication of his general theory of knowledge and specific phenomenological account of how knowledge of nonmaterial or nonsensual reality is possible is outside the purview of this book. Suffice it to say Willard spent much of his philosophical energy on the topic and that in his view, there is a path to knowing things as they are on an appropriate basis of thought and experience, and there are no limits a priori to the subject matters we can come to know in this manner.[23] Willard's ontology of knowing is what paved the way for him to contend in lectures, sermons, and writings of all manner that we can make epistemic contact with ultimate reality.

A DIRECT REALISM OF THE SPIRITUAL LIFE

Willard's theory of human transformation is predicated on invisible things being real and personal: the triune God and his kingdom, above all, but also things such as truth, soul, morality, goodness, and so on.[24] Because these are part of reality and have a personal signature, you can go to them in thought and experience—you can know them—and if you do, *they will change you*. What emerges theologically from these metaphysical, personalist, and epistemic claims is a particular type of mysticism and a deeply relational approach to spiritual formation.

In Willard's reading of Husserl, the Austrian-German phenomenologist never retracted the basic position he staked out in his earliest

---

[23]For those interested in studying this further, I recommend starting with one of Willard's lesser-known writings. See Dallas Willard, "Comments on Articles by Nelson, Slife, Reber, and Richardson," *Journal of Psychology and Theology* 34, no. 3 (2006): 266-71. For a more technical treatment, and one in which he expressly uses Husserl as his guide, see Willard, "Knowledge," in *The Cambridge Companion to Husserl*, ed. Barry Smith and David W. Smith (Cambridge University Press, 1995), 138-67.

[24]"The biblical tradition teaches that reality consists of a personal God and his kingdom (all he arranges for), and that every subject matter of human thought, along with human thought itself, exists within that overarching reality." Dallas Willard, "The Bible, the University and the God Who Hides," in *The Bible and the University*, ed. David Lyle Jeffery and C. Stephen Evans (Zondervan, 2007), 21. Having stated in *Knowing Christ Today* that Jesus was a personalist, Willard continues, "Trinitarian personality is, for him, the last word on the universe. This ultimate person, God, is the only one who can say without qualification, 'I am'" (50).

writing.²⁵ The same can be said of the basic assumption underlying Willard's earliest theological writing. In the first book of his pentalogy, *In Search of Guidance*, two chapters titled "Our Communicating Cosmos" and "The Still, Small Voice and Its Rivals" provide Willard's argument for a direct realism of the spiritual life, predicated on a personalist view of reality and the universe. I will attempt an exegesis of his argument here since it is foundational for his interpersonal approach to formation and thus underlies the rest of his pentalogy and religious writings.

Willard begins by asking, "*What kind of world do we live in? and How does God relate to us enclosed within it?*"²⁶ He contends that the prevailing view in the university, the de facto adjudicator of knowledge in modern society, is one of a closed universe. Humans are entirely on their own, enclosed within a material world. If a divine higher being does exist, then it is outside or beyond the material world, which entirely runs on its own.

Yet the Bible presents a different view of the cosmos, says Willard, one in which humans "live and move and have our being" (Acts 17:28) in a God who self-subsists as unbodily, limitless personal power.²⁷ As a nonspatial being unrestricted by time, everything is accessible to God; he does not need to go through any intervening physical reality to reach humans. "The material world in which we are placed by [God]," writes Willard, "permits him to be 'nearer' to us than even our own eyes, ears, and brain."²⁸ Moreover, there is no established truth in science that prevents this from plausibly being the case. To the contrary, it would seem contemporary physics (namely, quantum mechanics) accommodates a

---

²⁵Willard, "World Well Won," 69.

²⁶Dallas Willard, *In Search of Guidance: Developing a Conversational Relationship with God*, 2nd ed. (HarperSanFrancisco, 1993), 63.

²⁷Willard, *In Search of Guidance*, 72-73. The fourth edition of the book adds an illuminating paragraph to this argument; see Dallas Willard, *Hearing God: Developing a Conversational Relationship with God*, 4th ed. (InterVarsity Press, 2012), 97. To hear him unpack these attributes of God in detail, see Willard, "The Biblical Understanding of the Reality of God" (April 24, 1990), MP3, 7:00.

²⁸Willard, *In Search of Guidance*, 73. Cf. "He is able to penetrate and intertwine himself within the fibers of the human self in such a way that those who are enveloped in his loving companionship will never be alone" (36).

view of the world in which the mental or spiritual side of reality interacts in efficacious ways with physical reality.[29]

Willard continues to lay the groundwork for how an intimate and experiential relatedness to God is epistemically possible by examining six ways God addresses people within the biblical record. These are: (1) a phenomenon plus a voice, (2) a supernatural messenger or angel, (3) dreams and visions, (4) an audible voice, (5) the human voice, and (6) the human spirit or the "still, small voice." This list includes both the objective means of communication (1, 2, 4, 5) and subjective means of communication (3, 6), if *objective* here is taken to be sense-perceptible and *subjective* to be non-sense-perceptible (or extra-sense-perceptible).

Willard maintains that the first four, often considered the "spectacular" means, are rarer in the Bible, while the last two—the human voice and the still, small voice—are the primary ways God addresses people in Scripture. God prefers these two modes of communication, both then and now, since they fully engage "the faculties of free, intelligent beings socially interacting with *agape* love in the work of God as his co-laborers and friends."[30] In other words, these communicable modes most deeply bond us in relationship with others and God.

God speaking through *the human voice* does not imply an essentially mechanical or passive relationship, in which God merely uses a human to speak forth his word to another. Such an arrangement is not beyond God's means, but it is not his usual modus operandi. Instead, the Spirit of God prefers to "mix and mingle His power with our own," resulting in our energies and abilities being heightened and expanded.[31] This may happen in various ways, but often the experience entails God and the person he empowers speaking conjointly; that is, God speaks *along with* human beings or, in other cases, *to* the person he is speaking *through*.

---

[29]Willard, *In Search of Guidance*, 74-75.

[30]Willard, *In Search of Guidance*, 98; cf. 102.

[31]Willard, *In Search of Guidance*, 98, citing Samuel Shoemaker, *With the Holy Spirit and with Fire* (Harper & Row, 1960), 27.

Intelligent Mysticism   89

On the other hand, *the still, small voice* is understood not as an audible word or soft whisper of some sort but rather as a mental or spiritual exchange in which God communicates to a human person through the inner thoughts of her own mind. Communication is simply the process of guiding someone else's thoughts, and as humans, we are limited to finite means of communicating with one another. We speak audibly so a person hears the sounds of words, or we write (or type) physically so a person reads our words. But God, as unbodily substance of limitless power, is infinite; he does not have to use finite means to communicate. God can guide a person's thoughts directly from within the experience of the person addressed.[32] (This obviously raises the question of discernment, something Willard discusses elsewhere in the book.[33])

Taken together, Willard's description of the communicable modes of the human voice and the human spirit presents a robust and normative account of experiential knowing in the divine-human relationship. By means of the human voice, God speaks through other people's speech by uniting his word with their word; and by means of the human spirit (or still, small voice) God converses directly with a person through their own consciousness.[34] Thus it is possible to experience "a life of personal, intelligent interaction with God," or, if

---

[32] This immediate, intimate means of conversation between God and humans is found repeatedly in the biblical record. Yet there is a decided shift in how the "still, small voice" voice is experienced after the appearance of Jesus in redemptive history. It is now spoken and heard *with a distinct accent*—that of the Son of God. According to Willard, a main reason Jesus spent forty days with his disciples between his resurrection and his ascension was to teach them how to recognize his voice *when they could no longer see him*. Jesus' actions in Acts 1 and Lk 24 (the road-to-Emmaus encounter) reflect a careful pedagogy toward this end, and one that "is absolutely central for our understanding of how he is with his people now" (Willard, *Divine Conspiracy*, 277). See also Dallas Willard, "General Introduction to Acts" (January 4, 1978), MP3, 31:45; Willard, "Spirituality and the Churches" (June 4, 2012), video, 1:07:00.

[33] See Willard, *In Search of Guidance*, 178-205. In a footnote (207n19), he also recommends Richard Foster's chapter on communal discernment in Foster, *Celebration of Discipline* (Harper & Row, 1978).

[34] Jesus' earthly ministry raises an interesting question of whether his first-century listeners experienced both modes of divine communication or only one through his speech. Jesus spoke with verbal words, which clearly qualifies as the human voice, yet in this instance the human voice was not an intermediary. In other words, Jesus spoke directly with the divine voice through his human voice. Furthermore, there appear to be instances in the Gospel narratives in which God (or the Spirit) communicates with persons through the still, small voice (e.g., Mt 16:17;

you will, *intelligent mysticism*.[35] It is mystical because it involves a conversational relationship with the divine; intelligent because its modes of communication are not at odds with human reason.[36] Moreover, Jesus forever remains the model of such intelligent mysticism. The Son of God, who "was supreme sanity," shows through his own relationship with the Father that the more spectacular the mode of communication with the divine, the less spiritually mature the person.[37] (This is, for Willard, a key principle of experiential knowing in relationship with God.) From Willard's view, then, it is the birthright of every child of God to hear the voice of the Father through the Spirit, and this takes place not through an abandoning of the intellect but a deepening of it.

Consequently, he has stern words for Christian leaders (and one author in particular) who do not, for whatever reason, lead those under their care into intimate relationality with God:

> It seems to me that one of the most damaging things we can do to the spiritual prospects of anyone is to suggest or teach that God will not deal with them specifically, personally, intelligibly, and consciously or that they cannot *count on* him to do so as he sees fit. Once we have conveyed this idea to them, it makes no sense to attempt to lead them into an honestly personal relationship with God.[38]

Lk 2:26-27). A robust trinitarian perspective assumes that Jesus, as the Second Person of the Trinity, was somehow involved in these exchanges, though they were void of verbal speech.

[35]Willard, *In Search of Guidance*, 106. Cf. Dallas Willard, "Q & A 1" (February 22, 1997), MP3, 19:30, where he describes how the voice of God comes to his people "in the form of intelligible content." The phrase "intelligent mysticism" comes from Scottish theologian John Murray, *Redemption: Accomplished and Applied* (Eerdmans, 1955), 169-70, but is quite fitting for Willard's direct realism of the spiritual life.

[36]Willard liked to assign Calvin's *Golden Booklet of the True Christian Life* in seminary courses he taught, in part as a preemptive response to certain so-called Reformed objections to experiencing God directly. *Golden Booklet* includes excerpts from Calvin's *Institutes* in which the Christian life is described as "mystical union with Christ." Citing the little book, Willard quips, "You mean Calvin talked about *that*? Hmm . . . sounds like mysticism." Dallas Willard, "Taking 1 Corinthians Seriously: Intending to Do It 1" (January 5, 2010), video, 1:30.

[37]Willard, *In Search of Guidance*, 114, citing E. Stanley Jones, *The Way* (Abingdon-Cokesbury, 1946), 283.

[38]Willard, *In Search of Guidance*, 107. This critique was originally leveled directly at Garry Friesen's book *Decision Making and the Will of God* (Multnomah, 1980), but the third and fourth editions remove the reference and thus generalize the critique.

This warning is reiterated a few pages later, with Willard turning the knife further:

> From the pastoral point of view, one of the greatest harms we can do to those under our care is to convince them that God is not going to meet them personally in their experience. . . . If our gospel does not free up the individual for a unique life of spiritual adventure in living with God daily, we simply have not fully entered into the good news Jesus brought.[39]

Willard recognizes the dangers inherent in encouraging people to hear from God directly and that some, as a result, may go off the deep end. Yet he believes we are equally wrought with the danger of going off the *shallow end*, which leads to what he calls "Bible deism," the dim view that once God gave us the Bible, he left us to our own devices to make of life what we could.[40]

Over against this, Willard proposes "the phenomenology of the Spirit's presence," which is a systematic investigation into what it is like to experience the Spirit and how such real encounters might be distinguished from mere emotion, self-deception, or divine silence.[41] In the essay "Hermeneutical Occasionalism," he argues that we must not rig this process by starting with the assumption that our biblical interpretation or churchly practice is already correct. In other words, phenomenological descriptions should not be biased by theological presuppositions or predetermined conclusions but instead offer independent grounds for assessing whether the Spirit is present in a given interpretation or moment. We should let experience speak on its own terms and be willing to revise our conclusions if the Spirit's actual presence (or absence) suggests otherwise. This could be done, he

---

[39] Willard, *In Search of Guidance*, 111.

[40] Willard, *In Search of Guidance*, 110-12. Willard compares Bible deism to the Sadducean doctrine that God stopped communicating directly and supernaturally (via angels, spirits, etc.) with people after Moses.

[41] Dallas Willard, "Hermeneutical Occasionalism," in *Discipling Hermeneutics: Interpretation in Christian Perspective*, ed. Roger Lundin (Eerdmans, 1997), 171.

suggests, with a rigorous, experience-based approach to discerning God's activity, grounded in historical Christian spirituality and tested through lived obedience rather than theoretical claims alone.[42] The goal is not absolute certainty but sound judgment on the movement of divine presence in a particular time and place—an extension of the intelligent mysticism modeled in Jesus and offered to every apprentice in the kingdom.

Turning now to the end of *In Search of Guidance*, Willard provides in the epilogue a summation of the resolute realism of the spiritual life he has argued for and its practical meaning for followers of Christ. Reflecting on Jesus' last words to his disciples before the ascension, specifically that he will be *with* them always (Mt 28:20), Willard writes:

> He is with us, and he speaks with us, and we with him. He speaks with us in our heart, which burns from the characteristic impact of his word. His presence with us is, of course, much greater than his words to us. But this presence is turned into *companionship* only by the actual communications between us and him, which frequently are confirmed by external events as life moves along. *This companionship with Jesus is the form that Christian spirituality takes as practiced through the ages.* Spiritual persons are not those who engage in certain "spiritual practices," but those who draw their life from a conversational relationship with God.[43]

How does this relational approach factor into discipleship and spiritual transformation? It means following Jesus cannot just be about following his example and doing what he did. If so, we would no longer need his presence because we have his example. Rather, following Jesus means entering into the same sort of relationship Jesus bore to his Father by the Spirit.[44] We learn from Jesus how to live life

---

[42]Not unlike older methods of discerning the experience of God's Spirit advocated by the likes of George Fox, Francis de Sales, Ignatius of Loyola, even Jonathan Edwards.

[43]Willard, *In Search of Guidance*, 239.

[44]Commenting on Jesus' announcement that the kingdom of God is "at hand," i.e., "available" (Mt 3:2; 4:17), Willard writes, "Now all humankind is invited to live in a *family*, made possible by Our Father in heaven, whom we address in prayer." Dallas Willard, *The Spirit of the Disciplines: Understanding How God Changes Lives* (Harper & Row, 1988), 243.

in his Father's kingdom by the Spirit, just as he did. Thus, becoming and being Christlike requires fellowship and engagement with the living Christ; we abide in him and he in us, in real time through the Spirit, as we develop "the mind of Christ" (1 Cor 2:16). Jesus actively and individually leads us, and this conversation or presence forms the basis of our "religion."[45] This is a crucial way Willard's theory differs from another predominant account of Christian formation, namely, virtue theory in Christian ethics. Accordingly, a few comments about this classic virtue paradigm and how it relates to and contrasts with Willard's are in order.

COMMONALITIES AND CONTRAST WITH VIRTUE ETHICS

There is a long tradition of virtue ethics in Christian theology focused on character formation, which has experienced something of a revival among both Catholics and Protestants in the last generation.[46] Drawing from ancient Greek philosophers such as Plato and Aristotle, this discourse found its fullest elaboration in Thomas Aquinas, who synthesized the thought of Aristotle and Augustine.[47] Well-known contemporary proponents of virtue theory include moral philosopher Alasdair MacIntyre and ethicist Stanley Hauerwas.[48] MacIntyre's elaborate and oft-repeated definition of *practice* is a cornerstone in

---

[45] For straightforward statements to this end, see the section titled "Life in the Spirit and the Kingdom of the Heavens" in *Divine Conspiracy*, 279-81. Willard's translation of Rom 8:14 is telling—"All who are interactive with the spirit of God are God's children" (280)—as is his assertion that "the kingdom of the heavens, from the practical point of view in which we all must live, is simply our experience of Jesus' continual interaction with us in history and throughout the days, hours, and moments of our earthly existence" (280).

[46] In this book, the terms *virtue theory* and *virtue ethics* are used interchangeably. For the subtle way in which some scholars differentiate between the two, see Nancy E. Snow, ed., *The Oxford Handbook of Virtue* (Oxford University Press, 2018), 1-2.

[47] See Thomas Aquinas, *Summa Theologiae* 2-2.49-67, trans. Fathers of the English Dominican Province (Ave Maria Press, 1948), 793-877.

[48] See Alasdair MacIntyre, *After Virtue*, 2nd ed. (University of Notre Dame Press, 1984); Stanley Hauerwas, *A Community of Character: Toward a Constructive Christian Social Ethic* (University of Notre Dame Press, 1981).

the discourse, and Hauerwas's emphasis on the believing community and the narrative it proclaims and abides by accentuates the communal side of virtue formation. Other theologians, such as William Spohn and Glen Stassen, take a decidedly Christocentric approach, situating acquired moral virtue in the discipleship of Jesus.[49]

Yet what these various streams have in common is a focus on practices and their formative potential, how they reorder thought patterns and habits and shape new ones.[50] Even those accounts that stress discipleship frame it primarily as following the ethical pattern and moral authority of Christ, as discerned in the New Testament witness and mediated through the Christian tradition. Jesus is understood as the "concrete universal of Christian ethics."[51]

Willard's view of spiritual formation has many commonalities with these recent views of virtue formation. Practices play a vital role in shaping character (MacIntyre), as do the narratives we abide by (Hauerwas)—especially those narratives we believe about God and his relation to his people—and discipleship to Jesus is the main context for Christian formation (Spohn/Stassen). All these approaches share what we might call "a long obedience in the same direction" understanding of sanctification (to borrow Eugene Peterson's phrase[52]), in which character growth is the result of slow, deliberate, habitual work in the Christian life. A handwritten note by Willard captures this well: "Spiritual growth not by information [or] infusion but by steady engagement—faith to faith."[53] This contrasts with what one might call an

---

[49]William C. Spohn, *Go and Do Likewise: Jesus and Ethics* (Bloomsbury Academic, 2000); Glen Harold Stassen, *A Thicker Jesus: Incarnational Discipleship in a Secular Age* (Westminster John Knox, 2012).

[50]See Angela Carpenter, *Responsive Becoming: Moral Formation in Theological, Evolutionary, and Developmental Perspective* (T&T Clark, 2019), 5.

[51]Spohn, *Go and Do Likewise*, 2.

[52]A phrase Peterson himself borrowed from Friedrich Nietzsche. See Eugene Peterson, *A Long Obedience in the Same Direction: Discipleship in an Instant Society* (InterVarsity Press, 1980); Friedrich Nietzsche, *Beyond Good and Evil* (1886), aphorism 188, many editions.

[53]Dallas Willard, "Following Christ in Everyday Life, or Training for Reigning" (handwritten notes, 1993), Dallas Willard Collection, 4.

Intelligent Mysticism

"instantaneous" view often shared by those in more charismatic circles who rely heavily on healing prayer and deliverance ministry to bring about spiritual and moral change, as well as a "faith alone" or more passive understanding of sanctification found among some Lutheran and Reformed thinkers, in which we merely wait on God in faith rather than perform faith through habitual practice and activity.

Nevertheless, while there is no outright conflict between his approach and virtue ethics, Willard does place the emphasis of formation elsewhere. His is a relational approach to discipleship, one in which disciples follow the historical witness of Jesus and belong to the historical community that grows from this tradition—but they also seek to converse and commune with the risen Christ in real time. For Willard, this is the crux of character formation for the Christian. Our personal relatedness to the triune God and our life as lived in God's kingdom are the main catalysts in spiritual and moral transformation. In his words, "What brings about our transformation into Christ-likeness is our *direct, personal interaction with Christ through the Spirit*. The Spirit makes Christ present to us and draws us toward his likeness."[54]

This constitutes a major methodological difference in their accounts of how persons become virtuous. In the case of Hauerwas, for instance, one's relationship with God is *always* mediated through one's relationship with the church, so that virtue formation in Christ is impossible outside of participation in the corporate body of Christ. He is fond of saying that just about the last thing he wants Christians to have is a personal relationship with Jesus.[55] Apart from the hyperbole

---

[54] Dallas Willard, "Looking Like Jesus," *Christianity Today* 34, no. 11 (1990): 30, emphasis added.

[55] See, e.g., Hauerwas's comments in these two interviews: "I really don't like the word 'personal.' It makes it sound like I have a relationship with Jesus that is unmediated by the church.... But the heart of the gospel is that you don't know Jesus without the witness of the church. It's always mediated"; and "But one of the great problems of evangelical life in America is evangelicals think they have a relationship with God that they go to church to have expressed but church is a secondary phenomenon to their personal relationship and I think that's to get it exactly backwards: that the Christian faith is mediated faith. It only comes through the witness of others as embodied in the church. So I should never trust my presumption that I know what my relationship with God is separate from how that is expressed through words and sacrament in the church." Laura Sheahen, "'Why Have You Forsaken Me?' Stanley Hauerwas on Atonement

of this statement, Hauerwas is serious. He believes modern Protestantism, especially its American form, has drunk deep of Enlightenment individualism and in so doing marginalized the central place of the church in shaping Christians. As we will see later, Willard too sees participation in the church as essential for Christlike formation, going as far as endorsing, in a qualified sense, the dictum "there is no salvation outside the church."[56] Nonetheless, my research leads me to assume that Willard would question whether Hauerwas has confused personal relationship with Jesus with a private one, thus making his polemic a red herring. He might also query, given the ethicist's extreme emphasis on the church and its practices, whether Hauerwas's thinking on formation is sufficiently theocentric.[57]

Further analysis of Hauerwas's theology would take us too far afield. My intention has simply been to show where recent views of virtue formation, of which Hauerwas is a leading proponent, differ significantly from Willard's approach. One last passage from Willard should make this abundantly clear. In a contribution to *The Renovaré Spiritual Formation Bible*, he writes: "Intimate, individual communication with God is something that cannot be done away with in spiritual formation. We must constantly seek out this intimate, individual communion. We need the full assurance of God's greatness and goodness that comes only from his direct presence. This, frankly, cannot be derived from any other source."[58] Consider this along with the previous quote about "direct, personal interaction with Christ through the Spirit."[59]

Theology, Mel Gibson's 'Passion,' and the 'Chilling' Meaning of Christ's Last Words," March 2005, www.beliefnet.com/faiths/christianity/2005/03/why-have-you-forsaken-me; Albert Mohler, "Nearing the End: A Conversation with Theologian Stanley Hauerwas," *Thinking in Public*, April 28, 2014, https://albertmohler.com/2014/04/28/nearing-the-end-a-conversation-with-theologian-stanley-hauerwas.

[56]Willard, *Renovation of the Heart*, 37.

[57]With typical candor, Hauerwas himself has pondered whether God is "missing from my work." Stanley Hauerwas, *Sanctify Them in the Truth: Holiness Exemplified* (Abingdon, 1998), 37.

[58]Dallas Willard, "People of God in Individual Communion with God," in *The Renovaré Spiritual Formation Bible*, ed. Richard J. Foster et al. (HarperSanFrancisco, 2005), 3.

[59]Willard, "Looking Like Jesus," 30.

Intelligent Mysticism 97

Herein Willard's metaphysical realism, personalism, and Husserlian phenomenology come to the fore and intersect with his radically realist Christology, meaning Jesus is alive and accessible today through the Holy Spirit to ordinary people who rely on him.[60] It is through extensive acquaintance with the fundamental reality of the living Lord on a direct, personal level that we are transformed, the very phenomenon alluded to by Paul: "And we all, with unveiled face, beholding the glory of the Lord, are being transformed into the same image from one degree of glory to another. For this comes from the Lord who is the Spirit" (2 Cor 3:18 ESV).[61] In Willard's theology, interpersonal relationship with the triune God is the main mechanism for virtue formation in Christ.

KNOWING CHRIST TODAY IN A SECULAR AGE

Much could be said about the relevance of Willard's metaphysical and epistemic realism for both academia and Christian practice, but our concern in this chapter is (1) how this factors into his understanding of spiritual formation and (2) its implications for the mission of the church today. My effort thus far has been explicating the first, so my attention is now given to the latter. In terms of churchly implications, certain aspects of Willard's ontology of knowledge present a reasonable epistemological account for knowing divine reality, which is crucial for how the church perceives and facilitates spiritual formation in a couple of ways. First and most importantly, it provides the foundational scaffolding for a relational approach to spiritual and moral change on which the rest of Willard's formational theology builds. The second implication is more suggested than argued: This account may offer some epistemological therapy for faith formation in an age of doubt.

---

[60]By contrast, Willard asserts that the theology of the "current Christian left" has rendered "the destruction of any workable sense in which God and Jesus are persons, now alive and accessible, standing in an interactive relationship with those who rely on them" (*Divine Conspiracy*, 53).

[61]For Willard's exegesis of 2 Cor 3:18 in this vein, see "Looking Like Jesus," 30.

With the renewal of interest in virtue ethics among Christian theologians and philosophers, a MacIntyrean-Hauerwasian understanding of virtue and practice has made strong inroads in many churches and congregations. Even if the leaders of these communities are not well versed in the technical language of virtue theory (e.g., MacIntyre's definition of *practice*) and have never read primary sources within the tradition (Aristotle, Aquinas, etc.), they have absorbed enough of its ideas from secondary sources and authors who have popularized its ideas.[62] In part to correct an overly individualistic view of Christianity, these authors see the church as the primary context for moral formation and emphasize the role concrete, shared practices play in such formation. This approach to character formation might be defined as the Holy Spirit working through social practices passed down from the Christian tradition to form Christlike communities that display the good news of God's reign before a watching world.

As we have seen, Willard's account of spiritual development shares much with these recent views of virtue ethics. A later chapter will reveal further cohesion, showing how he emphasizes the efficacy of habitual practice in formation, drawing from the ascetic traditions of both Christianity and ancient philosophy. However, one point of divergence that has emerged is Willard's interpersonal approach to discipleship and thus character formation. In his view, direct, personal interaction with Christ through the Spirit is the *primary* way persons are formed in Christlikeness. This does not displace the role of

---

[62]In addition to works by Hauerwas, MacIntyre, Spohn, and Stassen already mentioned, a broad and diverse sampling of Christian writings that advocate key themes of virtue theory includes James K. A. Smith, *Desiring the Kingdom* (Baker Academic, 2009); Jennifer A. Herdt, *Putting On Virtue* (University of Chicago Press, 2008); Lesslie Newbigin, *The Gospel in a Pluralist Society* (Eerdmans, 1989); Darrell L. Guder, ed., *Missional Church* (Eerdmans, 1998); David E. Fitch, *Faithful Presence* (InterVarsity Press, 2016); Rod Dreher, *The Benedict Option* (Sentinel, 2017); Samuel Wells, *Improvisation* (Brazos, 2004); and Nancey Murphy, *Beyond Liberalism and Fundamentalism* (Trinity Press International, 1996). While not all of these authors are explicitly associated with virtue ethics, their works strongly align with important aspects of the tradition.

community and tradition in the formative process, but it does lessen its singular importance. I cannot say here everything I need to concerning communal formation since this also will be discussed later in greater detail. Yet I submit here that a commitment to practicing the faith in real (local) communities where social-ecclesial practices reflect a living tradition and form a plausibility structure that supports that tradition—a chief tenet of contemporary Christian virtue ethics—can and should be integrated with Willard's insistence on the primacy of direct interpersonal relationship with God in spiritual formation.

I use the word *should* because of our pluralistic and increasingly secularized context. In a society like America today, in which there remains fewer and fewer reflexive elements in culture for the Christian faith, forming people of virtue in the way of Jesus means Christians must belong to communities anchored in the great tradition (MacIntyre/Hauerwas) *and* have their own direct experience of the divine (Willard).[63] Metaphysical skepticism and epistemological uncertainty pervade contemporary Western culture. To attempt to follow Jesus without being socially embedded in a Christian community with concrete practices that revolve around the narrative of God leaves a person vulnerable to the reigning narratives of the dominant culture. On the other hand, to neglect one's direct, personal relatedness to God and instead look entirely to the community for discipleship and faith formation through socialized processes is

---

[63]This is a claim that must be qualified. There is little doubt that Willard would strongly critique certain aspects of this MacIntyrean-Hauerwasian approach. In fact, he had planned to include a full-dress critique of MacIntyre's account of tradition-constituted rationality in a philosophical monograph he was working on at the time of his death. The monograph, *Disappearance of Moral Knowledge*, was completed and published posthumously in 2018 by three authors who were former students of Willard's. Although it does include an entire chapter on MacIntyre, it is one of two chapters almost entirely written by the former students (see editors' note on 337). Its highly redacted character makes it not as reliable for understanding Willard's argument as other contents in the volume—but there is a paper trail one can follow to piece together his view of MacIntyre, and the redacted chapter is a helpful step in that direction. However, my claim is that we need to work with insights from both methods if we are to construct a personal and collective approach to spiritual formation with "epistemological etiquette," to borrow a term from Esther Lightcap Meek; see her *Loving to Know: Covenant Epistemology* (Cascade, 2011), chap. 15.

to forgo the intimate communion with the Father that Jesus invites us into through the Spirit. Relinquishing this communion also leaves us vulnerable since secondhand experience of the divine alone may not be able to sustain living faith in Christ in a society that seeks transcendent experience in the secular and technological rather than the sacred. Christian spiritual formation in a secular and disenchanted age requires both a *robust plausibility structure* that only communities of praxis can provide, and *intelligent mysticism* in which God is directly and intimately known.

Allow me to further clarify. A churchly plausibility structure without intelligent mysticism results in forms of Christianity that offer institutional strength and social belonging but lack spiritual vitality. It produces churches that are organizationally impressive (whether shaped by high-church liturgical heritage or low-church entrepreneurial energy) yet existentially hollow, offering rituals or answers but not encounter. On the other hand, intelligent mysticism without a solid plausibility structure tends to drift into privatized spirituality. It is rich in experience but thin in friendship and accountability, unanchored in a shared way of life, and ill-equipped to contribute meaningfully to the renewal of the world. Formation in Christ today requires both—a thick community life in which belief is made livable and believable, and personal communion with God that is intimate and sustaining in the face of cultural disenchantment. It has been said before but bears repeating: Our relationship with God is personal but never private. To this we must add: Our relationship with God is communal but never merely a crowd.

The secondary implication pertains to how Willard's approach to faith formation, and the missional vision behind it, might elicit a genuine missionary encounter with modern Western culture. Lesslie Newbigin, a longtime missionary to India and one of the most influential thinkers in missional Christianity, sought to help the Western church recover its identity and vocation in the rubble of Christendom. For this reason, he was deeply concerned about knowledge and the gospel as public truth in a pluralistic context, a constant theme in his post-India writings.[64] In a paper delivered on the topic of our missionary responsibility in late modernity, he attests, "Plainly the fundamental issue is epistemological: it is the question about how we can come to know the truth, how we can know what is real."[65] While numerous theologians have taken up many of Newbigin's concerns in works published over the past three decades, the epistemological crisis is one that has received little extended reflection, despite how central it was to Newbigin's project and to what he felt was necessary for engaging our culture with the gospel. One of the few serious works written expressly from a missional perspective that attempts to build further in the area of epistemology is *To Stake a Claim: Mission and the Western Crisis of Knowledge* (1999), coauthored by a team of scholars.

Although *To Stake a Claim* is somewhat dated, I bring it into the discussion because it responds to Newbigin's challenge to the church concerning epistemology and its proposals are still quite relevant. Second, it is explicitly written as a collaborative work between missiologists and philosophers. Willard would feel right at home with its cross-disciplinary tone, even if he could not endorse all its philosophical positions.[66] The book's editors state succinctly why epistemology is a crucial matter for a missiology of the West: "If there is no agreed epistemological basis for judging the adequacy of particular beliefs and values, it would seem to follow that the claims that Christians make for the gospel are no more valid than any other religious

---

[64]A case in point, the first five chapters of Newbigin's magnum opus, *The Gospel in a Pluralist Society*, are essentially about epistemology. Many more of his books and essays could be listed as examples.

[65]Lesslie Newbigin, *A Word in Season: Perspectives on Christian World Missions* (Eerdmans, 1994), 104.

[66]I should add that it is surprising that a comparative work has not yet been produced on Newbigin and Willard. They had different theological methods, for sure, but they share a deep concern about the status of moral knowledge in the West and of the gospel as public truth in a pluralist society. Furthermore, their critical analyses of modernity and pluralism are strikingly similar. Willard references Newbigin only once in his writings (*Knowing Christ Today*, 2), quoting from one of Newbigin's earliest books, *A Faith for This One World* (SCM Press, 1961).

or secular claims," and "If the universality of the gospel vanishes in the face of epistemological relativism, would not the mandate to make it known universally have to be rejected as epistemological imperialism?"[67] These authors go on to explain that although the claims of logical positivism have been thoroughly refuted, "a quasi-positivist suspicion of religion and traditional metaphysics" remains prevalent in analytic philosophy departments, from which it then trickles down to Western cultural thought at large.[68] (As a university professor, I can attest these observations still hold true.)

These are undoubtedly critical missional issues for reaching those *outside the church*, but there is an equally important a priori question concerning epistemology and spiritual formation *inside the church*, among "members of the household of God" (Eph 2:19 NRSV). If intimate knowing within the divine-human relationship is essential for spiritual formation, how can God's people be formed in Christ and participate in his mission unless epistemological uncertainty—of the sort that says we cannot know whether there is a transcendent God or, if there is a transcendent God, we cannot know him by acquaintance—is adequately dealt with and overcome?

Willard's ontology of knowing deserves our attention for at least this reason. As Charles Taylor and others have argued, our age is one of disenchantment and doubt. Secularization does not just mean there are more people who do not have faith; secularization also changes the faith of the faithful. The options are no longer "believe" or "doubt." Rather, a person of faith believes while doubting.[69] In this sense, secularity represents a *different consciousness*. It is a particular way of being—of thinking, seeing, feeling, and acting.[70] The formidable

---

[67]J. Andrew Kirk and Kevin J. Vanhoozer, eds., *To Stake a Claim: Mission and the Western Crisis of Knowledge* (Wipf & Stock, 1999), xvi.

[68]Kirk and Vanhoozer, *To Stake a Claim*, 5.

[69]"Naïveté is now unavailable to anyone, believer or unbeliever alike." Charles Taylor, *A Secular Age* (Harvard University Press, 2007), 21.

[70]Gordon T. Smith, *Wisdom from Babylon: Leadership for the Church in a Secular Age* (IVP Academic, 2020), 15.

challenge in a secular era, then, is not that people outside the church will not find their way inside, but that people inside the church will no longer have the capacity to imagine the possibility of divine action and transcendence.

Willard does not minimize the need for divine revelation to make up for our human inability to grasp something beyond "a closed universe," or to cleanse our consciousness, so to speak, if it has been thoroughly secularized.[71] Yet he is also hopeful about the philosophical project and the way that reason, as a divinely given human ability, can assist faith formation in a secular age.[72] He would not have taught a metaphysics class nearly every year at a place such as USC if he did not think progress could be made. If Willard's ontology of knowledge presents a reasonable account for understanding the nonperceptual dimension of reality—and perhaps even for experiencing it, as I have intimated—then it offers *epistemological therapy* in a secularized, pluralistic society.[73]

This implication is proffered with a lighter touch, not because it is less important, but because it may require readers to grant more philosophical assumptions than they are prepared to. I will thus not press the point further since one does not have to accept the entirety of Willard's ontology of knowing and philosophical realism—all premises and positions to boot—to endorse his relational approach to formation, which is the more important implication. My point is that Christian spiritual formation in our day needs a healthy epistemology. My analysis of this secondary implication only scratches the

---

[71] On the necessity of revelation, see Dallas Willard, "Postmodernism: Philosophical & Historical Roots 4" (August 19, 1992), MP3, 1:14:15.

[72] To be more precise, he thinks revelation and reason are not only compatible but consistent: "Here's another one of the popular mistakes, the idea that reason and revelation are opposed. They're not opposed. Revelation does not mean you 'lose your mind.'" Dallas Willard, "The Morally Responsible Skeptic" (April 5, 1995), MP3, 1:16:00.

[73] "Epistemological therapy" is another term borrowed from Esther Meek, *Loving to Know*, chap. 1. For Willard's recommendation of her earlier work, *Longing to Know: The Philosophy of Knowledge for Ordinary People* (Brazos, 2003), see Willard, *Knowing Christ Today*, 220n19; *Disappearance of Moral Knowledge*, 46n15.

surface but hopefully will provoke further scholarly reflection on the meaning of Willard's philosophical work to this end.[74]

In this chapter and the prior one, we examined the first two themes of Willard's formational theology, namely, the eschatological dimension of formation, or training for reigning, and the transformative efficacy of epistemic interaction with spiritual reality, aptly called intelligent mysticism. Now that we have view of the larger framework and foundation of his model, we are ready to explore his formation theory proper, asking how individuals and communities are transformed into Christlikeness.

---

[74]For those interested in researching this, I especially commend the transcribed lectures of his 1993 Metaphysics course at USC (available in the Dallas Willard Collection), the recorded lectures of his 2003 Ontology of Knowledge course at Biola, and, of course, his various commentaries and writings on Husserl.

PART 2

THEOLOGY OF FORMATION PROPER

FIVE

THE HEART OF THE HUMAN PROBLEM

IN A FEW PLACES, Willard indicates there are two reasons he emphasizes spiritual formation as *spiritual*.[1] First of all, this is a formation *of* the human spirit (will or heart) everyone receives, religious or not, by virtue of being human. He often remarks, "Everyone receives spiritual formation, just as everyone gets an education. The only question is whether it is a good one or a bad one."[2] More common terms for this phenomenon may be *moral formation, character formation*, or *virtue formation*. But for Willard, this is fundamentally *spiritual* formation since it deals with the shape of the inner, nonphysical dimension of a person. From his view, the direction in which one's spirit develops is most determinative in who a person becomes and what becomes of her.

Second, it is *spiritual* formation because it is *by* the Spirit, the third member of the Trinity. This occurs in a Christian's life, under the direction of the Spirit, and is upheld by God's sustaining grace. Whenever Willard accentuates the Holy Spirit's role in formation, he is shifting

---

[1]Dallas Willard, "Spiritual Formation in Christ: A Perspective on What It Is and How It Might Be Done," *Journal of Psychology and Theology* 28, no. 4 (2000): 254-55; Willard, *Renovation of the Heart: Putting On the Character of Christ* (NavPress, 2002), 19-22; Willard, "Spiritual Formation as a Natural Part of Salvation," in *Life in the Spirit: Spiritual Formation in Theological Perspective*, ed. Jeffrey P. Greenman and George Kalantzis (IVP Academic, 2010), 45-46. In this first article, his most lengthy discussion of the terminology, he distinguishes between three different meanings or senses of *spiritual formation* in Catholic and Protestant circles. Yet one of those meanings—training in certain specifically religious practices—is not how he himself uses the term.

[2]Willard, "Spiritual Formation in Christ," 254.

the focus from the *domain* of formation to its *agency*. More often than not this is simply implied in his use of "spiritual formation," but it is especially signaled by his language of "Christian spiritual formation," "spiritual formation in Christ," or, more precisely, "formation in the Spirit." No longer is this merely the universal experience of a person's inner life taking specific shape; now in view is the divine Spirit forming one's inner life more in the image of the Son.[3] For Willard, this certainly does not negate human agency in the formative process, nor does it mean the Spirit will always have its way in a person's life, as if the person's volition were then canceled out. The direct presence of the Holy Spirit does not override human choice, but it does bring a special grace or empowerment that is lacking in the universal spiritual formation everyone gets.[4]

Willard's twofold understanding of Christian spiritual formation—as the shaping *of* the human spirit *by* the Holy Spirit—provides the basic structure for part two of this book (this and the next two chapters). The present chapter, then, centers on the pivotal role of the human will (or spirit) in God's sanctifying work, reflecting the *domain* of formation. However, to discuss this intelligibly we need to understand the place of the will in his overall philosophical anthropology. Willard's complex anthropology pervades his theological

---

[3]This accounts for *Christian* spiritual formation but leaves open the question of who or what is the (main) actor of the spiritual formation everyone gets. Is the Spirit involved? Or is it demonic? Or something in between? Although not specific to the issue of human formation, in one place Willard writes, "The fact that God is a being whose most basic nature is *agape* love for *all* human beings, *regardless* of their religious or culture, means that he cares for *all* human beings. . . . Since he is the God of all, he *cares* for all. He does not sit in splendid isolation demanding that all worship and obey him. He reaches out to them, calls them to himself. His grace is an active principle in his universe." Dallas Willard, *Knowing Christ Today: Why We Can Trust Spiritual Knowledge* (HarperOne, 2009), 176-77.

[4]Willard holds there is a *common grace* at work in the spiritual formation everyone gets, stemming from God's gracious design of human persons and the world. That means there is divine agency in back of it and responsible for it, but it is common in that one need not engage directly with God as God to experience the formative process. Things such as getting good sleep, exercise, good nutrition, taking ten deep breaths, going for a long walk in nature, and fasting, for instance, tend to work whether a person seeks God or even believes in God, for God has ordered phenomena in the world to operate in certain law-governed ways (e.g., when we get good sleep we tend to flourish), and anyone can partake of these processes.

work and is the main subject of one of the pentalogic books (*Renovation of the Heart*), warranting an entire study in itself. Here my task is limited to outlining its contours and clarifying its importance for his theology of formation, before turning to the will as the focal point of God's redemption of the person. The next two chapters, corresponding to the *agency* of formation, explore the interplay of the Holy Spirit and the human person in sanctification. Taken together, the chapters in part two examine Willard's view of formation proper, that is, his understanding of the theological and phenomenological dynamics involved in the spiritual transformation of persons and communities.

SANCTIFICATION PRESUPPOSES ANTHROPOLOGY

The nature of the human person receives major attention in *Spirit of the Disciplines* and *Renovation of the Heart*, but the subject underlies all of Willard's work in spiritual formation. As he states, "Any understanding of human development will turn upon assumptions about the essential dimensions ('parts') of the human being, and mistakes concerning those dimensions will undermine efforts at modifications of human life in desired directions."[5] In his view, sanctification presupposes anthropology. I will therefore focus on two main aspects of his mature theological anthropology as it relates to his theory of formation (I will explain what I mean by his "mature" view).

To begin, the human self is a complex whole composed of multiple dimensions working in close conjunction with one another; second, the human will (spirit or heart) is the central and most critical part of our personhood but is accessed and governed (and thus necessarily limited) by the mind. Willard argues that if we are to apprehend not just how humans are formed but how they might be transformed, we must understand each of these different dimensions, how they relate to one another—especially the relation between the will and

---

[5]Dallas Willard, "Engaging the Will in Personal Transformation" (presented paper, November 7, 2008), Dallas Willard Collection, 1.

mind—and what is necessary for them to align in such a way that character change is possible. "The ideal of the spiritual life in the Christian understanding," he writes, "is one where all of the essential parts of the human self are effectively organized around God, as they are restored and sustained by him."[6] We will explore each of these points in turn, but before doing so, I will say something about Willard's commitment to dualism, as it is foundational to his anthropology.

A MODERATE ANTHROPOLOGICAL DUALISM

In the introduction to this chapter and elsewhere I have followed Willard in referring to the "inner life" of the self as a way of describing our spiritual (nonphysical) side. The core of this inner life or hidden world of the self is a person's spirit/will/heart. I will momentarily parse this idiosyncratic term of his (spirit/will/heart), but a more basic issue to address is the dualist view implied in such language and conception of the human person.

The mind-body problem has been a major subject of debate since at least the Enlightenment, but anthropological dualism has especially come under criticism in modern times.[7] Willard has little trepidation weighing in on the debate. His position is one of moderate or soft dualism, despite self-identifying at times as a "stark raving dualist."[8] Moderate dualism, in this context, affirms a fundamental ontological distinction between body and mind, while eschewing any radical separation. This stands in contrast to monist views, such as materialism and nonreductive physicalism, that rule out any immaterial aspect of the human person. Willard resists such accounts

---

[6]Willard, *Renovation of the Heart*, 31.

[7]E.g., Lynne Rudder Baker, *Persons and Bodies: A Constitution View* (Cambridge University Press, 2000); Nancey Murphy, *Bodies and Souls, or Spirited Bodies?* (Cambridge University Press, 2006); Joel B. Green, *Body, Soul, and Human Life: The Nature of Humanity in the Bible* (Baker Academic, 2008).

[8]The passage in full: "I'm a stark raving dualist. And the first dualism is between God and the physical creation. . . . Now I also believe that the mind is not identical with the brain." Dallas Willard, "Spiritual Formation as a Natural Part of Salvation" (April 17, 2009), MP3, 1:14:00.

because, in his view, they cannot do justice to the full reality of personhood or to the nature of spiritual formation.

His full philosophical argument for the unity and substance of the self and for why some degree of mind-body independence cannot be ruled out proceeds from the ontological nature of intentionality and a phenomenological account of consciousness.[9] Accordingly, he builds on Aristotelian and Thomistic metaphysics (substances, properties, relations, etc.), but his approach is decidedly Husserlian in that he posits mental acts have intentional properties—they are *of* or *about* things other than themselves—and these mental acts form larger mental wholes, up to the level of the whole person. Thus it is from Husserl that he gains an account of the *substantiality of the self*.[10] But Willard's full argument is not our concern here. What is our concern is why he considers at least some commitment to dualism important to spiritual formation.

First of all, Willard insists that the great contrast that runs throughout the biblical narrative is between the visible and invisible.[11] At the heart of this contrast is a dualism between God and his creation. God is pure spirit and substance. That is, he is unbodily personal power and the source of all else that exists. It follows that all that is visible (matter) comes from and is subject to the invisible

---

[9]Two resources on his philosophy of mind are especially helpful. See Dallas Willard, "Intentionality and the Substance of the Self," *Philosophia Christi* 13, no. 1 (2011): 7-19; Willard, "On the Mind's Independence from the Body" (unpublished paper, n.d.), Dallas Willard Collection. The latter paper was posthumously edited by Brandon Rickabaugh and published under both authors' names as "Intentionality Contra Physicalism: On the Mind's Independence from the Body," *Philosophia Christi* 20, no. 2 (2018): 497-515.

[10]Willard, "Intentionality and the Substance," 16. On the intentionality-substance of a person he writes, "Its independence, made so much of in the philosophical traditions, need not be absolute, but a matter of a certain high degree, in contrast to 'dependent particulars' (modes, tropes) and perhaps universals, which supposedly cannot exist outside a true substance" (16); and, "Issues of the *dependence* (in some degree or in some respects) or independence of spiritual or personal substances seem to me to require *prior* elaboration of what a spiritual substance would be like. The logical order here is commonly disregarded. Similarly, or even more so, in discussions of mind/brain *identity*. What exactly is it that is claimed to be identical with the brain or some of its states or states of the central nervous system?" (17-18).

[11]Dallas Willard, "God in Himself—Part 2" (February 12, 1989), MP3, 11:00.

(spirit). Furthermore, our interaction with God is in and through the spiritual/invisible realm. This is precisely what faith is in Scripture, says Willard—it is the currency by which humans engage God and his kingdom. To fail to recognize the "substantiality of the spiritual" is to saw off the branch we sit on for not only formation in the Spirit but relationship with the Spirit.[12]

Second, we are spiritual beings. More specifically, the "human person is a nonphysical (spiritual) entity that has an essential involvement with a particular physical body."[13] If we begin with the above understanding of God's nature, to say we are spiritual beings in an analogous sense is to acknowledge that immaterial realities such as mental acts or events (which have intentional properties) are most constitutive of a person.[14] A person's relation to their body is, Willard says, analogous to how God occupies and overflows space but is not localized in it. Every point of space is accessible to God's mind and will, and in such a way that he can choose to manifest his presence in any spatial location he so desires—but without limiting his presence to or being found in only that location. In a similar way, we occupy our body and have consciousness of and agency in its movements and features—not least through our thoughts, feelings, and will—yet this "very *unity of experiences* that constitutes a human self cannot be

---

[12]Dallas Willard, *The Divine Conspiracy: Rediscovering Our Hidden Life in God* (HarperSanFrancisco, 1998), 81-82; see also Willard, *In Search of Guidance: Developing a Conversational Relationship with God*, 2nd ed. (HarperSanFrancisco, 1993), 235.

[13]Dallas Willard, interview by David O'Conner, "Gray Matter and the Soul," *Christianity Today* 46, no. 12 (2002): 74.

[14]I am aware that some thinkers associate personhood primarily with our relational dimension (Gunton, Zizioulas, Grenz, etc.). But there are others who do not, at least not in that robust way. In other words, Willard has notable company. See, e.g., French Thomist personalist Jacques Maritain, *The Person and the Common Good* (University of Notre Dame Press, 1972). And while Willard does place primacy on the individual rather than community (a theme explored in later chapters), it is inaccurate to label his personalism as *individualistic*. See Dallas Willard, "Postmodernism: Philosophical & Historical Roots 3" (August 19, 1992), MP3, 12:00, for his critical discussion of "the threefold competence of the individual that is worked out in European intellectual history" through Luther (religious), Descartes (epistemic), and Adam Smith (economic). A major shortcoming of this individualism, he says, is its "rejection of authority as a principle of life" (13:00).

located at any point in or around this body through which we live, not even in the brain."[15]

Such a view per se is not disparaging of the body or physicality. To be sure, we have plenty of examples in Christian history of dualistic conceptions of the soul, largely inherited from Greek thought, that render the mortal body merely a container for the immortal soul or, worse, its prison house. But Willard is adamant that the body is an essential dimension of personhood and is in fact part of the *imago Dei*, as we will see. So, his distinction between the physical and the spiritual in the human person does not devalue the former but rather clarifies the relationship between the two and what truly runs or rules human life.[16] Just as spiritual reality rules over material reality in the universe at large—that is, God rules over his creation—so within each human person the spiritual, unseen dimension rules over that which is physical/visible. To misunderstand this fundamental axiom about our existence, Willard believes, is to sabotage the work of spiritual transformation from the get-go, at least from our end. Said differently, the assumption of physicalism will prevent understanding of the nature of formation.[17] For Willard, physicalism just will not work when it comes to understanding the nature of change,

---

[15]Willard, *Divine Conspiracy*, 75.

[16]"Runs or rules" does indeed suggest a hierarchy. But this alone does not devalue the body. Willard's view of the human person is straightforwardly hierarchical. There is a clear sense in which the body is *less important*—but that does not mean it is *unimportant*. A simple example to illustrate this is that my own children are more important to me than other people's children. That does not mean other people's children are unimportant to me or that I would be unwilling to help them at great cost to myself. So, to deem Willard's view of the human person as implicitly Manichean because it is hierarchical is absurd.

[17]As do some contemporary philosophers of mind, Willard often uses the terms *physicalism* and *materialism* interchangeably to describe positions that require no appeal to any nonphysical substance to explain mental phenomena. See Dallas Willard, "Knowledge and Naturalism," in *Naturalism: A Critical Analysis*, ed. William Lane Craig and J. P. Moreland (Routledge, 2000), 24-48; Willard, "Naturalism's Incapacity to Capture the Good Will," *Philosophia Christi* 4, no. 1 (2002): 9-28; Willard, "Non-Reductive and Non-Eliminative Physicalism?" (unpublished paper, 1995), Dallas Willard Collection. By describing Willard's view as "moderate" dualism, as I have, it should be acknowledged that his is one of many intermediate positions between radical dualism and reductive physicalism. In certain important respects, then, he may have more in common with a nonreductive physicalist position than a radical dualist one. That said, he does not

and understanding is the basis of care. Recall that the young Willard, as a pastor, decided to pursue further academic studies because he felt ignorant of God and the soul and thus deemed himself a *hazard* to his parishioners.

Lastly, although it might seem otherwise, Willard's insistence on the existence of the human soul as a spiritual substance is an attempt to keep the *person* as the ultimate unit of analysis. We will see that Willard conceives of the soul as the principle that uniquely orders human life and is thus inclusive of the whole person—similar to how it is viewed, he contends, by classical thinkers (Plato, Aristotle) and in the biblical sources (e.g., when the psalmist addresses his soul in the third person, such as Ps 42:5; 103:1-2).[18] Thus, it is the soul that unifies within an individual the personal and the biological, the visible and the invisible.

Some thinkers who deny mind-body independence run the risk of reductionist conceptions of the human person, something Willard thinks both robs personhood of its dignity (its preciousness and uniqueness) and has devastating consequences for the ethical dimension of life. Again, from his view, dualism is the only anthropology that prevents the *disappearance of the self*—and when the self disappears from the discussion, the person disappears. The following passage evidences his outlook:

> In our sermonic and idealistic and moralistic moments we make much of respecting and loving and valuing persons. We say, or at least many do, that life cannot go on in this earth unless we learn to treasure persons. I submit that a part of our problem in this respect derives from an implicit view of what a human being [is]. If a human being is only an ambulatory, oblong piece of meat and bone, a dense electron cloud, or a natural feedback mechanism of great complexity, you can

---

make a distinction between reductive and nonreductive physicalist positions since, for him, the stakes are still high even in the nonreductive forms.

[18]Dallas Willard, "Spiritual Disciplines, Spiritual Formation, and the Restoration of the Soul," *Journal of Psychology and Theology* 26, no. 1 (1998): 103-4.

talk of respect, admiration, love for such a thing all you wish, but the reality of such emotions and maturations will come forth only if you succeed in thinking of human beings as something a great deal more than just that.[19]

Willard's commitment to a soft dualism, then, is a way of recognizing and valuing the human person. He gets quite detailed in his description of the various dimensions of the human self—to which we now turn—but he does so knowing that he is describing something (or rather, some self) that is irreducible, and that any aspect of the person must be ultimately defined by the whole person.

WILLARD'S PHILOSOPHICAL ANTHROPOLOGY (IN SHORT ORDER)

Willard attempts to ground his anthropology in a biblical account of the human person, and this account remains a main point of reference. And while this anthropology is every bit as theological as it is philosophical and thus can be referred to as either in this book, it is best thought of as a philosophical anthropology looking for biblical justification.[20] (It should also be viewed as a *pastoral* anthropology, for reasons that will become apparent.) Some exegetes and theologians will no doubt take issue with how he goes about this, but the biblical referent of personhood is a first principle in his anthropology.

---

[19]Willard, "On the Mind's Independence," 24-25. I might add that Willard thinks the disappearance of self-knowledge goes hand in hand with the *disappearance of moral knowledge*. In an essay on moral rights and responsibilities, he writes, "Clearly, knowledge of moral distinctions depends upon knowledge of the human self. What Elizabeth Anscombe said decades ago about the need to quit doing moral theory until we have an adequate 'moral psychology' seems very sensible in the light of how knowledge is now understood in the institutions of knowledge. . . . We can never regain the self (will, character) as a subject of knowledge so long as we insist in forcing the self into a scientific ('naturalistic') mold. Moral knowledge disappears with authentic self-knowledge." Dallas Willard, "Moral Rights, Moral Responsibility, and the Contemporary Failure of Moral Knowledge," in *Guantanamo Bay and the Judicial-Moral Treatment of the Other*, ed. Clark Butler (Purdue University Press, 2007), 175-76.

[20]This is because if it is a theological anthropology and his theology or exegesis fails, then it fails as a theological anthropology. Yet if it is a philosophical anthropology, then he might get the theology or exegesis wrong, and it would still be an accurate account for philosophical reasons.

This is made clear in how he introduces his view of the human self in a speech to a gathering of psychologists: "What might be called a *descriptive*, non-theoretical view of the essential dimensions of human personality develops within biblical writings and culminates in the teachings of Jesus."[21]

Before describing these essential dimensions in greater detail, I should mention that Willard's anthropology developed and changed over the course of his career, arguably more than any other area of his theology. This is exemplified in that he has a very different method for working out his anthropology in *The Spirit of the Disciplines* (1988) than in *Renovation of the Heart* (2002). In the former, Paul's writings are his point of departure, the material and immaterial aspects of the person are tightly wound together, and emphasis is particularly on the body as the identity of a person and the locus of spiritual change. In *Renovation of the Heart*, none of these points are undone, but each is augmented or slightly modified. His main scriptural reference is Jesus' double-love commandment, the material and immaterial are wound together but in a looser manner for the sake of analysis, and emphasis is especially on the human will (heart or spirit) and on how all the essential elements of the self must work in unison for spiritual change.

The biggest difference between the two books, however, concerns his view of *spirit* and *soul*. When writing *Spirit of the Disciplines*, he makes no effort to differentiate between these two terms but by and large uses them (along with *mind* and *will*) interchangeably. This is also the case in public talks given during this era and prior.[22] In the mid-1990s this begins to shift as he starts equating the human "spirit" with the "will" or the "heart" and describing this as the innermost core of a person, as distinguished from the person's "soul," which he

---

[21]Willard, "Engaging the Will," 3. See also Willard, "Spiritual Disciplines, Spiritual Formation," 102.

[22]E.g., Dallas Willard, "The Soul as a Factor in Mental and Physical Health—the Revenge of the Soul That Was Lost" (January 26, 1990), video.

portrays as the source of life within an individual but especially as its coordinating principle. His most lengthy explication of this arrives in *Renovation of the Heart*; from thereon he would espouse this view, though his usage of *soul* remained somewhat fluid even after its publication in 2002. Sometimes it refers to one of the main five aspects of personhood, while at other times, such as when he has dualism debates in mind, it simply denotes the spiritual (nonphysical) substance of a person. Since *Renovation of the Heart* reflects his more mature view and was the method he consistently took when teaching on human nature the last two decades of his career, I will focus my analysis there.

Willard often cites Jesus' words in the great commandment as instructive for the nature of the human person: "You shall love the Lord your God with all your heart, and with all your soul, and with all your strength, and with all your mind; and your neighbor as yourself" (Lk 10:27 NRSV). In his exegesis, he suggests that if *strength* is taken to refer to the body and *neighbor* represents the social dimension, then along with heart, soul, and mind, this passage touches on five basic aspects of human life.[23] Willard does not treat this passage as a prooftext for a theological anthropology, let alone as some magical formula, since he holds "there's no worked out, consistent biblical psychology" that can be extracted straight from Scripture.[24] Given the amount of teaching he does on this subject his last two decades, this point needs to be emphasized. As he explains in a talk,

> Now, the Bible does not give us a systematic psychology or anthropology. . . . It doesn't give us a systematic treatment, and so many of

---

[23]Dallas Willard, "Considering the Whole Person: Heart, Soul, Mind, Strength and Neighbor" (January 4, 2010), video, 36:15. Here is an example of where his exegesis might fail but his anthropology still be largely correct. In other words, even if Willard is wrong in his exegesis of Lk 10:27, there can still be good philosophical reasons (and other biblical or theological reasons) for his anthropology. To take one example, it may be that the philosophical arguments for moderate mind-body dualism are stronger than the exegetical arguments.

[24]Dallas Willard, "Spiritual Formation as the Key Component of Leadership" (June 22, 2009), MP3, 38:30.

the terminology that we need to understand—*soul, heart, body,* and so on—is not given in a form that you can cleanly say, "It's all laid out right here." We have to work to do that. But there is a system of the human self in the Scripture. It is not given systematically, but there is a system there, and we have to understand it.[25]

Willard believes the great commandment is a profound summative statement on this scriptural "system of the human self" and, furthermore, one that indicates what is required for whole-life transformation in the Spirit. In his view, Jesus' words express an essentially Hebraic understanding of personhood in that they denote differentiated aspects of the whole self, similar to Old Testament passages such as Psalm 16:7-9.[26] Such a perspective has more in common, Willard contends, with a classical or Hellenistic understanding of the person than many modern Western understandings, which he considers on the whole to be reductionistic.[27]

He especially has in mind modern views that reduce a person to the purely physical or to social constructions. His critique of the former comes out, for example, in any number of talks in which he describes a fictional brain-transplant scenario.[28] Suppose a live

---

[25] Dallas Willard, "Changing the Depth of the Heart" (April 1997), MP3, 9:30.

[26] More specifically, Willard believes Jesus derived his notion of personhood from the Old Testament but "tweaked" and "updated" it ("Considering the Whole Person," 13:30). On this psalm he comments, "Note how many aspects of the self are explicitly involved in this passage: the mind, the will, the feelings, the soul, and the body. A major part of understanding spiritual formation in the Christian traditions is to follow closely the way the biblical writings repeatedly and emphatically focus on the various essential dimensions of the human being and their role in life as a whole" (*Renovation of the Heart*, 31).

[27] In this area and in others, Willard is a defender of classical Greek thought. Nevertheless, he does not withhold critique of the Greek conception of the self when he feels it is necessary. Any extreme dualism in which spirit and body are radically separate and spirit is all that really matters misses the mark by a long shot, in his estimation. See, e.g., what is lost by "a Platonic imposition upon the biblical view of personality." Dallas Willard, *The Spirit of the Disciplines: Understanding How God Changes Lives* (Harper & Row, 1988), 82. But even with this implicit danger, Willard believes the Hellenistic understanding of personhood is still more sophisticated and balanced than a host of reductionistic modern views that treat persons as just their brain or behavior or social constructs. There is no place for the spirit or the soul in such anthropologies, and that, for Willard, is a theological (and philosophical) wasteland.

[28] This thought experiment is not original to Willard but is standard fare in the philosophy of mind.

surgery could be performed in which a person's brain was transplanted into another person's body. Who, Willard asks, would wake up—the one who had the brain or the one who had the body? Often he does not answer his own question but lets the audience wrestle with the implicit cultural bias (and their own) to assume it is the one who had the brain. But on some occasions he shows his hand, such as this 1993 lecture:

> Number one, the person who wakes up will be very confused, I am sure. But the second thing I want to say to you is—I'm telling you this not as a prophet but as someone who spends a lot of time working in the field . . . the person who wakes up, if anyone wakes up, will be the person who had the body, not the person who had the brain. The brain is just another piece of meat, that's all it is. Some people eat brains and scrambled eggs together. And when they do, they're not eating a person. The brain is an organ, it's like the heart.[29]

His critique of social constructivism is just as sharp.[30] He describes it as "the opinion that human beings do not actually have a nature and that all classifications of them . . . are 'social constructions' with no reality apart from the judgments and motivations of social groups or cultures."[31] It should also be noted he began writing in the 1990s but never finished a book-length critical treatment of the philosophical roots of deconstructionism (provisionally titled *The Rage Against*

---

[29]Dallas Willard, "Bringing the Kingdom into Our Life" (August 12, 1993), MP3, 32:30. While it would take us too far afield to discuss the many interesting questions engendered by these remarks, it can at least be said that Willard, in pushing back against the notion "you are your brain," wants to either (1) identify personhood with one's soul diffused throughout the body or (2) stress that the body is what houses the immaterial (spirit) side of personhood that is most uniquely *us* and that cannot be equated with one organ (brain) or bodily system (central nervous system). To my knowledge, Willard does not address to what extent he thinks the brain has to do with one's personality and thus what the hypothetical brain swap would mean for memory loss, personality difference, etc. So, one can agree with him that personal identity does not depend on the brain yet remain agnostic about just how much functioning depends on a particular brain.

[30]See, e.g., his treatment of it in a four-part seminar on postmodern theory for Biola University faculty, *Christian Critical Perspectives on Postmodernism* (August 19, 1992), MP3.

[31]Willard, *Renovation of the Heart*, 29.

Identity) that likely would have dealt with some of the underlying metaphysics of this view.³² All told, he saw naturalism and constructivism as equally disastrous, whether for formation or for human life in general.

As others have argued, the attention Willard pays to anthropology is unusual because many, if not most, contemporary resources on Christian spiritual formation present a fairly nebulous picture of the human person.³³ Terms such as *soul, mind, spirit, flesh, heart,* and *character* are used in fuzzy ways, and accordingly, there is a vagueness to how these aspects of the person are distinct from yet interrelated in the sanctifying process. In contrast, Willard rigorously seeks an intellectually sound understanding of the human person that can hold its own in the world of philosophy and psychology, and he gets quite specific and detailed about what he considers to be the five essential aspects of personhood and their interrelatedness.

In the 1990s, he workshopped various iterations of a diagram that shows how these five aspects each have their own properties or qualities while remaining deeply interwoven and working together. The final (and now well-known) version was published in *Renovation of the Heart*.³⁴ He prefers to speak of these not as "parts" but "aspects" or "dimensions," for although they are distinguishable, they are inseparable.³⁵ When he does use the language of "parts," it is either because he is discussing personhood in light of larger metaphysics and

---

³²See Dallas Willard, "Proposed Project for Sabbatical Leave for Fall 1992" (ca. 1992), Dallas Willard Collection; Willard, "Sketch of Outline for *The Rage Against Identity*" (ca. 1992), Dallas Willard Collection. One clue that *Rage Against Identity* would have addressed the constructivist view of personality is found in *Renovation of the Heart*, 28. See also Willard, "Postmodernism: Philosophical & Historical Roots 1" (August 19, 1992), MP3, 49:30–52:00.

³³Steven L. Porter, "An Overview of Willard's Primary Writings: The Willardian Corpus," in *Until Christ Is Formed in You: Dallas Willard and Spiritual Formation*, ed. Steven L. Porter et al. (ACU Press, 2018), 46-47. There are, of course, many detailed treatments of the human person in contemporary theology. However, this is not the case in the literature of Christian spiritual formation. In Diane J. Chandler's *Christian Spiritual Formation: An Integrated Approach for Personal and Relational Wholeness* (IVP Academic, 2014), 279-80n6, the author herself notes Willard's unique contribution amid this yawning gap.

³⁴Willard, *Renovation of the Heart*, 38.

³⁵According to Gary W. Moon, Willard once quipped, "The only way to actually separate these dimensions was in writing the chapter titles for [*Renovation of the Heart*]." Moon, *Becoming*

thus means the term in a Husserlian sense (the whole of something consists of parts with properties, etc.) or because he is using the word in a nontechnical way for mere convenience's sake.

The *will/spirit/heart* is the fundamental dimension of personhood. This is the aspect of a person that connects to God, initiates action, and most expresses character. *Will*, *spirit*, and *heart* all refer to the same entity but to different senses or emphases of it. Perhaps in this respect it can be thought of like a diamond with different facets. The *will* refers to its power to initiate and create, to bring about what did not exist before. The *spirit* refers to its unbodily nature, that it is distinct from physical reality. And *heart* refers to its position at the center; it is meant to drive or govern all the other aspects.

The *mind* consists of both thought and feeling because they always work in concert. That is to say, there is no thought a person has that does not have a feeling attached to it. Thus, for Willard, the mind operates on a much deeper level than mere cognition, or at least how cognition is generally understood; it is not merely cerebral but also deeply visceral.[36] How the mind is ordered in relation to the will/spirit/heart is one of the more difficult ideas to grasp in Willard's model. But it is crucial to his theory of transformation, so it is something to which we will need to return.

The *body* is the physical aspect of the human person, but it is much more than just our organs and bone and blood; it is our personalized "power pack" that gives us strength to live out our existence in the world and fulfill our God-given vocation in it. As such, Willard contends the body is part of the *imago Dei* and lies right at the center of the spiritual life.[37] (Earlier, I noted that he says the will/spirit/heart is

---

Dallas Willard: The Formation of a Philosopher, Teacher, and Christ Follower (InterVarsity Press, 2018), 215-16.

[36]For further discussion, see Rick Yount, "The Mind: Discipleship That Forms the Thoughts of Christians—Reflections on Dallas Willard's Thinking on the Mind (Thoughts)," *Christian Education Journal* 16, no. 1 (2019): 54.

[37]Although this is a special point of emphasis in *Spirit of the Disciplines* (see 53), Willard maintains this view throughout; see *Renovation of the Heart*, 165-66.

positioned at the center of the *person*; here, he has in mind the body's position in the *spiritual life*.) The body also houses our habits, as it contains ingrained grooves formed through repeated practice of some sort, which is a key reason it is significant for spiritual formation.

The *social context* is the relational aspect of personhood. It is our interface with others—family, friends, coworkers, neighbors, strangers—and without it we cannot interact with others, including God. That means social context, or relations with others, is part of a person rather than separate from or outside of her. It is woven into her very identity.

Lastly, the *soul* is the source of life and, simultaneously, what integrates all these dimensions into a single life. That means the soul not only makes a person alive but is also the cohering or adhesive aspect that holds a person together. In a lot of Christian writing and discourse, *spirit* and *soul* are used synonymously, but as previously mentioned, Willard's mature view is that it is important we see their different functions. The spirit *directs* the whole person, whereas the soul *unifies* the whole person. The spirit is the *center* of a person, while the soul is *comprehensive* of the person. He compares the soul to a computer's operating system: It runs in the background at all times, and when it is out of whack nothing works the way it should.[38] But, as the organizing principle of the person, it means the converse is also true: If one of the other dimensions is out of sorts, then the soul may also become disordered.

It should be stated that Willard does not provide much exegetical support from Scripture for distinguishing so clearly between spirit (Hebrew: *rûaḥ*; Greek: *pneuma*) and soul (Hebrew: *nepeš*; Greek:

---

[38]Willard, "Spiritual Disciplines, Spiritual Formation," 104; Willard, *Renovation of the Heart*, 37. Willard was aware that a metaphor as such is not an argument, nor can it replace an argument. Nevertheless, in respect to the multifaceted nature of human personality, he remarks, "We really do need analogies for all of this, because the only alternative is to write a long book of philosophy that no one would understand." Dallas Willard, interview with Lyle SmithGraybeal, "A Conversation with Dallas Willard About *Renovation of the Heart*," *Perspective* 12, no. 4 (2002): 4.

psychē), something that leaves his model open to critique. Now, he engages plenty of scriptural passages when describing these dimensions of personhood in *Renovation of the Heart* and elsewhere, and his goal in so doing is to provide a clear, rational depiction of the human person that is consistent with biblical teaching, not to produce some model through prooftexting. Nevertheless, he does not supply textual analysis or exegesis to show that the Bible itself speaks of the soul in distinction from the spirit.[39]

There is, however, a certain hermeneutical sensitivity and humility in his method. After describing characteristics of the soul that can be learned from carefully studying how it is portrayed throughout Scripture, he adds a caveat: "Now, I don't think we can find a passage in the Bible that says that. We have to read and study how it addresses the soul, . . . [but] we cannot just get out of the Bible a definition of the soul."[40] Again, this is what makes his anthropology more philosophical, or perhaps it is an integrative anthropology resulting from concomitant philosophical reflection and biblical/theological work.

On a related note, it is important we see Willard offers his theological anthropology as a heuristic, a working mental model aimed at helping people better grasp the complex nature of human personality in order to more fully love God and neighbor with the whole self. To be clear, his anthropological dualism is *not* a heuristic; it is a hill he is willing to die on. His fivefold model, on the other hand, is one plausible explication of this dualism. This is in keeping with his practical theological approach; in his most substantive treatment of the human person, he explicitly states his aim is "intensely practical."[41] (I would argue *Renovation of the Heart* is the most practical of the pentalogy, even more so than *In Search of Guidance*.)

---

[39] Here is another example of where his exegesis might be lacking but his philosophical reasoning may still be sound. That is, there may (or may not) be good reasons apart from biblical exegesis for distinguishing between soul and spirit/will/heart. In other words, the question does not hang just in the balance of exegetical arguments.

[40] Willard, "Conversation with Dallas Willard," 4.

[41] Willard, *Renovation of the Heart*, 25.

He does not claim his model is flawless or even exegetically normative. Instead, he views it as his best attempt at explaining the multidimensionality of the human person in a holistic way, and he encourages others to develop comprehensive, sophisticated models of personhood that do justice to both the scriptural account and human experience. In reference to his diagram, he explains,

> Now, we could get in a long fight about the essential elements of the human being, but I beg off, because I need simply to make a point. If you want to divide the whole person up in other ways, be my guest. I do think that this little diagram is an adequate presentation of the self for making the point I need to make. And that is that *spiritual formation is a matter of reworking all aspects of the self*.[42]

And elsewhere, "If you want to do it in a different way, blessings on you. . . . Please don't feel cornered by this. But for goodness's sakes, work out something *for you*, so that you will know what it means to love God with all your mind . . . and then your body [and so on]."[43] The practical and pastoral are paramount for Willard's theology, and his anthropology deserves to be interpreted in that light. Yet, even with this proviso, we must conclude that his insistence on delineating between spirit and soul is unsubstantiated on a textual level in his work. Likewise, his mature view of the soul, as one of the five main aspects of the self, lacks conceptual precision and thus remains blurry in his model, something even those who most champion his work have admitted.[44]

---

[42] Dallas Willard, "Spiritual Formation in Christ Is for the Whole Life and the Whole Person," in *The Great Omission: Reclaiming Jesus' Essential Teachings on Discipleship* (HarperSanFrancisco, 2006), 55-56. I have cited the revised version of this article because its wording on this point is clearer. However, subsequent citations will refer to the original version with the same title, in *For All the Saints: Evangelical Theology and Christian Spirituality*, ed. Timothy George and Alister McGrath (Westminster John Knox, 2003), 39-53.

[43] Dallas Willard, "Life in the Kingdom 4/Understanding the Person 1" (October 13, 2011), MP3, 48:45, 50:00. See also Willard, "How Spiritual Formation Empowers and Informs Kingdom Living" (November 4, 2004), MP3, 19:30.

[44] See J. P. Moreland, "Body and Soul: Tweaking Dallas Willard's Understanding of the Human Person," in Porter, Moon, and Moreland, *Until Christ Is Formed*, 55-75.

The Heart of the Human Problem   125

These few critical remarks reveal limitations of his anthropology, but they by no means render it without merit. To see what potential it might offer for understanding spiritual formation, we will now examine his analysis of the human will, its relation to the mind, and the place of its redemption within the transformation of persons.[45]

THE CENTRALITY OF THE WILL

For Willard, transforming the will/heart/spirit is the key to Christian formation. How does he derive this conclusion? When thinking about the redemption of the self, he insists it is a mistake to begin with *justification*, as much Protestant thinking does. The proper place to begin is with *creation* since justification, along with the other doctrines of salvation—not least of all glorification—is aimed at restoring what has been lost and fulfilling what was originally intended.[46] Since God's intention from the beginning was for human persons to co-reign with him over the rest of creation, he designed human life with the power for self-determination.

Recall that Willard identifies the *imago Dei* most closely with "creative will." The will is the capacity to initiate courses of reality or action. It is the place of freedom and creativity and the source of our dignity—that is, what makes us priceless and unique.[47] Moreover, it is this inner yes or no in response to situations that decides the eventual character of a person. The will (spirit or heart) is therefore the aspect of

---

[45]To help the reader follow the flow of my argument thus far, here is how Willard distinguishes the essential from the nonessential: Dualism is *essential*; five parts of the person is *nonessential*; and now, as we get to Willard's understanding of the will, we are back to *essential*.

[46]Willard, "Considering the Whole Person," 00:45.

[47]In *Disappearance of Moral Knowledge*, Willard locates himself within the moral philosophical tradition that focuses "upon the will and the role of the will in the organization of the 'ideal self.'" Dallas Willard, *The Disappearance of Moral Knowledge*, ed. Aaron Preston, Gregg Ten Elshof, and Steven L. Porter (Routledge, 2018), 362. He mentions some who stand in this long tradition: Aquinas, Immanuel Kant, and T. H. Green, among others. But his reflections more generally on the will reveal he is tapping into a broader tradition that includes Aristotle, Augustine, William James, and perhaps Jonathan Edwards. While he is more forthright about the influence of some (e.g., Aquinas, James), I would venture to say his study of all the aforementioned thinkers contributed to his view of the will.

personhood that is distinctly *us*. Its primacy to God's redemptive purposes is further shown in how he speaks of "spiritual transformation" as synonymous with "the renovation of the human heart."[48]

To return to and expand on an earlier point, Willard is not saying human thoughts, feelings, beliefs, values, bodies, and social relations are unimportant to our personhood. It is just that if persons have the thoughts, feelings, beliefs, values, bodies, and relations they do because they are determined by forces outside themselves, then what makes that person the person she is has nothing to do with her. It has to do with whatever sort of determinism is at work (divine determinism, biological determinism, social determinism, etc.). On a deterministic view, what makes you *you* is whatever forces have shaped you. For Willard, the will is what makes you *you* because your choice is the ultimate ground of your thoughts, feelings, beliefs, values, bodies, and social relations. To the extent we are conditioned from the outside and to the extent our will is conditioned therein, we still have the ability to choose or not choose to increase our agency. Thus, your will is unique to you. It is unshareable.

As the power to initiate human action, the will is needed to worship God. It is also needed for any other act of love, since for Willard, to love is by definition to will the good of another. To say God is love, then, is to say God always wills what is good. So the human will functions properly only when it is aligned with God's good will. This is why sin, which at least initially involves choice, is at its most basic level a turning from God—the antithesis of worship. In an exegesis of Romans 1, Willard describes the downward spiral of "pervasive soul corruption [that] begins with the heart (or will) deflecting the mind from God."[49] (The intimate interworking between the will and mind is likewise crucial in a person's first move back from ruin.) Departure from the knowledge of God (i.e., interactive relationship with God)

---

[48] Willard, *Renovation of the Heart*, 20.

[49] To the following, Willard, *Renovation of the Heart*, 50-57; quotation on 51. Cf. Dallas Willard, "Man's Blindness to God" (1988), MP3.

quickly skews the mind's ability to discern truth and reality, especially in relation to God's goodness and rightful claim on our lives. This moral blindness then leads one who has turned from God to in the end place herself in the position of God. Self-idolatry ensues, and soon after, desire or sensuality becomes king.[50] This is because the body, the sphere we primarily have control over and can act independently through, becomes our overriding focus when we live apart from God. All attention turns to satiating the body's appetites and desires; feelings, which have their proper place in God's design of the person, are now considered one and the same with these appetites and desires.

Once this happens, will (for good) and desire (for want) become entangled to the point that a person cannot differentiate between the two. This is what Willard calls *vital* or *impulsive will*.[51] The person moves toward what they want or desire, with little thought to what is good or better—both for the person and for others. It is a *vital* will because it is the experience of a newborn who is moved only by what she wants. Yet unless a person grows out of this, she will remain ruled by the *impulsive* will, forever justifying a want alone as warrant for action.

This is in contrast to *reflective will*, which is oriented toward the good. Here is where choice comes in: Alternatives are weighed and considered as a person discerns what is good, better, or best, rather than only homing in on what is wanted or desired.[52] Neither of these

---

[50] Willard's position that "Your desires are not your friends" appears to stand in stark contrast to that of Christian philosopher James K. A. Smith. Dallas Willard, "Spiritual and Emotional Maturity," in *Renovated: God, Dallas Willard and the Church That Transforms*, by Jim Wilder (NavPress, 2020), 18. I will comment further on the supposed conflict between their views later in this chapter. For Willard's more nuanced reflections on desire, see Willard, interview with Mike Yaconelli, "Spirituality Made Hard," *The Door*, no. 129 (1993): 15-16, during which he states, "Desire itself is not bad. God has desires. Even angels have desires," but immediately adds that human desire is often malformed, requiring suspicion. See also Willard, "Why Am I Here? The Four Great Questions in Life" (October 12, 2010), video, 23:45, where he contrasts a Christian view of desire with Buddhist and Stoic attempts to extinguish it altogether.

[51] To the following, Dallas Willard, "Spiritual Formation and the Warfare Between the Flesh and the Human Spirit," *Journal of Spiritual Formation & Soul Care* 1, no. 1 (2008): 83-84.

[52] Willard was influenced here by William James's understanding of volition and mind in *The Principles of Psychology* (1890), which I will say more about momentarily.

states of the will—impulsive or reflective—is exclusive to life apart from Christ or life in Christ. But even if a person can perceive what is truly good, which is not a minor accomplishment, apart from Christ the reflective will eventually finds itself ensnared in the battle between, in Paul's terms, the human spirit and human flesh. (The biblical notion of "flesh," for Willard, is not innately sinful or depraved but rather is the natural life apart from God. Those who "walk in the flesh" live from and rely on their own resources instead of God's.) The human spirit (the will) alone is simply no match for desire; thus when there is direct confrontation "between what is desired and what is good, *sin wins*."[53] Hence the dilemma described by the apostle as not doing the good we want to do, and doing the evil we do not want to do (Rom 7:15). Yet when the reflective will is at work in one who is not only alive in Christ (born "from above") but also aided by the instruction of the law, presence of the Spirit, and fellowship of God's people, then it becomes possible for the reflective will to stay its course and guide the rest of one's psychology and life. In such cases, real growth and transformation in Christlikeness is possible and probable. But for it to become actual, two things must happen simultaneously from a theological and phenomenological standpoint.

First, our relationship with Christ must include *cruciformity with Christ*. As Willard explains, "The meaning of the cross of Christ in human experience is that it stops any mere 'I want to' from functioning as an adequate reason for action. The cross is therefore central to the moral life of humanity."[54] Jesus models this in the Garden of Gethsemane as he prays, "My Father, if it is possible, may this cup be taken from me. *Yet not as I will, but as you will*" (Mt 26:39).[55] Here we find the Son of God in his earthly experience, submitting his will and

---

[53]Willard, "Spiritual Formation and the Warfare," 85.

[54]Willard, "Spiritual Formation and the Warfare," 83.

[55]Although it does not affect the point being made, it deserves mention that Willard interprets this verse quite differently from the standard exegesis. See Dallas Willard, "The Craftiness of Christ" (unpublished draft chapter, 2004), Dallas Willard Collection.

wants to the greater will and wants of his Father.[56] Often Willard describes cruciformity as *mortification of the flesh*, something he insists can only be done with the Spirit. Attempts to go it alone account for much misery in the church's history, since mortification is "essentially divine work, though we also must act."[57] We act by surrendering our impulsive will and retraining our body and its reflex-like responses through intentional practice.

Second, we must *walk in the Spirit*, which means we look to and expect the unbodily personal power that is the triune God to enable us to do the good we know we are to do. In other words, we count on our connection to the Trinity rather than on our natural abilities and resources alone. This is where walking in the Spirit overlaps with cruciformity: As Willard puts it, "To mortify the deeds of the flesh just means to learn how to live from a *source* that is superior to and outside of your natural abilities."[58] In so doing, we gradually deepen our fellowship with God and our participation in what he is doing in the world. Willard is fond of saying that at the beginning of Genesis, God not only creates but creates co-creators. The will/spirit/heart is what allows us this creative freedom, and its gradual alignment with the Father's will to accomplish his good work is not only the purpose of spiritual formation but the meaning of human life. The ultimate goal is for our will to be conformed to God's, for there to be a sort of communion of wills, so that in this relational harmony we will the same good for the sake of that good.[59] These two sanctifying acts of

---

[56]Regardless of whether we think Jesus possessed one divine will (monothelitism) or possessed both a divine will and human will (dyothelitism), this passage shows that Jesus experienced a deep inner struggle concerning his impending death, a struggle that ultimately was resolved in him relinquishing his will to that of the Father's. And, I might add, this was nothing new for Jesus. He had been entrusting his will/spirit/heart to the Father every moment of his life. For further discussion on this from Willard's view, see Steven L. Porter, "Will/Heart/Spirit: Discipleship That Forms the Christian Character," *Christian Education Journal* 16, no. 1 (2019): 85-87.

[57]Willard, "Spiritual Formation and the Warfare," 85.

[58]Dallas Willard, "Authentic Leaders for Christ" (February 22, 1997), MP3, 6:15.

[59]Porter, "Will/Heart/Spirit," 85. Porter points out that we find in the Gospels this sort of relational unity between Jesus and his Heavenly Father; e.g., "My food is to do the will of him who sent

cruciformity with Christ and walking in the Spirit, meant to engender and reinforce each other, will be further illustrated in the coming chapters. But we note here that this twofold scheme is, says Willard, how the reflective will can win out over the impulsive will in a person's life.[60]

Willard mentions a third state: *embodied will*.[61] Unlike impulsive will and reflective will, embodied will is neutral in and of itself. It is simply what happens when either the impulsive will or the reflective will becomes settled in the body to such an extent that a person automatically does what it dictates. The human will is constituted in such a way that free will becomes less free over time. That is to say, what at first requires conscious deliberation becomes over time more unconscious and automatic. For Willard, then, a main goal of God's redemptive work in his people is for Christ's will to become our embodied-reflective will. "Christian spiritual formation," he maintains, "is the process through which the embodied/reflective will or 'spirit' of the human being takes on the character of Christ's will," and again, "It is, above all, this spirit (or will) that must be reached, cared for, and transformed in spiritual formation. The human will is primarily what must be given a godly nature and must then proceed to expand its godly governance over the entire personality."[62]

The question of how the will is "given a godly nature" (i.e., regeneration) will be addressed in the next chapter. There is still more to be said, however, about Willard's understanding of how the will

---

me and to accomplish his work" (Jn 4:34 ESV); "I do nothing on my own authority, but speak just as the Father taught me" (Jn 8:28 ESV).

[60]In *Renovation of the Heart*, Willard presents a more elaborate fourfold scheme for the "progression toward complete identification of our will with God's" (150), which consists of surrender, abandonment, contentment, and participation. His descriptions of these first two more or less align with cruciformity and walking in the Spirit, although elements of the latter two are also folded into walking in the Spirit. Yet the main difference is that the fourfold scheme is focused more on *stages* of the will's progression in sanctification and less on *steps* we take in that progression. Another difference is that the twofold scheme derives from his exegesis of Paul's counsel on the matter.

[61]To the following, Willard, "Spiritual Formation and the Warfare," 83-84, 86.

[62]Willard, "Spiritual Formation and the Warfare," 84; Willard, *Renovation of the Heart*, 34.

functions in human life, especially in relation to the mind and then to the other essential dimensions of the self.

YET THE WILL CANNOT BE TRANSFORMED DIRECTLY

In a 1989 talk, Willard summarizes the human person in the following way: "You are primarily a mind with a will in a body, and that will is the center of your being."[63] We have seen that his anthropology is complex and difficult to categorize, so, obviously, this statement captures only a sliver of the whole. But its brevity sheds light on how he perceives human personality effectively functioning. Now, considering his emphasis on the will and its role in directing the rest of the self, we might have expected he would say "You are primarily a *will*. . . ." So why does he instead foreground the mind yet still emphasize the centrality of the will?[64]

The will (spirit or heart) remains the most fundamental aspect of a person, the pinnacle of personhood, we might say, because it directs the rest of one's life. As the capacity to choose, it is also most determinative of who we become (our character) and makes us morally accountable in a way no other creature on earth is. Yet, the will is deeply connected to the mind (thoughts and feelings) since we must have a mind in order to have a will. A will cannot just run on its own. Furthermore, choice is the exercise of the will, but when the will is in bondage—enslaved by lustful/obsessive desire (*epithymia*)—our ability to choose what is truly good and godly becomes severely distorted. As noted, it is quite possible to live in a state of contradiction with oneself—what Willard calls the "splintered will"—or for a person to be ruled by the body's feelings and appetites.[65]

---

[63]Dallas Willard, "Why Such Lack and Evil?" (February 26, 1989), MP3, 47:30.

[64]One possible answer is that when Willard made this statement, his anthropology had not yet reached its most mature expression. However, he is clear in *The Spirit of the Disciplines* (1988) that creative will is the *imago Dei* and the aspect of our humanity that most needs reform. So, the fact that his anthropology was still evolving does not explain why he says a person is primarily her mind. This statement, then, is right in line with his mature thought.

[65]Willard, *Renovation of the Heart*, 145-46; cf. 40.

Lastly and most critically, while the will is sovereign over all the other parts of our psychology, it is not *immediately* sovereign in many or even most instances. For example, if a person who is prone to be anxious wants instead to become more joyful and content, this will not simply happen by exerting her will to experience joy and calmness in the moment anxiety swells up inside her. Any project aimed at genuine spiritual transformation "is bound to fail if it focuses upon the will alone," states Willard.[66] We must instead take the path of *indirection* and begin with the mind, the flow of thoughts and emotions that constitutes our conscious experience, and then with bodily practices that retrain our reflex-like responses.

In the case of anxiety, this person can purposely choose to engage in practices that foster her connection with God and awareness of his loving presence in her life. She might, for instance, begin consciously reflecting on her life and the specific ways in which God has provided for her. She could regularly meditate on scriptural passages that speak of God's gracious care for his children and the kingdom provisions always available to her. Perhaps she starts practicing sabbath as a way to rest in God's goodness and increase her enjoyment of his presence. Fellowship with other believers and conversational prayer are other important disciplines in which she could engage. Whenever she feels anxiety rising in her, she could be prepared to repeat to herself, "I am always safe in the kingdom of God," or to gently remind herself to release outcomes and results to God. In all of these instances, she is using her mind and body via her will in ways that give rise to certain psychological conditions that, over time, can habituate an inner state and disposition of joy and contentment. But she is not depending on her will to do this in the moment of anxiety; even in the example of bringing something before her mind in the moment of her struggle ("I am always safe in the kingdom of God"), she has *prepared* to do so. She is using her will indirectly, then, to arrange for

---

[66]Willard, *Renovation of the Heart*, 39.

her mind and body to participate in activities that over time change her character.

On this principle of indirection, Willard goes as far as to say the will is *entirely* dependent on the mind since we can only choose in accordance with the contents of the mind. "The will is hemmed in," he writes, "by what our thoughts and feelings actually are at the time of willing." He goes on:

> There is a kind of "back and forth" here, which is very important to understand for our purposes of spiritual formation. Obviously, the thoughts and feelings that the will depends on in any given moment of choice cannot be changed *in* that moment. But the will or heart can change the thoughts and feelings that are to be available to it in *future* choices. . . . Will alone cannot carry us to change. But will *implemented through changing my thoughts and feelings* can result in my becoming [a different kind of person].[67]

Willard's teaching on the relationship between the will and the mind, especially in terms of what he calls "the psychology of redemption," owes much to American philosopher and psychologist William James. In a section on the psychological nature of the volition in his *The Principles of Psychology* (1890), James writes, "The essential achievement of the will, in short, when it is most 'voluntary,' is to ATTEND to a difficult object and hold it fast before the mind."[68] He

---

[67]Willard, *Renovation of the Heart*, 142-43. See also Willard, "Spiritual Disciplines, Spiritual Formation," 105. In lectures given in the late 1980s and early 1990s, we hear Willard wrestling with how to describe the dialectical structure of the will and mind: "The heart . . . is the executive center of the personality, it is the domain of choice, but it is not separable from the domain of mind because you cannot choose if you do not think. You have to understand—even misunderstand—in order to choose. . . . You've got to think something." Dallas Willard, "Spiritual Reality: God and the Human Soul" (May 30, 1992), MP3, 48:15. In some of these lectures, he also presents primitive versions of his diagram of personhood in which the mind is in the innermost circle, rather than the spirit. One handout shows he initially placed the spirit in the innermost circle but then marked it out, replacing it with the mind. Willard, "Seminars on Creative Ministry in Times of Crisis" (handout, 1987), Dallas Willard Collection, 8. He would, of course, ultimately decide to place the spirit in the innermost circle, followed by the mind. But these various iterations of the diagram serve as a historical illustration of the "back and forth" between the mind and spirit Willard here describes.

[68]William James, *The Principles of Psychology* (Holt, 1890), 2:561.

describes the drama involved in the volitional process as wholly a "mental drama," an intimate affair between the mind and its ideas—yet one that also includes consent and an essential element of choice.[69] But where that choice lies, he makes clear in his conclusion:

> To sum it all up in a word, the terminus of the psychological process in volition, the point to which the will is directly applied, is always *an idea*. There are at all times some ideas from which we shy away like frightened horses the moment we get a glimpse of their forbidding profile upon the threshold of our thought. The only resistance which our will can possibly experience is the resistance which such an idea offers to being attended to at all.

James punctuates this with his closing remark: "To attend to it is the volitional act, and the only inward volitional act which we ever perform."[70]

This Jamesian notion shows up in Willard's philosophy of mind and consequently in his model of spiritual transformation. "The primary freedom we have," he asserts, "is always the choice of where we will place our minds."[71] If we are to, by God's grace and through the Spirit's power, undergo real character transformation, then we must, says Willard, begin with *the mind*. The will is accessed most readily through the mind and, more specifically, through the thoughts we bring before the mind. This is not a narrowly cognitivist view since, again, he also recognizes the will dictates what is brought before the mind. But the intentionality of consciousness is a basic fact of human life for Willard—it is *the* primary freedom we have. In his first theological book he writes, "We all live at the mercy of our ideas."[72] When describing Eve's temptation in the garden, he points out that Satan "did not hit her with a stick, but with an idea."[73] And in *Divine*

---

[69]James, *Principles of Psychology*, 2:564.
[70]James, *Principles of Psychology*, 2:567, italics slightly adapted for clarity.
[71]Willard, "Spiritual Disciplines, Spiritual Formation," 108; cf. Willard, *Renovation of the Heart*, 95.
[72]Willard, *In Search of Guidance*, x.
[73]Willard, *Renovation of the Heart*, 100.

Conspiracy he states, "The killing fields of Cambodia come from philosophical discussions in Paris."[74] So, while the mind is not what directs or unifies one's personality, it is the dimension of the self we must give the most attention to if we are to experience a thorough renewal of our personality. Where the mind goes, the life will follow.

The last part of Willard's shorthand for the self (a mind with a will in a *body*) is also essential in Christian spiritual transformation. Reshaping the will with the mind requires the body since the human body is the reservoir of finite independent power God has granted us as living beings.[75] Every human function, ability, or activity—whether mental, emotional, or physical—takes place in and through the body. The ability to choose, create, and self-determine thus cannot be exercised without a body. Willard often points out the irony that all spiritual disciplines are bodily behaviors. This is why Paul, when admonishing the Christians in Rome to be "transformed by the renewing of your mind," urges them to offer their "*bodies* as a living sacrifice," not their *minds* or *wills* (Rom 12:1-2). Furthermore, our body is inherently social since it is the vehicle or means by which we interact with creation (inorganic and organic), other human creatures, and the Creator.[76]

So, how is all this brought together? Willard contends the plasticity of the body is how habits come to be (more on this later). Most of what happens in the body is habitual. What does not yet happen by

---

[74]Willard, *Divine Conspiracy*, 7. There is empirical evidence behind this chilling line. Over one million people were executed in Cambodia between 1975 and 1979 by the communist regime in power at the time, with the total population of the country only eight million people. When the leader of this regime, Pol Pot, was in his twenties, he spent three years in Paris as a student—during which he read and was deeply influenced by the Marxist writings of Lenin and Mao. And he was not alone. There was a whole group of Cambodian leftist students in Paris (now known as "the Paris student group") who became part of Pol Pot's government.

[75]Dallas Willard, "Afternoon Session" (August 4, 1987), MP3, starting at 6:15; cf. Willard, *Spirit of the Disciplines*, 53-54.

[76]Willard's conviction that a person exists only in relation to others through their body accounts for why he does not include social context as one of the essential dimensions of the self in his earlier work. This relationality is subsumed in what he says about the body, for instance, in *Spirit of the Disciplines*.

habit requires the will—but the will, in turn, requires the mind, since the will is necessarily limited by what our thoughts and feelings actually are in the moment of willing. Hence, there is a cascading dependence here. Through repetition, what once required conscious thought and volition (mind and will) becomes habituated/automatic in the body. It is as if the body has an unconscious mind and will of its own, but in reality, this only further reveals the holistic nature with which God designed the human person. And though Willard does not mention the soul in his condensed anthropology ("You are primarily a mind with a will in a body, and that will is the center of your being"), we might add that the soul is what integrates all this dimensionality—mind, will, body/relations—into a whole. If these aspects of the self are not aligned but at odds in any way, a disjointedness will be experienced throughout.

It should be clear at this point that Willard does not hold a *strictly cognitivist* view of the human person.[77] This is pertinent since an anthropology overly calibrated toward cognition would risk rendering spiritual formation essentially a process of indoctrination. Such a view would operate on the premise that right knowledge will produce right desire and action, something Willard explicitly critiques in the "education" models of Plato and Aristotle.[78] Pedagogies in the church and seminary that lean this intellectualist way, often emphasizing the importance of a Christian worldview, have come under attack in recent decades for this very reason, not least by philosopher James K. A. Smith. However, it would also be a mistake to associate Willard with those who subscribe to an *affective* view of the person, such as Smith. Considering the wide reception of Smith's

---

[77] *Strictly cognitivist*, for lack of a better term, though *intellectualist* also works. On a personal level, Willard was certainly someone we would call "heady," and his teaching style was nearly as theory-oriented as you can get, something seen in how few personal stories and examples he shared in lectures or even in sermons. But these idiosyncrasies of personality and pedagogy alone do not render his view of the human person an intellectualist one.

[78] Willard, "Spiritual Formation and the Warfare," 80-81; cf. Willard, "Spiritual Disciplines, Spiritual Formation," 103-4.

more Augustinian anthropology and his critique of "bobblehead" Christianity, a comparison of his and Willard's views would be informative but obviously cannot be pursued here.[79]

Let me only suggest that while their anthropologies have much in common,[80] there are important differences in their views of personhood that lead to significant points of disagreement in their proposals for the church.[81] In Willard's view, one cannot plow around the life of the mind and expect to grow in sanctification. God has fashioned human nature with a dialectical structure, so knowledge is meant to be the foundation of volition, yet the mind cannot act on its own but requires the will's cooperation—or at least this is how human

---

[79]See especially the first two volumes of his Cultural Liturgies project: James K. A. Smith, *Desiring the Kingdom: Worship, Worldview, and Cultural Formation* (Baker Academic, 2009); Smith, *Imagining the Kingdom: How Worship Works* (Baker Academic, 2013). To what extent Smith accurately represents (or does not) Augustine cannot be taken up here.

[80]First off, they both feel it is crucial that the church reclaim a vision of *the human being as embodied*. Second, they both posit *the heart as the pinnacle of personhood*. Also, they both see *imagination/vision as what fuels real life-change*. Further correlation can be seen by comparing Smith's diagram of the human person (*Desiring the Kingdom*, 48) side by side with Willard's VIM pattern (Vision, Intention, Means; *Renovation of the Heart*, 85-91).

[81]Willard would likely question the degree to which Smith separates the cognitive and the affective in his anthropology and then prizes affectivity as the preeminent locus of formation. It is especially the latter that Willard would contest. On this point Smith states it is not his intention to place the intellect and affectivity in a duel (*Desiring the Kingdom*, 28n11), and his appropriation of Charles Taylor's concept of social imaginary is one way he attempts to hold the two together in dynamic tension. But his sustained critique of a rationalist picture of the human person and overwhelming praise of an affective one does little but in the end create a dichotomous relationship between the two. He bluntly asserts we are "fundamentally noncognitive" and "primarily affective" (53), while depicting the heart (*kardia*) in entirely affective terms (24-25). Then there is the way Smith explicitly equates *love* with *desire*, "eschewing any distinction between *eros* and *agape*" (51n20). Given Willard's parsing of the will/spirit/heart and its relation to the mind (both thought *and* feeling), and his warnings about desire and careful delineation between it and genuine love, he would find these moves highly problematic. Unpacking these points in detail is worthy of its own essay, so perhaps this will be taken up by someone in the future. Until then, I offer the following summary. On the first point, Willard places feeling in the mind and not on equal grounds with but subordinate to thought. This is very intentional on his part. It means when it comes to renewing/reshaping the mind, we need to first address thought; feeling should be a clear second. Further, for Willard, the human heart is the will; it is not something affective. Accordingly, it is paramount, from his view, that we delineate between *love* and *desire*. Love is "will-to-good"; it is to will the good of the object loved. Thus, much of what we say we "love" is motivated not by love but desire. Willard's favorite illustration to invoke here is chocolate cake. We may say we love chocolate cake but actually all we want is to eat it; we have confused desire for love.

life is meant to function. Willard's anthropology may be thought of as some hybrid of the cognitivist and affective views or perhaps as a different configuration altogether; but his position cannot be labeled as one or the other without serious qualification.

UNDERSTANDING THE PERSON IS THE BASIS OF CARING FOR THE PERSON

I readily admit this chapter has not done justice to the depth and nuance in Willard's philosophical anthropology and psychology. His view is complex and hopefully will receive a full exposition by a future researcher. My purpose here has been much more modest, as I have focused only on the areas of his anthropology most critical for understanding his theory of spiritual formation.

For Willard, spiritual formation is *spiritual* in that it is the formation of the most precious part of a person—the spirit/will/heart. This is the aspect of our being at the core of who we are and thus must be surrendered to God if our character is to be shaped like Christ's. But this entails a holistic approach, one aimed at re-forming the will by indirection (via the mind and body) and always with reference to the whole person. The mind is particularly important in this process since we can only authentically will what we authentically think or imagine.[82] At the same time, the direction of our thoughts is crucially dependent upon our choices. This dialectical structure of the will and mind is woven into the very fabric of human life and therefore into the possible transformation of human life.

Why Willard thought knowledge is important for spiritual formation, a theme covered in the prior chapter, extends here to his concern about anthropology and specifically the human spirit. As he explains,

> Understanding is the basis of care. What you would take care of you must first understand, whether it be a petunia or a nation. If you would

---

[82] Walter Hopp, "Dallas Willard on Knowledge and Its Role in Transformation" (paper presented at the Hildebrand Project Summer Seminar, June 30, 2022).

care for your spiritual core—your heart or will—you must understand it. That is, you must understand your spirit. . . . If you would form your heart in godliness or assist others in that process, you must understand what the heart is and what it does, and especially its place in the overall system of human life.[83]

In essence, without a genuine understanding of something, we cannot expect to adequately care for that something. In fact, without understanding there is a chance we might harm the very thing we intend to care for. Thus to experience genuine personal transformation in the Spirit and to assist others in this, it is important that we have a practical knowledge of the self, how it is ordered, and how it can be, by God's grace, transformed. To that event of personal transformation we now turn.

---

[83]Willard, *Renovation of the Heart*, 27.

SIX

THE METAPHYSICS OF GRACE

TAKING AS OUR CUE Willard's second reason for emphasizing spiritual formation as *spiritual*, namely that it is formation *by* the Holy Spirit, we now turn to questions of the agency and dynamics involved in formation. Germane to any biblical account of Christian spiritual formation is how to parse God's sovereign work and the disciple's obedient participation in the sanctifying process. Does human volition and effort play an important or inconsequential role? Is transformation primarily by divine prerogative, by affective relationship to God, or by sharing in the divine nature—or are the Spirit's workings too mysterious for us to meaningfully understand? This subject deserves careful and nuanced reflection, for, as Singaporean theologian Simon Chan states, understanding the relation between God's grace and human effort "is perhaps the most problematic issue for the development of a Protestant spiritual theology."[1]

Closely connected are questions about the means and contexts that best facilitate characterological growth. What human phenomena—practices, settings, circumstances, and so on—shape a person's spirit in the image of Christ, and how does the divine Spirit work in and through such phenomena? And does the divine-human relationship displace the significance of other human relationships in the formative process, or are such relationships central to how one grows in godliness?

---

[1]Simon Chan, *Spiritual Theology: A Systematic Study of the Christian Life* (IVP Academic, 1998), 79.

There is no lack of interest on the part of contemporary theological scholarship in these issues.[2] However, I should state from the onset that Willard's theory of spiritual formation proper is more theological-phenomenological than systematic-theological. By this I mean his main concern is to elucidate the dynamic theological process of transformation in Christlikeness in such a way that ordinary people can intelligibly grasp its nature and responsibly act for it themselves, always with the Spirit's assistance and through the empowerment of grace. This will become apparent as we proceed. But let us begin by plotting Willard's view of sanctification on the larger Protestant spectrum as a point of reference.

WILLARD'S POSITION WITHIN THE PROTESTANT WORLD

In the introduction to *Christian Spirituality: Five Views of Sanctification* (1989), Donald Alexander describes three main perspectives on sanctification across the Protestant spectrum. The first is those who stress *faith alone*, represented most clearly in Lutheran and some Reformed theology. The second is those who stress *faith and the believer's responsible participation*, a position many within Reformed and Baptist traditions hold. And the third is those who stress *the unique role of the Holy Spirit*, exemplified by Wesleyans and Pentecostals.[3]

Although a case might be made that Willard aligns with the third perspective, given his strong affinity for John Wesley's and Charles

---

[2]E.g., Simeon Zahl, *The Holy Spirit and Christian Experience* (Oxford University Press, 2020); Kelly M. Kapic, ed., *Sanctification: Explorations in Theology and Practice* (IVP Academic, 2014); Steven L. Porter and Brandon Rickabaugh, "The Sanctifying Work of the Holy Spirit in Christian Virtue Formation," in *Faith and Virtue Formation: Christian Philosophy in Aid of Becoming Good*, ed. Adam C. Pelser and W. Scott Cleveland (Oxford University Press, 2021), 123-45. For an example from the perspective of moral theology, see Jennifer A. Herdt, *Putting On Virtue: The Legacy of the Splendid Vices* (University of Chicago Press, 2008).

[3]Donald L. Alexander, ed., *Christian Spirituality: Five Views of Sanctification* (IVP Academic, 1988), 10. Certainly there are more than three variations of belief within Protestantism on this complex doctrine, but Alexander limits himself to those represented by the volume's contributing authors. Accordingly, his mapping of these positions, while not comprehensive, does run the gamut from those stressing God's sovereignty to those emphasizing human responsibility.

Finney's theologies of the Spirit, he is most at home with the second: faith and the believer's responsible participation. The third perspective, at least within Alexander's framework, encompasses more charismatic teaching on the subject along the lines of instantaneous change via God's Spirit with an emphasis on heightened spiritual experience and, for some, the second blessing of the Spirit. Willard thinks there is theological validity to these special operations of the Spirit and that they should be sought in special cases, such as when a person's soul has been deeply wounded or an addictive behavior has become so all-consuming that deliverance is required, but that such an approach is not normative in the New Testament for growth in godliness.[4]

This much cannot be said for the first position—faith alone—if this is taken to mean we can do little more than listen to God's declaration of our justification or wait on divine fiat to bring about our transformation.[5] Willard did not believe there is biblical warrant for such passivity in the spiritual life.[6] In an essay titled "Spiritual Formation as a Natural Part of Salvation," he addresses this head-on:

> Salvation is by grace through faith. That is a foundational truth. But it is usually understood to mean that nothing you do contributes to salvation. With this, a *pervasive passivity* enters the scene. You will even be told by some that your very faith in Christ as the sacrifice for your sins is not something you do, but something God just produces in you (or not). It is not just that grace is "unmerited favor," but that it is

---

[4] "Characteristically, you see, you have groups that will emphasize the action of the Holy Spirit— [but] the Holy Spirit *will not do* Christian maturity for you. It will not. You can be baptized in it, you can be filled with it and do all sorts of things, but your character will not change except insofar as you engage your will in the process." Dallas Willard, "Authentic Leaders for Christ" (February 22, 1997), MP3, 10:30.

[5] In the volume of collected essays edited by Alexander, *Christian Spirituality*, this position is represented by Lutheran theologian Gerhard O. Forde ("The Lutheran Position," 13-32). The theme of Forde's essay is that sanctification is "getting used to justification"; he writes, "It is what happens when we are grasped by the fact that God alone justifies. It is being made holy, and as such, it is not our work" (14). For character formation, then, his only admonition is that we "listen" to God's unconditional announcement of forgiveness and new life (22).

[6] Nor is there, from Willard's standpoint, ontological warrant for such a view. Why would God change a person into someone or something the person never intended to become?

something exterior to you—an event involving God in heaven, a transfer of merit from Christ to your account. . . .

The conclusion I draw from all of this is that a view that takes salvation to be the same thing as justification . . . *cannot* come to see spiritual formation as *a natural part* of salvation. The result of that will be the routine omission of spiritual formation unto Christlikeness as a serious objective of individuals and groups who hold a mere "justification" view of salvation.[7]

Willard asserts it is, in Karl Barth's words, "an absorption of Christology into Soteriology" that is largely to blame for this misconstrual of salvation.[8] That a "pervasive passivity" now plagues much of evangelical Protestantism should come as no surprise since God's righteousness, from this perspective, is *merely* imputed. Personal transformation is thus inconsequential to salvation. Willard insists, to the contrary, that salvation in the New Testament is the transferal not only of Christ's merits but also of Christ's life. Accordingly, he saw the retrieval of the doctrine of regeneration as a possible remedy to this theological conundrum.

REGENERATION AND THE ALLURE OF GOD'S GENTLENESS

Regeneration means, in Willard's view, that *salvation is a life*. To be saved is to be *born again*, as evangelicals are apt to say, yet "birth and life of course go together."[9] And *life*, ontologically speaking, is self-initiating, self-directing, and self-sustaining—it is something that grows. Through God's work of regeneration, a person possesses the

---

[7]Dallas Willard, "Spiritual Formation as a Natural Part of Salvation," in *Life in the Spirit: Spiritual Formation in Theological Perspective*, ed. Jeffrey P. Greenman and George Kalantzis (IVP Academic, 2010), 48-49, emphasis added on *"pervasive passivity."*

[8]Dallas Willard, *The Divine Conspiracy: Rediscovering Our Hidden Life in God* (HarperSanFrancisco, 1998), 403n8.

[9]Willard, "Natural Part of Salvation," 49. Cf. "For all of the talk about the 'new birth' among conversative Christians, there is an almost total lack of understanding of what that new birth is in practical terms and of how it relates to forgiveness and imputed or transmitted righteousness" (Willard, *Divine Conspiracy*, 42).

divine life "from above" (Jn 3:3 NRSV), hence the righteousness of Christ is not only imputed; it is *imparted*.[10] As a deposit of the Holy Spirit, Christ's righteousness—the very *life* of Christ himself—works itself out existentially in the life of the believer. As Willard states:

> Simple inductive study of the New Testament will, I believe, convince anyone that its primary way of understanding salvation is in terms of a divine life that enters the human being as a gift of God. There is then a new psychological reality that is God acting in us and with us.... Eternal life in the individual does not begin after death, but at the point where God touches the individual with redeeming grace and draws them into a life interactive with himself and his kingdom. A new, nonhuman activity becomes a part of our life. Speaking thus we must make it clear that we are not just "talking something up," but referring to the concrete reality of regenerate existence.[11]

Willard's understanding of salvation as eternal living, beginning here and now, is undergirded by "a non-forensic model of Grace as relational." In the seminar handout in which this line appears, he highlights the example of Abraham in Genesis 15:6 ("And he believed the LORD; and the LORD reckoned it to him as righteousness" [NRSV]), adding to his personal copy of the handout this handwritten note: "Believing God is a *relationship*, not a qualifying status."[12] This framing informs how Willard understands *ordo salutis*, for he suggests forgiveness of sins is subordinate to regeneration since the gift of new life, God's very indwelling life, is what brings about forgiveness.[13]

---

[10] Dallas Willard, *Renovation of the Heart: Putting On the Character of Christ* (NavPress, 2002), 224. This is categorically different from the Thomist notion of "infused moral virtue," which Thomas contrasts with "acquired moral virtue." For Willard, virtue that is divinely imparted/infused does not cancel out its being acquired by human effort.

[11] Willard, "Natural Part of Salvation," 50.

[12] Dallas Willard, "Seminars on Creative Ministry in Times of Crisis" (handout, 1987), Dallas Willard Collection, 10.

[13] Dallas Willard, "Christ-Centered Piety," in *Where Shall My Wond'ring Soul Begin? The Landscape of Evangelical Piety and Thought*, ed. Mark A. Noll and Ronald F. Thielmann (Eerdmans, 2000), 30; Willard, "Regeneration and the Heart Jesus Wishes to Give Us" (August 25, 2000), MP3, 8:15. Cf. Willard, "Attention to Christology and Atonement" (March 16, 2011), video, where he says

The Metaphysics of Grace 145

How regeneration relates to *faith* is crucial for Willard. Though powerless in itself, faith is the way one apprehends the new life from above.[14] It is not the case that God rewards salvation to those who exhibit faith, as if faith were a righteous act itself—something the term *saving faith* may imply. Instead, faith is, according to Willard, a *confidence that compels*. It is no mere mental act but necessarily involves the will and the body.[15] So, when we have faith that Jesus really is Lord of all, our will (spirit or heart) puts us into relational contact with that reality, and, as covered earlier, epistemic interaction with spiritual reality is transformative.[16] This is how those who were dead in their trespasses and

---

God no longer holds the sins of regenerated persons against them because "they have come out of the position of rebellion" (37:45). My use of *ordo salutis* should be understood in terms of differentiations, not separations, within soteriology. This is in keeping with Willard, who describes atonement in the following way: "It is not separable from our faith in Christ or from justification. This is rather difficult to make clear, but justification is not just a forensic act. It is a declaration before God, but it is not just a credit transfer; it is God's act of entering our life." Quoted in Gary W. Moon, "Getting the Elephant Out of the Sanctuary: An Interview with Dallas Willard," *Conversations Journal* 8, no. 1 (2010): 15. He later adds, "Justification, atonement, and salvation are three aspects of one thing" (16).

[14]Willard does speak of faith as "a power and a life" but does so to distance it from mere mental activity and especially to show the vital role it plays in regeneration, which he considers the real source of salvific power and life. Dallas Willard, *The Spirit of the Disciplines: Understanding How God Changes Lives* (Harper & Row, 1988), 39. It should be noted that it is not all that clear from his writings where he places faith on the continuum of knowledge, belief, commitment, and profession, which he describes in *Knowing Christ Today*, among other places. See Dallas Willard, *Knowing Christ Today: Why We Can Trust Spiritual Knowledge* (HarperOne, 2009), 15-18. At times he seems to simply equate faith with belief (*Knowing Christ Today*, 19, 20; *Divine Conspiracy*, 91). Yet at other times he describes faith—or at least biblical faith—as something weightier and more substantive. In these instances, faith is "confidence grounded in reality" (*Renovation of the Heart*, 129) or a "distinctive life force" (*Spirit of the Disciplines*, 41) that expands with experience and the use of reason. As such, it is situated between knowledge and belief or is a powerful pairing of knowledge and belief. I think it is clear he has two different types of faith in mind. Since he does not define the term as precisely and consistently as the others on the continuum, I suggest "mere faith" and "living faith" accurately describe these two types, respectively.

[15]See Willard, "Natural Part of Salvation," 52, where he refers to faith as "hearty confidence." Considering he understands the heart and the will as nearly identical, *hearty* confidence has to do with a person's will (not just mind).

[16]In Willard's view, knowledge rests on truth in a way that faith (or belief) does not, while faith (or belief) involves the will in a way that knowledge does not. He therefore firmly rejects the notion that knowledge and faith are incompatible or at odds in any significant way, since, he argues, they are combined in living faith. E.g., "Faith is not opposed to knowledge; it is opposed to sight"; "An act of faith in the biblical tradition is always undertaken in an environment of

sins are made alive in Christ (Eph 2)—by placing their hearty confidence in the God who is the giver and sustainer of life.

Yet Willard also contends that such faith is not possible apart from divine assistance. Initial faith in the Son of God as one's savior comes only by the Word and Spirit of God penetrating the human spirit (will or heart), a salvific work wrought by the sovereign initiative of God. Faith is in the end a gift of God. Faith increases as a person obtains more evidence and experience of God, yet faith can never be *produced* by human effort. It forever remains a divinely initiated gift of grace.

In a 2000 lecture, Willard expounds on how God's sovereign act of regeneration brings about new birth in a person's spirit, the centermost part of one's being.

> When we think of spiritual formation, it all begins with the Word and Spirit of Christ coming in, through the mind, to the spirit. And the natural response would be to evoke faith in Christ, which reestablishes communion with God. Now, that is something that is far beyond our ability to do. That is the new birth; we are born of above at that point. That's regeneration. That means there is a new life in the center of the soul; in the spirit there is new life.[17]

So now we must qualify what has just been said. In Willard's view, regeneration is a *relationally* sovereign work of God. It is sovereign because the sending of the Word and Spirit is a unilateral divine act, and it is relational because it requires a natural response of faith that is up to the person's will.

---

knowledge and is inseparable from it"; "Although faith often goes beyond knowledge, it never works—on the biblical model—outside of a context of knowledge." Dallas Willard, *In Search of Guidance: Developing a Conversational Relationship with God*, 2nd ed. (HarperSanFrancisco, 1993), 209; Willard, *Knowing Christ Today*, 20; Willard, "The Failure of Evangelical Political Involvement," in *God and Governing: Reflections on Ethics, Virtue, and Statesmanship*, ed. Roger N. Overton (Pickwick, 2009), 85.

[17]Willard, "Regeneration and the Heart," 29:30. Cf. the line representing how the "Word and Spirit of Christ" enters the human person in Willard's diagram of the human person in *Renovation of the Heart*, 38. That grace comes "through the mind, to the spirit" is even clearer in his hand-drawn rendition of the diagram on a transparency he used in his annual Fuller Theological Seminary course (available in the Dallas Willard Collection).

God's relational sovereignty accounts for (1) how the human person, in her fallen condition, is truly lost and will not turn to God on her own accord: "There is no one righteous, not even one" (Rom 3:10). We are *depraved enough*, says Willard, to require God's gratuitous intervention for a person to be capable of submitting herself to God.[18] Yet it also accounts for (2) how faith is a response to this grace and not a result of it. As Willard states above, "it all begins with the Word and Spirit of Christ coming in," to which "the natural response would be to evoke faith in Christ." Faith is the *natural* response, not the *automatic* or *predetermined* response. This is beyond our ability to do because without prevenient grace the human will would be unable to respond,[19] but the will can still resist the overtures of the Word and Spirit. Even in regeneration the will has some agency, even if it is tiny; it must either receive or resist the gift of enlivening grace. Thus grace, to remain gracious, cannot be irresistible or imposed.

This point should not be glossed over. The divine conspiracy, as Willard conceives it, is predicated on God as a respecter of persons and their freedom,[20] for the will is the only basis for developing an

---

[18]When asked about the doctrine of total depravity, Willard would answer that he believed in "enough depravity." Dallas Willard, "Vision: The Cooperative Friends of Jesus" (November 4, 2004), MP3, 1:33:00.

[19]On the doctrine of prevenient grace, see Willard's interview with Luci Shaw, "Spiritual Disciplines in a Postmodern World," *Radix*, no. 3 (2000): 30-31, where he remarks, "I do believe that God is constantly moving in gentle ways around people (except possibly those who have absolutely hardened themselves in their own self-will to the point where God isn't going to bother them). I think he's constantly eliciting in us the desire for himself.... The prevenient grace of God, as the theologians call it, has usually long been at work, and at a certain point it emerges to a conscious desire to know God." Elsewhere, he describes prevenient grace as "God is on the march even before you're awake." Dallas Willard, "Spiritual Formation and the Disciplines" (June 7, 2012), video, 52:45. Let it be noted that Willard does not associate prevenient grace exclusively with Wesleyan theology but sees it (rightly or wrongly) as a Calvinist doctrine as well. See Willard, "From the Greeks to the Barbarians—Even to the Scythians" (July 25, 1974), MP3, 53:00.

[20]"You cannot overestimate the importance of God's respect for our nature as creative, spiritual being as will." Dallas Willard, "The Spirit and the Heart" (October 11, 1993), MP3, 59:45. This is another notion he gains from William James. From James's view, says Willard, "The only thing that is uniquely you are your consents—what you consent to and what you don't. That's your contribution to reality. That is why you and your will is absolutely unique and God will not

interpersonal relationship with God and the moral character necessary to responsibly share in his redemptive project now and in the future. Numerous passages of Willard can be cited in support, not least the first three chapters of *Divine Conspiracy*. For instance, in an unpublished paper on theodicy, he writes, "Producing people with character without giving them choice is impossible because the capacity to choose is a part of character," and "the moral development of personality is possible only in a world of genuine freedom."[21] Willard believed that many theological missteps on sovereignty and freedom—missteps that, in his view, have made "many people miserable"—stemmed from erroneous assumptions, even among giants such as Augustine and Calvin, whom he respected but ultimately regarded as "very confused about it."[22]

In an academic yet lucid address delivered at Biola University on the nature of the spirit, Willard recommends Thomas's *Summa Theologica* and Charles Finney's writings but gives particular praise to Scottish philosopher C. A. Campbell's *On Selfhood and Godhood* (1957) and endorses in a more qualified sense Presbyterian minister John Wood Oman's *Grace and Personality* (1917). Based on Campbell's Gifford Lectures, the first champions a metaphysical view of free will as foundational to selfhood and moral responsibility, asserting that moral choice requires the ability to transcend determinative influences, whether divine or natural.[23] The second book addresses the doctrine of grace, with Oman arguing for a personalistic understanding of the workings of grace as emanating not from an overriding force but from a Father. He contends that grace, as a relationship

---

override it because he has chosen to allow you a creative role in the world." Willard, "The Transformation of the Mind: Thoughts and Feelings 1" (January 7, 2010), video, 3:00.

[21]Dallas Willard, "God and the Problem of Evil" (unpublished paper, 1993), Dallas Willard Collection.

[22]Dallas Willard, "Metaphysics," PHIL 460 (transcript, University of Southern California, fall 1993), Dallas Willard Collection, 496.

[23]See especially lectures 8 and 9 in C. A. Campbell, *On Selfhood and Godhood* (Allen & Unwin, 1957).

between persons, upholds human freedom and personality, offering a path between two extremes: a deterministic view that diminishes human agency and a Pelagian emphasis on earning favor.[24] That Willard considers *On Selfhood and Godhood* "one of the best things I know of" on the topic and *Grace and Personality* "a very rich study"[25] suggests he may have been influenced by these authors or at least found strong kinship in their portrayal of the human soul as free, rational, and responsible—and of grace as God's empowering presence that preserves rather than denies our agency and integrity, a concept I am calling Willard's position of relational sovereignty.

It makes sense for Willard, then, that God's way of working in history and in human persons is, in a word, *gentle*. Gentleness is his nature, but it is also a profound strategy. "The Spirit is the kind of being that doesn't force itself on others," says Willard, for God "knows that he cannot bring out of human life and history what it's all about unless he gives distance so that people have room to decide what they want and to pursue that. But the promise is there: Anyone who seeks God will find him. And the truth is he'll find them—but you have to seek it."[26] Again, we see the centrality of the human will in God's redemptive project, first in whether a person receives the gift of enlivening grace and second in that person choosing to participate in God's larger redemptive work in the world.

So, what *precedes* or *prepares* a person for regeneration, according to Willard, is a unilateral divine act of God's relational sovereignty. But there is a sense in which *regeneration itself* is a unilateral act, but now in respect to its target (not agent): It initially affects *only* a person's spirit. The new life that regeneration produces in a person's spirit

---

[24]"In a right relation of persons, especially of father and child, the help of the one does not end where the effort of the other begins." John Oman, *Grace and Personality* (Cambridge University Press, 1917), 73.

[25]Willard, "Spirit and the Heart," 32:15, 33:30. But he adds the disclaimer: "I can't guarantee you that [*On Selfhood and Godhood* is] readable."

[26]Dallas Willard, "Bringing the Kingdom into Our Life" (August 12, 1993), MP3, 3:45; cf. 52:30; Willard, "April 2012 Interview" (April 17, 2012), MP3, 16:45.

enables him or her to then partner with God in reclaiming the rest of the person's being and life. This reclamation project is sanctification proper. It is not possible without the enlivening of the will by God, yet it will not happen without responsive human effort.

Returning to the lecture from 2000 cited earlier, Willard goes on to illustrate how spiritual transformation happens in an individual's life, after and on account of regeneration, with an analogy of the Israelites in the Promised Land. This illustration later appeared in *Renovation of the Heart*,[27] but its meaning is more forthright in this talk combined with a second analogy of Jesus' method of healing in the Gospels. Of course, no analogy can stand on all four legs, and the relationship between divine grace and human effort will always remain partially mysterious to us. Nevertheless, what we can grasp of our life in Christ via the Spirit, we grasp by means of analogy: father/child, vine/branch, groom/bride, and so forth. And Willard was intent on making this intelligible—or as intelligible as possible—for the church.

Discussing how once the divine Spirit has enlivened the human spirit, this does not instantly heal the rest of one's personality (thoughts, feelings, bodily habits, etc.) from the sin that resides therein, he says:

> Being born again does not solve all these problems. And it does not put you on an automatic path to spiritual transformation. And I want to just pause on that because that is really fundamental.
>
> I'll give you this analogy to think of. The first city that was taken by Joshua was what? Jericho. What happened to the walls of Jericho? They fell down. Was there any other city whose walls fell down after that? No. What did they have to do for the other cities? They had to take them, didn't they? Did they take them by themselves? No. If God didn't go with them, they couldn't take them, they found out to their sorrow. But on the other hand, God didn't take them and say, "Now come on in, guys."
>
> The walls of Jericho fell down flat. No more. The rest of them, you take them. Jesus said, "Without me you can do nothing." And I will guarantee you that if you do nothing it will be without him. It's just

---

[27]Willard, *Renovation of the Heart*, 42.

The Metaphysics of Grace

that simple. Now, it's not a matter of earning. But it is a matter of acting. We have to act.

Ask yourself how many of the miracles of Jesus required that the person assisted do what they could not do. Here's a man with a withered hand: "Stretch forth thy hand." "Well, it's withered, you see." Here's a man borne of four [i.e., carried by four friends]: "Take up thy bed and walk." "Well, why do you think they carried me in here? I can't do it!" What do you think if that guy had just said, "No, I can't. I'll just lie here." He'd still be lying there. A man is blind: puts mud on his eyes, tells him to go wash in the Pool of Siloam. Now, I don't know if you know this, but the Pool of Siloam was a good distance from where he'd got the mud on his eyes. Most tourists ride down there in a bus. Isn't there some place closer he could have washed the stuff off?

So now you have to understand this about spiritual disciplines and about the transformation of the self. All of this has to be transformed. The function of the spirit is to take the initiative, having been brought to life, and begin to work with the mind and the feelings and the body and the social relations and the soul to transform them so that they all function well.[28]

Willard's understanding of the metaphysics of grace becomes all-important here. He often encourages his readers or listeners to do an inductive study of a key term or phrase in the Bible.[29] This is never more so than with the word *grace*.[30] He believed if people carefully traced how the word is used throughout the whole of Scripture, they would see for themselves that biblical grace is not merely God's forgiveness but is constitutive of all God's action, similar to the Wesleyan

---

[28]Willard, "Regeneration and the Heart," 31:00.

[29]Lying behind this traditional Bible study method, for Willard, is the complex phenomenological method of *conceptual analysis*, which he gained from his study of Husserl. For his explanation of conceptual analysis, see Dallas Willard, "Translator's Introduction," in *Philosophy of Arithmetic: Psychological and Logical Investigations—with Supplementary Texts from 1887–1902*, ed. Edmund Husserl (Kluwer Academic, 2003), xv. See also Michael Stewart Robb's astute discussion of Willard's appropriation of this method in *The Kingdom Among Us: The Gospel According to Dallas Willard* (Fortress, 2022), 85-86.

[30]E.g., Dallas Willard, "Spiritual Disciplines and Means of Grace: Contrast or Continuum?," interview, *Modern Reformation*, no. 4 (2002): 43.

notion of grace as both pardon and power. He remarks in an interview, "This misunderstanding of grace as a mere transfer of credit just totally destroys the teaching of grace in the New Testament."[31] At its most basic level, grace is the action of God doing for humans what they cannot do on their own. That includes forgiveness of sins but also, and critically, divine empowerment or enablement bestowed on human actors.[32] Willard's quip that saints use more grace than sinners is well known.[33] It sprang from his view that grace is simply how anything happens in the kingdom of God; it is both the foundation and the ongoing energy behind holy living and obedience to Christ.

He summarizes this quite bluntly in another lecture: "Character issues are not settled by unassisted grace." To which he adds, "Now, if you're a Lutheran, you're apt to say, 'synergism,' and rush out the door. But you know all you have to do to go to hell is do nothing."[34]

SYNERGISM THAT SHUNS WORKS RIGHTEOUSNESS

We must, at this point, discuss the topic of synergy and Willard's particular flavor of it since he has been accused of semi-Pelagianism by at least one theologian.[35] Willard borrowed from myriad Christian traditions, but, as we will see momentarily, he situated his doctrine of sanctification proper within classic Reformed theology.[36] If we

---

[31] Dallas Willard, interview by Keith Giles, "Authentic Disciples of Jesus," in *Subversive Interviews* (Subversive Underground, 2011), 18.

[32] As he puts it: "We all know that grace is unmerited favor, right? Everyone can say that: grace is unmerited favor. The problem with that description is it doesn't tell you what form it takes. . . . Often people present grace in such a way that it never touches the life." Dallas Willard, "My Grace Is Sufficient" (May 2, 2003), MP3, 27:00.

[33] "The true saint burns grace like a 747 burns fuel on takeoff." Dallas Willard, "Spiritual Formation in Christ Is for the Whole Life and the Whole Person," in *For All the Saints: Evangelical Theology and Christian Spirituality*, ed. Timothy George and Alister McGrath (Westminster John Knox, 2003), 50.

[34] Dallas Willard, "Spiritual Formation as the Key Component of Leadership" (June 22, 2009), MP3, 19:15.

[35] Joseph M. McGarry, "Christ Among a Band of People: Dietrich Bonhoeffer and Formation in Christ" (PhD diss., University of Aberdeen, 2013), 212.

[36] My usage of *Reformed theology* is meant to be taken in a broad sense rather than equated with a specific designation such as Calvinism. For a preliminary description of the Reformed

conclude this classification is correct, as I contend we should, then it is possible to interpret his teaching on the divine-human interchange that makes spiritual transformation in Christlikeness possible as a Reformed variant of synergism.

Willard does not use the term *synergy* or *synergism* in his published writings, and I have found only negative references to the term in his recorded talks, with one exception. By *negative* I do not mean he himself disavows the concept. To the contrary, these are instances when he is clearly teaching a synergistic view of sanctification he knows some may be uncomfortable with and thus invokes the "synergism" label to preemptively beat them to it. This is a case of anticipating his audience's concerns. For example, when asked in a question-and-answer about whether we have any role to play in what Paul describes as "the washing of water" that brings about holiness (Eph 5:26; 1 Cor 6:11), Willard responds:

> If you mean you don't do anything, I would say *wrong*. If you mean you couldn't do it if God didn't help you, I would say *right*. . . .
>
> The question is whether or not it is okay for you to be active. I want to tell you it is okay for you to be active and necessary for you to be active. But the moment you put your trust in that, you're dead. You act and you trust. "Trust and obey, for there is no other way to be happy in Jesus than to trust and obey." See, the *obey* part is what we really have trouble with today. The form of religion that we have inherited from the Reformation is one that makes it very difficult for us to get serious about doing something. So I ask you to dwell on the Twenty-Third Psalm.[37] Well, again, God isn't going to do that for you. You have to do it.
>
> Now, if you have a theology that says all human effort is sinful, probably you're going to be paralyzed. And many people have that theology. And so in some theological circles the word *synergy* is a dirty word.[38]

---

tradition that recognizes the diversity therein and is not narrowly defined by the Canons of Dort, see Paul T. Nimmo and David A. S. Fergusson, eds., *The Cambridge Companion to Reformed Theology* (Cambridge University Press, 2016), 1-7.

[37]Earlier in the talk, he encouraged the audience to dwell on this psalm as a spiritual practice.

[38]Dallas Willard, "Q & A" (Fall 2003), MP3, 1:00:30.

While researching Willard's unpublished papers in the Dallas Willard Collection at Westmont College, I came across a document titled "Becoming a Disciple of Jesus," likely written around 1990.[39] Although the majority of its content differs little from what can be found in *Divine Conspiracy* or post-1990 talks focused on discipleship, the document has two unusual features. The first, which does not directly concern us here, is a pair of notes: one at the top of the document stating, "*NOT FOR GENERAL DISTRIBUTION*," and one at the end that may indicate why.[40]

The second feature is its positive usage of the word *synergism*. After introducing the idea that disciples of Jesus ought to expect "kingdom manifestations" in their lives and that such manifestations need not be spectacular, he states, "But our aim should be to learn to live in *synergism* with God and His spiritual realm." He then explains,

> This word, with a usage established in the New Testament writings and developing in the Greek language as the early church fathers attempted to find language to express kingdom experience, is defined in dictionaries as: "cooperative action of discrete agencies such that the total effect is greater than the sum of the two effects taken independently." The scriptural record is filled with events where divine and human effort coalesce or fuse into one event with an outcome beyond human capacity. It is this that we are learning in learning kingdom manifestation. In practical terms, we study with Jesus how to speak (and listen) to God in such a way that our prayers are answered, and we study how to act trusting God for an outcome beyond our power. The specific manifestations of kingdom presence, of the very "life that is in God" (Eph. 4:18) pervading our actions, will not be the same for all. But

---

[39]This date is my best educated guess based on some of the phrases and concepts he uses and when he would have developed those phrases/concepts.

[40]Dallas Willard, "Becoming a Disciple of Jesus" (unpublished paper, ca. 1990), Dallas Willard Collection. The note at the end reads, "{*PLEASE NOTE:* This material should not be taught to the usual communicant without approximately one year of straightforward teaching of the gospel which Jesus himself preached preceding it. The 'non-churched,' however, will generally make sense of it more readily. But there is no point in presenting material in such a way that the well-intentioned will merely feel attacked.}"

there is a life of divine *synergism* for every one of Jesus' pupils. That is what it means to *live* in the kingdom of the heavens.[41]

It is not clear what "usage" of synergism in the New Testament Willard is referring to since he does not provide scriptural passages, but we may assume he has in mind *synergos* or *synergeō,* which can denote both divine-human and human-human relationships. When this Greek word is used in Scripture to denote a divine-human relationship, such as in 1 Corinthians 3:9 ("For we are God's co-workers" [NAB]) and 1 Thessalonians 3:2 ("Timothy, . . . our brother and co-worker in God's service in spreading the gospel of Christ"), it is in the context of ministry and mission rather than salvation and sanctification. And this is precisely how Willard uses the term in this document. At least here, where he unabashedly endorses synergism, using it in a positive, affirming sense, the cooperative action in view is that of a disciple synergistically working with God to manifest the kingdom to serve God's purposes. This is also the case in the one recorded talk in which he uses the term approvingly.[42] To be clear, Willard taught that there is a human side to holiness, that we must be active in pursuing Christlikeness, but he does not use the word *synergy* to describe that phenomenon. Instead, his preferred term is *effort.*

We noted earlier that in Willard's theology, grace constitutes all God's action in our lives. Hence it logically follows that grace is not opposed to effort but to *earning,* as he famously stated, since earning is an attitude, whereas effort is an action.[43] It is impossible to overstate the importance of this distinction in Willard's theological phenomenology of spiritual formation. He insists God's grace and human effort do not stand in opposition but go hand in hand; in fact, God designed humanity from the beginning with and for this capacity. That is to say,

---

[41] Willard, "Becoming a Disciple," 8-9.
[42] Dallas Willard, "The Foundations of Confidence: Work" (August 15, 1987), MP3, 1:10:45.
[43] Willard's earliest written articulation of this is "The Spirit Is Willing: The Body as a Tool for Spiritual Growth," in *The Christian Educator's Handbook on Spiritual Formation,* ed. Kenneth O. Gangel and James C. Wilhoit (Baker, 1994), 225.

God's abundantly bestowing grace on humanity is not a makeshift plan after the fall. If Adam and Eve had never sinned, they would have still needed divine grace to fulfill the vocation given to them by God.

Grace corresponds, then, with creation and human nature, not just redemption. Willard believes few things have been more detrimental to post-Reformation Christianity than a failure to recognize this and to instead teach that "effort" is a Pelagian-like move in the doctrine of salvation.[44] In one of his earliest recorded sermons he states,

> Many times we hear a teaching of grace which goes something like the following: "There's nothing you can do to receive the grace of God." Well, what do you do then? Nothing. You don't do anything because you've been told there's nothing you can do to receive the grace of God. There's all kind of confusion around grace and works and its role in salvation. Let's just remember that when we are told that we cannot *earn* salvation, that does not mean that there is nothing we can do to *receive* it.
>
> A person who wishes to give me a gift must find circumstances which I can fulfill in order to receive it. A gift is not an imposition. I can't give you something by dumping it on your head. You have to receive it.[45]

Much later he writes, "We must stop using the fact that we cannot *earn* grace (whether for justification or sanctification) as an excuse for not energetically seeking to *receive* grace. Having been found by God, we then become seekers of ever-fuller life in him."[46]

Willard compares this synergistic reality in the spiritual life to the simple act of eating a meal.[47] When a person lifts food to her mouth with a fork, she has not earned anything, but she does get to eat. Likewise, nothing is merited or earned when we act on and with God's grace, yet

---

[44] In his words: "The single most harmful obstacle to spiritual growth in Western Christianity today is a misunderstanding of grace that keeps it out of daily life and obedience" (Willard, "Contrast or Continuum?," 43).

[45] Willard, "From the Greeks to the Barbarians," 16:45.

[46] Dallas Willard, "Spiritual Formation in Christ: A Perspective on What It Is and How It Might Be Done," *Journal of Psychology and Theology* 28, no. 4 (2000): 257.

[47] To the following, Dallas Willard, "What Does Holiness Look Like Shorn of Its Legalistic Expressions? 2" (January 4, 2010), video, 16:30.

such action *is* how we enter and live in the kingdom of God. Anyone who contends otherwise, he says, does not consistently *live out* their theology. And such a disconnect between professed theology and lived theology will manifest itself in problematic ways since well-directed effort based on understanding is key to transformation. A second "crude metaphor" he offers on this is that of power steering in automobiles.[48] He recalls as a young boy when a person driving had to strenuously tug and pull on the steering wheel to maneuver it alone. But when power steering came along, there was suddenly another and greater force aiding the driver. However, the person driving still has to do something or nothing will happen, since power steering does not act on its own. So it is in the spiritual life: "You do something and then something bigger than you takes over. The way you know the presence of the Spirit in human life is the outcome is incommensurable with the input."[49]

Staying with metaphors, to get at the same point but from the reverse side, Willard uses the analogy of God dancing with a lifeless dummy to describe the doctrine of divine monergism held by some. God's redeeming work requires our active participation, he argues, and "there is no inconsistency as long as we don't try to think about it mechanically. But some people present the spiritual life as it were like dancing with a mannequin or something, and you're the mannequin. . . . It just isn't like that. It is *interactive*. And it does not lessen the glory of God that it should be so."[50]

SANCTIFICATION PROPER

Because Willard's theological account of spiritual transformation is more phenomenological than systematic, he only occasionally addresses the doctrine of sanctification proper. *Renovation of the Heart*

---

[48]To the following, Willard, "Cooperative Friends of Jesus," 1:26:45.

[49]Willard, "Cooperative Friends of Jesus," 1:27:15. Of course, we now do have fully self-automated cars, so we might update the metaphor to compare three views of divine-human interaction with driving: complete human passivity (self-automated steering), complete human action (pre–power steering), and cooperative human action (power steering).

[50]Willard, "Q & A," 1:05:00.

is where he does so most directly in his writings. The doctrine is treated in three succinct, sequential sections in a late chapter of the book.[51] What is unusual is the extent to which he quotes and footnotes others—approximately half of his treatment is quotations—as well as the theologians he quotes and draws from, as they are notably different from his usual sources (such as Finney, Wesley, Calvin, George Fox, Lewis, Francis, Augustine, William Law, and E. Stanley Jones). We would profit from listening to "some older authors," he explains, since sanctification "is a matter that used to be much better understood than it is now."[52] Yet it is not the antiquity of these authors that stands out but the distinctly clear theological tradition they represent.

Willard's main source is Augustus Hopkins Strong's (1836–1921) *Systematic Theology*, first published in 1907. An eminent Reformed Baptist scholar, Strong was seen by some as a stalwart preserver of classical Reformed theology and by others as a mediator between theological liberalism and orthodoxy.[53] On the doctrine of soteriology, he was decidedly Calvinist.[54] In addition to Strong, Willard quotes four other theologians from the same era, all of whom are cited by Strong himself: Swiss Protestant Frederic Louis Godet (1812–1900), Presbyterian Archibald Alexander Hodge (1823–1886), and two "now unknown" authors Willard does not name but who are American Baptists O. P. Gifford (1847–1932) and William Newton Clarke (1841–1912). The one contemporary source he quotes is Reformed theologian Wayne Grudem (b. 1948).

In these three short sections, Willard builds up to and then upon Strong's particular definition of the doctrine of sanctification, "that

---

[51]Willard, *Renovation of the Heart*, 224-26.

[52]Willard, *Renovation of the Heart*, 224.

[53]Grant Wacker, *Augustus H. Strong and the Dilemma of Historical Consciousness* (Mercer University Press, 1985), 7-8.

[54]See Augustus H. Strong, *Systematic Theology*, 8th ed. (Judson, 1993), 777-886. Cf. William H. Brackney, *A Genetic History of Baptist Thought: With Special Reference to Baptists in Britain and North America* (Mercer University Press, 2004), 328.

continuous operation of the Holy Spirit, by which the holy disposition imparted in regeneration is maintained and strengthened."[55] After adding a subtle qualification concerning the difference between the sanctifying process (spiritual formation proper) and the settled state of righteousness in a person resulting from this process (sanctification proper), Willard summarizes his own position on sanctification as "a consciously chosen and sustained relationship of interaction between the Lord and his apprentice, in which the apprentice is able to do, and routinely does, what he or she knows to be right before God because all aspects of his or her person have been substantially transformed."[56] His overall argument—which he uses these mostly "older authors" to support—centers on, first, the inseparability of justification and sanctification, and, second, an understanding of sanctification as something imparted by God in regeneration but requiring human cooperation and appropriation.

Again, it is the latter point—the human contribution to holiness—that Willard thinks contemporary evangelicalism is confused on. I will describe in a later chapter what he believes are the historical causes of this confusion and how they are a departure from earlier evangelicalism. What I want to point out here is how Willard implicitly yet deliberately situates his doctrine of sanctification within the classic Reformed theological tradition—or at least a curated version of it—by means of the theologians he chooses to cite in explicating the doctrine. I would venture to say one reason he does so is to demonstrate that this tradition is quite compatible with the view that effort is needed in sanctification. Similar to Paul's rhetorical move on the Areopagus ("as even some of your own poets have said," Acts 17:28), here Willard relies on Reformed voices to fortify his case. While the passage from *Renovation of the Heart* is admittedly a small sample size within his corpus, it is his most direct treatment of the

---

[55]Willard, *Renovation of the Heart*, 225, citing Strong, *Systematic Theology*, 869.
[56]Willard, *Renovation of the Heart*, 226.

doctrine in the pentalogy. More importantly, it is consonant with what he says elsewhere on spiritual formation in the Spirit. Those who would contest Willard's self-association with this tradition and instead posit that he teaches a view of sanctification outside the bounds of historic Reformed thought will need to show exactly how. Because if synergism is taken to mean "cooperative action of discrete agencies such that the total effect is greater than the sum of the two effects taken independently,"[57] then the burden of proof rests on those who claim there is no place for synergism in the Reformed heritage, let alone in the New Testament account of growth in the Spirit and participation in God's redemptive project.

Now that we have covered Willard's view of sanctification proper, including the intimate interplay between God's Spirit and a person's spirit in character transformation, it is time to examine the practical tools he developed to help people actively engage in this transformative process. As I have argued, Willard is a theologian of the Christian life, and for him, such practical concerns are not peripheral to the theological task but lie at its center. From his view, theology must be clinical—grounded in the realities of people's lives—if it is to have any meaning at all. And this grounding is precisely what his heuristics for spiritual transformation aim to provide.

---

[57]Willard, "Becoming a Disciple," 9.

SEVEN

HEURISTICS FOR SPIRITUAL TRANSFORMATION

I MUST REITERATE THAT part two of this book does not present Willard's systematic theology of spiritual formation but instead his theological phenomenology of it. He does not engage in many of the finer points concerning the doctrine of redemption that dogmaticians take up, or at least he does not dwell there. Rather, he is intent on explaining how transformation in Christlikeness *actually happens*—the dynamic process involved—and in a way that helps instruct ordinary people how to experience this reality.

This intention, as well as his frustration with theologians content to keep things on an abstract level, comes through in a 1985 paper presented to a group of Christian philosophers. Citing multiple passages from Reinhold Niebuhr's *An Interpretation of Christian Ethics* (1935) in an effort to summarize the book's practical value (or lack thereof) for assisting in moral transformation, he comments:

> How characteristic these pretty words are of writings by Christian moralists in the twentieth century! A fine discussion could be mounted of what, if anything, they really mean for practice. But they do not seem to address with any *realism and practicality* the problem of moral and spiritual enablement; and they seem to be in some wholly different vein from the rigorous advice on life handed out on the pages of the New Testament and by the church throughout most of its history. They are, I believe, a form of the Protestant delusion that the fellowship of the church or of Christ infuses in us the power to do as we ought to

do without our undertaking a rigorous, individualized program of "exercise unto godliness" (1 Tim. 4:7).[1]

In an effort to teach about transformation with "realism and practicality," Willard developed two key heuristics. Especially in his last decade and a half, his teachings are replete with "VIM"—what he considers the general pattern for growing as apprentices of Jesus—and the "golden triangle" of spiritual transformation, which is a methodology on the means of formation. The first (VIM) focuses on how personal change is congruent with the nature God created us with, while the second (golden triangle) illustrates the dynamic relationship between God's empowering grace and human action. Treating each in turn not only further elucidates his doctrines of regeneration, divine grace, and sanctification but gives legs, if you will, to his theological phenomenology of transformation and thus rounds out our picture of his formation theory proper.

THE MODUS OPERANDI OF CHARACTER CHANGE

The acronym VIM stands for *vision, intention,* and *means,* and Willard posits any advance made in the spiritual life will follow this basic structure.[2] He also notably contends VIM is the general pattern of *all* personal transformation, spiritual or otherwise. It is as pertinent for learning to play tennis, speak Swahili, or stop smoking as it is for learning to discern God's movement, walk in the Spirit, or exercise the power of Christ in daily life. VIM is a "structure of personality" that one must go through to grow in any area of life.[3]

Willard understands each of these elements in the following way. *Vision* is the mental and visceral sense of what life would be like if a

---

[1]Dallas Willard, "Asceticism: An Essential but Neglected Element in the Christian Theory of the Moral Life" (presented paper, March 1985), Dallas Willard Collection, 8, emphasis added.

[2]For his most substantive written treatment of VIM, see Dallas Willard, *Renovation of the Heart: Putting On the Character of Christ* (NavPress, 2002), 82-91. For a succinct, lucid account in a talk, see Willard, "Spiritual Transformation" (November 5, 2004), MP3, starting at 27:45; for a more lengthy exposition, see his three-part lecture series in Scotland titled *V.I.M.: Renovation of the Heart* (2002).

[3]Dallas Willard, "Discipleship as Life in the Kingdom" (October 13, 2010), video, 1:10:30.

certain goal were achieved and its outcome materialized. *Intention* is the aspiration and motivation for that vision to be fulfilled, which is inseparable from the decision to pursue it. The *means* are specific steps or activities taken to realize the vision—life arrangements put into place to foster a path toward its fulfillment. Willard insists these three conditions are necessary for any substantial change on the level of personality regardless of the intended goal.

In terms of spiritual formation, VIM is the modus operandi of character change in Willard's theology; that is to say, inward transformation into Christlikeness comes about only when it is *envisioned*, *intended*, and *cultivated*.[4] The gospel forms a vision of the good life as life in the kingdom with Jesus. One senses the pervasive goodness that comes from living under God's gracious rule and care, the central message Jesus preached.[5] This compelling vision then gives way to a serious intention to live as Jesus did, as a kingdom person who routinely does the sort of things Jesus taught. More than anything, this is expressed in a person trusting/relying on Jesus—something indivisible from the person actually acting on that trust/reliance, because motivation to live into a vision must be accompanied by the decision to carry it through. Otherwise, it is merely

---

[4]Some readers may bristle at the word *only*, fearing it excludes divine grace, exaggerates how often (or rather, how rarely) these steps are consciously followed, or overlooks other catalysts of transformation such as community, sacraments, or suffering. Regarding the first concern, enough has been said, and there is more to come, to make clear that Willard's theology is not human-centric or mechanistic but utterly grace-dependent. As for the second and third, VIM need not be consciously understood to be efficacious; the pattern may unfold subconsciously, as in the lives of many saints throughout history who never explicitly named the steps. Further, Willard does not deny the formative power of things like community or suffering, but would say that transformation through such realities still follows the pattern of VIM, even if not explicitly recognized.

[5]Such a vision of the good life cannot be conjured up on our own but must "be *given* to humanity by God himself, in a revelation suited to our condition" (*Renovation of the Heart*, 87). Yet Willard suggests this revelation has *already* been given, first to the Jewish people and then through them to the rest of humanity, with the revelation reaching its "fullest flowering" in the person of Jesus (87). However, it is not clear in his brief note whether he is suggesting this vision is therefore not something persons must await to receive on an individual basis, at least not from God, or whether he more generally means the vision has been received by humanity as a whole, i.e., through special revelation in redemptive history.

something wished for or wanted as opposed to intended.[6] Lastly, a strong vision of the kingdom and solid intention to live into it will naturally lead to seeking appropriate means for bringing such a life to pass. These means, the disciplines of the spiritual life, are the resources to effectually put on the character of Christ through practice and cultivation.

When a person is not advancing in Christlikeness, Willard suggests it is because at least one of these (vision, intention, means) is missing. The three are hardly of equal importance, however. The means are only the caboose, so to speak, in spiritual transformation. Vision runs the show, and the process will not get off the ground unless a person's will/spirit/heart is in it (intention). So, while all three are essential, the first two are fundamental.

Willard devised the VIM acronym quite late, presenting it first in a lengthy section of *Renovation of the Heart*. But one can see the framework developing in his earlier writing. In a section on Paul's "psychology of redemption" in *Spirit of the Disciplines*, the three areas of vision, intention, and means appear but are described in different and decidedly theological terms. He suggests a three-stage process of personal redemption can be discerned in Paul's letters, most notably Romans 6–7. Because VIM is integral to Willard's theory of spiritual formation and his treatment of it here is explicitly theological, this earlier iteration deserves to be explored in some detail.

The first stage is baptism into Christ or "experiential union" with him.[7] The new life that results from this communion is a profound psychological freedom from sin manifested in the ability to choose otherwise. This is similar to the Augustinian view of humanity in a

---

[6] As he writes in a handout on how to practically live a day with Jesus, "You must make the decision to have Him live with you. You cannot *drift* into a life of constant companionship with Jesus. Decision is an inward resolve, made at some time, that you will do whatever is necessary to bring something to pass." Dallas Willard, "How to Live One Day with Jesus" (handout, 1993), Dallas Willard Collection, 2.

[7] Dallas Willard, *The Spirit of the Disciplines: Understanding How God Changes Lives* (Harper & Row, 1988), 114.

post-regeneration state of grace,[8] in which sin no longer is the controlling force or, as Willard puts it, the fuel running one's life engine. Our participation in the death and resurrection of Christ is not merely a forensic fact but a *psychological reality*, for "this is a matter of what we find in our conscious experience." Psychological reality is more than cognition for Willard; it also and importantly includes volition, the wellspring from which one's choices flow. Because of the new life brought about through baptism into Christ, we can now see sin for what it is, and this sight gives us "a real alternative" to the world's sin system as the way to orient and satiate our natural desires.[9] In this phenomenological description of regeneration, one can discern the connections with Willard's later conceptualization of *vision* in VIM. An essential element of regeneration, he thought, is a new psychological condition (cognitive and volitional) brought about through experiential union with Christ.

In the second stage of redemption, this psychological condition fuses with *intention* to become a settled and enduring attitude in the redeemed person. Willard identifies this as the Pauline doctrine of *reckoning*, based on the apostle's admonition that we reckon ourselves "dead to sin but alive to God in Christ Jesus" (Rom 6:11). This is a conscious, deliberate act of disassociating ourselves from our old life and its sinful tendencies. It entails bringing before our minds, with a settled disposition, the new life we have in Christ and how this union has spelled death to the "old person." That this has in fact become our new center of gravity—we must purposefully regard it as so. The new psychological condition is imparted by *God alone* (first stage). But reckoning it with resolute consciousness (second stage) is something *we must do*, for it will not be done for us. Again, Willard is not yet

---

[8]See *Enchiridion* 31.18, in *Augustine: Confessions and Enchiridion*, trans. Albert Cook Outler (Westminster John Knox, 2006), 409-10. In a later writing, Augustine describes Adam (humanity) before the fall as *able not to sin*, after the fall as *not able not to sin*, after regeneration as *able not to sin*, and in the gloried state as *not able to sin* (see *Admonition and Grace* 10.26–13.42, many editions).

[9]Willard, *Spirit of the Disciplines*, 114-15.

formulating this as VIM, but we learn that it is through intention that vision is grabbed hold of and made good on. He writes:

> So, with his doctrine of "reckoning," Paul has capitalized upon the first effect of "the light of the glorious gospel of Christ" upon our personalities. This effect is that we now vividly see and are gripped by an alternative to sin. With the life imparted by this vision we love what we see and are drawn to it. In this vision and the power it provides lies our freedom to determine who we shall be.
>
> And this is the standpoint from which the reign of sin over our bodies and lives can be broken. We have the simple power, communicated by the gospel, to think in a certain way and to count upon things being as we then think of them. Paul teaches us to think of ourselves as if the world's sinful motivational system were nothing to us, were dead to us, because of the vision of that alternative life present with us in Christ. When we so think, then his life enables us to live independently of the world's values. We can be dead to them.[10]

The third and final stage of personal redemption takes place as we *submit our members to righteousness*. Willard explains this as directing our bodily, socialized selves in a manner that ensures righteous behavior will eventually become instinctual. Just as sin was once automatic, so it will be with righteousness; such is the result of "habitual reliance upon God." Here he explicitly has in mind the practice of spiritual disciplines and activities as the indirect yet essential means by which we submit our body and its members to God as instruments of righteousness. This and "reckoning" (second stage) comprise our contribution to sanctification—though we can be assured that our efforts will always be accompanied by "gracious strength beyond ourselves."[11]

At the beginning of this chapter in *Spirit of the Disciplines*, Willard sets out to elucidate what Paul means by "exercise unto godliness" (1 Tim 4:7). His commentary on these three stages of personal

---
[10]Willard, *Spirit of the Disciplines*, 116.
[11]Willard, *Spirit of the Disciplines*, 117-18.

redemption is an attempt to do so and roughly corresponds to what he would later frame as VIM.[12] God is active in all three stages, and though human persons have some responsibility in the first stage (a gift must be received, Willard tells us), it is minimal and limited compared to the second and third stages. If regeneration is thus a relationally sovereign divine work that produces a new psychological condition in a person (first stage), then the second and third stages involve "working out what God has worked in," but always with divine empowerment.[13] As he remarks elsewhere, "Spiritual growth comes in response to *intelligent, informed effort*. That's the human side of holiness. We have to learn and we have to make the effort. And if we do nothing, then nothing will happen."[14]

VIM is the general and natural pattern of all personal transformation, according to Willard. God has created human life and the world in such a way that persons can grow if vision, intention, and means work in concert. Biblical growth in godliness follows this natural pattern too but includes a special strength or grace lacking in the non-Christian's VIM. Through regeneration, God brings about a new psychological reality in a person, enabling them to envision God and his kingdom in ways otherwise not possible. Sanctification relies therefore on both common grace and special grace, and it is wrought by divine action but is inextricably participatory.

So, how do we participate in this sanctifying work? What does "intelligent, informed effort" on our part actually look like? For this we turn to Willard's golden triangle of spiritual transformation.

---

[12]Cf. where he states that these three stages are "the rigorous form of life mandatory for excellence" (*Spirit of the Disciplines*, 121). One significant difference between the three stages and VIM is that the former is *sequential stages of growth*, whereas the latter is *essential elements for growth*, i.e., they are the necessary conditions for growing. Nevertheless, it seems clear that VIM and the three stages are drawn from and modeled after each other.

[13]Willard, *Spirit of the Disciplines*, 118.

[14]Dallas Willard, "What Does Holiness Look Like Shorn of Its Legalistic Expressions? 2" (January 4, 2010), video, 15:15.

A PROCESS AS PRECIOUS AS GOLD

In a 1990 article, Willard presents a working model of character transformation through a word picture. Responding to the question of *how* the inner character of Christ can be formed in us so that our faith and love resemble his, he writes:

> While it is in one sense a result of God's presence within us, the New Testament also describes a process behind our "putting on" the Lord Jesus Christ. It is repeatedly discussed in the Bible under three essential aspects, each inseparable from the other, all interrelated. This process could be called "the golden triangle" of spiritual transformation, for it is as precious as gold to the disciple, and each of its aspects is as essential to the whole as three sides are to a triangle.[15]

In later writing and lectures he represents this triangle as a visual image, using it extensively and in various iterations.[16] There is inherent risk in the pedagogical use of diagrams, as they can easily oversimplify and become a caricature of the complex subject or process they are meant to illuminate. This is likely why he used so few of them in his teaching, despite the volume of talks delivered and breadth of material covered. Yet the few diagrams and images he did use, he used with gusto. That was certainly the case with the golden triangle. He employed it to explain the method and procedure of what he called a "curriculum for Christlikeness." In relation to the VIM principle (the conditions of growth), the triangle concentrates on the *means*. In other words, if there is already a vision and intention to put on the character of Christ, the triangle presents a methodology one can follow to progress toward that end.[17]

---

[15]Dallas Willard, "Looking Like Jesus," *Christianity Today* 34, no. 11 (1990): 30.

[16]Most notably in Dallas Willard, *The Divine Conspiracy: Rediscovering Our Hidden Life in God* (HarperSanFrancisco, 1998), 347.

[17]The triangle will be of little worth, however, if there is not a vision and intention to grow in Christlikeness. A curriculum for Christlikeness must begin, Willard holds, with "enthralling the mind with God" (*Divine Conspiracy*, 323), which corresponds most closely to *vision* in VIM. In talks he frequently quotes William Law's admonition to "first and last, think magnificently of God," once adding "this is the root of spiritual formation in Christlikeness." Dallas Willard,

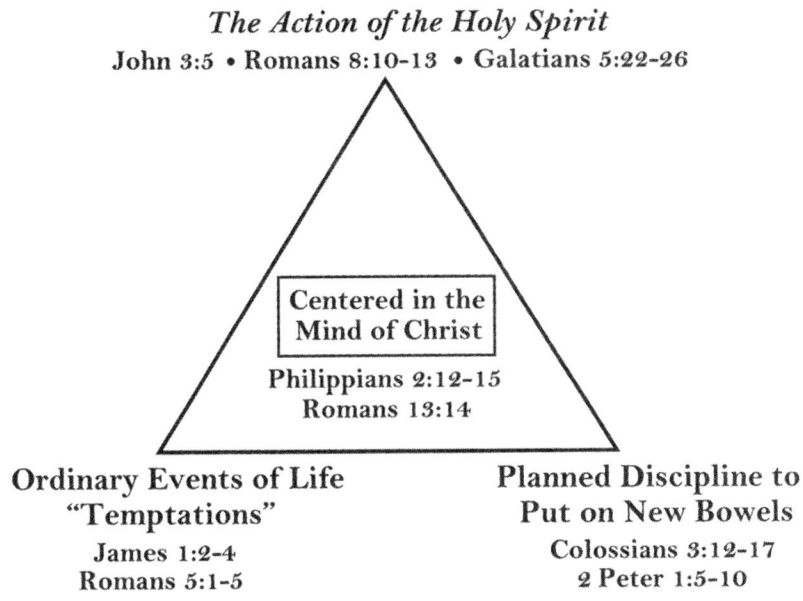

Figure 7.1. Willard's golden triangle of spiritual formation. *Source:* Dallas Willard, transparencies for "Spirituality and Ministry," GM 720 (1993-2012), Dallas Willard Collection

How Willard intends for this diagram to be understood is made clear by a playful yet pointed note on the transparency above, which he frequently used when teaching: "This is NOT a phone booth. (Superman)."[18] The triangle does not depict a magical wand to instantly transform a person into a super-Christian, nor does it capture all that is involved in one's life with God and in the world. Rather, it presents growth in godliness as a gradual, interpersonal process and presents the key elements that facilitate such growth. Centered in the middle of the image is *the mind of Christ*, implying it is the

---

"The Calling and Resources of the Pastor" (July 6, 2010), MP3, 54:45. That said, Willard also thought the two primary objectives of the curriculum—ravishment with God and character conformity to Christ—should be pursued simultaneously, given the holistic and integrative way God created us, with our mind working interactively with our body and social context (*Divine Conspiracy*, 322-23).

[18]The transparency version of the triangle also differs from that in *Divine Conspiracy* by using *bowels* instead of *heart*, a detail I will discuss momentarily.

immediate goal toward which the formative process moves. The "mind" here is not strictly the mental/visceral dimension of the self, as it is in Willard's fivefold model of the human person, but instead is meant in the sense that Paul uses *phroneō* ("mindset" or "attitude") to describe the "inmost character of Jesus" we are also to have.[19] Willard thus treats the apostle's exhortation to "put on the Lord Jesus Christ" (Rom 13:14) as synonymous with putting on the mind of Christ (Phil 2:5).[20]

In keeping with Willard's relational approach to formation, *interaction with God's Spirit* is placed at the apex of the triangle to signify its primacy in the entire process.[21] Some may understandably feel it unwise to place the Holy Spirit within any model since, they would insist, God is over everything. Yet this is Willard's very point: *Christianly* spiritual formation is saturated with God's grace (action). The more we become open to the activity of the Holy Spirit in our lives by relying upon God to act in and around us, the more his divine life is manifested in ours through the gifts and, most importantly, the fruit of the Spirit. "You grow in the grace and knowledge of our Lord Jesus Christ," he writes, "as your life is increasingly dominated by interactive relationship to Christ in everything. That's what it means to grow in spiritual and moral maturity."[22]

When referencing the triangle in lectures, Willard often notes that while the Spirit's activity is integral for formation, we can underemphasize or ignore the human contribution. He believed this was

---

[19] Willard, *Divine Conspiracy*, 346.

[20] Willard, "Discipleship as Life in the Kingdom," 1:00:30.

[21] In his earliest iteration of the triangle (Willard, "Looking Like Jesus," 30), which does not include a visual image, he refers to this as the "second side" of the triangle because he had not yet conceived of it as the apex.

[22] Dallas Willard, "The Failure of Evangelical Political Involvement," in *God and Governing: Reflections on Ethics, Virtue, and Statesmanship*, ed. Roger N. Overton (Pickwick, 2009), 89. Cf. "The eternal fact of our lives is that we are constantly being upheld by God's direct action upon us.... And we can become aware of his constant work and presence only by experiencing individual communion with God." Willard, "People of God in Individual Communion with God," in *The Renovaré Spiritual Formation Bible*, ed. Richard J. Foster et al. (HarperSanFrancisco, 2005), 3.

presently the case in many Christian circles. As he remarks in one place, "Many people say, 'Well, where is the Holy Spirit in all of this?' The answer is: *all over the place*. But I can't talk about that now because I've got to talk about some other stuff that we don't talk about enough."[23] For there to be genuine progress in godliness, "the action of the Spirit must be accompanied by our response, which . . . cannot be carried out by anyone other than ourselves."[24] The whole process of Christian formation is saturated with the Spirit; yet, that does not mean we can simply relegate the whole process to the Spirit. Since we have been designed as free creative wills, sanctification requires our response to and cooperation with the Spirit's work. If we neglect the other two indispensable aspects represented on the triangle, we do so to our own detriment—for these are the main avenues by which human persons tap into divine grace and participate in what the Spirit is doing. Hence, Willard felt it "necessary to assert boldly and often that becoming Christlike never occurs without intense and well-informed action on our part."[25]

The bottom left angle represents our response to *ordinary life events* in general and *everyday problems* in particular. This encompasses all moral decisions we make, however big or small, stemming from the particularities of our life. If character is habituated will, then the decisions we repeatedly make end up making us. Such is the formative power of volition in the human creature. Yet here, Willard has in mind particularly the more challenging moments and circumstances of ordinary life, what Scripture refers to as *temptations*, *trials*, and *tribulations*. For the shape of one's character, more is at stake in these situations. Temptations disproportionately affect who we are becoming because they present a starker moral crossroads. So, if we

---

[23]Dallas Willard, "Pastors as Teachers of the Nations" (March 30, 2007), MP3, 49:00.

[24]Willard, *Divine Conspiracy*, 348.

[25]Dallas Willard, "The Spirit Is Willing: The Body as a Tool for Spiritual Growth," in *The Christian Educator's Handbook on Spiritual Formation*, ed. Kenneth O. Gangel and James C. Wilhoit (Baker, 1994), 225.

intend to become like Christ, we must learn to faithfully accept what problems come our way and "see every event as an occasion in which the competence and faithfulness of God will be confirmed to us."[26] In Willard's model, daily struggles are fertile ground for growth in godliness.

This ordinary-events-of-life side of the triangle grounds Willard's approach to spiritual growth in concrete worldly life rather than esoteric experiences or abstract theories. His is a spirituality of the ordinary, we might say, meaning one need not run off to a monastery to experience God's presence and advance in the spiritual life. Engaging in normal human affairs—and seeking God in so doing—is more than enough to elicit such holy activity. Willard insists this can be gleaned from Jesus' own spiritual life, describing it in one of his last essays as *incarnational spirituality*.[27] In this instance, *incarnational* does not denote the coming together of Christ's divine and human natures but rather a spiritual life that unites the divine and earthly realms. Previous remarks in chapter four about Willard's mysticism should also be understood in this light.

Compared to the other elements represented by the triangle, the human response to ordinary life events does not receive as much attention in his teachings and writing. Willard may have assumed his audience would grasp what he was getting at through brief description and exegesis of particular biblical texts or, more likely, felt only so much could be said (in terms of instruction) about *unplanned* discipline in the spiritual life, given the circumstantial nature of this dynamic in the formative process. Regardless the reason, he does not offer nearly as many examples or as much instruction as he does for the last angle (spiritual disciplines). Yet Willard once commented that he came up with the golden triangle to counter the idea that "you can just do the disciplines and that's all there is to [spiritual

---

[26]Willard, *Divine Conspiracy*, 350.

[27]Dallas Willard, "Jesus," in *Dictionary of Christian Spirituality*, ed. Glen G. Scorgie (Zondervan, 2011), 59.

formation]."²⁸ Elsewhere he says the triangle "simply tries to help us see and balance everything that is involved, because spiritual disciplines *are not the answer to everything*."²⁹ God's Spirit is the primary agent, and our part in spiritual formation is not merely proactive but also profoundly reactive, in that "our reactions and choices to what God puts before us" will indelibly shape our character over the long haul.³⁰ Therefore the importance of this dimension of formation to his overall theory must be stressed, especially since much of the spiritual formation literature does not substantively address it.³¹

The last angle in the triangle is *planned discipline to put on new bowels*. In *Divine Conspiracy* the word *heart* appears instead of *bowels*, but only because Willard's editor felt squeamish about *bowels* and convinced him to replace it.³² However, he continued to use *bowels* when lecturing on the triangle. This choice of verbiage may indicate that Willard, in his mature anthropology, envisioned some combination of the heart (spirit or will), the mind, and the body—or more simply, that he used *bowels* in the King James sense to symbolize the embodied depth from which strength and transformation arise. Either way, it reinforces his conviction that spiritual disciplines are at their core bodily disciplines.³³ More importantly, they are intended to institute kingdom habits throughout the body in how one naturally

---

²⁸Dallas Willard, "The Larger Self & the Disciplines for Spiritual Life" (October 12, 1993), MP3, 00:45.

²⁹Dallas Willard, "Authentic Leaders for Christ" (February 22, 1997), MP3, 5:15. His own pedagogical use of the triangle proves this, as he, dating back to his earliest teachings on it, always began with the "ordinary events" side and only then moved on to the "planned discipline" side. See, e.g., Willard, "The Virtuous Life: The Substance of Holiness" (November 1989), MP3, starting at 47:30; Willard, "Looking Like Jesus," 30; Willard, *Divine Conspiracy*, 347-64.

³⁰Willard, "People of God in Individual Communion," 2.

³¹Interestingly, by contrast, many general books on Christian living talk a lot about the role of ordinary life events—how to deal with everyday challenges, how struggles build character, and so on—yet focus less on discipleship and spiritual formation.

³²Dallas Willard, "Life in the Kingdom 4/Understanding the Person 1" (October 13, 2011), MP3, 21:30.

³³Willard prefers we think of these as "disciplines for the spiritual life" rather than "spiritual disciplines" since, he argues, the disciplines are not *spiritual* in and of themselves. But in actual practice, "spiritual disciplines" is his common nomenclature.

and routinely thinks, feels, and acts. Such disciplined training "is to make our body a reliable ally and resource for the spiritual life."[34]

Formation through discipline is what is historically known as asceticism. Christian asceticism differs from secular and other religious forms of asceticism in that the disciplines are understood as "means of grace" (Wesley), or, as Willard describes, human activities that create space and foster the conditions for the divine to accomplish in us what we cannot accomplish on our own. Thus, spiritual disciplines work by indirection. They are practices that put us into contact with a force and reality mightier than ourselves, capable of transforming us into what we cannot become through effort alone. But our proactive participation in this process is essential. We must choose to engage in these disciplines and commit to practicing them—it cannot be outsourced.

Let us return to Willard's conviction that spiritual disciplines are fundamentally *bodily* disciplines. The body houses a person's habits, which is to say, habits become ingrained in our very flesh and manifest as automatic responses. William James's influence is once again evident, this time regarding the physical basis of habit.[35] His understanding of habituation is much more informative for Willard than that of, say, Aristotle or Pierre Bourdieu. James describes the body and its nervous system as living matter with a property he calls *plasticity*—"a structure weak enough to yield to an influence, but strong enough to not yield all at once."[36] For Willard, this insight underscores the purpose of spiritual disciplines: to eliminate sinful habitual patterns *in the body* that reside even on the epidermal level and emerge as a person's initial responses. More positively, the disciplines train the body to depend on and trust God, deepening relationality

---

[34]Willard, *Divine Conspiracy*, 354.

[35]See Willard, "Asceticism," 6-7.

[36]Willard, *Spirit of the Disciplines*, 92, citing William James, *The Principles of Psychology* (Holt, 1890), 1:105. Cf. Dallas Willard, "Human Effort, Human Character and Divine Grace: Why Grace Requires Effort 2" (January 6, 2010), video, 32:30.

Heuristics for Spiritual Transformation

with him. Through intentional practice and the passage of time, the body undergoes a transformative process that it retains. So, if a person desires genuine transformation, she must intentionally work with both the body and the mind to replace old habits with new ones.

Willard's standard list of spiritual practices is rooted in the life of Jesus and his followers down through the ages.[37] This list, which he divides between disciplines of abstinence and disciplines of engagement, is not meant to be definitive or comprehensive but to provide an idea of the special activities proven to be conducive for spiritual growth in the way of Christ. He does contend, however, that a few practices are indispensable for discipleship, such as solitude, silence, and worship. Yet his main point is that students of Jesus, if they intend to become like their rabbi, will have "a life plan for spiritual growth."[38]

The bottom two sides of the triangle—ordinary life events and planned discipline—are the main avenues by which we engage with and participate in the action of the Holy Spirit. Taken together they comprise, so Willard thought, a one-two punch for spiritual formation, an around-the-clock curriculum for Christlikeness. Yet how each specifically relates to *character* is quite different.

In general, our character is *manifested* in our response to ordinary life events but *trained* through planned and habitual practice. How a person reacts to being reprimanded by her boss, for example, says volumes more about the person's character than what spiritual disciplines she regularly practices. This is because character, understood as habituated will, largely resides in the automatic and unconscious regions of personhood. Deliberate, rational thinking comes only after our automatic, unconscious response. But the way to change how we react "on the spot" is through training "off the spot."[39] In other words,

---

[37] Willard's survey of the disciplines in *Spirit of the Disciplines* (158) is identical to the one in *Divine Conspiracy* (417-18n18), except that the latter adds a sixteenth discipline: "watching."

[38] Willard, *Divine Conspiracy*, 418n18.

[39] Willard, *Renovation of the Heart*, 90. Cf. Dallas Willard, "The Biblical View of the *Imago Dei*" (January 15, 1985, MP3), 51:00.

the way to gain control of automatic, unconscious responses is through deliberate, intentional practice that becomes habit.[40] For instance, in fasting we abstain from eating (and possibly drinking) for a period of time. We can learn a lot about ourselves and our automatic responses when we are deprived of something we want and are accustomed to having. One function of fasting as a spiritual discipline, then, is that it retrains how our mind, body, and spirit react when we encounter situations in the world in which we do not get our way.

These three sides of the golden triangle, oriented toward developing "the mind of Christ" in the disciple of Jesus, comprise the practical side of Willard's curriculum for Christlikeness. However, he acknowledges that he is merely building on historical masterworks of Christian living. After a long discussion of this curriculum, he writes,

> If you examine landmark works such as Calvin's *Institutes* or John Wesley's standard two-volume set of *Sermons*, you will discover nothing new in what I have said here about a curriculum for Christlikeness, except possibly some points of organization. And certainly what I have said remains much more shallow, both theologically and practically, than these masterworks of the spiritual life.[41]

PNEUMATOLOGICAL ASCETICISM

We are now prepared to take a step back and, in view of what we have covered in this chapter and the previous two, offer a provisional evaluation of Willard's theory of spiritual formation proper. Since we are also interested in how his formational theology might serve the church in its mission, I will do this by descriptively analyzing the pedagogy behind his theory of formation. By *pedagogy* I mean this: If a person or community desires to grow in Christlikeness, what instruction and counsel would Willard's theory provide? Is there an implicit or explicit curriculum one could follow? And how would that

---

[40]Hence Willard emphasizes the difference between *trying*, which occurs "on the spot" without practice, and *training*, which requires deliberate, intentional practice "off the spot."
[41]Willard, *Divine Conspiracy*, 370-71.

instruction and curriculum best be characterized? Combining his view of the concurrence of divine and human action involved in spiritual transformation with his way of parsing the complex interplay of dynamics at work in such moral growth (understood within his theological anthropology) and the practical heuristics of personal change he developed to explain these phenomena, what emerges is a *pneumaascetic* pedagogy of spiritual formation. If this term strikes you as overly technical or obscure, I ask you to bear with me. I believe it aptly names something essential about his approach.

The *pneuma* descriptor indicates how, in Willard's theology, the Holy Spirit is the primary actor through and through. Regeneration of the human spirit is a relationally sovereign work of the Spirit; divine grace, as God's activity in our lives, is a metaphysic of reality pervading not only the phenomena of salvation but the entire Christian life; and interaction with the triune God on a personal, relational level is the main means by which individuals grow in character to resemble Christ and are empowered for holy living.

Yet the primacy of the Spirit by no means displaces human agency. The *ascetic* descriptor indicates the human side to holiness, and Willard never tires of telling us that grace and effort are compatible rather than competitive. What sets the human person apart from all other creatures is the will/heart/spirit. This divinely given capacity to choose and have "say-so" is the most precious part of the person, according to Willard; it is the *imago Dei* in the human creature. For a person who has received the new life from above (Jn 3:3), the structure of personal change (illustrated by VIM) still requires that she exercise her will in conjunction with the mind and manifested through embodied action. With time and practice, the person's body yields to the new nature imparted to her by God's gift of regeneration. As he explains,

> The human body is, then, the plastic bearer of massive intentionalities of will, feeling, and perception, which do not depend for their

functioning upon self-conscious awareness or direct effort, but rather provide the essential foundation of such awareness and effort. The body thus understood is not transformed by religious conversion or ritual alone, much less by mere intellectual enlightenment, but by intense, large-scale, and long-run experience, and especially by ascetic practices or spiritual "disciplines." Such a transformation is essential to bring us to the point where we effectively do what we would (or ought) do and do not do what we would (or ought) not do.[42]

Spiritual formation in Christlikeness, as described by Willard, corresponds with the type of creatures we are and the law-patterned world we live in. The ascetic side of formation—the human contribution to holiness—reflects the realities of creation and our creatureliness.

Willard is well aware of past abuses of ascesis in the history of the church, describing numerous examples of what he calls "consuming asceticism," which feeds, among other things, "body hatred."[43] Over against this, he contends the New Testament contains an "incipient philosophy of the body."[44] This philosophy, thought Willard, is a percipient view of the human body and its positive contribution to moral transformation. In a lecture on spiritual disciplines he counsels,

> Don't torture yourself. I'm one of those people who really believes that there's very little gain from pain. I think that comes from a masochistic view of God and human nature. And I sure know that there's a lot of pain from which there's no gain. So when you go to practice the disciplines like solitude, don't try to make it hard on yourself. Don't feel like you've got to sit on a rough log in a cold wind. Be comfortable.[45]

---

[42] Willard, "Asceticism," 7.

[43] Willard, *Spirit of the Disciplines*, chap. 8; Dallas Willard, "Seminars on Creative Ministry in Times of Crisis" (handout, 1987), Dallas Willard Collection, 22. Some readers may find it surprising I use the word *ascetic* to describe Willard's view, given his strong criticism of asceticism in certain places, not least in the cited chapter. However, deeper study of his thought reveals that he critiques a specific form of asceticism, while his own theory of formation is in fact brimming with a distinctly different approach to it.

[44] Willard, "Asceticism," 5.

[45] Willard, "Larger Self," 35:30. Cf. this handwritten note: "If 'no pain no gain' means 'if pain then gain' it is just false" (Willard, "Seminars on Creative Ministry," 22).

For the Christian, ascesis (or a disciplined life) is meant to reform a person's character through *interactive relationship with the Spirit of God*.[46] Grace empowers human effort so that the effect of a person's action exceeds anything that could be accounted for alone by human personality or effort. It begins with regeneration, the birth of new life in the will/spirit/heart of a person. This grace, which is God's own presence within us, requires our constant effort in response. As a person responds through her renewed spirit, she joins the Holy Spirit in working to renew the rest of her existence—her thoughts, feelings, body, social relations, and soul—via planned discipline, or off-the-spot training. Ascesis is the human contribution, always with divine assistance, to the redemption of the self. And, to repeat once more, it is done through friendship with God. "Holiness is not something that is our project. Holiness is not something we get; virtue is not something we get," states Willard. "It is a relationship which we maintain. We maintain a relationship with God, and in that we know holiness."[47]

In the introduction of *Divine Conspiracy*, Willard says there is little that is novel contained in his book, even if it has been forgotten or neglected. He contends his ideas about God, the kingdom, the human soul, and so on can be found in the works of past luminaries such as Athanasius, Augustine, Anselm, Thomas Aquinas, Luther, and Calvin.[48] Let us not pass over this comment too quickly. Willard's

---

[46]Having said this, Willard also recognizes ascesis is positively formational even for those who are not in interactive relationship with the Spirit of God. Thus there is, for lack of better terms, both a *natural* and *supernatural* role for ascesis in his view. Our focus here is on the latter, but for comment on the former, see Dallas Willard, "Can Wisdom Be Taught?," *Roundtable* (1971): 16-17.

[47]Willard, "Virtuous Life," 17:30.

[48]Willard, *Divine Conspiracy*, xvii-xviii. This is not just a formal nod to these luminaries. Careful review of Willard's writings and recordings shows his study of these authors is the tip of his theological-reading iceberg. Willard became a voracious reader early on and by the time of his graduation had read every book in the high school library. Asked about this in an interview, he gives a caveat about the library ("Of course, it wasn't very large") but then says, "I just read everything that was there. That's been something that has gone with my . . . devotion to Christ. . . . It meant as I grew, I'd just read anything that had the slightest smell of Christian on

project has strong correlation with what many church fathers and later masters were doing: a theology that is rooted in spiritual formation. Due to the parameters of this book, I can only intimate this relationship. But Christian writers with a strong and lifelong interest in spiritual maturation will always look a bit similar. And though it would be illuminating to trace specific connections between some leading lights and Willard as well as to explore the various ways their ideas influenced his own project, I would argue for a more obvious source, and the one Willard himself names as his ultimate reference: "the teachings . . . that lie richly upon the pages of the Bible itself."[49] Willard's realist biblical hermeneutic, something hardly unique to him, is how he arrives at an ascetic pneumatology of spiritual transformation. Whether his account of transformation is theologically and exegetically responsible is a separate issue to be argued for or against. My point here is that Willard's pedagogy of formation has antecedents in historical theology and is above all deeply resonant with biblical motifs.

A ROOMY THEOLOGY OF FORMATION

We have unearthed much in Willard's view of formation proper, but what are the specific implications for the church today? Recalling Chan's claim that "the nature of grace is perhaps the most problematic issue for the development of a Protestant spiritual theology," this warrants extended discussion.[50] Willard offers a theological-phenomenological account of how persons can grow in the character of Christ, by first recognizing the centrality of the will—by God's design—in determining the moral shape of a person, given God's purposes for humanity to exercise their creative will as co-rulers with

---

it. And so that broadened me out a lot." Dallas Willard, "Interview with Dallas Willard" (May 5, 2003), MP3, 4:00.

[49]Willard, *Divine Conspiracy*, xviii.

[50]Simon Chan, *Spiritual Theology: A Systematic Study of the Christian Life* (IVP Academic, 1998), 79.

him. God desires to mature people to the point where he can give them what *they* want because their "wanters" (hearts) have been so thoroughly renewed that they resemble that of Christ's.[51] Such transformation in the *imago Christi* is possible only by God's grace, beginning with the relationally sovereign divine act of regeneration, which brings new life, then through a person's responsive (and ascetic) effort in conjunction with the Spirit's continual empowerment. Willard's heuristics for this latter dynamic, the human side of holiness, offer individuals and churches a clear framework (VIM) for understanding the structure necessary to experience personal change and a practical curriculum (golden triangle) for organizing one's life around that structure to foster genuine growth in Christlikeness.

Considering the primacy of the divine Spirit and the necessity of ascesis for spiritual growth, the pedagogy that undergirds Willard's formation theory and is embedded in the heuristics is a pneuma-ascetic one. This pneumatological asceticism is a *roomy* theology for the church as it seeks to form disciples of Christ who resemble him in character and purpose. This is because it makes more room for our action in the work of sanctification and mission without it being meritorious. A concentration on forensic justification as the core of soteriology, characteristic of much twentieth-century Protestant theology, leaves very little room for our participation in God's great divine conspiracy, both in terms of the spiritual renovation of the self and of the Spirit's larger redemptive work in the world.[52] Yet without this participatory element, our theology of human transformation in (and co-mission with) the Spirit is either rendered unintelligible or does not do justice to how God designed humans in the first place. As Willard asserts, "A philosophically clarified understanding of ascetic

---

[51]Dallas Willard, "Session 1—Part 3" (March 9, 2004), MP3, 34:30.

[52]I would like to thank the late Lutheran theologian Robert W. Jenson, a professor I studied under in graduate school, for suggesting "roominess" as a theological category, although my appropriation of the concept here is quite different from the one that appears in his work. See his *Systematic Theology*, vol. 1, *The Triune God* (Oxford University Press, 1997), 226.

practices that are psychologically and theologically sound is needed if we are to understand the meaning and process of the redemption of human personality."[53] This roominess in Willard's formational theology may go a long way in helping the church recover a biblically grounded and theologically sound approach to discipleship and Christian growth.

Allow me to elaborate on this point. The extreme anxiety over works righteousness shared by many modern Protestant thinkers has played no small part in the development of a reductionistic soteriology and corresponding intellectualist approach to spirituality prevalent in Western Christianity. Willard's theology of formation, with its interplay of heart and habits, virtue and action, is an important corrective. The Holy Spirit is the initiator and main actor. Yet this reality does not diminish or displace human persons in the process of their growth in holiness. On the contrary, God's regenerating grace—which requires consent—brings new life to a person's will, enabling the person to respond to and join the Spirit's activity in renewing the rest of the person's life. We cannot do what only God can, yet God will not do what we must do. Willard contends this synergistic view of sanctification has a rich theological heritage and is above all rooted in the New Testament.

Since the relation of divine grace and human agency can be a contentious doctrine, I will share my own evaluation: Willard is not sloppy on the matter. His account of human transformation, focused on life (action/practice) in the Spirit and grounded in a kingdom gospel, represents, to put it plainly, a theologically and pastorally responsible version of synergism that is not Pelagian. Moreover, his understanding of salvation as "participating in the life that Jesus is now living on earth," and spirituality as "union in action with the triune God,"[54] is a potential bridging theology to missional Christianity and

---

[53]Willard, "Asceticism," 9.

[54]Dallas Willard, interview by Keith Giles, "On the Gospel of the Kingdom," in *Subversive Interviews* (Subversive Underground, 2011), 70; Willard, "Spiritual Formation in Christ Is for the

its watchword, "There is no participation in Christ without participation in His mission."[55] Also, Willard's distinction between merit and effort and his careful reflection on how the latter is integral for Christian living aligns well with the recent turn toward the priority of practice in contemporary theology.[56] In Willard's view, the will is transformed by lived experience, not information or mere belief,[57] and action is not for merit but for participating in the life of Christ and his work in the world. Willard is a theologian of the Christian life with a unique formational grammar, and the descriptors "theological phenomenology" and "ascetic pneumatology" are befitting for his roomy theology of formation.

UNCHARTED DIMENSIONS

Before moving to the final part of this book, a few further thoughts are in order. Considering the overtly eschatological dimension of

---

Whole Life and the Whole Person," in *For All the Saints: Evangelical Theology and Christian Spirituality*, ed. Timothy George and Alister McGrath (Westminster John Knox, 2003), 45.

[55]This declaration, issued at the end of the 1952 Willingen Conference, sits at the heart of the *missio Dei* tradition and was later picked up and expanded on by Lesslie Newbigin, David Bosch, Darrell Guder, Christopher Wright, and a host of other mission scholars. For its original formulation, see Norman Goodall, ed., *Missions Under the Cross: Addresses Delivered at the Enlarged Meeting of the Committee of the International Missionary Council at Willingen, in Germany, 1952* (Edinburgh House, 1953), 190. I also suggest Willard's formational theology resonates strongly with Michael Gorman's recent work in missional hermeneutics. Gorman argues that union with the triune God is both the telos of human existence and the means of God's mission. His notion of "missional theosis," drawn mainly from his close readings of Pauline and Johannine literature, posits that participation in the *missio Dei* is not merely a consequence of transformation in Christlikeness *but also effects* such transformation. See Michael J. Gorman, *Becoming the Gospel: Paul, Participation, and Mission* (Eerdmans, 2015); Gorman, *Abide and Go: Missional Theosis in the Gospel of John* (Cascade, 2018). However, Gorman's express purpose in these writings is to explicate theosis as the *goal* of the gospel and the *means* of God's mission rather than explain the *process* by which theosis produces missional communities and individuals. Willard's work could therefore be an important complement to these discussions.

[56]E.g., Miroslav Volf and Dorothy C. Bass, eds., *Practicing Theology* (Eerdmans, 2002); James K. A. Smith, *Desiring the Kingdom* (Baker Academic, 2009); Smith, *Imagining the Kingdom* (Baker Academic, 2013); Bonnie Miller-McLemore, "The Theory-Practice Distinction and the Complexity of Practical Knowledge," *HTS Theological Studies* 72, no. 4 (2016): 1-8; Kevin W. Hector, *Christianity as a Way of Life* (Yale University Press, 2023). See also Pete Ward, ed., *Perspectives on Ecclesiology and Ethnography* (Eerdmans, 2012), 1-12.

[57]Dallas Willard, "The Self/Spiritual Transformation and Discipline" (May 17, 2000), MP3, 1:24:30.

Willard's formational theology, covered in an earlier chapter, spiritual disciplines—from worship and prayer to Scripture memorization and confession—are not ends in themselves but *means to a missional end*. These practices are for training, and this training is ultimately for reigning with God. Nevertheless, this is not apparent in his rendering and explanation of the golden triangle. This is perhaps understandable since he intends for the triangle to illuminate the main phenomena involved in Christian transformation rather than its telos—in other words, the "what" of spiritual formation rather than the "why." But considering how prominent the triangle became in his teachings (especially mid-1990s onward) and how it has come to symbolize and summarize his approach to formation, not to mention how it has taken on a life of its own,[58] the triangle's latent missional dimension deserves to be further explored in future studies on Willard's theology.

On a more critical note, the bottom two sides of the triangle (ordinary life events and planned discipline) are, in Willard's mind, the main avenues by which we engage with and participate in the action of the Holy Spirit. But where is the role of community in this? We can now see Willard's model is one in which the planned practices and everyday responses of an *individuated* life are the gymnasium for spiritual formation. His golden triangle, with its individual approach to on-the-spot and off-the-spot training, exemplifies this. This is perhaps where his model is most in tension with what some scholars would argue is the inherently *communal* nature of sanctification in Scripture. The next chapter examines a related issue more closely, specifically Willard's view of how individual character change leads to larger societal change but not vice versa. Let me preliminarily state

---

[58]It is beyond the scope of this book to document the extent to which his golden triangle and its threefold dynamic have been appropriated by others. To illustrate with two examples from popular literature, see James Bryan Smith's "triangle of transformation" in *The Good and Beautiful God: Falling in Love with the God Jesus Knows* (InterVarsity Press, 2009), 24; and John Mark Comer's "working theory of change" in *Practicing the Way: Be with Jesus, Become Like Him, Do as He Did* (WaterBrook, 2024), 102, which is a minor reworking of Smith's version.

here, however, that while Willard's model of spiritual formation may need some refinement on this point, his work offers vital insights into how individuals can experience personal transformation that could greatly benefit the church today.

Furthermore, given my analysis of Willard's missional vision, another question arises about his triangle and the formative process it seeks to explain: Where is missional engagement with the world? We might suppose Christian vocation and witness are subsumed under "ordinary life events," but Willard stresses the reactive element of formation at work in this dimension, whereas the proactive is stressed in the "planned discipline" side of the triangle. So, again, where does proactive, externalized engagement with the world factor into our formation? Or does the relationship between formation and mission in Willard's theory move only in one direction: from formation to mission? In a later chapter, I will make a case that Willard's view—best understood as "mission by formation"—is essential to a holistic understanding of the Christian life. But here let me suggest that a robust formational theology must recognize that there is also "formation by mission" and that this sort of formation is essential for growing in Christlikeness. An account of spiritual formation through engagement with the world as God's witness is lacking not only from Willard's work but from nearly *all* the major Protestant views of spiritual formation. This is why it is crucial, not merely for my project but for the future of spiritual formation in the church, that Willard's model be critically engaged and further developed.

In part two, we examined Willard's theory of spiritual formation proper through the lens of his philosophical anthropology (chap. 5), theological phenomenology (chap. 6), and heuristics for personal transformation (chap. 7). These chapters provide a comprehensive understanding of how Willard envisions transformation into Christlikeness, but our analysis is not yet complete. Part three will turn to the broader implications of his approach, focusing on the societal and communal dimensions beyond the individual. How does Christian spiritual formation connect to and affect the larger domains of human life? Furthermore, what role does the church play in all this? And if Willard's formational theology is indeed inherently missional, as I claim, then does he understand discipleship and evangelism as separate endeavors or as a unified calling for the church?

PART 3

THE CONSEQUENCES OF FORMATION

EIGHT

RECTIFICATION OF THE SOCIAL ORDER

WILLARD BELIEVES THAT God's redemptive work is aimed at both the personal and the public, but in proper order. Heart change in individuals is what fosters social change on a larger scale. He does not see heart change alone as sufficient, yet he does view it as *the* essential foundation for social change. Characterological transformation leads to societal transformation, not vice versa, for justice and well-being will not prevail, he thinks, until there are enough just and good people dispersed throughout society. The revolution of the social order thus rides on the coattails of the renovation of individual lives. Willard also believes the reverse is true: The renovation of individual lives is influenced by the social order, either positively or negatively. But as we will see, he has his reasons for not granting the same gravitas to this side of the equation.

His viewpoint on individual/societal change involves a distinction between symptoms and causes, a practical and personalistic approach, a theory of leaders and their role in institutions, and a particular interpretation of the moral aim of Jesus' ministry and the gospel. Other concepts and ideas surely factor into his position, but these points most clearly guide his thinking on the redemption of the social order.

SYMPTOMS VERSUS CAUSES

Nicholas Wolterstorff's account of *justice*, and by extension *a just society* from a theistic and specifically Christian view, may serve as a reference point for our discussion. Wolterstorff writes, "A society is just insofar as its members enjoy the goods to which they have a right," and such right(s) are "ultimately grounded in what respect for the worth of persons and human beings requires."[1] That God's redemptive work includes and is even ultimately aimed at the creation of a just society is something Willard continually alludes to. As he puts it in a 1971 lecture, "The intention of God in history is to create an all-inclusive community of loving and happy persons dwelt in by God himself."[2] Much later he writes that Jesus "set afoot a *perpetual world revolution*," and "as this revolution culminates, all the forces of evil known to mankind will be defeated and the goodness of God will [pervade] every aspect of human life."[3] Lest we think he has in mind here a revolution that merely or mainly takes place in the spiritual realm, Willard lays his cards on the table: "We have to aim at the renovation of society at all levels; that is *exactly* what Jesus had in mind."[4]

Christian hope has eternal consequence but is also profoundly this-worldly, encompassing not only individual lives but also the social structures within which humans live. The pressing question, however, is how such a vision can be realized. For Willard, social justice is ultimately a byproduct of changed lives, for "an authentic

---

[1] Nicholas Wolterstorff, *Justice: Rights and Wrongs* (Princeton University Press, 2008), xii. Wolterstorff offers his theory of "justice as inherent rights" over against what he calls "justice as right order" (1). There are many ways to define justice, and Wolterstorff's articulation of it is by no means without its detractors, yet a line must be drawn somewhere for our present discussion, and I have chosen to draw one that aligns with Willard's personalist (and trinitarian) view of the universe. I should note that in an article on Jesus and the civil law that Willard cowrote with Robert Cochran Jr. shortly before Willard's death, the two authors draw from Wolterstorff's account of justice. See Robert F. Cochran Jr. and Dallas Willard, "The Kingdom of God, Law, and the Heart: Jesus and the Civil Law," in *Law and the Bible: Justice, Mercy, and Legal Institutions*, ed. Robert F. Cochran Jr. and David VanDrunen (IVP Academic, 2013), 154-55. It is clear from a footnote that Willard is not in complete agreement with Wolterstorff's view (154n8), and my correspondence with Cochran confirmed that it was originally his (Cochran's) idea to cite Wolterstorff's book (personal communication, July 6, 2022). Nevertheless, Willard saw no problem in using Wolterstorff's general account of justice as a basis for their argument.

[2] Dallas Willard, "The Kingdom Comes in Power" (November 28, 1971), MP3, 3:15.

[3] Dallas Willard, *Renovation of the Heart: Putting On the Character of Christ* (NavPress, 2002), 14-15.

[4] Dallas Willard, "How Kingdom Values Impact Leadership" (February 22, 1997), MP3, 1:14:15.

spiritual life always pushes one back into the world."[5] And along with the heart change produced by an authentic spiritual life, moral knowledge and wisdom are an additional, essential attainment. A person must be motivated to love but also be equipped to discern what love requires (knowledge) and what love looks like in particular situations (wisdom/practical knowledge).

At the heart of Willard's conviction is a distinction between the symptoms and the causes of social ills that plague human life. Eighteenth-century philosopher Jean-Jacques Rousseau famously purported that society, not the soul, was the true problem.[6] Willard's view is the exact opposite. His most extensive treatment of this is in the last chapter of *Spirit of the Disciplines*. A recurring theme there is how *the readiness within individuals to do evil* is what lies at the core of and sustains evil in the world *in all its forms*. This is not to say that the whole (social injustice) is merely the sum of the parts (individual bad actors). Structural evils, impersonal as they are, take on a life of their own and wreak havoc on human life incommensurable with their individual inputs. And yet, structural evils exist solely, Willard insists, because godly character in enough individual persons does not.[7] After describing a number of specific instances of systemic sins, he writes, "The social structures exhibited in such cases are, strictly speaking, not *in* any individual, but in the world where we live, though they totally depend for their existence and power upon the *readinesses* that are in us individually," and again, "The impersonal

---

[5]Dallas Willard, interview by John Ortberg, "What Makes Spirituality Christian? Dallas Willard Thinks It Is as Important to Live the Truth as It Is to Believe it," *Christianity Today* 39, no. 3 (1995): 17.

[6]For Rousseau's most mature articulation of this, see *The Social Contract* (1762), many editions. Cf. his *Letter to Beaumont* (1763) for his repudiation of the doctrine of original sin: "There is no original perversity in the human heart."

[7]Willard holds that evil spirits (the devil and the demonic) inhabit the world and act on human beings, both collectively and individually. To what extent these evil spirits animate structural evils is inconsequential for our present discussion, however, since he maintains that individuals are ultimately responsible for resisting evil in all its forms. For Willard's clearest articulation of his demonology, see Dallas Willard, "The Kingdom of Evil on Earth" (1988), MP3; Willard, "Angels and Demons" (August 19, 1987), MP3.

power structures in the world are, though independent of any one person's will and experience, nevertheless dependent for their force upon the general readiness of normal people to do evil."[8] Thus, no amount of just legislation or societal pressure (e.g., honor and shame) can hold back the tide of evil deeds on the social level, as long as this readiness remains and individuals are easily moved in the wrong direction.[9]

As a case in point, Willard references the bloody history of revolutions in the nineteenth and twentieth centuries as indicative of the inadequacy of strategies that seek to radically rectify the social order but fail to address individual character and the proclivity of the human heart to harm others out of fear, pride, lust, or indifference. Large-scale reform can undoubtedly do some good, but he considers the belief that the answer to humanity's problems lies in new societal arrangements, in the form of legislative and social reform, to be "the Holy Grail of modernity."[10] Willard regards liberation theologies and the like on the whole as strong on analysis but weak on solution. This comes across quite clearly in a personal letter written in 1986 to his friend Trevor Hudson, a South African pastor, in discussing how best to combat and overcome apartheid. He writes,

> I can, I believe, enter into you [sic] feelings about the social and political conditions in your country. In general, it seems to me that the Left's criticisms of the *status quo* are usually well founded in the actualities of peoples [sic] lives. I wish I could say the same for what the Left has to say about what should be done. I do not much believe in programs or political reforms that are directly supposed to transform the human condition, although there *is* an obvious time and place for them, and

---

[8] Dallas Willard, *The Spirit of the Disciplines: Understanding How God Changes Lives* (Harper & Row, 1988), 229, 231.

[9] Advocates of a systemic-injustice perspective would argue that the problem lies not merely in the readiness of individuals to *do* evil but in their inability to *see* or *define* it. Often Christians have done evil while they thought they were serving Christ (e.g., colonialism, killing "pagans"). In other words, the problem may be that our moral vision is at least partly shaped by society and culture, and these are not neutral. There is much more ground to cover in Willard's view of the social order, so I ask the reader to wait to decide whether he sufficiently addresses this dynamic.

[10] Willard, *Spirit of the Disciplines*, 234.

some people are even called by God to give their lives for them. . . . Hence, while I enjoy the liberation theologians or Ron Sider or John Yoder or Jeremy Rifkin or [etc.] as well as the Marxists of various persuasions, I have no confidence at all in their recommendations—except in a rare case with reference to some specific, localizable issue.[11]

PRACTICAL AND PERSONALISTIC

Two things should be kept in mind at this point. First, once again we see Willard's approach is eminently *practical*. Some Christians, especially those within the evangelical tradition since the end of the nineteenth century, have held that social justice is subordinate to the church's primary calling of evangelization and discipleship for *theological reasons*. Leaders such as D. L. Moody, Billy Sunday, and Billy Graham gave theological rationale for prioritizing "spiritual" matters over "social" issues in their ministries.[12] This is in contrast to those, like Willard, who emphasize discipleship ministry for *practical reasons*, with the belief that character transformation is the only means for building a truly just society. He explains:

> The worldly system of understanding tries to produce justice, peace, and prosperity directly in people's lives by placing restraints upon what would harm them. But the effort, besides being ineffective, *also proves impractical.* The gospel of Christ, by contrast, comes to create a new person pervaded by the positive realities of faith, hope, and love—toward God primarily and therefore toward all men and women and

---

[11]Dallas Willard, letter to Trevor Hudson, October 6, 1986, Dallas Willard Collection.

[12]Michael O. Emerson and Christian Smith, *Divided by Faith: Evangelical Religion and the Problem of Race in America* (Oxford University Press, 2000), 41, 46-47. In the case of Graham, although he showed concern about many social issues, his premillennialism gave him a rather gloomy outlook toward social progress. As Emerson and Smith write, "According to this view, the present world is evil and will inevitably suffer moral decline until Christ comes again. Thus, to devote oneself to social reform is futile. The implications of this view were clearly expressed by Billy Graham. In response to King's famous 'I Have a Dream' speech that his children might one day play together with white children, Graham, who had been invited but did not attend the 1963 March on Washington, said: 'Only when Christ comes again will little white children of Alabama walk hand in hand with little black children.' This was not meant to be harsh, but rather what he and most white evangelicals perceived to be realistic" (47).

creatures. From this positive transformation of the self, justice, peace, and prosperity can result as God's rule is fulfilled in human life.[13]

Again, the question for Willard is not whether worldly justice matters but how it may be truly realized. We must deal with the root causes of injustice, not just the symptoms. Can we aspire to create a good world without first becoming good people? The only plausible way for radical societal transformation to come about, he believes, is for enough mature disciples of Christ, formed by the disciplines of the spiritual life and empowered by God's grace, to be dispersed throughout society and especially in positions of leadership and power.[14] Not only does Willard think character change is the key to social change, but he also thinks persons of good character need to act locally, so to speak. In numerous places in both his philosophical and theological writings, he describes who the good person is and what she does.[15] A good person seeks to bring about good that is in her effective reach—in other words, good that she is positioned to do something about. If persons of good character seek the good with which they are in effective contact, the world will become a just place.

Second, Willard's *personalistic philosophy and anthropology* play a significant role in his emphasis on the individual. In his view, the human person is a social being who never exists in isolation. Willard was, in terms of metaphysics, an organicist rather than an atomist.[16] Yet a person's body, directed by one's will and mind, is the most basic unit of potential energy in a social system. In his words,

---

[13] Willard, *Spirit of the Disciplines*, 221, emphasis added.

[14] Willard, *Spirit of the Disciplines*, 241. See also Dallas Willard, "Being Church" (August 14, 2011), MP3, 22:00.

[15] E.g., Dallas Willard, *The Disappearance of Moral Knowledge*, ed. Aaron Preston, Gregg Ten Elshof, and Steven L. Porter (Routledge, 2018), 358-62; Willard, *Knowing Christ Today: Why We Can Trust Spiritual Knowledge* (HarperOne, 2009), 53.

[16] "The human self requires rootedness in others. This is primarily an ontological matter—a matter of *being* what we are. It is not just a moral matter, a matter of what *ought* to be. And the moral aspect of it grows out of the ontological" (Willard, *Renovation of the Heart*, 36). For Willard's discussion of organicism versus atomism, see Dallas Willard, "Human Effort, Human Character and Divine Grace: Why Grace Requires Effort 1" (January 6, 2010), video, 39:00.

> Certainly the social dimension of life is essential to spirituality. *Of course* I should not disregard social evils and should oppose them when it is strategically possible to make some difference. . . . But how can I succeed in doing this? Concretely, the only place where I can "fight the good fight of faith, lay hold on eternal life" (1 Tim. 6:12) is in and through *the management of my body*, dealing rigorously and wisely with it and depending on God's help.[17]

The social system can exert tremendous influence on and shape individual persons, but the social system in the end derives all its life from those individuals. As he states in a lecture, "There is no such thing as *evil* structures or *wicked* structures or *sinful* structures—there are *harmful* ones. Organizations do not have a will; that is why they cannot repent. . . . They don't have feelings. Individuals have that."[18] It is with individual persons who have feelings and, most importantly, a will that we must begin if we are to possibly bring about societal transformation. This is ultimately an ontological argument stemming from his personalism. "Individual change *is* the answer, even though many believe strongly the answer lies in social change."[19]

Having said that, in Willard's anthropology the mind, the body, and the social dimension are intricately connected, continually interface, and exert mutual influence. There are multiple inlets into the human soul that can reinforce each other to various degrees.[20] For

---

[17] Willard, *Spirit of the Disciplines*, 125, emphasis added on "*the management of my body.*" See also Dallas Willard, "The Matrix of Mission 1" (May 1985), MP3, where he describes the human body of the believer as the "womb" of mission.

[18] Dallas Willard, "The Transformation of the Mind: Thoughts and Feelings 1" (January 7, 2010), video, 8:00.

[19] Willard, *Spirit of the Disciplines*, 233. See also Dallas Willard, "Q & A 1" (February 22, 1997), MP3, 12:15: "There's a conspiracy under the aegis of the social sciences to set will aside and replace it with causation."

[20] In discussion of the dimensions of personhood that comprise the human soul, Willard writes: "Acts and states within the range of these distinctive capacities are essentially interrelated. . . . Out of the rich texture of interrelationships within and between the various capacities and dimensions of the human being there arises the individual human personality and its life." Dallas Willard, "Spiritual Disciplines, Spiritual Formation, and the Restoration of the Soul," *Journal of Psychology and Theology* 26, no. 1 (1998): 103.

example, consider how an experience (body and social) reinforced with speech (mind and body) can be extremely powerful in shaping the soul. If a teenager is followed in a store by an employee, its formative impact on his soul is exponentially increased by an awareness that the majority surrounding culture and its authorities view him with suspicion because of his skin color. So, while Willard holds that true societal change comes about only through the revolution of individual character, he also maintains that the social dimension is undeniably a major inlet in shaping the human soul. Personal formation always takes place within a public context (family, church, government, education, etc.), so if the public context is not good, individuals will struggle to become good persons.

INSTITUTIONS, LEADERS, AND THE PROFESSIONS

Closely connected to this last point are Willard's view of institutions and subsequently his theory of leaders. In a 1992 talk on the topic of truth, he discusses the importance of *belief* in everyday life since it enables us to act as if something is true even if we cannot immediately know or prove its truth. For instance, to hold a bank account requires one to trust (a trust founded on belief) that funds that were previously deposited can be withdrawn in the future even though those funds are not presently seen and in fact *cannot* be seen, since there is no place within the bank where *your* actual dollars are being stored. So much of modern life, says Willard, requires this sort of trust in institutional systems, and it cannot be otherwise:

> Given that we can't, by and large, set out to confirm all of the truths that we need for our lives to run on, we have to take our beliefs from the institutions that surround us. Institutions are organizations that survive transgenerationally, that is, they go through history. Individuals that fill them up at one time go away, but the thing is still there. . . .
>
> Of course, institutions can die. They come into existence and they die. But what I want to say to you is that we fundamentally must take beliefs by which we live . . . from our institutions. . . . And these

institutions carry beliefs about how things are and beliefs about what things are valuable, what things are good or bad or right or wrong.[21]

In other words, institutions help define reality for a society and socialize individuals into that reality. Willard goes on to give examples of institutions, ranging from the simple (*The Los Angeles Times* newspaper) to the more abstract (art and burial customs). The family can also be seen as an institution, but he suggests it is a more fundamental social form, since the family is the primary way institutions themselves are transmitted.[22]

His point is that we all live within and around institutions that form us in significant ways. The reason institutions exist to a large degree is to shape us to such an extent that we do not have to make decisions all the time. Yet most people remain unaware of this socio-formational phenomenon. In a lecture delivered a decade later, he remarks, "I think we are, as people in the United States, at least, we're very simple-minded about institutions. We really don't understand them. Above all, we often think we're not involved in them, that we're just out there being individuals. And yet the institutional hand is heavily governing what we are attempting [and] what we can do."[23] Institutions are powerful influences of unconscious ideas, of what goes without saying. This is akin to the notion of *plausibility structures*, which sociologists such as Peter Berger and others describe as systems of ideas and practices embedded in sociocultural contexts that determine what beliefs are plausible and normative.[24] Plausibility structures are a byproduct of cultural institutions, yet they also reinforce and further shape cultural institutions. The reigning plausibility structures of a

---

[21]Dallas Willard, "Truth" (February 21, 1992), MP3, 24:15, 27:00.
[22]Not unlike how some sociologists think of the family as a meta-institution.
[23]Dallas Willard, "Naming the Issues" (May 19, 2000), MP3, 12:15.
[24]See Peter Berger, *The Sacred Canopy: Elements of a Sociological Theory of Religion* (Doubleday, 1967). While Willard himself does not use the language of plausibility structures, his description of institutions in one place is materially the same: "An institution is a pattern of recognized actions and reactions that survives across the generations." Dallas Willard, "Starting from Community and Human Realities" (May 19, 2000), MP3, 17:00.

society form what Willard elsewhere refers to as the Zeitgeist, the spirit of the age, a concept we will return to.

Willard is interested in how institutions define reality for societies, in that they serve as authorities for knowledge. But he is especially interested in how institutions of higher education (i.e., colleges and universities) are *the* authority for knowledge today in Western society, and what it would mean for the public state of knowledge if these institutions were to lose their way. "Because of the intimate interweavings of knowledge with institutions," he writes, "knowledge can be lost or become unavailable to those who need it. It can 'disappear' as a publicly available resource. Changes in the institutions of knowledge can have that effect."[25] This vanishing act is in fact what he thinks has happened to moral knowledge over the past century and a half. Institutions deeply shape people's beliefs and values, for they are responsible for preserving, refining, and transmitting bodies of knowledge, not least moral knowledge, to the members of a society.[26] So, if our institutions are failing to adequately present knowledge of what is good and right, to guide us in being and doing, where do we begin to recover moral knowledge? Would Willard still say "individual change *is* the answer" when it comes to reforming institutions to serve the public good?[27] Yes, but in a very specific sense. Here is where his theory of leaders emerges, as well as his interest in the professions. And both relate to a particular interpretation of late modernity and the (over)sophistication of its social structures.

In the 1992 talk cited above, Willard reflects on how "life was very simple" in rural Missouri, where he was born and raised during the first half of the twentieth century. "We didn't have a lot of reality to deal

---

[25] Willard, *Disappearance of Moral Knowledge*, 21.
[26] "Now, the human world is one in which knowledge is made available to people in general *through institutions* of one kind or another," writes Willard. "Important things that might very well be known and acted upon by individuals and groups will not be known, and therefore not acted upon, if knowledge concerning them is not made publicly available by groups and institutions that stand before the public for that purpose" (*Knowing Christ Today*, 200).
[27] Willard, *Spirit of the Disciplines*, 233.

with, and we didn't need a lot of beliefs to deal with it." But that sort of existence, he thinks, is nearly impossible today because we are caught in a system that "is incredibly complex."[28] Similarly, in *Renovation of the Heart* he writes, "We now live within the life form called 'modernity,' where revered ritual and personal relations do not smoothly govern life, because human solidarity (in family, neighborhood, school, workplace, church) has been pulverized. There are few things of equal significance to this fact for serious Christians to understand today."[29] Willard indicates in a footnote that he is drawing here from sociologist Anthony Giddens's *The Consequences of Modernity* (1990), which he commends as "one of the best introductions to modernity and what it means for life today."[30] What one finds in Giddens's book is an institutional analysis of modernity that is decidedly different from analyses largely focused on epistemological and philosophical changes (Lyotard, Foucault, etc.). He argues that a modern society is essentially one with institutions that are so complex that only experts can directly deal with them. As a result, modern life requires we trust in *expert systems*, by which Giddens means "systems of technical accomplishment or professional expertise that organise large areas of the material and social environments in which we live today."[31] This leads to one of his main theses: "The disorientation which expresses itself in the feeling that systematic knowledge about social organisation cannot be obtained, I shall argue, results primarily from the sense many of us have of being caught up in a universe of events we do not fully understand, and which seems in large part outside of our control."[32]

On this note, Giddens contends that the *local community*, as a particular place in time that provides a familiar milieu to its members, has been replaced in modernity by *abstract systems* as a means of stabilizing

---

[28] Willard, "Truth," 21:45, 22:15.
[29] Willard, *Renovation of the Heart*, 126.
[30] Willard, *Renovation of the Heart*, 262n3.
[31] Anthony Giddens, *The Consequences of Modernity* (Stanford University Press, 1990), 27.
[32] Giddens, *Consequences of Modernity*, 2-3.

relations across indefinite spans of time and space.³³ The growing complexity of life in our contemporary world, which owes no small part to these abstract systems, is one of the defining features of modernity. For example, consider the legal system in the United States (or in any other Western nation). It is now so complex that the average person cannot really deal directly with it—only experts can. And we must trust the experts if we are going to have any chance in the legal system. The same is true for other areas of societal life. The institutions of modernity have rendered the navigation of life unmanageable without those with professional expertise. Yet this was not the case in premodern society; most of these abstract systems did not exist, and most individuals were capable of engaging society on more or less the same level.

Willard's perennial emphasis on the role of leaders and the importance of professions is due in part to his Giddens-like understanding of modernity. Willard is not hopeful that the average person can affect much change on an institutional level.³⁴ Perhaps one had a greater chance of doing so in the past, but not today. As he states in his 1992 talk, "Nobody can just go out and reinvent it all, any more than you can go out and reinvent chemistry. You can't go out and reinvent culture. You take it from your institutions."³⁵ There is no way around the expert systems (institutions) of modernity. However, the experts or leaders working within these various systems do wield tremendous responsibility, and rightfully so, in Willard's opinion. Those with knowledge in a certain

---

³³Giddens, *Consequences of Modernity*, 101-3.

³⁴See Willard, "Starting from Community and Human Realities." His sober outlook is due not only to the growing complexity of institutions but also, and relatedly, to the loss of a "real-life basis" (22:15) once shared by the citizenry of a place. This common life has been replaced by "systematic isolation" (24:15), which he considers "a new phenomenon in human history" (25:15). In his view, "individualism has ripped the guts out of the fundamental structures of society" (32:00); he further comments, "If you go back as far as Plato or Aristotle and you look at what they have to say about community, it always addresses a situation where people are dependent on one another and live together and have much in common. Even from Aristotle all the way to Rousseau, the assumption was you couldn't have a genuine community if it was beyond a certain size. Because you had to have some significant degree of face-to-face relationship before you could have community" (25:30).

³⁵Willard, "Truth," 28:45.

area should be the ones entrusted to act, teach, supervise, create policy, and so on pertaining to their subject matter, since knowledge alone confers this authority.[36] These are individuals, certainly, but they are a specific kind of individuals: *leaders in the professions*.

Willard maintains that God has ordered human life and affairs in such a way that leadership is a good and necessary social structure. Leadership is, broadly defined, "a matter of bringing the activities of many into coordination for a common end or good," and a profession can be understood as "a *practice* (action or advice) on the behalf of others of some activity of great importance to the well-being of society generally."[37] So, if the complex web of social structures that make up a modern society is going to change, it will change largely because of and through the leadership of professionals working within institutions.[38] This provides us a major clue as to why a philosopher with expertise in Husserlian phenomenology chose to frequently teach college courses on the professions and their place in the public life—a pairing I dare say we would not intuit.

In the syllabus for his 2010 USC course "Professions and the Public Interest in American Life," Willard introduces the course's main themes and content in the following way:

> In 1968 the distinguished American sociologist, Talcott Parsons, wrote that the professions have "become the most important single component in the structure of modern societies." This is even more true for the America of the 2000's, as the increasing complexity of life makes it increasingly difficult for the individual or the public *to know itself and its needs*.... A *philosophy of society* adequate to contemporary life

---

[36]Willard, *Disappearance of Moral Knowledge*, 20.

[37]Dallas Willard, "Leadership as Love of God and Neighbor" (May 15, 2000), MP3, 44:15; Willard, "Professions and the Public Interest in American Life," PHIL 141g (syllabus, University of Southern California, spring 2010), Dallas Willard Collection, 26.

[38]Willard's theory of leaders does not just apply to the traditional professions (law, medicine, religion) but to all persons who have some level of say or authority that other people do not have. It thus includes business leaders, political leaders, educational leaders, finance leaders, media leaders, and so on. Yet when it comes to his view of large sociocultural change, special emphasis is on leaders in the professions because of their proximity to institutions.

therefore requires an understanding of how the professional substructures in society operate and how they can best serve.³⁹

The next paragraph elucidates some of the "philosophy of society" that will be taught in the course, explaining how "certain qualified individuals" are to serve the common good within the institutional structures of modern society:

> By public interest (or "the public good") we understand those goods which *all* members of society may reasonably be presumed to benefit from, directly or indirectly, or at least have access to. For example, the public has an interest in commerce, legal institutions and processes, public order, health care, education, housing, transportation, and information flow. That there should be corresponding activities in society, and that they should be well conducted by certain qualified individuals, is, precisely, in the public interest.⁴⁰

Later on in this rather lengthy course description, Willard explicitly states his position on the moral responsibility of leaders, both in their personal life and in the larger public sphere: "It will be maintained that the specifically *moral* dimension of professional life is fundamental to its nature and function," which implies "the professions must also be considered as avenues of moral fulfillment and meaningful human existence."⁴¹ He suggests that not every occupation is a profession, for the latter entails a special and irreplaceable function within societal life. This does not mean professionals are better than nonprofessionals. Willard claims such an egoistic aura is insidious and would grossly distort the meaning of the professions over time. Nevertheless, he insists, "The major goods in society upon which your well-being depends are in the hands of these professional people."⁴² In short, professionals are trustees of the public good.⁴³

---

³⁹Willard, "Professions and the Public Interest," 1.
⁴⁰Willard, "Professions and the Public Interest," 1.
⁴¹Willard, "Professions and the Public Interest," 3.
⁴²Willard, "Professions and the Public Interest," 27.
⁴³There may be a Kuyperian dimension here, especially since I found a handwritten reference to Abraham Kuyper in Willard's notes from 2009 on discipleship and the redemption of the social

Willard's emphasis on the transformative potential of leadership—specifically Christly leadership—is vividly illustrated in a handout he distributed to Christian audiences on multiple occasions, in which he identifies a critical issue facing the church today: "We have been trying to deal with world evangelism while ploughing around non-Christian leadership in societal institutions." In response, he proposes a bold remedy: "Human society in the contemporary age demands Christian leadership and standards in all of its institutions. Christianity is *not* one thing and business/government another. Only as Christians can we succeed. The *best* leader is the Christlike leader, for nothing less than Christian vision and character will suffice as the substance of *organizational life*."[44]

Together, these passages from his syllabus and handout are valuable for filling in gaps between his view of institutions in late modernity and his theory of leaders and their responsibility in societal life. This connection also sheds light on Willard's particular focus on the profession of pastors/clergy, a theme in his Christian teaching and writing that only grew with time. He has a high view of the pastorate, something I will return to in the next chapter. As we can see, Willard's approach is not as straightforward or simple as I previously stated, namely that the renovation of individual character leads to the revolution of social order. For him, societal transformation happens only with the formation of virtuous individuals, particularly those in leadership roles. Institutions and professions depend on such individuals to embody and enact Christly leadership, which in turn influences broader social change. Even so, individual character formation is still where it all must begin for Willard.

---

order, notes I will discuss momentarily. This would add an additional lens to how we view Willard's social theory, but I cannot pursue the question further here.

[44]In the Dallas Willard Collection, this single-page handout, titled "Creative Ministry Today Must Aim to Transform Social Institutions Through Christly Leadership," appears both on its own and as part of larger handouts. Its earliest appearance is Willard's 1987 South Africa trip; see Dallas Willard, "Seminars on Creative Ministry in Times of Crisis" (handout, 1987), Dallas Willard Collection, 32. It also appears in a 2003 presentation at Church of the Saviour in Washington, DC.

HEART CHANGE TO SOCIETAL TRANSFORMATION

Before turning to Willard's interpretation of Jesus' moral aim, let us consider two of his relatively unknown writings—one unpublished and the other coauthored shortly before his death—to ensure we have properly outlined his theory of social change. In my research of his unpublished papers, I discovered the manuscript and notes for a 2009 lecture on the topic of discipleship and mission delivered to a group of pastors, a lecture that unfortunately was not recorded. I will engage with this more extensively in chapter ten, so I will not detail it here; instead, I want only to comment on one point that indicates the direction and flow of social redemption Willard assumes is biblically normative and historically operative. Describing what type of Christian faith results when discipleship to Jesus drops away as an essential—which he claims is our present predicament—he writes, "The outcome is a Christianity that does not deal with (I) Transformation of Character, (II) Exaltation of Vocations, and (III) Rectification in Righteousness of Social Processes and Structures."[45] A scribbled note next to the word *structures* indicates he has in mind social institutions of various kinds: "family, education, financial, arts, media, labor, business."

Two minor notes found in his handwritten draft of the lecture[46] indicate more precisely how he sees these three realities of the characterological, vocational, and societal relating to and impinging on one another. Below the line about I, II, and III (Character, Vocations, Structures), he writes, "The latter two are firmly rooted in the first," and "How these 3 interlock and depend 3 on 2 and 2 on 1."[47] I have reproduced Willard's notes just as they appear, but even in their shorthand,

---

[45] Dallas Willard, "Discipleship to Jesus vs. the Missional Church" (printed lecture, 2009), Dallas Willard Collection, 1.

[46] It was Willard's custom to work out what he wanted to say first on yellow pads and transfer the finished or nearly finished product to typewriter or computer. This was the case with not only his lectures but also essays and whole books.

[47] Dallas Willard, "Discipleship to Jesus and the Missional Church" (handwritten notes, 2009), Dallas Willard Collection, 3.

rough form, it is clear what he has in mind. The rectification of the social order comes about only through personal transformation. Yet vocations—by which we can assume he means the professions but also other occupations and callings—are the social bridge between transformed individuals and the redemption of the larger social realm, which he more or less equates with institutions here.

Willard's last essay before his death, cowritten with law professor and friend Robert Cochran Jr., is a rare piece of political theology and as such offers further insight into his view of individual/societal change. Published in a volume titled *Law and the Bible: Justice, Mercy and Legal Institutions* (2013), the essay examines Jesus' teaching about the priority of heart change in God's kingdom and how this relates to his call for both justice and love, the ways in which civil law and God's moral law overlap but also deviate from each other, and the meaning all this has for the institutions of law and government.

The authors build their argument in part through interacting with a wide range of sources, from legal scholars and justice activists to classical theologians (Augustine, Aquinas, Calvin, Luther) and modern ones (O'Donovan, Hauerwas, Volf), and by distancing themselves from certain theological traditions on the church's relationship to the political/legal sphere, specifically Anabaptism and Lutheranism. They contend Jesus is to the utmost concerned with the condition of people's hearts because of, not in spite of, his concern for justice and righteousness in the public realm. Personal transformation is the only true basis for love and justice to be upheld in society. But what is particularly valuable about their argument is how it fleshes out some of the specific social and institutional implications of Willard's social architecture, that is, his view of the relation between individual and societal change and the order in which they unfold.

> The transformed heart can do much for law. Those with transformed hearts will be far more likely to comply with most aspects of law than

those who do not have such a heart. They will go beyond the requirements of law. . . . Moreover, a changed heart will lead one to be greatly concerned with justice, and thus with law. Justice alone will never do justice to justice, but a heart of love will promote and require justice (and much more).[48]

Willard has a number of one-liners that indicate his disdain for many current notions of justice, such as this phrase that "justice will never do justice to justice" or his suggestion that one can satisfy "equal rights" by hating everyone equally.[49] During Willard's four-decade tenure at a public university teaching philosophy and ethics, one can imagine all the treatises on justice and human rights that came across his desk. The essence of his grievance is the separation of justice from love—love understood as the condition of a will that is oriented toward the good of the other.[50] He tackles this issue directly in *Knowing Christ Today*, among other places, arguing that justice is a foundational human good, but without love it will always fall short of what needs to be done.[51] Love is the fundamental virtue, the center of moral reality, from which true justice flows.[52] (This explains why he is more prone to talk about the nature and implications of love rather than justice.) In the present article, this point is made in

---

[48]Cochran and Willard, "Kingdom of God, Law," 157.

[49]Dallas Willard, "The Good Life" (September 30, 2006), MP3, 59:15. For another instance of "justice will never do justice to justice," see Willard, "What Is the Kingdom of God?" (October 13, 2010), MP3, 42:45.

[50]For one of his fullest articulations of the concept of love, see Dallas Willard, "Getting Love Right" (presented paper, September 15, 2007), Dallas Willard Collection, esp. 3-4.

[51]Willard, *Knowing Christ Today*, 84. For his more philosophically substantive argument, see Dallas Willard, "Faith, Hope and Love as Indispensable Foundations of Moral Realization" (presented paper, March 25, 1987), Dallas Willard Collection, 5-6.

[52]To hear more of his rationale, consider this statement: "The New Testament depiction of love as the fulfilling of the law seems to preclude it from being one character trait among others and to place it in the position of an overall quality of life within which the various character traits that are virtues, along with their corresponding actions, are sustainable and even 'natural'" (Willard, "Faith, Hope and Love," 11). Willard has a sophisticated view of the virtue of *agapē* love as a "presence" (though he notes "the ontology is not clear") in human persons, one that is communicated to them via the indwelling of God's very own presence. For those interested, see Willard, "Faith, Hope and Love," 18-19.

respect to the responsibilities of public leaders; quoting William Temple, the authors define justice as "the primary form of love in social organizations."[53]

The authors also discuss how law might be organized around the value of Christian love in practical (but not "cuddly") ways so it does not merely keep order among citizens but actually aids good character development in those citizens. "Law creates habits, good and bad, and these habits can become virtues and vices—good and bad moral habits. Young people can be formed by law, especially when they see law as good, sensibly exemplified in elders."[54] Yet they also recognize there is a significant limit to what law can do to influence a person's character since character development, good or bad, requires the exercise of free choice. Wise law must allow adequate space for this developmental process to occur, while also protecting citizens and reinforcing the practices of the good.

In addition, the essay addresses the role of leadership and power in societal transformation *apart from* heart transformation, though the authors never state it in such dichotomous terms. They write, "Unlike Luther we believe that Jesus' teachings have much to teach governing officials about how government power should be exercised" and, "The development and enforcement of wise laws can be among the most loving acts in which a person can engage." Here they align closely with Calvin (as well as Augustine), echoing the Reformer's view that "the magistrate is minister of God for our good."[55] This implies "good people" in government wielding their power and thus exerting force when needed.[56] For example, we all know that one person who seeks

---

[53]Cochran and Willard, "Kingdom of God, Law," 173.

[54]Cochran and Willard, "Kingdom of God, Law," 169.

[55]Cochran and Willard, "Kingdom of God, Law," 164-65, 171, citing John Calvin, *Institutes* 4.20.17.

[56]One might ask what Willard would have to say about Christian leadership in a context in which a Christian has power over non-Christians. He likely would ask what better arrangement is there than for those who have developed Christ's character to be in positions of power over Christians, non-Christians, or people of any faith persuasion. Personally speaking, I have been influenced by the Anabaptist tradition, so I might then ask whether Willard thinks this tradition has something to teach us here. Certain aspects of Willard's ecclesiology align well with Anabaptism, but

evil can do more harm than ten people who seek good. At some point, then, the godly will have to wield power over the ungodly and force them into abiding by the law. In other words, we cannot escape the idea that societies are changed, to some extent at least, not by character formation but simply by power. Again, the authors do not put it as baldly as this, but they clearly wrestle with the issue over a number of pages.[57]

But true to form, in the end Willard and Cochran are adamant that "true righteousness requires a changed heart living interactively with God," and yet such heart change "is not merely a private event, as is so often thought, but has a vast range of insuppressible implications for life, including life as a citizen."[58] This drumbeat emphasis is the same one found throughout Willard's theory of social change and reflections on leaders. Although the essay does not detail what other capacities lawmakers and legal administrators need in addition to changed hearts to promote justice and love, one can combine its argument with what he says elsewhere about moral knowledge and practical knowledge. Citing a study on human rights in the developing world, the authors describe how "many of the greatest injustices to which poor people in developing countries are subjected are not a result of the content of their countries' laws. Their laws prohibit slavery, extortion, land grabbing, human trafficking, child labor and prostitution, but no one enforces these laws."[59]

---

he would, I surmise, find little value in the Anabaptist view of and response to power. Power is, he would say, simply a reality in human life. Some have more of it than others; it can be used well or abused, or it can be rejected (though not all apparent rejections of power are truly that, as even Anabaptists have learned; see also the history of John Howard Yoder). Willard may have his own naivetés when it comes to Christians wielding power, but his thinking in this area may expose a certain naiveté in the Anabaptist position on power, just from the other side.

[57]See Cochran and Willard, "Kingdom of God, Law," 164-74; e.g., "In our view, the best resolution of conflicts between love and justice at the institutional level may be the traditional Christian formulation: 'justice tempered with mercy'" (174). See also their discussion of Jesus' critique of political leaders who use their power to "lord it over" people (Mt 20:25) rather than to serve them (168).

[58]Cochran and Willard, "Kingdom of God, Law," 159, 164.

[59]Cochran and Willard, "Kingdom of God, Law," 167.

What is needed first and foremost, Willard would say, is changed hearts in the leaders of these countries so that they will put the well-being of their citizens above their own interests. Yet this is not enough. Along with the motivation to love (heart change), these leaders also need to see what love requires (knowledge) and what love looks like in particular instances (wisdom) if they are to lead competently in the areas of policy making, law enforcement, and so on.[60] Heart change is essential, but it alone is not adequate for significant social change. And no one knew this better, Willard claims, than Jesus of Nazareth. But in one of the great ironies of history, Jesus' revolutionary message, wherein a framework is offered for lasting societal transformation, is co-opted and squandered by many who profess him.

THE FAILURE OF FALSE GOSPELS

Often Willard comments on what he calls "gospels of sin management," distortions of the Christian message that deal solely with the effects of sin but not its source. These truncated gospels have two main theological formulations, one liberal and the other conservative.[61]

His critique of *the gospel on the left* is that its proponents put the cart before the horse by seeking social justice before or entirely without spiritual transformation. Although fond of Walter Rauschenbusch,

---

[60] In an exegesis of Ps 85:10 ("Mercy and truth are met together; righteousness and peace have kissed each other" [KJV]), Willard states, "The form that mercy and truth in community takes now is . . . *a sufficient number of the right people, in the right places, to see to it by the power of God that things go as they should.* Now what I'm giving you here is not a secret. Any social grouping, whether it's a family or whatever, that is going to function as it should, must have in it people who know what to do, when to do it, and have the resources to get it done." Dallas Willard, "The Desire of All Nations" (May 1985), MP3, 10:15. He then adds, "And what I'm giving you here is nothing but a projection of the system of judges in the Old Testament" (11:30). There are clear connections here between Willard's social theory and his teleology of formation (see chap. 3).

[61] Willard's fullest treatment of this in print is Dallas Willard, *The Divine Conspiracy: Rediscovering Our Hidden Life in God* (HarperSanFrancisco, 1998), chap. 2. Yet his most substantive argument as to why both gospels—the left and the right—are incapable of producing true social transformation is in *Spirit of the Disciplines*, 234-35. In his writings and in most of his talks he focuses on these two misconstrued gospels, though in the last decade of speaking he began including a third, what he calls the gospel of "churchmanship." This will be further discussed in the next chapter.

often considered the father of the social gospel, and how his ministry united together personal spiritual concern and social concern, Willard believes the generation after Rauschenbusch veered from this vision, separating personal change from social justice and equating the latter with the gospel.[62] This is the fundamental problem, he thought, with modern liberal theology and churches as well as left-leaning parachurch ministries such as Sojourners.[63] Social action thus becomes a way to dodge or ignore personal change. And once an interactive relationship with Jesus is exchanged for a social ethic based on his example, the "gospel" becomes incapable of producing the character change in persons needed to motivate and sustain true justice work.

The gospel on the right does not fare any better, according to Willard. He roots the history of both the right and left gospels in the modernist-fundamentalist controversy of the early twentieth century. On the right side, conservative Christians felt threatened by the increasing secularization of Western society and in response put all their eggs, so to speak, in the basket of religious belief/doctrine. This led, in due time, to an intense focus on what was perceived to be the most important salvific belief: the atonement. There are certainly differences on the theological right over how exactly to understand Christ's atoning death and how precisely its merits are attained, but there is near-universal agreement that salvation is about justification, forgiveness, and entry into heaven upon death or judgment, which God bestows on those who profess faith in Jesus (i.e., have orthodox belief). The gospel is essentially good news

---

[62] Willard, "What Makes Spirituality Christian?," 17; Dallas Willard, "Session 1—Part 2" (March 9, 2004), MP3, 1:45.

[63] It deserves mention that Willard was also fond of Jim Wallis, the founder of Sojourners, once referring to him as "a sweet, wonderful man," and instead levels his critique against "the people who usually read *Sojourners* [the magazine]." Dallas Willard, "What Does Holiness Look Like Shorn of Its Legalistic Expressions? 2" (January 4, 2010), video, 43:30. Keep in mind that as a professional philosopher, Willard had no qualms about critiquing others in his field but, as a general rule, did not critique living theologians.

about the remission of sins wrought by Christ's death; salvation is a legal status rather than a living status.[64] Yet forgiven people does not equal just people. So, once again, we are left with the question, how do people *become* just?[65]

Willard's own answer to that question reframes personal salvation as a transformative and missional reality. In a 1984 talk, he articulates what we might call a tripartite view of salvation, which stands in stark contrast to the reductionistic gospel he heard in the Southern Baptist churches of his youth. Salvation in the New Testament, he maintains, consists of three main parts: (1) forgiveness of sins, (2) transformation of character, and (3) significant power over evil, exercised by both the individual and the church.[66] After an extended critique of the gospel he inherited—a gospel raised on the knee of dispensationalism and the Scofield study Bible, effectually rendering the Gospels and Jesus' teaching on the kingdom "totally irrelevant" for our present age—he states:

> Salvation comes in the following of the Lord Jesus Christ in a new life, which has the power to transform the world, which indeed Jesus said meant the casting down of the evil powers of heaven—which is the beginning of the movement of that stone cut out without hands which shall eventually crush the kingdoms of this world until they are become the kingdoms of our God and of his Christ.[67]

---

[64] At the heart of this rendering of the gospel is a one-sided understanding of *righteousness* (*ṣədāqâ* in Hebrew, *dikaiosynē* in Greek) as "right standing with God" without reference to justice. Willard's rendering of *dikaiosynē* in Mt 6:33 as the "rightness" of God (*Divine Conspiracy*, 212) may serve as a corrective and should be compared with the interpretive translations of other contemporary theological works, such as David P. Gushee and Glen H. Stassen, *Kingdom Ethics: Following Jesus in Contemporary Context*, 2nd ed. (Eerdmans, 2016), chap. 7; David J. Bosch, *Transforming Mission: Paradigm Shifts in Theology of Mission* (Orbis, 1991), 72-73.

[65] Willard's polemic, in sum: "What right and left have in common is that neither group lays down a coherent framework of knowledge and practical direction adequate to *personal transformation* toward the abundance and obedience emphasized in the New Testament, with a corresponding redemption of ordinary life" (*Divine Conspiracy*, 41, emphasis added).

[66] Dallas Willard, "You Can't Have One Without the Other" (May 14, 1984), MP3, 23:00; cf. Willard, *Spirit of the Disciplines*, 39-40.

[67] Willard, "You Can't Have One," 21:30.

A mouthful of a description of salvation indeed. Yet this, Willard says, is what is missing not only from the gospel he heard in his youth but from most churches today. And it is precisely this vision of transformation and kingdom power that Jesus intended for his revolution.

THE REVOLUTIONARY NATURE OF THE TRUE GOSPEL

In a lengthy footnote in *Renovation of the Heart*, Willard quotes historian Will Durant's assessment of Jesus:

> Jesus is not concerned to attack existing economic or political institutions. . . . The revolution he sought was a far deeper one, without which reforms could only be superficial and transitory. If he could cleanse the human heart of selfish desire, cruelty, and lust, utopia would come of itself, and all those institutions that rise out of human greed and violence, and the consequent need for law, would disappear. Since this would be the profoundest of all revolutions, beside which all others would be mere *coups d'état* of class ousting class and exploiting in its turn, Christ was in this spiritual sense the greatest revolutionist in history.[68]

This particular interpretation of Jesus' ministry and the revolutionary nature of the gospel deeply resonates with Willard. In short, Willard considers Jesus to be the most revolutionary revolutionist because he (Jesus) sought the *spiritual transformation of persons* that would in turn bring about lasting social and political transformation.[69] Movements that seek revolution primarily or solely on a social level are, he thinks, akin to the teachers of the law and Pharisees cleaning the outside of the cup and dish while leaving the inside filthy (Mt 23:25). But the sociopolitical ethic of Jesus comes at it from the other way around: If people can be changed from the

---

[68]Willard, *Renovation of the Heart*, 257n1, citing Will Durant, *Caesar and Christ* (Simon & Schuster, 1944), 566.

[69]Quoting the Durant passage again some years later in a lecture, Willard adds, "You only understand that if you *do* know who Christ was and if you understand the message he brought and the reality of the kingdom of God. . . . Jesus is the true revolutionary." Dallas Willard, "Living in the Knowledge of Christ and His Kingdom" (February 16, 2010), MP3, 40:30.

inside out, then there is potential for this *upside-down* world to be turned *right-side up*.

We thus arrive again at Willard's christological realism and interpersonal view of spiritual transformation, themes introduced in chapter four. Jesus is the ever-present teacher, accessible through the Spirit, leading his apprentices in all matters of life. As these students of Jesus exercise their trust in him, they undergo a renovation of their personhood, beginning with the spirit/will/heart, and are gradually transformed into his likeness by means of interactive relationship with God in Christ and living in his kingdom. Then, as these redeemed personalities are distributed throughout society, Christ's character and wisdom infiltrate the outer forms of our existence—families, communities, institutions, governments, and the like—establishing just relations and structures and stabilizing what evil remains in human hearts and systems.

Allow me to connect the dots here. Willard's tripartite understanding of salvation—as forgiveness, formation, and kingdom power—both reorients our understanding of personal salvation and propels the broader threefold movement of redemption he believed was normative: the transformation of character, the exaltation of vocations, and the rectification of social structures. The first triad is soteriological and the root; the second is societal and the result. So, if the *back end* of God's strategy for overwhelming evil with goodness—the divine conspiracy—is for righteous (just) persons to be dispersed throughout society, then the *front end* is the formation of those righteous (just) persons. For Willard, the revolution of Jesus is first and foremost a revolution of individual character.

THE PERSONAL IS POLITICAL

Willard's approach to individual and societal change is not "either/or," as is typical among some Christians, but neither is it merely "both/and." It is a qualified "both/and" since it is also "first/then." Characterological transformation *first, then* societal change, for the personal always precedes the public in God's redemptive work. Yet, because personal formation always takes place within a public context (family, church, government, education, etc.), social institutions too have profound effects on the personal.

There is something of a resurgence among theologians today focusing on the communal nature of the Christian life. Many scholars now view community, rather than the individual, as the starting point for our relationship with the triune God as well as our participation in God's redemptive work. This shift reflects a broader turn in contemporary Protestant theology to a more communitarian understanding of the faith, countering what was deemed to be a preoccupation with the individual in Western thought in the wake of the Enlightenment. Does Willard's theory of spiritual formation offer something to our understanding of societal transformation, or will his emphasis on the individual merely exacerbate the situation by reinforcing the sort of individualistic thinking that contemporary theology deems inadequate? His approach does indeed have something important to offer here, but it also needs to be augmented by a fuller conception of community in the process of spiritual formation.

For Willard, the personal is political. If reality is personal at its core, then we cannot look to impersonal structures and systems to solve our most pressing social problems. Instead, redeemed personhood must be central to whatever solution is sought. Transformed individuals engaged in public issues, especially those in leadership positions, is how the larger social level is punctured. "I think we finally have to say," Willard concludes, "that Jesus' enduring relevance is based on his historically proven ability to speak to, to heal and empower the *individual human condition*."[70] As Jesus heals and puts individual persons back together, they are then called and empowered to join him in putting the world back together. This includes the rectification of social structures, but it all hinges, Willard believes, on the actions and moral aptitude of

---

[70]Willard, *Divine Conspiracy*, 13, emphasis added.

the individuals involved in those social structures. To ignore this reality is to abdicate our responsibility and whistle in the wind. In a teaching he states, "Individual responsibility and stewardship is God's plan for managing the world in such a way that the needs of people are met—needs for justice and food and clothing and opportunity and all that."[71]

His framing of the situation, I suggest, can be represented as two levels, illustrated in figure 8.1. Within Willard's social architecture, individuals are the means by which the larger social realm is reached and possibly transformed. What is missing, however, is *the role of community* as the intermediary between the two levels.

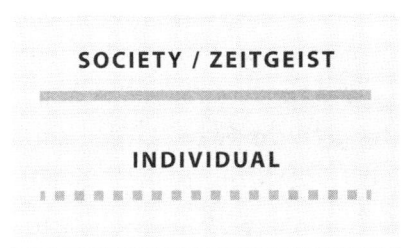

Figure 8.1. The social architecture in Willard's theory of spiritual formation

Consider Willard's argument in the final chapter of *Disappearance of Moral Knowledge*.[72] Willard understood the power of the Zeitgeist—the pervasive thought patterns—in a given society, especially in terms of shaping people's understanding or lack thereof of moral knowledge.[73] The purpose of the Zeitgeist is to serve the common good within that society, in conjunction with the efforts of individual persons and the

---

[71]Dallas Willard, "Evangelism" (June 21, 2002), MP3, 19:00.

[72]Willard, *Disappearance of Moral Knowledge*, chap. 8, esp. 358-74. Since this chapter in Willard's book is important for my analysis, and it was previously mentioned that the book was edited and published posthumously, I should explain why I deem it a reliable representation of Willard's view. The final chapter (chap. 8) is reconstructed from two separate drafts written by Willard and a number of published and unpublished papers. Steve Porter, the editor responsible for compiling the chapter, was gracious to share these with me along with a color-coded version of the final version that shows the original source material of each section. After reviewing these documents, I can say two things. First, the chapter is redacted from these sources with no interpolations minus connecting words to smooth transitions between otherwise independent original material. Second, the final version both honors what Willard had planned for the chapter in the prospectus he wrote for the project early on (to use Levinas as a foil for a kind of phenomenology of moral intuition that grounds moral knowledge) and amplifies it significantly with what he wrote and said about the shape of moral knowledge elsewhere. If Willard had lived to write the chapter, it likely would have grown in proportion and scope to at least what it is in this posthumous form.

[73]Willard draws his sense of the Zeitgeist from the work of historian W. E. H. Lecky (1838–1903); see *Disappearance of Moral Knowledge*, 6-7.

effects of other social mechanisms. This might be thought of as the overall cultural project of a society. Yet he considered the Zeitgeist, like other societal forces, an impersonal and nonrational reality, too abstract to be governed or changed directly by human persons. So what is to be done when the Zeitgeist or other reigning plausibility structures become distorted and no longer serve the common good?

When Willard turns from diagnosis to prescription in his treatment of the disappearance of moral knowledge in the West, he suggests we find exemplary individual persons to serve as surrogates for what should be a collective cultural project.[74] In other words, the cultural project of a given society should involve individuals, institutions, social mechanisms, the Zeitgeist, and the like acting in concert toward a common good, but in lieu of the failure of these societal entities to uphold their moral place and responsibility in this project, we must look to the only personal actor among them—individual humans—to regain the moral guidance necessary for the health and flourishing of a society. Exemplary individual persons become surrogates for larger societal entities, in that they act as the authoritative models for the moral life. "In short," Willard argues, "people who possess a good will are those who can restore moral knowledge to the public arena."[75]

Part of his reasoning is that one's immediate station in life and relation to others is where the range of that person's effective will can make a difference for the good. He writes:

---

[74]Willard, *Disappearance of Moral Knowledge*, 358-77. To be clear, this is my interpretation of Willard's strategy in the last chapter of *Disappearance*. He never states it in this exact manner. Also, it is important to note that the proposals he makes in *Disappearance* are aimed not at transforming the social order as a whole but rather specifically at regaining moral knowledge on the social and institutional level. Nevertheless, they illustrate his "first/then" method to individual and societal change and thus are a microcosm of his general approach.

[75]Willard, *Disappearance of Moral Knowledge*, 377. This move to look to individual agents is, in Willard's mind, the only option given the disappearance of moral knowledge in culture. In other words, this is not how he thinks it *should* work, but it is one of the only ways knowledge *can* be received when institutions are not presenting morality as knowledge. So, in a sense, this is a very social, nonindividualistic move. He does not think we can recover moral knowledge without exemplars of moral goodness; it would be best to have this enculturated in institutions, but without that available, we look to good persons.

One's job or position is morally significant, as a concrete setting to influence goods. As Bradley and others before him clearly saw, "my station and its duties" is nearly, but not quite, the whole moral scene, and can never be simply bypassed on the way to "larger" and presumably more important things. One of the major miscues of ethical theory since the 1960s has been, in my opinion, its almost total absorption in social and political issues. Of course, these issues also concern vital human goods. They are important, and we should always do what we can for them. But. . . . they do not essentially involve the center of moral reality, the will, and its settled direction.[76]

By "settled direction," Willard means character. Social and political issues are impersonal realities and therefore will always be secondary to and dependent on the will and character of human persons involved in those issues. Thus, no amount of modifying, refining, or even perfecting of the periphery can in the end transform the center, whereas good persons with good habituated will (character) can potentially transform the social issues and entities they encounter through their station and its duties. Hence, again, the personal is political.[77]

COMMUNITY AS THE MISSING LINK

Yet Willard does not seem to take account of how thin such a solution ultimately is. It is thin because, first, it miscalculates to what extent unorganized personal good can overcome organized evil.[78] In other

---

[76]Willard, *Disappearance of Moral Knowledge*, 368.

[77]As Willard is purported to have said, "The true social activist is the person who lives as an apprentice of Jesus in his or her ordinary relationships." See James Bryan Smith, *The Good and Beautiful Community: Following the Spirit, Extending Grace, Demonstrating Love* (InterVarsity Press, 2010), 13-14.

[78]Recall from the section "Symptoms Versus Causes" above Willard's 1986 letter to Trevor Hudson expressing skepticism that programs and political reforms could overcome apartheid. Years later, Hudson observes, "Disorganized good offers weak opposition to organized evil. Personal concerns for good, if they are going to effectively counter institutional evil, must be corporately organized for creative action." Writing in the context of his church's struggle against apartheid in South Africa, Hudson goes on to emphasize the need for communally organized intercession, organized protest, and organized resistance. Trevor Hudson, *Christ-Following: Ten Signposts to Spirituality* (Revell, 1996), 200-201.

words, he overestimates the potential of mere individuals, no matter how exemplarily, to affect direct change on a broad sociocultural level. Community is needed as the go-between, for individuals must be organized and act together to make a dent in the public realm. Otherwise, the chasm between the individual and the society is simply too vast. This is true even if, in addition to exemplary individuals, there are exceptional leaders in the professions. In the two-level reconstruction of Willard's thought, these leaders form the bridge to the larger societal realm. In his view they are, through their management of complex institutions for the public good, our best hope for piercing the Zeitgeist. But he neglects to give enough attention to the collective base needed for leaders and professionals to work from to steward change within the expert systems of modernity. In contrast, sociologist James Davison Hunter contends that significant social change happens not merely through professionals but *networks* of professionals and *communities* that support them. A central tenet of his social theory in To Change the World (2010) is that culture is generated and changed within well-developed networks of elites working near or within institutions, in opposition to the view that history and culture are the result of the "great man," that is, individual genius.[79]

Perhaps we may say it like this: God's own mission essentially takes a communal effort. Redemption and restoration are not the activity of an individual but an entity working in one accord, though each individual has their own role/expertise/function toward the goal. Societal change requires individuals who "will (the same) one thing" and become in essence a single entity working toward that one thing.[80] It is telling, I

---

[79]"Against individualism, which influences us to view the autonomous and rational individual—even if a genius—as the key actor in social change, we now see the power of networks and the new institutions that they create, and the communities that surround them that make the difference." James Davison Hunter, To Change the World: The Irony, Tragedy, and Possibility of Christianity in the Late Modern World (Oxford University Press), 44-45. Following contemporary social analysis, Hunter uses the term *elites* in a nonevaluative manner to connote a powerful minority affecting the public sphere, rather than in the classical sense of superiority ("the cream of the crop").

[80]An intentional riff on Søren Kierkegaard's definition of purity of heart as "to will one thing."

might add, that Jesus himself came from a community and became a leader who formed a community intending to change the world.

Second, Willard's strategy is thin due to its exclusion of an essential mechanism for how the virtuous life is cultivated in persons. Plausibility structures, as social realities, work on the communal level, and plausibility structures are needed to sustain belief and practice. When structural evils, even in their more subtle forms, have a hold on society, meaning they are broadly accepted and practiced as normative, those who would resist and live differently must have the socio-structural support to do so. Again, community is needed—this time as the social fabric that holds together patterns of belief and practice and nurtures civic virtues among those who will work toward transforming our most serious social issues. Willard does not underestimate the way culture (the amalgam of community, institutions, and traditions) shapes and habituates us. But he does seem to underestimate what is needed for individuals to resist this (mal)formation in a given culture. Individuals cannot overcome cultural forces without some cultural forces of their own; as the saying goes, fight fire with fire. The communal layer does at times factor into his strategy, but mainly only in terms of instructing and guiding individuals.[81] There is little ontological weightiness given to community outside this function.[82]

Something that is *personal* can be either *individual* or *communal*. This means Willard's commitment to personal experience, personal change, and so on does not fully account for his tendency to think of the individual before the community. However, his commitment to

---

[81] It bears repeating that Willard places significant emphasis on the role and responsibility of the "institutions of knowledge" in our society, i.e., higher education and its university system (as well as research centers, academic journals, professional associations, etc.), to impart moral knowledge in the public sphere. Yet a large part of his thesis on how Western society lost moral knowledge has to do with universities abdicating this responsibility, and he is not optimistic that they will return to and reclaim this role. See Willard, *Disappearance of Moral Knowledge*, 377; cf. Dallas Willard, "Moral Rights, Moral Responsibility, and the Contemporary Failure of Moral Knowledge," in *Guantanamo Bay and the Judicial-Moral Treatment of the Other*, ed. Clark Butler (Purdue University Press, 2007), 161-78.

[82] What meaning Willard does ascribe to community, especially the *ekklēsia*, will be dealt with in the next chapter.

the personal (as well as the practical) is why he begins with individual change rather than societal change—because he views sociocultural structures as impersonal realities. Community is the missing link here, for it can be personal *and* efficacious on the societal (impersonal) level.

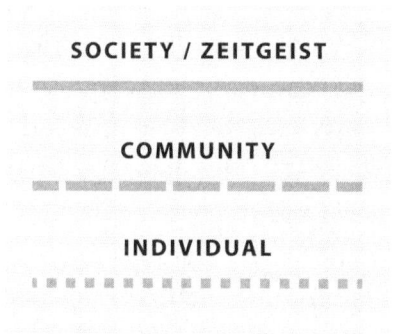

Figure 8.2. Community as the intermediary layer between society and individual

Considering this amendment to his model (see fig. 8.2), I should mention a 2002 essay by Willard on how the moral foundations of rationality might be restored in modern culture at large and in the modern university in particular, since he explicitly states that the solution we must seek is *community*. The majority of the essay is quite technical as he describes reason and the reasonable person (one who lives the life of reason); the intricate relationships between truth and logic on the one hand, and reasonableness and moral goodness on the other; and the process by which universities shifted their focus from knowledge to research (information) and, accordingly, implemented new methods or logics that depart from rational method and sound reasoning. With the descriptive and diagnostic out of the way, he then attempts to respond to one mounting question. If reason and logic are to survive as living, social practices, they must rest on a foundation of moral character; yet the cultivation of such moral character rests on an accessible body of moral knowledge, and there is no recognized body of moral knowledge in our culture today.[83] So how can moral knowledge as a body become accessible to the public?

---

[83]The statement "yet the cultivation of such moral character rests on an accessible body of moral knowledge" needs to be qualified. Willard's view of the importance of knowledge to life in general often goes like this: While there are ways to do things without knowledge, broadly speaking things go better with knowledge than without knowledge. The same applies to moral character formation and to public moral knowledge (see *Disappearance of Moral Knowledge*, 3-4, for

Quoting the last lines of MacIntyre's *After Virtue* about awaiting another St. Benedict, Willard admits he has never fully known what MacIntyre intends by this statement, but he interprets it to mean "that community must come, somehow, *before* virtue, and subsequently provide the support for rationality and the life of reason, among other things." He then adds, "The details are far from clear to me, but I think something like the development of a community of moral understanding in the Christian tradition must be the answer to our current situation."[84] In other words, given our cultural moment, the only thing capable of nurturing the moral identity that makes the life of reason possible is community that provides the social structure for moral knowledge to serve as a foundation and guide for life. Does this neutralize or perhaps even refute my critique that community is the missing link in Willard's model? At first blush it would appear so. However, I think there are a few reasons why his proposal in this essay does not significantly move the needle away from virtuous individuals and toward communities of character as the focus and centerpiece of his social architecture.

First, the type of community he has in mind here is *not* the local church or even a more general sense of shared life among apprentices of Jesus but is more of an intellectual think tank of leaders, a community of "professionals, academics and intellectuals" devoted to restoring moral knowledge to our academic culture.[85] He does think the Christian tradition offers the best resources for this community and that it likely

---

Willard's analogy between moral life/moral knowledge and electricity/knowledge of how electricity works). Cases of this are widespread: A child develops the virtue of honesty without knowing that honesty is a virtue and despite a social context in which honesty is not presented as a virtue. Such a child would, Willard thinks, do better with moral knowledge himself and with a social context of moral knowledge, but it is not necessary. Furthermore—and here is where the electricity analogy breaks down—due to God's grace, the Spirit's formative work still exists *and* has effects even if we do not have knowledge of it. So, the cultivation of moral character ultimately rests on an accessible body of moral knowledge, but God condescends to our epistemic weakness, i.e., the Spirit works even when we are ignorant.

[84]Dallas Willard, "How Reason Can Survive the Modern University: The Moral Foundations of Rationality," in *Faith, Scholarship, and Culture in the 21st Century*, ed. Alice Ramos and Marie I. George (Catholic University of America Press, 2002), 190-91.

[85]Willard, "How Reason Can Survive," 191.

will be a product of the capital "C" church, but the church itself (whether capital "C" or lowercase "c") is not in view. Second, his concern here is not with the rectification of social structures per se but with, very specifically, the restoration of moral knowledge in society.[86] The two are obviously connected in his thought, but they are not identical. He is not positing, therefore, that community is the only way virtuous individuals are formed or that it is the primary intermediary between the two levels of the social order. Third, his argument here is two pages long, and it differs from the more detailed proposals he makes elsewhere—whether society as a whole is in view or just the institutions of moral knowledge—such as in *Spirit of the Disciplines* and *Disappearance of Moral Knowledge*. I am not aware of other places where he supports the claim that "community must come, somehow, *before* virtue." And here he only tentatively supports this claim. It would appear, then, that this is a molehill compared to the mountain of his focus on individual transformation. Even with this suggestive essay serving as an appendix to our overall analysis of his social theory, the communal remains 1B in his model, always subservient to the 1A of individual actors.

FAITHFUL PRESENCE, FIRST AND FOREMOST

Willard is right to insist that personal transformation must precede societal transformation since impersonal realities are always at the mercy of personal ones. The degree of personal transformation required will depend upon the area of social life and the goal in mind. For example, poverty reduction or justice may not require explicitly Christian character formation, but it will require some level of benevolent character formation so that enough persons will value and work for these goods in a given society. Moreover, it will require some level of benevolent character formation in *leaders*.[87]

---

[86]As it is in *Disappearance of Moral Knowledge*, which I have noted. This differs, then, from Willard's focus in other works, namely, *Spirit of the Disciplines*, *Renovation of the Heart*, and (with Cochran) "Kingdom of God, Law," among others.

[87]Plato's *Republic* is clearly a starting point for Willard on both these points. But he also sees the limits of Plato's proposal, namely that Plato and the Greeks could not surmount the problem of

Additionally, there is something to his conviction that the larger social level is too abstract to engage with and transform directly. Especially in late modernity, the complex institutions we live within and the expert systems they depend on make it nearly impossible for citizens of a society to really change the fabric of the sociocultural order. Since leaders within the professions are responsible for the direction and management of institutions, and these institutions form us in profound ways, Willard's concern for leaders and the shape of their moral lives is an incisive and important part of his social theory. Nevertheless, his proposal that the formation of virtuous individuals is the way to affect societal change is in the final analysis too lean by itself, even if these individuals are leaders within the professions. It fails to recognize that mere individuals working for the common good, whether from the center or the periphery of institutions, are inadequate to bring about substantial change on the larger social level, nor does it recognize the extent to which these individuals remain vulnerable to the reigning plausibility structures in a given society. What is needed is a more formidable understanding of the role of community, as an organized body with virtue-forming potential, as an intermediary layer situated between the societal and individual levels, through which social issues are effectively engaged.[88]

Willard's formation theory would also benefit from a more substantive theology of the "powers."[89] The biblical, especially Pauline, concept of principalities and powers (Eph 6; Col 1–2; 1 Pet 3) refers to sociostructural and spiritual realities originally created good but now fallen and often oppressive—forces that must be resisted and can ultimately be

---

how to best achieve the character formation they upheld as the ideal (see Willard, *Knowing Christ Today*, 53). As for whether the theological virtues (faith, hope, and love) can be formed in non-Christians, see Willard, "Faith, Hope and Love," 17-20.

[88]For a somewhat similar framing of community as the intermediary between individual and societal interests, see Wendell Berry's essay "Sex, Economy, Freedom, and Community," in *Sex, Economy, Freedom & Community* (Pantheon, 1992), 117-73.

[89]Such as that found in Hendrik Berkhof, *Christ and the Powers* (Herald, 1962); Walter Wink's *Naming the Powers* (Fortress, 1984), the first in his trilogy; and Marva Dawn, *Powers, Weakness, and the Tabernacling of God* (Eerdmans, 2001).

redeemed. Willard acknowledges the powers from time to time but does not think naming and engaging them is of first importance for spiritual formation and for our partnership with God in the divine conspiracy. On the whole, he takes a more individualist, Screwtape-like view of demonic involvement that pays secondary attention to how cultural forms of oppression and distortion are guided or strengthened by the demonic. He sees the world, the flesh, and the devil (Eph 2:1-3) as separate realities that interrelate and get entangled within individual and corporate life but thinks they can most often be clearly distinguished and, importantly, that it is the flesh and the world that are the main culprit for humanity's struggles.[90] I should add that Willard is hardly alone on this; an underdeveloped theology of the powers is characteristic of the spiritual formation movement in general. Thus, a more thorough biblical understanding of this dynamic could go a long way if integrated into an approach to Christian spiritual formation.

In spite of this critique of the social architecture in Willard's theory of formation, I do not want to portray his thinking in this area as simplistic. It is anything but. The introduction and final chapter of *Disappearance of Moral Knowledge* and the syllabus from his Professions course at USC alone prove there is much more scaffolding behind his conclusions than I presented in this limited space. Yet I believe I have sufficiently outlined the contours of his basic position and have paid close attention to his philosophical works in this area. I mention this latter point because much of the nuance in his position (e.g., the role of institutions, the emphasis on professions) is found in his philosophical rather than theological reflections.[91] So, while my treatment is not comprehensive, it is representative of the whole, including the fine print.

---

[90]Dallas Willard, "Bringing the Kingdom into Our Life" (August 12, 1993), MP3, starting at 58:30, esp. 59:00. For a more balanced treatment of the "trinity of evil" and of the interconnectedness of its members, see Willard, "The Gospel of the Kingdom and Spiritual Formation," in *The Kingdom Life*, ed. Alan Andrews (NavPress, 2010), 47-48.

[91]His philosophical work was intended for a very different audience from his theological work, namely, for professional philosophers and philosophy majors in college. It is understandable, therefore, that we would find more nuance there. But despite his attempt to make his theological

Lastly, having earlier noted the dissonance between Willard's social theory and James Davison Hunter's, I should mention that their proposals for social change, at least where they begin, are strikingly similar. This is significant since one might assume Willard would be implicated in Hunter's critique of the individualist "hearts and minds" position held by many evangelicals, a position he, Hunter, summarizes as "cultures change when people change."[92] Both men recognize the tremendous power cultural institutions have in shaping people's values and views of reality (their hearts and minds) and the vital role that professionals/elites play in producing cultural capital (albeit Hunter is alone in stressing the need for networks and communities here), yet they both emphasize the need for *individual Christians* to simply attend faithfully to what is in front of them—to practice "faithful presence," as Hunter says—rather than set out to change culture or society per se. Recall Willard's concern that to jump over one's immediate context for the sake of larger goods is to avoid becoming a good person. Good persons act from where they are located; to reach beyond is to avoid the responsibilities in front of oneself. This point is where their approaches especially harmonize:

> I would suggest that a theology of faithful presence *first* calls Christians to attend to the people and places that they experience directly.... The call of faithful presence gives priority to what is right in front of us—the community, the neighborhood, and the city, and the people of which these are constituted. For most, this will mean a preference for stability, locality, and particularity of place and its needs. It is here, through the joys, sufferings, hopes, disappointments, concerns, desires, and worries of the people with whom we are in long-term and close relation—family, neighbors, coworkers, and community—where we find our authenticity as a body and as believers. It is here where we learn forgiveness and humility, practice kindness, hospitality, and charity, grow in

---

books more accessible to a lay audience, they are certainly not dumbed down. I submit, then, that the differing audiences do not fully account for this discrepancy.

[92]Hunter, *To Change the World*, 16.

patience and wisdom, and become clothed in compassion, gentleness, and joy. This is the crucible within which Christian holiness is forged. This is the context within which shalom is enacted.[93]

These are Hunter's words, though they could have easily been written by Willard.[94]

Once there is clarity on how God's redemptive purposes for the world unfold, the next question becomes: What is the church's role in this? Could Willard's lack of emphasis on community be that he does not see the visible church in its current form as being much help in this? Or could it be that, in his view, the *ekklēsia* is a unique communal reality and thus should be thought of quite differently from other human communities? This analysis of Willard's understanding of the relation of spiritual formation to individual and societal change therefore necessarily leads to discussion of his ecclesiology, the next area of his theology to be explored.

---

[93] Hunter, *To Change the World*, 253.

[94] Where their proposals eventually diverge beckons back to the differences in their social theories at large, for Hunter goes on to stress that the "institutional aspect to faithful presence" entails forming networks and mobilizing resources among leaders (see *To Change the World*, 270-71).

NINE

THE CHURCH AS A DIVINE SOCIALITY AND SCHOOL OF LIFE

CONSIDERING WHAT I HAVE JUST SAID about Willard's view of community, it may come as a surprise that Willard develops a dynamic ecclesiology that continually comes through in his writings and lectures. It is by no means systematic, however; his doctrine of the church is mostly implicit and tacit. When he does speak about the church, it is generally to stress how local churches (and by extension their pastors) are called to pursue spiritual formation above all else and how the gospel proclaimed there must naturally lead to this outcome. Unsurprisingly, his intended audience on these occasions is pastors and church leaders rather than theologians. Since a full examination of his ecclesiology is outside the purview of this book, in the present chapter I attempt to make explicit what is implicit—namely, his core ecclesiological convictions—while analyzing the church's place in his overall theory of spiritual formation.

EVANGELICAL, ECLECTIC, AND ECUMENICAL

At its most basic level, Willard's ecclesiology derives from a congregationalist model in which the church is a loose association of those who profess Jesus as Lord. Membership in this visible community is based on an individual's personal choice and confession of faith. The invisibility of the true church is simply accepted as fact, since only

God knows the depths of the human heart/spirit/will.[1] All of this is fairly in line with the evangelical, Baptist, and free-church circles that nurtured his faith early on and as a young minister. However, other aspects of his ecclesiology are not as easily categorized or directly tied to this tradition, for, similar to what is found elsewhere in his theology, Willard's doctrine of the church has an eclectic streak.

For instance, Willard considers the local church the people of God in a given area; what are commonly thought of as churches or congregations, he sees instead as *assemblies* or *manifestations* of the *one* local church.[2] This gives his ecclesiology a distinct ecumenical style—not just in theory but also in practice, as he counted his own church membership to be among *all* the churches in the region of Southern California where he lived.[3] It follows that the division typical between churches (assemblies) in an area is, he holds, a serious ecclesiological and missiological problem. Such disunity shows blatant disregard for Jesus' prayer that we be one for the sake of our witness (Jn 17) and means the body of Christ presently lives "in an unintentionally schismatic condition," standing in contradiction to God's objective of bringing forth a people who live in deep harmony with him and one another.[4] This problematic may be overcome only by recommitting ourselves to the church's essential calling, which is

---

[1] Dallas Willard, "Local Congregations as Schools of Discipleship" (March 31, 2007), MP3, 2:45.

[2] Willard describes three different meanings for the word *ekklēsia* in the New Testament. These are (1) a single congregation, such as a church in someone's house; (2) all the Christians in a certain city or area, such as the church in Corinth; and (3) the cosmic or invisible church that extends through time and space. Dallas Willard, "The New Testament Theology of the Church" (June 19, 2005), video, starting at 20:15. But he adds that the second meaning—all the people of Christ in a given area—"probably . . . is the closest meaning of the New Testament concept of the local church" (21:30). See also Willard, "The Purpose and Problems of the Church Today" (August 7, 1993), MP3, 1:30.

[3] Perhaps this sounds like standard evangelical ecclesiology, in which the church as an institution is relativized on account of the invisibility of the true church. No doubt, the heavenly citizenship and invisibility of the church are a major theme of Willard's, but his view also contains a certain ecumenism that is not typical among Protestants, let alone evangelicals. For example, he often said the *most* important spiritual discipline for pastors is to pray for the success of the other churches in their area (Willard, "New Testament Theology of the Church," 27:00–28:00).

[4] Willard, "New Testament Theology of the Church," 19:15; cf. 23:00.

itself grounded in the church's essential nature. "In a sense," says Willard, "we have to bring the *church* back to the *churches*."[5] So what exactly is the church's essential nature and calling?

DYNAMIC TENSION

At the center of Willard's ecclesiology is a twofold dynamic of the church as a sociality of divine presence and an academy for transformative discipleship in the way of Jesus. Other images for the church are employed—such as a spiritual hospital or a beachhead of the kingdom[6]—but none are as important to his formational theology as divine sociality and "school of life." The first is ontological, the other functional; together they form a dynamic tension. Each will be treated in turn, before analyzing their inherent interrelatedness to one another.

Sociality of the trinitarian reality. The church is the sociality of the trinitarian presence from which divine power flows.[7] A key biblical text for Willard in this regard is Jesus' words in Matthew 28:19 and, more specifically, the second clause of the passage, that disciples from the nations are to be baptized in the name of the Father and the Son and the Holy Spirit. Willard contends that the *name*, biblically speaking, is the reality of the thing named.[8] And to be *baptized* in or into something is to be surrounded by or immersed in that something.[9] For instance, when Paul speaks of those who were "baptized into Moses" (1 Cor 10:2), he is referring to how the Israelites, upon leaving Egypt, were surrounded by the presence of Yahweh

---

[5] Dallas Willard, "Our Current Situation and the Four Great Questions of Life" (July 25, 2000), MP3, 48:00.

[6] Spiritual hospital: Dallas Willard, *Renovation of the Heart: Putting On the Character of Christ* (NavPress, 2002), 234. Beachhead of the kingdom: Willard, introduction to *The Great Omission: Reclaiming Jesus' Essential Teachings on Discipleship* (HarperSanFrancisco, 2006), xiii.

[7] How sociality is being defined here will become clearer as Willard's position is explicated.

[8] Willard, *Renovation of the Heart*, 267n4.

[9] Dallas Willard, "The Heavens Were Opened" (1987), MP3, 32:00. Willard makes no distinction between being baptized "in" versus "into" something.

that had accompanied Moses.¹⁰ Thus to be *baptized in the name of the Father, the Son, and the Spirit* is to be immersed in the trinitarian reality and presence.¹¹

Willard affirms the ecclesial practice of water baptism as a sign of regeneration for those who have made a decision to follow Jesus, yet he interprets the baptismal charge in the Great Commission as categorically different, pointing to a broader, ongoing immersion into the kingdom life.¹² This sort of submersion is not a one-time event but a continuing "engulfment" in the Spirit of God, made possible by Pentecost, that forms the basis of the with-God life.¹³ Water baptism, then, is a rite marking one's entry into this reality.¹⁴ But how does one *actually* enter and experience this reality? Through immersion in the church, the social embodiment of God's presence on earth. To be baptized "in the name of Jesus means to be surrounded by the community of his people, which he inhabits," for the trinitarian presence is the very "atmosphere" of the church gathered.¹⁵

---

¹⁰Dallas Willard, "Being Kingdom People in the Character and Power of Jesus" (August 2, 2000), MP3, 12:00; cf. Willard, "Baptisms" (1987), MP3, starting at 15:00.

¹¹Dallas Willard, "The Current Captivity of the Church" (July 26, 1974), MP3, 27:45. See also Willard, "The Failure of Evangelical Political Involvement," in *God and Governing: Reflections on Ethics, Virtue, and Statesmanship*, ed. Roger N. Overton (Pickwick, 2009), 90.

¹²He seems to have developed this view of the Great Commission in his later years. For instance, it does not appear in two 1987 sermons on baptism, which are his most detailed treatment of the subject. Yet he does state in these sermons, "The primary baptism is simply the engulfing of the people of God in the presence of God" (Willard, "Baptisms," 33:30), and "Christian baptism is a matter of being engulfed by the Spirit of God, which is chiefly identified through the presence of God's people, and the presence of God's people carries with it the Spirit of God into which we are to be baptized" (Willard, "Heavens Were Opened," 32:15). In a 2000 lecture he reflects on his early view of the Matthean passage: "I was raised a Baptist, and . . . really all we knew was when you got 'em wet you said, 'In the name of the Father and Son and Holy Spirit.' It took me some time to understand that this does not just refer to what we call baptism. This is not a ritual, [but] a ritual might serve as a nodal point in accomplishing what this says" (Willard, "Our Current Situation," 34:00).

¹³Dallas Willard, *The Divine Conspiracy: Rediscovering Our Hidden Life in God* (HarperSanFrancisco, 1998), 278-288.

¹⁴Willard, *Renovation of the Heart*, 267n4.

¹⁵Willard, "Being Kingdom People," 12:45; Dallas Willard, "How to Establish and Lead a Community of Jesus' Disciples in a Congregation of Spiritual Formation in Christlikeness" (May 24, 2006), MP3, 25:30.

Humans were made to be inhabited by God, Willard maintains, and until that inhabiting takes place, they are incomplete.[16] To be *inhabited by* means, in this context, to *live intimately with*. Since the beginning of creation it has been God's intention to dwell with human persons—to live in close proximity and co-labor with them. Willard sees this as a key principle running throughout the biblical account.[17] This principle accelerates after Christ's ascension, as his disciples become "a dwelling in which God lives by his Spirit" (Eph 2:22), and will reach its complete fulfillment when Christ returns at the close of human history: "Now the dwelling of God is with human beings, and he will live with them" (Rev 21:3 NIVi). Yet no one person is ontologically capable of holding the full presence of the triune God; persons must come together for the Trinity to live in them, for God inhabits his people *communally*.[18] This is again by God's design, since human personhood is innately social, modeled after the trinitarian life of Father, Son, and Spirit.[19] Therefore the Trinity cannot fill a person, only a people. As Willard explains in an early teaching on the book of Acts,

> There is no individual which is large enough to receive the Spirit of God by himself. It's true that some people have unusual blessings, but these are always limited, and [if] you find a person like that, you will not find the kind of thing which happened in the book of Acts. It

---

[16] Willard, "Being Kingdom People," 16:45.

[17] Willard, *Renovation of the Heart*, 246. See also "A General Introduction" in *The Renovaré Spiritual Formation Bible*, ed. Richard J. Foster et al. (HarperSanFrancisco, 2005), xxvii-xxviii. While the introduction was the result of an editorial team, Willard was the primary drafter for the section titled "Catching the Vision."

[18] Willard, "New Testament Theology of the Church," 9:45.

[19] An example of bad grammar but good theology is when Willard writes, "Some people wonder what God was doing before He created the world—as if He didn't have anything to do. I often get asked that question on college campuses. I always reply, 'He was enjoying themselves.'" Dallas Willard, "The Gospel of the Kingdom and Spiritual Formation," in *The Kingdom Life*, ed. Alan Andrews (NavPress, 2010), 38. Elsewhere he describes the Trinity as "a glorious company, a loving society of three persons so united, so together in love and understanding and knowledge and in enjoyment of one another, that they're in fact inseparable." Willard, "Morning Session" (August 4, 1987), MP3, 1:05:00.

requires a group of people. We are social beings, whether we like it or not. . . .

"In whom the whole building, fitly framed together groweth up into a holy temple in the Lord. In whom ye also are framed, are fitted, are buildeth together for inhabitation of God through the Spirit" [Eph 2:21-22 KJV]. God does not indwell us individually. He indwells us together—and until we learn this and live according to it, we are simply frustrating the grace of God.[20]

Despite his enduring emphasis on one's *personal relationship* with God, something indispensable in his model of formation, Willard thinks this can and has been taken too far in some quarters of evangelical Christianity, such that one's *communal relationship* with God is seen as inconsequential. In a 2001 interview he remarks, "In our notions of evangelism today, being converted has nothing to do with community; it just has to do with your 'personal relationship' with God."[21] This is further illuminated by a 1973 seminar handout in which he addresses the importance of social relationality in the New Testament church. Following a list of biblical passages on "the life of God in the group committed to him," the handout reads:

The Principle involved:

That *many* individuals are required to sustain and communicate the person of God, because God is love—a love which cannot be known by *statement* or by *talk about it*, but only by its *presence* in the midst of flesh and blood human beings.[22]

What is the church, then, at its most fundamental level? It is a people inhabited by God's manifest presence. Willard states, "Metaphysically

---

[20]Dallas Willard, "The New Community of God Reaches Out in Power to the Old Jewish Community" (December 5, 1971), MP3, 21:45.

[21]Dallas Willard, "Rethinking Evangelism," *Cutting Edge* (Winter 2001): 11.

[22]Dallas Willard, "Justification of Faith by Experience" (handout, 1973), Dallas Willard Collection, 5. See also the handout from a seminar held a year earlier on the topic of forgiveness within the body of Christ, which contains this line: "The kingdom of God is *above all* a life together with other human beings, with and in God the Divine Center." Willard, "Jesus' Good News of God's Kingdom" (handout, June 18–September 10, 1972), Dallas Willard Collection, 12.

and theologically God is present everywhere, but the *manifest presence of God is his gift to his people*," and "The presence of God in the midst is the only sure mark of the true *ecclesia*."[23] If spirit is unbodily personal power, and God is ontologically pure spirit, then the manifest presence of God is replete with divine power. And when that manifest presence dwells among a people, there is limitless power to redeem and transform human lives.[24] This power is experienced, in phenomenological terms, not through spatial proximity but social relationality. That is to say, the power that emanates from the manifest presence of the Trinity resides in the social relations of God's people. As the sociality of the trinitarian presence, the church is a communal body/substance pulsating with divine power and the completion of God's intent for creation.

Excursus: The Influence of Dietrich Bonhoeffer's *Sanctorum Communio*

It is here that the influence of Bonhoeffer's doctoral dissertation-turned-tome, *Sanctorum Communio*, should be briefly discussed.[25] While describing the social dimension of personhood in *Renovation of the Heart*, and specifically how the human person exists only in relation to others, Willard adds the following footnote: "On this point nothing more helpful has been written than Dietrich Bonhoeffer's excellent study of the texture of the church, *The Communion of Saints: A Dogmatic Inquiry into the Sociology of the Church*

---

[23]Willard, "Local Congregations as Schools of Discipleship," 46:45; Willard, *Renovation of the Heart*, 245.

[24]To illustrate the *negative* consequences of this, Willard suggests Ananias and Sapphira *died of church* in the book of Acts: "The current of God's reality was flowing around them so mightily that when they got crosswise of it, it killed them." A further illustration is Paul's words in 1 Cor 11:30 about "people dying of the Lord's Supper" (Willard, "Being Kingdom People," 40:45, 41:45). Elsewhere he says, "Because the presence of God is upon that community, you'd better be careful about taking the Lord's Supper because you are apt to bite into a five-thousand-volt line that will do you in" (Willard, "Baptisms," 9:00). Cf. also Willard, *Renovation of the Heart*, 267n4.

[25]Bonhoeffer defended his dissertation in 1927, then revised and published it in 1930. I will primarily discuss and cite the revised version, *Sanctorum Communio* (Fortress, 1998); the dissertation version is cited as SC-A.

(New York: Harper & Row, 1963), especially chap. 2."[26] Willard returns twice more to *Sanctorum Communio* in later chapters, quoting specific passages to illuminate how sin isolates one from community and turns the self in on itself, and then to argue for the spiritual unity of the invisible church.[27] I note these later references simply to show that his praise in the footnote is not hyperbolic.

Although Willard's note there is brief, I posit it is key to understanding his view of the church as the sociality of the trinitarian reality. If one compares Willard's personalist approach to ecclesiology side by side with *Sanctorum Communio*, Bonhoeffer's influence is apparent.[28] This influence is in fact one reason I am using the language of *sociality*, a crucial term for the German theologian, to describe this dynamic in Willard's ecclesiology. By using this term, I may risk sounding overly technical or pseudo-scientific since it is not a theological word or even a common sociological word. In spite of this, I deem the risk worthwhile since it connects Willard's implicit ecclesiology with Bonhoeffer's explicit one and communicates how the church is, in Willard's view, simultaneously a fully human community and a reality of the trinitarian presence.[29]

---

[26] Willard, *Renovation of the Heart*, 258n2.

[27] Willard, *Renovation of the Heart*, 57, 186.

[28] Speaking of this in terms of influence implies Bonhoeffer's book shaped the *development* of Willard's thought, but this may be an inaccurate designation since it is unknown when Willard first read *Sanctorum Communio* and thus what role it played in shaping his ecclesiology. There are reasons to think he read the book quite late, in either the 1990s or early 2000s. We find this enthusiastic note in *Renovation of the Heart* (2002), but if he had read the book earlier, it likely would have appeared in prior works, such as *The Spirit of the Disciplines* (1988). If we accept a late date, then I surmise Willard had been teaching his immersion theology of the church for some time and then read *Sanctorum Communio*, which confirmed his convictions in a roundabout way through Bonhoeffer's quite sophisticated argument. Yet if this were the case, I am surprised he did not start assigning the book in his annual DMin Fuller class or mention it in later lectures (2002 and beyond) on the nature of the church. Willard's personal copy, now stored at Westmont College, is the 1963 English edition rather than the more respectable 1998 English edition, and it is heavily annotated—something characteristic of his pre-1990 years when he had more time to study. So, he may have read it earlier but never repeated his praise of it, perhaps because of the tension he felt between his ontological view of the church and his fear of ecclesiocentrism—which I'll return to later—or simply because he was not in the habit of recommending texts to his churchy audiences that are notoriously difficult to understand, which *Sanctorum Communio* certainly is.

[29] Akin to Bonhoeffer's twofold claim that the church "is simultaneously a historical community and one established by God" (*Sanctorum Communio*, 126).

It would be a misnomer, however, to say their views on the social ontology of the church are identical.[30] Bonhoeffer's usage of *sociality* is conceptually complex, involving particular views of personhood, community, and social relations, drawn from theological analyses of sociology and social philosophy.[31] Nevertheless, both Bonhoeffer and Willard contend (1) the human person is made for personal-social existence in community with God and other human beings; (2) sin has deeply ruptured this social integrity between humans and God and between humans themselves; but (3) in Christ, God has restored this integrity in the distinct sociological reality that is both Christ's body in the world and the sociality where God and humanity live in communion, the church.[32] One would likely not find much divergence from these first two points among orthodox theologians, but the third is more atypical. From the viewpoint of these two men, the church is "Christ existing as church-community"[33] and "the continuing incarnation of Christ."[34]

Willard does not work out the full ecclesiological implications of this, certainly not to the extent that Bonhoeffer did, considering some have argued that sociality serves as the programmatic scheme for the latter's theology.[35] Yet Willard's references to *Sanctorum Communio*, albeit sparse, prove to be valuable for reconstructing his position and

---

[30]One notable difference, at least in respect to the early Bonhoeffer (*Sanctorum Communio*), is Willard's method of beginning first with God as person, rather than humans—hence, the church is a sociality of *trinitarian presence* instead of a human sociality, as Bonhoeffer refers to it.

[31]For an in-depth analysis of sociality in *Sanctorum Communio* and Bonhoeffer's social theology, see Clifford J. Green, *Bonhoeffer: A Theology of Sociality*, rev. ed. (Eerdmans, 1999).

[32]Willard's three citations of *Sanctorum Communio* in *Renovation of the Heart* correlate, respectively, with these three points. For Bonhoeffer's discussion of the church as a distinct sociological reality, see *Sanctorum Communio*, 252-67.

[33]Bonhoeffer, *Sanctorum Communio*, 141.

[34]Dallas Willard, letter to Roy M. Carlisle of Harper & Row (concerning *The Spirit of the Disciplines*), November 15, 1981, Dallas Willard Collection. See also Willard, "The Acts of the Apostles and the Kingdom of God" (1974), MP3, 46:00; Willard, *Divine Conspiracy*, 336; Willard, *Renovation of the Heart*, 37.

[35]As Bonhoeffer writes in the preface to his original version of the dissertation (from 1927), his aim is "to show that an inherently Christian social philosophy and sociology, arising essentially out of fundamental concepts of Christian theology, is most fully articulated in the concept of the church" (*Sanctorum Communio*, SC-A, 22).

interpreting what he says elsewhere about the ontological nature of the church.[36] In Willard's ecclesiology, God's manifest presence and transformative power are described in a theological phenomenology of sociality.[37]

"School of life." The second dynamic of Willard's ecclesiology is the church as an academy, a place of teaching and training, that prepares disciples of Jesus to live out their vocation before a watching world. If the image of a sociality of the trinitarian presence has to do with the church's essential *nature*, then this image of a school of life concerns its essential *function*. This implies the church's primary calling is pedagogical and focused on forming mature Christians who resemble their Lord in all matters of life. Willard leaves little ambiguity here in his description of spiritual formation in Christ as "the exclusive primary goal of the local congregation."[38]

The imagery of an academy is most vivid in *Spirit of the Disciplines*, especially the last chapter, where Willard discusses what ministers should prioritize. In reference to Ephesians 4:12, he remarks that pastors have "something much more important to do than pursue the godless," since their main task is to "equip saints until they are like

---

[36] It should be noted that Willard also had a deep appreciation for Bonhoeffer's *Life Together*, a text he assigned in his seminary courses and cited frequently in talks. See his lengthy quotations from and engagement with this "indispensable book" in *Divine Conspiracy*, 236-37. One finds many more references to *Life Together* than to *Sanctorum Communio* in the Willardian corpus. Nevertheless, I submit the latter, with its sophisticated philosophical-theological method, with which Willard would have felt at home, was more influential for his ontological understanding of the church.

[37] Another topic worthy of research but cannot be pursued here is how Willard's recurring emphasis on the scriptural ministry of the laying on of hands relates to his ecclesiological conviction about the transformative power that flows through the church as the sociality of God's manifest presence. See, e.g., Dallas Willard, "Studies in the Book of Apostolic Acts" (handout, November 28, 1971–January 30, 1972), Dallas Willard Collection, 10-11; Willard, "Jewish Persecution Drives the New Community to the Gentiles" (December 19, 1971), MP3, 28:45; Willard, "The Best News You'll Ever Hear" (1986), MP3, 51:45; Willard, *The Spirit of the Disciplines: Understanding How God Changes Lives* (Harper & Row, 1988), 121-23; Willard, "Being Kingdom People," 29:45.

[38] Willard, *Renovation of the Heart*, 235.

Christ."[39] He goes on to explain what this amounts to for local congregations and their role in God's larger divine purpose.

> The local assembly, for its part, can then become an academy where people throng from the surrounding community to learn how to *live*. It will be a school of life (for a disciple is but a pupil, a student) where all aspects of that life seen in the New Testament records are practiced and mastered under those who have themselves mastered them through practice. Only by taking this as our immediate goal can we intend to carry out the Great Commission.[40]

Elsewhere he states that the *ekklēsia* "is intended to be a school of love,"[41] and the fellowship it offers with other disciples is both a means and an end of this formation: "When we gather 'in the name' of Jesus, we gather to love one another and to be loved, to serve one another and be served.... So when we 'go to church,' we go to love those who are there and to be loved with his *agape* love. But that love is not confined to when we are 'in church.' It is for everywhere in life. Church is for catching it and practicing it."[42]

Willard ends the aforementioned chapter in *Spirit of the Disciplines* by highlighting the monastic communities of St. Antony in the fourth century, quoting Athanasius's glowing description of them as "a multitude of ascetics, all with one set purpose—virtue."[43] There is hardly a better description of Willard's functional ecclesiology. The church is a community of students gathered in Jesus' name with the singular purpose of learning to live more deeply in God's kingdom—or, more

---

[39] Willard, *Spirit of the Disciplines*, 246.

[40] Willard, *Spirit of the Disciplines*, 247. Cf. "Our local assemblies must become academies of life as it was meant to be" (xii); "If we as Christ's people genuinely enter Christ's Way of the Heart, ... Christian assemblies will become what they have been in many periods of the past and what the world desperately calls for today: incomparable schools of life" (Willard, *Renovation of the Heart*, 25).

[41] Willard, "Failure of Evangelical Political Involvement," 78.

[42] Dallas Willard, *Knowing Christ Today: Why We Can Trust Spiritual Knowledge* (HarperOne, 2009), 157-58.

[43] Willard, *Spirit of the Disciplines*, 250.

precisely, *learning to become the sort of people* who live deeply in God's kingdom.

Willard laments this is not presently the case for much of the visible church, that it is rare to find a congregation that functions de facto as a school of life for apprentices of Jesus. In the next chapter I examine the historical and theological factors he thinks are to blame for this, at least within Protestantism. But here, I note how his conviction about the church as academy (i.e., his functional ecclesiology) connects to his view of church unity and the ecumenical thrust behind his work in spiritual formation. In numerous places he suggests that obedience to Christ is the "true ecumenism."[44] By this he means that true Christian unity results only when people from different backgrounds, traditions, and denominations commit to follow Jesus until they become like him. And we must not forget that for Willard, such *obedience, following*, and *becoming* takes place in the context of an ongoing, deeply interpersonal relationship with the triune God. In a 2009 interview, when asked whether he felt called to help bridge the divide between Protestants and Catholics, he replied that he did believe he had some role to play, adding,

> What I have found, when dealing with Catholics or Protestants, is that living the spiritual life is common ground. If you get into transubstantiation, consubstantiation—all those "stantiations"—that's the end of the discussion. But when you're talking about prayer, holiness, virtues, following Jesus, living the life—you're right on common ground. I've come to call obedience to Christ the true ecumenicity. Because that *is* the meeting place. And as long as people focus on that, there will be very few arguments.[45]

There will be no genuine ecumenicism—not among the various Protestant denominations, nor among the main ecclesial traditions

---

[44]E.g., Dallas Willard's interview with Luci Shaw, "Spiritual Disciplines in a Postmodern World," *Radix*, no. 3 (2000): 26; Willard, "Spiritual Formation in Christ: A Perspective on What It Is and How It Might Be Done," *Journal of Psychology and Theology* 28, no. 4 (2000): 257-58.

[45]Dallas Willard, interview with Patricia Hanlon, "The Man Behind the (Divine) Conspiracy: A Conversation with Dallas Willard," *Stillpoint* (Spring 2009): 9.

(Catholic, Orthodox, Protestant)—unless the many assemblies of the one, holy, catholic, and apostolic church regain an understanding of themselves as academies for kingdom living.

This understanding about the church's primary function is also the reason Willard places such emphasis on pastors as "teachers of the nations."[46] This designation indicates the pastor's unique role in the Great Commission, to make disciples of *all nations*, which Willard understands to mean people of *all kinds*. Although he especially has in mind *pastors* as those entrusted to lead congregations, he uses the term more broadly to include all Christian leaders and spokespeople for Christ. Since the church is an academy and school of life, pastors are primarily teachers tasked with educating and forming its members in the way of Jesus. All their ministerial duties—from preaching, baptizing, and administering communion to visitation, catechesis, counseling, and presiding over weddings and funerals—serve that one end. Thus, knowledge of how to live the way of Jesus, and of the foundational realities of God and his kingdom that undergird this knowledge, must be the minister's domain of specialty. One need not be an expert in this (is expertise even possible?) to be a teacher of the nations, yet Willard insists that competence in the pastorate demands firsthand knowledge of the truths of these realities.[47] In other words, pastors must be apprentices themselves who are steadily growing (even if slowly) in Christlikeness through relational discipleship to Jesus.

VESSEL WORSHIP = ECCLESIOCENTRISM

We should examine one last aspect of Willard's ecclesiology before turning to the implications of his view of the church for spiritual formation. Willard is suspicious of ecclesiocentrism, believing it is a case of misplacing the "vessel" for the "treasure." This theme of the vessel (or pot) versus the treasure, drawn from imagery in

---

[46]See, e.g., the chapter "Pastors as Teachers of the Nations," in Willard, *Knowing Christ Today*, 193-212. See also Dallas Willard, "Teaching the Teachers of the Nations" (printed lecture, January 2004), Dallas Willard Collection.

[47]Willard, *Knowing Christ Today*, 200.

2 Corinthians 4:6-7, continually surfaces in his work.[48] In the original context of the epistle, Willard explains, the apostle Paul applies the distinction of vessel/treasure to his physical body and the world's toil on it (vessel), and the renewed spirit within him that comes from the Spirit of Christ (treasure). One is temporary and decaying, the other eternal and sustaining. Willard suggests this same Pauline principle can and should be applied to our local churches and their larger denominations or traditions. These vessels, marked by human and cultural contingencies, are necessary. But all too often they eventually become the focal point and are thereby mistaken "for the treasure of the real presence of Christ in our midst."[49] The feeble vessel overwhelms the priceless treasure. Thus Willard: "Our various groups become over time nearly 100-percent vessel. That is, what they seem to regard as essential and what they devote almost all their attention and effort to, has to do with human, historical contingencies that have attached themselves to individuals brought up in a certain way."[50]

The surest sign a vessel has replaced the treasure is when the survival of the church or denomination becomes the predominant focus for the majority of the people involved. Willard goes so far as to say vessel worship is "a primary satanic strategy in defeating the cause of Christ on earth."[51] Historically, Satan's tactic here is one of distraction: Skew the vision, and the group will exist to perpetuate itself rather than to produce disciples who resemble Jesus. This is why Willard continually adds the qualifier *early* when speaking of past groups that, in his estimation, experienced profound individual and social transformation in Christ's name—the early church, early monastics, early

---

[48]For an early example (1974), see Willard, "Acts of the Apostles and the Kingdom of God," 46:15. For a much later example, see Dallas Willard, "What Does Holiness Look Like Shorn of Its Legalistic Expressions? 2" (January 4, 2010), video, 4:30.

[49]Willard, *Renovation of the Heart*, 237. Cf. Dallas Willard, "Church Communities" (July 14, 2004), video, 45:45: "The treasure is Christ living in the group."

[50]Willard, *Renovation of the Heart*, 237.

[51]To the following, Willard, *Renovation of the Heart*, 243-44; quotation on 243.

Quakers, early Methodists, to name a few—but at a certain point lost the plot and hence no longer seek formation in Christlikeness but conformity to a particular tradition. In light of this, Willard insists that a primary counterstrategy of God's people must be to sift out the merely human and historical contingencies from the enduring principles and absolutes of the New Testament church.

As previously mentioned, in his last decade or so Willard began adding a third "partial" gospel to the two he treats extensively in *Divine Conspiracy*. He refers to this as the gospel of "churchmanship," summarizing its message as, "You take care of your church and your church will take care of you."[52] The older form of this is expressed in the sacramental system of the Catholic Church, by which the sacraments administered by ordained priests in the church are treated as salvific.[53] However, Willard contends there is a newer, more Protestant form, in which belonging to the church or denomination with right doctrines or social ethics is treated as salvific.[54] The false gospel of churchmanship is the message that underlies vessel worship, as a nonessential is taken as an essential. But because it is also an improper dependence on the church as savior in a way it is not, the false gospel of churchmanship directs itself against the ontological dynamic of ecclesiology (not just the functional dynamic) in a way that the other two false gospels do not.

ECCLESIOLOGICAL DYNAMISM BETWEEN THE LINES

In Willard's twofold-dynamic ecclesiology, the second dynamic presupposes the first and builds on it as its basis. The power that flows from God's manifest presence (first dynamic) is the most potent ingredient for personal character change in the Christian life. The

---

[52]Willard, "Failure of Evangelical Political Involvement," 77.

[53]To this and the following, Willard, "What Does Holiness Look Like Shorn of Its Legalistic Expressions? 2," 45:00.

[54]In a sense, this newer form of the third gospel may be a variation of either of the first two distorted gospels: the gospel on the right (correct beliefs) and the gospel on the left (social activism). The difference is that here the accent is on *belonging to the right group*.

church cannot therefore effectively function as an academy for transformative discipleship (second dynamic) unless God dwells in the midst of a people. Similar to his theology of formation proper, in which the divine Spirit is the primary actor through and through, so it is with his account of the church proper: God is the first and real actor in Willard's ecclesiology.

This dual dynamism also denotes something of the divine/human agency involved in spiritual formation in the church. The first dynamic (sociality of trinitarian presence) is largely God's work in transforming the church through his presence and power. As such, it "is the single major component of the prospering of the local congregation" and completely dependent on *divine prerogative*.[55] The second dynamic concerns more the *human side* of the equation. The church as a training ground or gymnasium for kingdom living requires that congregants have a vision and intention for growth in godliness and that pastors teach the knowledge this growth requires. Such training "is clearly the main, ongoing function of the local congregation, so far as human effort is concerned."[56]

Willard's understanding of the ontological nature of the church as a sociality of the trinitarian presence (first dynamic) also delineates his ecclesiology from some Protestants who view the church more or less as an aggregate of regenerated believers, but who by themselves as individuals are "spiritually" complete. This version of ecclesiology amounts to little more than what Robert Bellah calls a "lifestyle enclave," a collective of like-minded individuals whose unity is formed around a shared interest, persuasion, or aim that is expressed in common practices.[57] For Willard, the divine Persons of the Trinity dwelling among a people is what most constitutes the church. As noted, this trinitarian presence is the "atmosphere" of the church

---

[55] Willard, *Renovation of the Heart*, 240.
[56] Willard, *Renovation of the Heart*, 240.
[57] Robert N. Bellah et al., *Habits of the Heart: Individualism and Commitment in American Life* (University of California Press, 1985), 72.

gathered.⁵⁸ Thus, what he lacks in a general ontology of community—what might be called a metaphysics of groups and which we surveyed in the previous chapter—he makes up for in his ontology of the church as the particular embodiment of community imbued with God's presence and power.

Furthermore, Willard's functional view of the church as an academy for discipleship (second dynamic) indicates how the people of God are transformed for godly living and witness, while avoiding the trappings of ecclesiocentrism, which turn the church into the sacrament of salvation, and the errors of "blueprint ecclesiologies"—abstractions of the church that ignore concrete reality.⁵⁹ There is a practicality to this dynamic of his ecclesiology that invites pastors and leaders to envision how their local congregations might become formational communities, centered upon the teachings of Jesus and the practices of the historical church.

Yet despite Willard having a dynamic ecclesiology, it remains in the background of his overall approach to spiritual formation. Similar to what we saw in the previous chapter, the individual comes before the community. In his earliest theology book,⁶⁰ he describes the church as "the glorious body of Christ, the living temple inhabited by God," stating that it is "the end and aim of all human history." But he immediately adds a caveat: "We must never forget, however, that the social and outward dimension of the church is not the whole—nor ultimately even the basic dimension—of redemption. The social dimension, in all its glory, is derived only from the *individual's communion* with God."⁶¹ Willard wants to ensure that one's relationship

---

⁵⁸Willard, "How to Establish and Lead," 25:30.

⁵⁹On blueprint ecclesiologies, see Nicholas M. Healy, *Church, World and the Christian Life: Practical-Prophetic Ecclesiology* (Cambridge University Press, 2000), chap. 2.

⁶⁰Although I generally cite from the second edition, *In Search of Guidance* (1993), in this section I cite from the fourth edition, *Hearing God* (2012), for its clarity.

⁶¹Dallas Willard, *Hearing God: Developing a Conversational Relationship with God*, 4th ed. (InterVarsity Press, 2012), 110-11. Later he reiterates, "No man or woman is an island, though we always remain much more than the sum of our relationships to others—even in the Christian

with the church adds to but never replaces one's relationship with God. Communion *in* the church is essential for communion *with* God, yet "we need to be careful with groups and not allow them to preempt any part of our soul."[62] Hence, he continually stresses God's immediate presence in the lives of his people, whether gathered or scattered, since for Willard, the individual comes before the community logically, not just chronologically.

This principle of the individual before the community works itself out methodologically in the other four books of his pentalogy. In terms of book structure, Willard deals with the church in the last chapters of each. He turns to ecclesiological matters only after he has thoroughly considered the individual. Placing primacy on the individual is by no means an unorthodox position in Christian theology; the ecclesiological question of whether the community or the individual comes first has long been debated by theologians. But it does explain why Willard's ecclesiology, despite its dynamism, remains peripheral or secondary in his approach to formation. How would his formational theology be conceptually different had he started with the church or at least had a more balanced approach?

In his critique of the Protestant evangelical tradition, Baptist theologian Stanley Grenz notes that evangelicalism "has never developed or worked from a thoroughgoing ecclesiology" and thus is best understood as a parachurch movement rather than a church one.[63] This judgment is based on how ecclesiology per se is and has been situated outside evangelicalism's essential theology. In this vacuum, a parachurch ethos developed.[64] Simon Chan refers to this problematic as

---

community. Our relationships to others, essential and helpful as they may be, must rest finally on our personal relationship to God himself" (112).

[62]Dallas Willard, "Why?," in *Great Omission*, 178.

[63]Stanley J. Grenz, *Renewing the Center: Evangelical Theology in a Post-Theological Era* (Baker Academic, 2000), 288.

[64]Grenz suggests a constellation of factors are behind this, including elements of Pietism and Puritanism, the emergence of congregationalism, and voluntary societies for missions, but none as important as denominationalism and an extreme focus on the invisible church that,

"the evangelical ecclesiological deficit."[65] Does Willard's implicit ecclesiology, with its focus on individual formation over communal formation, succumb to this criticism?

I contend that the dynamic nature of Willard's ecclesiology mostly escapes this criticism. The church functions as an academy for discipleship, but behind this functionality is the ontological reality of the church as a sociality of the trinitarian presence. Formation in Christlikeness can happen only within the context of our social relations with one another. Emphasis is placed on the invisible spiritual fellowship of the eternal church, but this does not negate the soteriological relevance of visible, local assemblies of the church. "Our very relation to Christ, our Savior, teacher, and friend, is located in the social dimension, along with our place in his body on earth—his continuing incarnation, the church," Willard writes. "Rightly understood, it is true that 'there is no salvation outside the church'—just not this 'church' or that 'church.'"[66] He treats the local church as indispensable, but always in view of the eternal, invisible church.

Yet, I stated that Willard's view of the church *mostly* escapes Grenz's and Chan's criticism. While the content of his ecclesiology is doctrinally coherent, its primary issue lies in its theological placement. This may lead some who read Willard to conclude his ecclesiology is underdeveloped or even inadequate. The church remains in the backdrop, playing something of a furtive role—especially in his writings—and is thus of secondary importance in his theory of spiritual formation. However, my research, which includes his recorded talks and unpublished papers, reveals that his ecclesiology is more robust than often recognized. The real need, then, is to rearrange its theological placement within his model of formation, something by

---

conversely, resulted in a deemphasis on the visible or institutional church (*Renewing the Center*, 290-300).

[65]Simon Chan, *Liturgical Theology: The Church as Worshiping Community* (IVP Academic, 2006), 15.

[66]Willard, *Renovation of the Heart*, 37.

no means unsurmountable, given the doctrinal coherence of his ecclesiology. I would suggest that future studies propose ways for Willard's ecclesiology to be brought to the forefront and amplified in his approach to spiritual formation for the church today.

I will return to this theme briefly in the final chapter to offer some additional reflection, but this is in fact a constructive theological work I hope to pursue in the coming years: to provide an ecclesiological center for Willard's theory of formation, drawing largely from his own work but also in dialogue with other theologians, and in a way that does not compromise Willard's commitment to personal relationality to God or his concerns about ecclesiocentrism. In so doing, communal formation and the communal spiritual practices that sustain it would be understood as the means by which God forms a people—not just individuals—to mediate his presence in the world.

Having covered both Willard's social architecture and his implicit ecclesiology in this portion of the book, we must now explore one last theme in his formational theory—a theme that centers on the outreach of the church but also concerns the very heart of the message it proclaims and lives by. In many ways, this final theme is the culmination or capstone of his work in Christian spiritual formation, in that it weaves together all the other themes to propel God's people forward in their participation in the divine conspiracy.

TEN

RESTORING EVANGELISM (AND THE GOSPEL) THROUGH DISCIPLESHIP

IN WILLARD'S THEOLOGY, evangelism is reimagined as inherently inclusive of spiritual formation—a transformative vision he terms "discipleship evangelism." He contrasts this with the "conversion evangelism" prevalent in the past century among evangelicals and other Protestants. Although he has something to say about the place of evangelistic ministry in the church and how it is practically approached, his focus is more upon evangelism's content than its method. In other words, he is primarily concerned not with evangelism per se but with the gospel conveyed therein. His teachings on the subject thus span both systematic and practical theology, offering a critique of contemporary ministry practices and a vision for discipleship evangelism with profound implications for soteriology, Christology, ecclesiology, and missiology.

But before delving into the history of evangelicalism—which Willard thought gave birth to conversion evangelism—one issue must first be addressed: his complex relationship with the tradition. Considering the diverse theological sources Willard engages with and the ecumenical character of his theological work, it is an open question whether he should even be considered an evangelical. Rarely did he refer to himself as such, though he would sometimes tell his listeners he was a Southern Baptist. Yet even this self-designation was usually not as it seems but rather a rhetorical move when commenting on a theological perspective or pastoral practice he was raised or trained in but had moved on from and was now openly critical of.[1] At the same time, the majority of churches and seminaries he was invited to speak at were broadly evangelical, and he was asked from time to time to address issues from an evangelical perspective or to comment on the state of evangelicalism, and so he did.[2] But on the whole, he was rather ambivalent about his association with evangelicalism. He had great admiration for the early evangelical tradition but was extremely critical of the movement from the post–World War II era up to the present. (Relatedly, he was not much a fan of Bebbington's quadrilateral, since he felt the British historian largely based his four distinctives on this later iteration of evangelicalism.[3]) In the end, given his own description of the essentials of evangelical faith and his reliance on the theologies of certain evangelical figures of the past (e.g., Finney, Wesley), it is fair to say Willard wrestles with evangelicalism from the inside.

DISCIPLESHIP EVANGELISM VERSUS CONVERSION EVANGELISM

Willard comments on the history of evangelicalism's relationship to discipleship in a number of places, most notably in a 2010 article for *The Oxford Handbook of Evangelical Theology*.[4] Following others, he

---

[1] E.g., "I'm Southern Baptist, and in that tradition we will preach to you for an hour that you can do nothing to be saved and then sing to you for half an hour trying to get you to do something to be saved." Dallas Willard, "The Redemption of Reason and the University in the Next Millennium" (February 28, 1998), MP3, 49:45.

[2] See, e.g., Dallas Willard, "The Failure of Evangelical Political Involvement," in *God and Governing: Reflections on Ethics, Virtue, and Statesmanship*, ed. Roger N. Overton (Pickwick, 2009), 74-91; Willard, "Christ-Centered Piety," in *Where Shall My Wond'ring Soul Begin? The Landscape of Evangelical Piety and Thought*, ed. Mark A. Noll and Ronald F. Thielmann (Eerdmans, 2000), 27-35; Willard, foreword to *The Post-Evangelical*, by Dave Tomlinson (Emergent, 2003), 11-12; Willard, foreword to *How I Changed My Mind About Women in Leadership: Compelling Stories from Prominent Evangelicals*, by Alan F. Johnson (Zondervan, 2010).

[3] Saying he was "not much a fan" puts it mildly. In an email correspondence with Gerald McDermott, dated December 24, 2008 (Dallas Willard Collection), Willard severely critiques three of Bebbington's four distinctives, finding common ground only on biblicism.

[4] Dallas Willard, "Discipleship," in *The Oxford Handbook of Evangelical Theology*, ed. Gerald R. McDermott (Oxford University Press, 2010), 236-46. See also Willard, "Failure of Evangelical

suggests a good marker for the origins of evangelicalism is when people began preaching outdoors at a time when such an act was viewed as extreme. That places the movement in the eighteenth century with George Whitefield and John Wesley on the British side and Jonathan Edwards and later Charles Finney (early nineteenth century) on the American side.[5]

The revivals of this era, stemming from the First and Second Awakenings, were, Willard contends, categorically different from the so-called crusades in the twentieth century. A revival was just that—it sought to revive faith in those who already had it, to grow churchgoers in overall holiness and devotion to God.[6] Increased evangelistic activity was one natural outcome of this, as those who experienced an awakening of their faith felt compelled to share that faith with others. Furthermore, evangelicals of this early period had the theological resources for such revivalism since they understood salvation as a new life (regeneration), not merely a forensic decree about one's life, and discipleship to Jesus as the process for working out this salvation "with fear and trembling" (Phil 2:12) by the quickening power of the Holy Spirit.[7] For these reasons, Willard considers early evangelicals to be heirs of Luther's radical faith.[8]

Political Involvement"; Willard, *The Divine Conspiracy: Rediscovering Our Hidden Life in God* (HarperSanFrancisco, 1998), chap. 2.

[5]Though Willard points out it was not Edwards's custom to "preach out of doors" ("Discipleship," 239).

[6]I should note that Willard also felt there was a dark side of revivalism since it focuses on *events* rather than *character growth*. As a temporary phenomenon, "it does not solve the problems of spiritual growth." Dallas Willard, "The Good Life and the Good Person Made Real by Jesus: Rethinking the 'Sermon on the Mount'" (October 10, 2008), MP3, 6:45. Cf. Willard, "Changing the Depth of the Heart" (April 1997), MP3, 1:07:30: "My background is revivalism. I was taught to believe that if you could just be there when the revival occurred, everything would be transformed.... I don't mean to knock this because I've been in revivals and I know what they do, but I just say this: Revivalism is not the answer to the question of spiritual formation and growth in Christlikeness."

[7]So writes Willard: "Evangelical Christians have a long history, and pre-WWII evangelicalism, especially in the eighteenth and the early nineteenth centuries, was, quite simply, a different kind of religion—with very different practices and theological assumptions" ("Failure of Evangelical Political Involvement," 75).

[8]Willard deems Luther, with his appeal to the Gospels (the "Evangels") over against the traditional institutions, the forerunner of evangelicalism. He contends "the basic genius of evangelicalism"

Yet starting around 1900 the emphasis of these revival meetings shifted toward reaching the lost, so that what had once been a side effect of revivalism now became its primary concern. Consequently, with the focus now on evangelizing those outside the church fold, the gospel espoused in such meetings ("crusades") centered on conversion as the forgiveness of sins wrought by Christ's death rather than whole-life transformation through union with Christ. Additionally, in the wake of the Second World War, a large contingent of fundamentalist Christians began treating correct doctrine as the demarcation for "saving faith," with little thought given to discipleship or character formation, at least in terms of salvation. The Christian life was therefore understood as substantively a mental activity, which rendered certain emphases of early evangelicalism, such as regeneration and sanctification, nonessential. Over time these two elements of *conversion as forgiveness* and *correct doctrine as salvific* combined to become the standard gospel of evangelicalism. Many converts were made under the pretense, says Willard, that one can be a Christian and never graduate to becoming a disciple.

A prime example, he suggests, is a threefold division of faith status made famous by the Navigators, a parachurch organization known, especially in the second half of the twentieth century, for "disciple making."[9] Those whom God has saved fall into one of the following groups: (1) Christians: those forgiven, (2) Disciples: those who can make Christians, and (3) Workers: those who can make disciples.[10] Although many evangelicals today would not spell this out in such formulaic and stark terms, the idea that one can be a Christian but not necessarily a disciple is pervasive.

---

that early evangelicals inherited from Luther and the Reformers revolves around two main convictions: (1) personal experience of conversion to and practical communion with God, and (2) devotion to Scripture as the ultimate authority and source of divine life ("Discipleship," 240-41).

[9]To the following, Willard, "Discipleship," 236-37.

[10]For an older example of literature published by the Navigators that lays this out explicitly, see LeRoy Eims, *The Lost Art of Disciple-Making* (Zondervan, 1978), especially the diagrams on 61, 74, 124.

So, the real problem with evangelism, as understood and practiced by many in the American church today, is not evangelism itself but "the theology that's in the back of it."[11] Evangelistic malpractice is in this case the result of a misunderstanding of soteriology and a misreading of Scripture: There is no essential connection between salvation and discipleship, nor between conversion and character transformation.[12] "What this most recent version of evangelicalism lacks," argues Willard, "is a *theology of discipleship*. Specifically, it lacks a clear teaching on how what happens at conversion continues on without break into an even fuller life in the Kingdom of God."[13]

Willard proposes "discipleship evangelism" as one way to right the ship. This is evangelistic outreach for the express purpose of making disciples.[14] In conversion evangelism, the central invitation is for people to give cognitive assent to the gospel—which, as previously noted, is generally taken to be Christ's sacrificial death on the cross for our sins. Discipleship evangelism, on the other hand, means people are invited to interact with the living Christ and the reality of his kingdom even before they "believe."[15] Such interactive knowledge is what constitutes the good news of the gospel. Thus, when a person comes to faith in Jesus, she has already established a relational rhythm

---

[11] Dallas Willard, interview by Keith Giles, "On the Gospel of the Kingdom," in *Subversive Interviews* (Subversive Underground, 2011), 69. This is not to suggest Willard was unconcerned about the actual practice of evangelism. It was imperative, he thought, that disciples of Jesus knew how to make disciples. He thus taught frequently on Mt 28:18-20, parsing its different clauses and indicating how they might be fulfilled today. Yet, as noted, he was far more concerned with the message of evangelism than the method, knowing the former largely shapes the latter. As he frequently stated, "Does the gospel I preach have the natural tendency to produce disciples? This is the bottom-line question, folks." Willard, "Session 1—Part 2" (March 9, 2004), MP3, 1:13:30.

[12] Dallas Willard, "Teaching the Teachers of the Nations" (printed lecture, January 2004), Dallas Willard Collection, 11; cf. Willard, "Failure of Evangelical Political Involvement," 75.

[13] Willard, "Discipleship," 245.

[14] Willard, *Divine Conspiracy*, 304-5. See also Dallas Willard, "The Place of 'Disciplines' in Christian Discipleship and Spiritual Formation 2" (January 7, 2010), video, 13:15.

[15] This does not minimize the meaning of Christ's sacrificial death on the cross, but it does displace it as the singular or even principal substance of the doctrine of atonement. For some of Willard's clearest teaching on the subject, see Dallas Willard, "Attention to Christology and Atonement" (March 16, 2011), video.

with him and is engaged in practices within redemptive community that can continue to foster her growth in Christlikeness.[16] Recast in this light, evangelism is about *getting people in motion* toward the kingdom, putting them in a position to expect God's action in their lives.[17]

This emphasis on embeddedness in a community of praxis and the habituation that comes through apprenticeship does resemble the logic of virtue ethics, especially as developed by MacIntyre and Hauerwas. But Willard goes much further. This is not merely about practicing something until it becomes a part of who we are (à la virtue ethics); it is about relating to Someone whose ongoing presence transforms us. Willard insists that apprenticeship entails an interactive relationship with a Master—the living Christ—whose presence and action are real and ongoing. Indeed, we see this in the Gospels, where some of Jesus' first disciples began following him and interacting with him as Master before they fully "believed" in him.

Willard suggests that the recent history of evangelicalism proves that if you aim at gaining converts, then that is what you will likely get, with perhaps some disciples thrown in. The strategy, therefore, ought to be reversed: Aim at making disciples so that is what you get, with some converts thrown in. Yet again, the real issue here is what gospel is proclaimed. The call of the gospel depends on the content of the gospel—so what exactly are people invited into?

TOWARD A (MISSIONAL) THEOLOGY OF DISCIPLESHIP

One resource to help answer that question is a 2009 talk Willard gave to a group of church leaders on the theme "Discipleship to Jesus and the Missional Church." Although he repeats many of the ideas elsewhere, this teaching is valuable since he (1) provides a succinct

---

[16] Trey L. Clark, "Dallas Willard's Theology of Evangelism," *Witness: Journal of the Academy for Evangelism in Theological Education* 30, no. 1 (2016): 16.

[17] Dallas Willard, "Living in the Knowledge of Christ and His Kingdom" (February 16, 2010), MP3, 1:01:15.

summary of the gospel of the kingdom of God, why it constitutes good news, and how it naturally leads to discipleship to Christ that is inherently oriented toward the world, and (2) directly addresses what makes a church missional.[18] For this reason and because the manuscript of the talk remains unpublished, I will quote it at length:

> Perhaps we would benefit from rethinking discipleship and rethinking how it relates to outreach/mission into the "outside the church" world.
>
> Could we start from the idea that the basic idea and reality for the Christ follower is a new kind of life? . . . There are various kinds of life, and one kind is "eternal living," the kind of life that comes from God and consists of interactive relationship with him. To "enter" the kingdom of God is to be engaged by and in this kind of life. The "kingdom" of God is simply what God is doing: his "reign." To seek the kingdom of God is to look for what God is doing and engage with it throughout life. A gospel that leads into discipleship is one that lets people know of *the accessibility to them of life now in the kingdom of God*: accessibility through putting their confidence in Jesus and therefore putting his words about the kingdom into practice. This is THE GREAT POSSIBILITY for human life: *the greatest opportunity anyone will ever have.*
>
> A disciple is someone who has been overwhelmed by the beauty, goodness and strength of Jesus, and, through him, of God.[19] Because of that they have chosen to be with him in every way possible, learning to be like him. They are learning from him how to live *their* life—all of it—in the kingdom of God, as *he* would lead *their* life if he were they. Discipleship to Christ is not a religious thing, though it covers that as well. It is a life thing. It is for the sake of life in the real world (which

---

[18]In this talk, *missional* is largely understood in terms of outreach and evangelism. The term appears a handful of other times in Willard's work, and this is generally true there as well. However, the accent is especially heavy on outreach/evangelism here because of how the topic and language of "missional" was initially framed for the talk by the pastor who invited him. See Bill Gaultiere's email correspondence with Willard, July 8, 2009, Dallas Willard Collection. Willard's understanding of mission certainly entails more than evangelism, yet this is conveyed usually not in his use of the word *missional* but rather under the rubrics of, for example, our role in God's divine conspiracy, what it means to reign with Christ, the church as a school of life, the vocation of the Christian, and the like.

[19]A handwritten note in the margin reads, "How to make a disciple."

God so loved) and not just the church. The church serves discipleship, as Matthew 28:18-20 makes clear. . . .

Outreach then is a natural part of what disciples do as they are in contact with others throughout their life. There is still plenty of need and room for special people and special efforts in outreach. There is no conflict between making disciples and cultivating them, on the one hand, and evangelization on the other. They are a perfect match.[20]

Earlier we noted Willard's judgment that modern evangelism lacks a *theology of discipleship*. He has provided the contours of that here, intimating the connections between discipleship and the gospel, soteriology, formation, Christian living, and mission. Therefore its main movements are rehearsed below and integrated with ground we have already covered.

First, a Christian is one who has not merely been forgiven but has been given new life. The New Testament speaks of this new life as "eternal life," yet since this phrase is often understood exclusively in terms of the quantitative—a person's fate after this life—Willard prefers the language of *eternal living*. His use of the present continuous tense ("living") indicates both its qualitative and quantitative nature: Eternal living begins concretely here and now and then extends into the afterlife, since the source of eternal living is interactive relationship with Jesus and his kingdom.[21] God's kingdom, as the sphere of his action and authority, has always existed; what was new in Jesus' message of the kingdom, then, was its radical availability to ordinary people through trusting him with their life. A person now looks to Jesus directly and in real time for how to live, and through this active discipleship comes to know God and his

---

[20]Dallas Willard, "Discipleship to Jesus vs. the Missional Church" (printed lecture, 2009), Dallas Willard Collection, 2.

[21]A key passage for Willard in this regard is Jn 17:3, "Now this is eternal life: that they know you, the only true God, and Jesus Christ, whom you have sent." In one of his earliest teachings on record, he comments that this passage shows Jesus "is faithful to the Jewish religion which is almost completely 'this-worldly' in its view of salvation." Dallas Willard, "Jesus' Good News of God's Kingdom" (handout, June 18–September 10, 1972), Dallas Willard Collection, 6.

power and to participate in what God is doing in the same manner that Christ did. The gospel is not just about what Jesus *has done* but what he *is doing*, for salvation is, as Willard says elsewhere, "participating in the life that Jesus is now living on earth."[22] And this participation, by nature, is oriented toward love. Discipleship to Jesus in the kingdom inherently leads to externalized, agapeic engagement with the world.

Willard's theology of discipleship thus makes little distinction between discipleship and mission. What distinction does exist is sequential; apart from that they are inseparable. A handwritten note accompanying Willard's manuscript makes this apparent: "If you implement discipleship in the N.T. sense you need have no concern about being missional. You will penetrate your community as never before with people from heaven."[23] He puts it even more succinctly in a 2012 lecture: "Being missional is an inevitable result of being disciples. You can't stop it."[24]

THE CHRISTOLOGICAL ISSUE

Willard's proposal of discipleship evangelism depends on understanding the gospel as the good news about the availability of God's kingdom and salvation as the impartation of new life. Yet such an

---

[22]Willard, "On the Gospel of the Kingdom," 70. Consider also this statement: "The atonement is *Christ himself*. Now that involves everything that he did, but it keeps us out of the position that the atonement is something he did that is detachable from him" (Willard, "Attention to Christology and Atonement," 1:02:30).

[23]Dallas Willard, "Discipleship to Jesus and the Missional Church" (handwritten notes, 2009), Dallas Willard Collection, 1. See also Willard, "Spirituality and Mission" (May 1985), MP3, 6:00: "There is an inward life, which is inseparable from an outward expression that constitutes our spirituality and makes mission not only successful; it makes mission inevitable."

[24]Dallas Willard, "The Kingdom and Its Instrumentalities" (June 6, 2012), video, 56:00. This recording is important because in the middle of a lengthy lecture on the with-God life and the kingdom of God, Willard is asked by a student about the relation between these biblical themes and the missional church. He responds with a quick summation of what, as he perceives it, instigated the missional church movement (53:15), then goes on to discuss many of the ideas touched on in this section and others in the chapter. I mention this because unfortunately no recording exists from his 2009 talk on the missional church. Since Willard's practice when delivering a talk was to offer extemporaneous comments in addition to his prepared notes, this 2012 recording is our best asset for knowing what unscripted material he may have discussed.

understanding of the gospel and salvation itself hinges on understanding Jesus as (1) a real-life personality who interacts, in real time, with his disciples, and (2) an intelligent teacher who knows the best answers to the most important questions of human life. Discipleship evangelism is therefore as much a consequence of Willard's Christology as it is his soteriology.

Divine Conspiracy opens with these memorable lines: "My hope is to gain a fresh hearing for Jesus, especially among those who believe they already understand him. In this case, quite frankly, presumed familiarity has led to unfamiliarity, unfamiliarity has led to contempt, and contempt has led to profound ignorance."[25] To explain how the church arrived at a place of "profound ignorance" in its understanding of Jesus, Willard turns again to the historical development of religious conservatives and liberals in the nineteenth and twentieth centuries.[26] According to his telling, liberals increasingly viewed Jesus as a great teacher and moralist during this period—but also as fundamentally wrong about central parts of his own message, such as expecting the imminent end of the world during his lifetime. In reaction, conservatives intentionally steered away from presenting Jesus as *teacher*, interpreting it as code language for "merely human," and instead elevated his status as divine Lord and Savior. What is missing in both accounts, Willard argues, is Jesus as expert and authority on all matters of life, and one who is alive and accessible today. As he writes, "We have come to accept 'Believe Jesus died for your sins' in such a way that does not involve 'Believe Jesus in everything.'"[27]

The implications of this for discipleship—and by extension evangelism—are seismic. How can we submit ourselves to and follow someone we believe, in the end, is uninformed about the issues that

---

[25] Willard, *Divine Conspiracy*, xiii.

[26] To the following, Willard, *Divine Conspiracy*, 55-57; cf. Willard, "Failure of Evangelical Political Involvement," 76.

[27] Dallas Willard, "Spiritual Formation in Christ Is for the Whole Life and the Whole Person," in *For All the Saints: Evangelical Theology and Christian Spirituality*, ed. Timothy George and Alister McGrath (Westminster John Knox, 2003), 52.

matter most to human life? Genuine discipleship to Christ requires we have *confidence* in his *competence*. This is what leads to Willard's claim that "our greatest challenge is to recover Jesus the Teacher."[28]

We must revisit Willard's Christology once more since his is a radically realist one, in terms of both ontology and epistemology. In chapter four I examined the epistemic realism of his Christology and the straightforward yet mystical implications this holds for spiritual formation. Here my focus is on the ontological realism of his Christology and what it means, in particular, about the personality and intelligence of Jesus and the nature of his resurrected body and life.[29] The epistemic and ontological are intertwined in his Christology but can and should be parsed separately to understand each more fully, as figure 10.1 illustrates. Yet it should be obvious that the epistemic is made possible only by the ontological. Personal interaction with Jesus after his earthly death depends, of course, on his bodily resurrection; otherwise he remains a corpse and thus merely a historical figure.[30]

---

[28]Dallas Willard, interview by Keith Giles, "Authentic Disciples of Jesus," in *Subversive Interviews* (Subversive Underground, 2011), 16. Elsewhere he asserts, "We have lost discipleship largely because in the evangelical tradition we have lost Christ as teacher" (Willard, "Christ-Centered Piety," 33).

[29]There is more to the ontological side of Willard's Christology that could be explored, such as the salvific meaning of Jesus as the face of God. See the section "Knowledge of the Glory of God in the Face of Christ," in *Divine Conspiracy*, 334-36. As Michael Stewart Robb explains, Willard's statements about Jesus' face are references to not his fleshy face (what he looked like) but his existential persona (who he was at the core of his personality). The incarnation accomplished many things, but its main purpose, according to Willard, was to correct humanity's shoddy theology about God. The Fourth Gospel thus declares, "No one has ever seen God, but the one and only Son, who is himself God and is in closest relationship with the Father, has made him known" (Jn 1:18), and Jesus himself states, "Anyone who has seen me has seen the Father" (Jn 14:9). For further discussion, see Robb, *The Kingdom Among Us: The Gospel According to Dallas Willard* (Fortress, 2022), 467-77.

[30]Depending on his audience and subject matter, Willard does occasionally limit his discourse to the intelligence and wisdom of the historical Jesus. See, e.g., Dallas Willard, "Nietzsche Versus Jesus Christ," in *A Place for Truth: Leading Thinkers Explore Life's Hardest Questions*, ed. Dallas Willard (InterVarsity Press, 2010), 153-68. This is a first step or stage in his ontological Christology, the second step being that the *resurrected* Jesus continues to guide and dispel wisdom to his people.

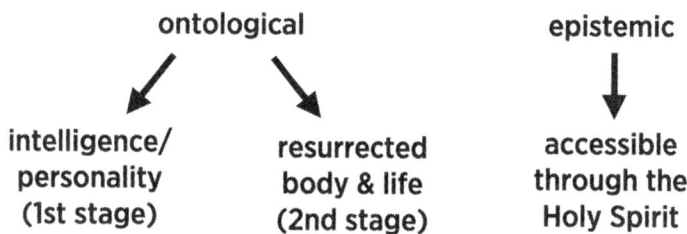

Figure 10.1. Willard's radically realist Christology (partial)

Willard posits that the resurrection of Jesus and its ongoing relevance rests on a few essential elements.[31] The Gospels attest that the resurrected body of Christ was similar to that of ordinary humans, yet also distinctly different in that his body could now relate to the space-time continuum and physical world in miraculous ways. This allowed Christ, as the second member of the Trinity but also a *human person*, to remain present and active in the world among his followers in the first century and beyond, continuing to be accessible to those who seek him and align themselves with him today.

This transition from Jesus' physical presence with his contemporaries to his spiritual presence with them and those who came after, for Willard, means nothing has altered the basic truth of Jesus' personality—that is, *his intelligence*. He frequently cites Colossians 2:3 as evidence that, in the eyes of the first Christians, Jesus holds within himself "all the treasures of wisdom and knowledge." Jesus is, in Willard's words, "the smartest person who ever lived" and "the premier thinker of the human race."[32] Willard reasons that this is, first and foremost, how Jesus should be seen because this is how he first revealed himself to us: Jesus came into the world as a teacher and luminary. Yet this is not just true of the historical Jesus, that is, the

---

[31]To the following, Dallas Willard, *Knowing Christ Today: Why We Can Trust Spiritual Knowledge* (HarperOne, 2009), 132-37.

[32]Willard, *Divine Conspiracy*, 94; Dallas Willard, "Jesus the Logician," *Christian Scholar's Review* 28, no. 4 (1999): 611.

thirty-something years of his earthly life in the first century. Because of the resurrection he is alive and well, and because of Pentecost and the Holy Spirit he continues to be accessible and available. Jesus remains the most brilliant personality in the world; his intelligence is the same yesterday, today, and forever (Heb 13:8).

If Jesus is received as anything less than the master teacher of life, says Willard, then the meaning of Christian discipleship significantly changes. It now becomes adherence to a tradition, a set of principles, or an institutional body. But this is not discipleship as practiced in the pages of the New Testament, which is adherence to Jesus as teacher through personal acquaintance.

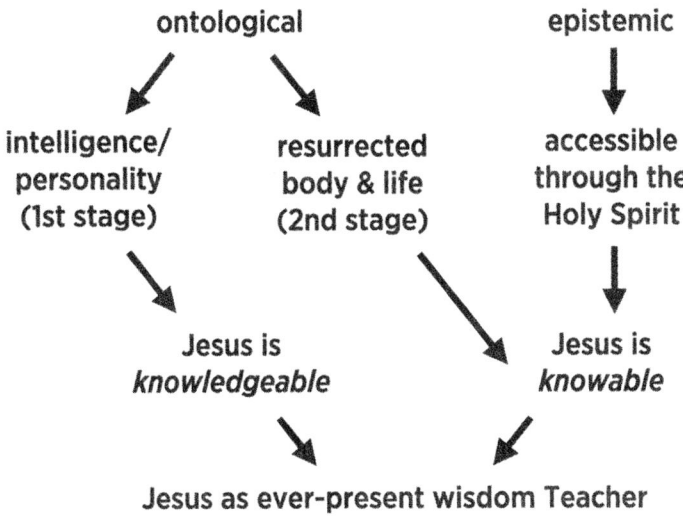

Figure 10.2. Willard's radically realist Christology (full)

What does this mean specifically for discipleship evangelism? It means, for one, that the church must present Jesus not only as *knowable* but as *knowledgeable*.[33] The epistemic realism of Willard's Christology

---

[33] See Willard, "Jesus the Logician," 611, where he contends a major problem today is "the way we automatically tend to think of Jesus himself. It is not just in what we *say* about him, but in how he comes before our minds: how we automatically position him in our world, and how in consequence we position ourselves."

stresses that we can personally know Jesus and be led by him in our moment-by-moment existence. The ontological realism of his Christology, with its focus on the personality and intelligence of Jesus and the nature of his resurrected body and life, indicates why this is good news. As the best-informed person in every domain of knowledge, Jesus is the expert and authority on becoming a good person and attaining the good life.[34] Therefore, the invitation of the gospel is to know him, above all, as ever-present wisdom Teacher (see fig. 10.2)—to place our trust in him, walk with him, and become like him as we live in God's kingdom.[35]

THE PRINCIPLE OF RADIANCE AND THE GROWTH OF THE REDEEMED

Earlier we explored the dual dynamics of Willard's ecclesiology, noting that the second dynamic—the church as an academy and school of life founded on the teachings of Jesus—constitutes its outgoing, sending movement. This is because the spiritual upbuilding of Jesus' disciples is not for their benefit, though they will certainly benefit from it; teleologically, it is for the benefit of the world.[36]

Yet in terms of centripetal and centrifugal direction, Willard understands the outgoing, sending movement of the church as primarily centripetal. This is true even when persons are explicitly sent out,

---

[34]"Jesus could produce matter out of thin air, he could suspend gravity. Most importantly, he understood how to take a wicked person and turn them into a good person. Shall I say that we are still working on that one?" Dallas Willard, "Jesus: Master of the Arts and Sciences 1" (April 22, 1998), MP3, 26:30.

[35]Willard makes his strongest case for viewing Jesus as expert in all areas of intellectual life in his 1999 essay "Jesus the Logician." But it should be noted that a rebuttal essay by Richard Riesen appeared some years later in the same journal; see Riesen, "'Jesus the Logician': A (Very) Modest Proposal," *Christian Scholar's Review* 34, no. 3 (2005): 341-51. Riesen takes issue with Willard's suggestion that Jesus be understood as a logician and a thinker on par with Aristotle, Kant, Heidegger, Wittgenstein, etc. He does not argue that Jesus was *not* highly intellectual or even the most intelligent person that ever lived, only that this is not the picture we are given of him in the Gospels. Instead, the Gospels present Jesus as "a very great deal more; and it is in the nature of that more that his uniqueness resides" (350). I mention this article because a comprehensive study of Willard's Christology, which cannot be done here, should take into account Riesen's counterargument.

[36]Dallas Willard, "Pastors as Teachers of the Nations" (March 30, 2007), MP3, 13:00.

such as in their vocation and workplace, since a *principle of radiance* is at work. If the church is the dwelling place of the trinitarian presence, and its members are being transformed by that manifest presence, then these persons will radiate God's glory and goodness wherever they go and to whomever they encounter.[37] As a result, those outside the faith will be drawn in by these radiant lives. Mission begins, therefore, in the household of God.[38] If character transformation is not happening there, then there is little hope, from a human perspective, for effective evangelization. History shows that God can work by other means, that his redemptive mission will not be thwarted; yet the "natural and God appointed way to be missional is through the incandescent lives of those who are 'here already'" in the church.[39]

Willard believes certain individuals are called and gifted for special evangelistic work, and also that cross-cultural or overseas missions is important. So there is a place for intentionally centrifugal direction in his missional vision. But it is not equal to the centripetal. A key text for his church-first or centripetal approach to evangelism is Jesus' prayer in John 17:23, "I in them and You in Me, that they may be perfected in unity, so that *the world may know* that You sent Me, and You loved them, just as You loved me" (NASB). Willard refers to this as "Jesus' method of mission" and "Christ's plan for world evangelization."[40] The radiance principle drawn from this passage and others, such as Philippians 2:15, is that "children of the light"—apprentices of Jesus resembling their

---

[37] Hence, as I argued in chapter nine, the second dynamic (academy for discipleship) depends and builds upon the first (sociality of trinitarian presence). In Willard's words: "The primary function of the church is not evangelism, but to be a place for the dwelling of God on the earth." Dallas Willard, "Rethinking Evangelism," *Cutting Edge* (Winter 2001): 11.

[38] Cf. this note in a handout for Willard's annual course at Fuller: "Our first main objective is to 'evangelize the church,' as Jesus came to Israel. 'To the Jews first.'" Dallas Willard, "Spirituality and Ministry," GM720 (syllabus and notes, Fuller Theological Seminary, 1993–2012), Dallas Willard Collection, 38.

[39] Dallas Willard, "Missional Church" (handwritten notes, 2009), Dallas Willard Collection. See also Willard, "Church Communities" (July 14, 2004), video, 40:00, where he describes the transformation of those inside the church spreading in a "virus-like way" to those outside it.

[40] Dallas Willard, "The New Testament Theology of the Church" (June 19, 2005), video, 32:45; Willard, "Evangelism" (June 21, 2002), MP3, 15:30.

Lord, who is himself the "light of the world"—will draw others toward Christ simply by means of their character. Yet this will be possible only if the church directs its efforts primarily toward the Christlike formation of its members, what Willard calls the work of *inreach*.[41] He remarks, "The ministry is given to the church *not* to convert the world; the ministry is given to the church for the perfecting of the saints," and, "In the mission of Christ there is one and one aim only . . . and that aim is to create new persons . . . to give them new life."[42] Or stated negatively, "If we put mission first, we . . . more or less go down in flames."[43] These statements should not be interpreted as pitting formation against mission or making mission a second step but rather as *mission by formation*. God forms a people under the lordship and in the image of his Son, and their very presence in the world is a witness to the gospel. Another handwritten note discovered in his papers puts it succinctly: "Discipleship [is] the only way to *be missional* in the framework Jesus set for his people."[44]

A further aspect of Willard's approach to evangelism, closely related to the radiance principle, is his redefinition of church growth as "the growth of the redeemed."[45] Similar to his "first/then" approach to individual and societal change, Willard thinks our churches today do not need *more* Christians but *larger* Christians; we need to stop

---

[41]"It is, I gently suggest, a serious error to make 'outreach' a *primary* goal of the local congregation, and especially so when those who are already 'with us' have not become clear-headed and devoted apprentices of Jesus, and are not, for the most part, solidly progressing along the path. . . . The most successful work of outreach would be the work of *inreach* that turns people, wherever they are, into lights in the darkened world." Dallas Willard, *Renovation of the Heart: Putting On the Character of Christ* (NavPress, 2002), 244.

[42]Dallas Willard, "Disciple or Christian?" (September 18, 1977), MP3, 57:15; Willard, "Spirituality and Mission," 37:15.

[43]Willard, "New Testament Theology of the Church," 42:30. Immediately prior to this statement he says, "Mission is not something that goes before, or you have to tack on after, the fullness of life in Christ with one another. I think it is something that will happen and you can't stop it. This is what Jesus was talking about when he said you can't hide a city and talked about us being the light of the world" (42:00).

[44]Willard, "Discipleship to Jesus and the Missional Church," 1.

[45]Willard, "Evangelism," 13:30.

counting the people in our congregations and start weighing them.[46] That is to say, churches need more people who have developed godly character through serious apprenticeship to Jesus. When (and whether) that happens, it will eventually result in more Christians—hence, "first/then"—since those living deep in the kingdom are themselves the ultimate apologetic and evangelistic witness to the faith.[47]

REFRAMING CHURCH MEMBERSHIP AND MINISTRY

Willard's approach to evangelism is grounded in the gospel of the kingdom and inseparable from the process of spiritual transformation through discipleship. If taken seriously, it would make active apprenticeship to Jesus not only (1) the central invitation of evangelism and (2) normative for the Christian life but also (3) the basis for membership in the visible church. Moreover, it would (4) reframe the American church as a ripe field for evangelism since many churchgoers, says Willard, have never taken the step to actively follow Jesus as a knowledgeable and authoritative guide for life. Considering these first two implications are intimated in what has already been said, I will comment on the last two—church membership and the need for the church to be evangelized—and the potential they hold for the future of spiritual formation in the church.

One inevitable ecclesial outcome of discipleship evangelism is that it would require a radical shift in how local congregations conceive of

---

[46] Willard, *Renovation of the Heart*, 244; Willard, *Divine Conspiracy*, 373; Dallas Willard and Dieter Zander, interview, "The Apprentices: What Is Spiritual Formation? And How Does a Church Do It? A Professor and Pastor Discuss the New Language of Making Disciples," *Leadership Journal* 26, no. 3 (Summer 2005): 22.

[47] On the notion of "ultimate apologetic," see Dallas Willard, "Lifting Doubts About Living and Acting with God in the Kingdom of the Heavens" (May 13, 1990), MP3, 55:45. For Willard, apologetics is an important ministry of the church, since questions raised by those living with doubt deserve thoughtful, rational, and *gentle* responses. He is critical of apologetics that are argumentative or aggressive, once referring to their proponents as "Bully-Boy Apologists" (Willard, "Authentic Disciples of Jesus," 19). In contrast, he defines apologetic ministry as "an activity in which one person helps another by answering real questions." Willard, "On Apologetics" (handwritten notes, 2007), Dallas Willard Collection. Although it overlaps with his view of evangelism—in that he believes the transformed life of a disciple is the best apologetic—he generally treats apologetics as a separate ministry.

their membership.[48] Churches must "be prepared to re-write the contract with everyone" based on the public identification of the church with discipleship.[49] In short, joining a local fellowship of Christ's body would require that a person commit herself to active apprenticeship to Jesus with that community of disciples. Churches that pursue such a vision should also be prepared to potentially lose a portion of their current "members" and attendees since some will likely interpret these measures as extreme. Nevertheless, Willard believes such redefining of what it means to belong to the local church would go a long way in restoring the integrity of church membership.[50]

There is nothing sacrosanct about church membership, Willard maintains[51]—and perhaps the language itself of *membership*, which does not appear in the New Testament, is not the most helpful.[52] But there needs to be some recognized way for people to commit themselves to following Jesus together and living under his lordship collectively in a particular place and time. However, this does not mean there will no longer be a place in the local church for those who are not committed disciples of Jesus. Willard understands that nondisciples (nominal Christians) will always be a part of the visible church. Such

---

[48] A fuller treatment of what church membership entails is unnecessary for the present discussion. Here it will simply be understood as a person belonging to a local congregation—a belonging that is assumed to be part of the normal Christian life.

[49] Dallas Willard, "Local Congregations as Schools of Discipleship" (March 31, 2007), MP3, 1:06:30; cf. 6:45. See also Willard, "What to Do 'in Church': Eternal Living Fostered by Church Activities" (August 5, 2010), MP3, 19:00; Willard, "Spiritual Formation as a Natural Part of Salvation," in *Life in the Spirit: Spiritual Formation in Theological Perspective*, ed. Jeffrey P. Greenman and George Kalantzis (IVP Academic, 2010), where he recommends "that efforts in evangelism and toward increasing 'church membership' be very purposively reoriented toward bringing people to the point of regeneration and discipleship" (60).

[50] Willard explicitly states he is not suggesting we *purify* the church, for the task of separating "weeds" from "wheat" (Mt 13) belongs entirely to God. Instead, he urges Christian leaders to *clarify* the church to itself, to make clear what full participation in Christ's body entails (Willard, *Renovation of the Heart*, 245).

[51] Dallas Willard, "The Shape of the Church Visible: Today and Tomorrow" (July 26, 2000), MP3, 33:15.

[52] Admittedly, Paul does often speak of Christians as "members" of Christ's body; but this has no direct parallel to the contemporary sociological concept of membership, whether used in relation to the church or to some other organization.

persons are welcome to participate in the life of the church, to come and see the goodness of God at work within the community. But attending to and attracting those uninterested in discipleship is not the express intent of the church. As schools of life founded on the person and teachings of Jesus, local congregations exist first and foremost to make disciples in his likeness. The energy and resources of these fellowships, and especially of their leaders, are to be channeled toward this end. Disciples produced in these congregations then carry the message of the gospel into the places they live, work, and dwell—and they do so primarily *via their character*. For Willard, truth is in the living, for apprentices of Jesus are the social manifestation of the gospel.

If Willard is correct that the gospel currently preached in most churches has no necessary connection to discipleship and character transformation, then one can see why he concludes that these churches are "the primary field of evangelism in our day." He believes that many, if not most, churchgoers have never decided to become apprentices of Jesus and experience God's kingdom here and now through his presence and power. And they have never done so because, "by and large, they have never been invited."[53] Again, the fundamental issue here for Willard is the standard gospel proclaimed in churches and the reigning soteriology and Christology from which such a gospel derives.

INCANDESCENT LIVES

This chapter not only completes our treatment of Willard's formation theory but is, from one perspective, its culmination since it draws from and integrates many of the other core themes, including his christological realism, kingdom theology, implicit ecclesiology, and deeply relational view of character growth in the Spirit.

According to Willard, active apprenticeship to the risen Christ should be not only the central invitation of evangelism but the basis for membership in the visible church. As we discovered, he makes

---

[53] Willard, "Church Communities," 55:30, 56:30; cf. Willard, "Natural Part of Salvation," 60.

little distinction between discipleship and mission in his theology since he claims that discipleship to Jesus in the kingdom inherently leads to externalized, agapeic engagement with the world. To have one's heart/spirit/will shaped like Christ's is to have, at the same time, one's heart/spirit/will oriented toward others in love and compassion. He contends this must not lead to an exclusivist view of the "real" or invisible church. Nondisciples are invited and welcome to participate in the life of the church—and we should expect them to come over time since those outside the faith will be drawn to the incandescent lives of God's people—but attracting these nondisciples must forever remain a byproduct rather than a focus of the church's mission. Much of this hinges, for Willard, on a radically realist Christology, for if Jesus is received as anything less than a real-life personality who interacts with and leads his disciples in real time and in all manners of life, then the meaning of Christian discipleship and, consequently, the gospel, is significantly altered. And though I began the chapter by stating Willard "reimagines" evangelism as inclusive of spiritual formation, it is more befitting to use the word *reclaims*, for in his view this is the philosophy of ministry one finds in Scripture and the high points of church history.

With our exploration of Willard's formational theology now complete, we approach the conclusion of the journey this book set out to undertake. From the outset I invited you to trek through the interwoven themes of Willard's thought, uncovering its theological depth and missional vision. Now, as we set our sights on the final chapter, we are ready to reflect on how his work might practically serve the church moving forward. What would it look like for local churches to embrace discipleship as their central invitation? How might the incandescent lives of Christ's apprentices transform not only the church but the world around it? As a theologian of the Christian life, Willard would expect nothing less.

ELEVEN

EXERCISE UNTO GODLINESS ... AND GODLIKENESS

Willard once suggested that every church must ask itself two questions: What is our plan for making disciples, and how is that going?[1] I submit that for many American churches today, these two questions are hardly on the radar. As the remnants of Christendom wane in our country—or completely dissipate in some parts—fewer people attend churches out of cultural expectations or norms. Yet this void of nominal Christianity has been filled by churches proclaiming a gospel with no intrinsic connection to actively following Jesus and being formed in his image. Such a gospel gives theological cover for one to forever be a Christian but never become a disciple, Willard observes. Small wonder, then, that we have so many "vampire Christians" who want Jesus only for his blood and nothing else.[2]

The widespread disconnect between Christian identity and discipleship is only one symptom of a broader formational failure—one that touches not just external behavior but our imagination, desires, and witness. In other words, it deeply affects the interior architecture of the Christian life: how we envision the good, what we long for, and how we live that out publicly. Willard's theology offers more than

---

[1] A former codirector of the Ecclesia Network, JR Woodward, remembers Willard saying this to a group of leaders over a table conversation at the network's 2010 national gathering in Chevy Chase, MD. JR Woodward, interview by author, December 20, 2022.

[2] Dallas Willard, *The Divine Conspiracy: Rediscovering Our Hidden Life in God* (HarperSanFrancisco, 1998), 403n8.

critique; it charts a constructive path across each of these realms. His questions about discipleship are ultimately about the very meaning of spiritual maturity, community, and kingdom living in an increasingly secular, post-Christendom age.

THE ONGOING SANCTIFICATION GAP

In many ways, what has come to be known as the spiritual formation movement was a response to this "sanctification gap" in twentieth-century Protestantism. An essay by church historian Richard F. Lovelace, published in the early 1970s, brought attention to this deficiency in evangelical theology and spirituality, painting it in stark terms and calling for spiritual renewal to close the gap.[3] Lovelace's assessment of American Christianity is as relevant now as when first penned. But what has changed is the locus of the sanctification gap, as the lack of Christlike character is experienced most acutely on the level of leadership today.

The moral failure of ministers and public leaders is nothing new in church history (see also the Donatist controversy in the fourth century), and we find this issue raised in the pages of the New Testament itself. For instance, Paul exhorts Timothy to "not be hasty in the laying on of hands" (1 Tim 5:22); in other words, to exercise caution when appointing and commissioning leaders to ensure they are spiritually mature and fit for their responsibilities. Nevertheless, there is something noticeably different about what we are witnessing today: a tidal wave of moral failures among Christian leaders—or perhaps a continuous storm of waves, as new ones keep coming.

What may be different today is not simply the existence of a character crisis but our collective awareness of it. With increased transparency, digital reporting, and broader platforms for victims and whistleblowers, what was once hidden is now exposed. In some ways, then, we are not facing something entirely new but rather encountering what has long

---

[3]Richard F. Lovelace, "The Sanctification Gap," *Theology Today* 29, no. 4 (1973): 363-69.

been true—only now with clearer sight. Still, the sheer scale and visibility of leadership failures in recent decades suggest a deeper problem in how we form leaders, how we define success, and what we are willing to tolerate for the sake of influence or numerical growth.

Especially since the advent of televangelist ministries in the 1980s, many high-profile pastors have become embroiled in controversies. But for at least a decade now, it seems we hear every month of a new scandal involving a pastor, clergy member, or public Christian leader. Stories of their abuse of power, sexual harassment, or financial mismanagement have become disturbingly commonplace.[4] These cases are far more numerous at the local level, within smaller churches, though many go unreported and draw no headlines. Nor is this crisis confined to leadership. What of those who are not in positions of authority—have they fared any better? Does the same formation gap extend across the pews? The urgency of addressing these patterns is clear, and we must recognize this is a deeply complex issue, shaped by cultural, institutional, and individual factors.[5] There is a critical need for the American church to devote more attention to the doctrine of sanctification and to the theological, psychological, and social causes underlying its present crisis of character.

Yet this character crisis extends beyond the church and into our society at large. In a penetrating article titled, "How America Got

---

[4]For example, in just 2024, in the Dallas metroplex—the area I grew up in—at least nineteen pastors, several of whom led prominent megachurches, either resigned, were removed, or came under investigation for misconduct, including five facing criminal charges. A local leader described it as "the unbuckling of the Bible Belt." See Ruth Graham, "Around Dallas, the Church Scandals Seem to Have No End," *New York Times*, October 3, 2024.

[5]A number of recent works document and analyze these factors. See, e.g., Daniel M. Doriani, "Above Reproach? Moral Failure and Godly Character in Pastoral Leadership," *Westminster Theological Journal* 85, no. 1 (Spring 2023): 53-68; JR Woodward, *The Scandal of Leadership: Unmasking the Powers of Domination in the Church* (100 Movements, 2023); Michael J. Kruger, *Bully Pulpit: Confronting the Problem of Spiritual Abuse in the Church* (Zondervan, 2022); Mike Cosper, *The Church in Dark Times: Understanding and Resisting the Evil That Seduced the Evangelical Movement* (Brazos, 2024); Katelyn Beaty, *Celebrities for Jesus: How Personas, Platforms, and Profits Are Hurting the Church* (Brazos, 2022). Coinciding with this epidemic of misconduct has been a steep decline in clergy trust, with the perception of pastors in the US falling to a record low. See Kate Shellnutt, "Above Reproach? Fewer Americans See Pastors as Ethical," *Christianity Today*, January 25, 2024.

Mean," cultural commentator David Brooks examines the steady erosion of moral virtues formerly valued in society, including empathy, humility, and decency.[6] In their place, troubling moral instincts have risen, including tribalism ("only my group is right") and emotivism ("whatever feels good to me is moral"). Given this situation in both the church and broader culture, the church needs to wholeheartedly renew its commitment to character transformation in the power of the Spirit. The church must once again become a people whose lives reflect the values and way of Jesus. Willard's two questions for every church are as relevant as ever: What is our plan for making disciples, and how is that going? I believe our study of Willard's formational theology provides crucial insights and tools to address this urgent need—not only in the realm of leadership but in the church's broader calling to cultivate Christlikeness in all of life, for the sake of the world.

The express goal of this book was to critically examine Willard's theory of spiritual formation, analyzing its core themes to determine its relevance and potential for Christian theology and, just as importantly, Christian living. Instead of merely summarizing the findings of our investigative journey, I wish to offer some constructive theological reflection as a way of putting a period on this study. But this punctuation mark should not be understood as ending the conversation but rather as opening it more fully. So think of the following reflections as three dots in an ellipsis rather than a hard-stop period. I have framed them as five formational reflections, beginning with kingdom apprenticeship—the signature of Willard's theological project.

KINGDOM APPRENTICESHIP: OR, TRAINING FOR REIGNING

Woven throughout Willard's understanding of spiritual formation is an eschatological dimension pointing toward God's ultimate purposes for creation; hence, this is the aspect of his theology with which

---

[6]David Brooks, "How America Got Mean," *The Atlantic* (September 2023): 68-76.

we began. We have been invited, Willard says, "to participate in the cosmic drama of God's eternal plan for the most glorious universe possible."[7] This vision involves co-ruling with God, a responsibility that necessitates a certain type of character. Our present life therefore serves as a training ground for becoming people God can entrust with this responsibility. For Willard, the eschatological logic of spiritual formation flows from the future back into the present: Reigning with Christ—the fulfillment of the original vocation given to humanity—requires we first have the agapeic character to handle such power.

Willard thus grounds the call of discipleship and the process of Christoformity not as an end in itself but as participation in God's comprehensive plan to overcome evil with goodness. It is within this sweeping biblical narrative that Willard develops a theology of kingdom apprenticeship to Jesus that conjoins spiritual formation with God's ongoing creative work in the present age and the one to come. His framing of character formation as training for reigning means there is a missional impulse kneaded into the whole of his theology—which may be what most distinguishes his approach within the spiritual formation discourse. And since this (eschatological) *reigning* is always defined in terms of the character of Christ, *training* is always directed toward cultivating, above all, the servant heart and *agapē* love embodied by Jesus—a formational telos that must never be forgotten.

The church exists, now as always, to produce people who resemble Jesus in values, beliefs, lifestyle, and purpose. If we are not doing that, one must ask: What exactly are we doing? This conviction has marked the most vital stretches of Christian theology, from the early church fathers to key figures throughout history who saw the theological task as ultimately ordered toward spiritual growth and moral transformation—figures such as Athanasius, Basil of Caesarea, John Cassian, Teresa of Ávila, Calvin, and Wesley, to name a few.[8] Willard joins this

---

[7]Dallas Willard, "Practicing the Presence of God" (August 11, 1993), MP3, 9:00.
[8]Of this lineage, Ellen Charry writes, "They were interested in forming us as excellent persons. Christian doctrines aim to be good for us by forming or reforming our character.... They seek

company, for he is eminently a theologian of the Christian life. From such a perspective, theology is the rules of the game, but the game itself is spirituality—the lived encounter with God in Christ through the power of the Spirit. In other words, theology exists to help people make contact with ultimate reality: God and his kingdom. And to truly make contact with these realities—to have *spiritual knowledge*, in Willard's terms—is to be transformed by them.

What Willard offers is not just a compelling vision of this transformation but a clear and coherent pathway toward it. His work enables us to bet the farm on apprenticeship to Jesus—to stake everything on it, pursuing it not as a vague aspiration or hollow platitude but as a concrete, attainable, grace-empowered way of life.

GRACE AND GRIT: A CONFLUENCE OF GOD'S ACTIVITY AND OURS

Many Christians struggle to understand how grace and effort fit together in spiritual growth. Some fear that emphasizing action leads to legalism, while others worry that stressing grace leads to passivity. Willard cuts through this tension, showing how spiritual formation is not about earning but actively participating in God's work in our lives. If grace is God acting in us to accomplish what we cannot do on our own, then in the lives of the saints it is not merely occasional (i.e., for forgiveness) but prevenient, pervasive, and always invitational. The Holy Spirit is forever the initiator and main actor; growth in godliness thus occurs only with divine precedence and empowerment. So let it be said once more that in Willard's theology, it is grace that does the heavy lifting.

Yet this grace does not eliminate the human side of holiness. Willard insists that sanctification requires the active participation of the will—or, more precisely, the will/spirit/heart as the executive center of the self—for

---

to form excellent persons with God as the model, and this in a quite literal sense, not as metaphors pointing to universal truths of human experience that lie beyond the events themselves. In other words, . . . the great theologians of the past were also moralists in the best sense of the term." Charry, *By the Renewing of Your Minds: The Pastoral Function of Christian Doctrine* (Oxford University Press, 1997) vii.

Exercise unto Godliness... and Godlikeness

it will not happen by divine prerogative alone; that is, God will not zap us into mature persons of Christ we ourselves have not chosen to become. To grow in Christlikeness is to consent to God's transformative action and respond with intentional effort. The Spirit empowers, but we must walk by the Spirit. Willard's account is therefore both profound and practical. It offers a clear picture of the human person and what is involved in shaping that person's character without oversimplifying either.

Since God has bestowed on individuals the power for self-determination—and since this aspect of the self is most distinctly *us*—the will/heart/spirit is in Willard's view the pinnacle of personhood and hence the fulcrum of formation in Christlikeness. Put differently, it is the critical aspect of a person that needs to be transformed for one's character to be thoroughly renovated. However, this transformation requires a holistic, bodily approach that especially accounts for the dialectical structure of the will and mind with which God has designed human persons.

For decades, Protestant theology has been shaped by serious concerns about works righteousness, often leading to an overly transactional view of salvation and a faith that remains mostly in the head. Willard counters this tendency by presenting a framework for the Christian life that integrates the heart, habits, and virtues into a daily apprenticeship to Jesus. The heuristics of VIM and the golden triangle make this process intelligible. While not explaining everything away, they do give form to the mystery of transformation. What emerges from all this is a noncompetitive understanding of grace and effort: God's action and human agency not in conflict but in concert. This has far-reaching implications not just for personal formation but for how we envision the church itself. Here, in relation to the workings of divine grace and human effort, especially our role therein, Willard's work is especially valuable for churches developing a theologically informed, practically viable approach to spiritual formation.

If seminaries, pastors, and leaders were to take seriously this metaphysic of grace, how might it change theological education? And how might it reshape life in the local congregation? What would we need to teach, model, or practice differently? These questions are not ancillary. They are central to what it means to form a people in the way of Jesus.

This same concerted logic extends to mission. Participation in the divine conspiracy is a Spirit-empowered, grace-sustained calling that also requires our effort—intentionality, risk, and courage. And for this, the church is indispensable. It is the soil in which this participatory life grows. For this reason, it is time we redefine and restructure our congregations around apprenticeship to Jesus rather than attendance or affinity. And so, ecclesiology.

FORMATIONAL ECCLESIOLOGY: BECOMING TOGETHER

While researching Willard's theory of formation for the better part of a decade, the area that most surprised me was his ecclesiology. At the outset, I assumed his theology of the church was quite lacking and perhaps insufficient, a critique that can be—and has been—levied against evangelical theology as a whole. And while it may be true that his broader social theory underplays the role of community in redemptive societal engagement and systemic transformation, this is untrue of his ecclesiology. His understanding of the church is actually quite weighty and substantial, as shown in chapter nine. For a researcher, discovering something that upends assumptions can be a joyful and humbling experience, and that is exactly what happened as I pieced together Willard's ecclesiology. Reconstructing it took care, for his ecclesiology flows just beneath the surface of his work, subtly supporting his broader vision without calling attention to itself. My interest in this goes beyond mere intellectual curiosity. As someone called to both academic and pastoral work, I'm deeply vested in the future of the church—and I believe its capacity to form people into Christlikeness is one of the defining challenges of our time.

Integral to Willard's ecclesial vision is a twofold dynamic of the church as a divine sociality and school of life. There is an inherent interrelatedness between these ontological and functional sides, for the power that flows from God's manifest presence in the *ekklēsia* (first dynamic) is the most potent ingredient for character growth in the Christian life. Hence, the church cannot effectively function as an academy for transformative discipleship (second dynamic) unless God dwells in the midst of a people.[9] Similar to Bonhoeffer, Willard views the church as a distinct sociological reality, unlike any other human community. This means the church possesses special resources for spiritual transformation—though the church possesses these by no means of its own accord but rather by God's possession of the church.

Since this ecclesial vision remains in the background of his formational theology, Willard does not spell out in detail how the manifest presence of God is actually *manifested* in the life of the church and how this catalyzes personal character transformation. But he has said enough for us to infer it is through the social relations of its members and, more specifically, through the giving and receiving of *agapē* love, toward both God and one another. Divine power is thus manifested in the *ekklēsia* as the members of Christ's body are engulfed in God's presence and in the goodwill of one toward another—or, put more tangibly, as they worship God and will the good of each other. Any robust approach to spiritual formation in the church must, then, prioritize this immersion into the trinitarian reality (Mt 28:19) for the upbuilding (schooling) of God's people.

My analysis of Willard's implicit ecclesiology shows the depth of his understanding of the church and its essential role in personal formation. Yet my treatment also reveals how ecclesiology plays a furtive role in his theology of formation, remaining nearly always in the background. There is a parallel here with the theological work of

---

[9]This is one further reason it is interesting that Willard does not give more attention to the possibility of malevolent nonhuman personalities dwelling within and having a stronghold on communities or other social phenomena. As noted in chapter eight, Willard does believe that demonic spirits can inhabit and act on human communities (not just individuals), yet he maintains that individuals are ultimately responsible for resisting evil in all its forms. So, there appears to be some inconsistency between this and his view on how a nonhuman personality (the Trinity) works within a particular human community (the *ekklēsia*), or at least he applies a different logic to each instance. On this latter intimation, it may be that the presence of *agapē* love—something possible only in human persons, Willard thinks, through God's indwelling Spirit—is the deciding factor.

Martin Luther. The sixteenth-century Reformer was chiefly concerned with reclaiming the message of the gospel, not the doctrine of the church.[10] The same is true of Willard. Both he and Luther sought to restore the gospel in their respective contexts, so when they do venture into churchly matters, it is always in view of this restorative desire. They hoped to establish the true *ekklēsia* once more on the foundation of the true *euangelion*, but the latter was clearly their aim.

While maintaining this focus on the message of the gospel, any constructive theological work in spiritual formation that builds on Willard's ideas will need to amplify his ecclesial vision and bring it to the forefront. This is because in today's pluralistic and increasingly secular context, where fewer reflexive supports exist for the Christian faith, forming people in the way of Jesus requires a thick plausibility structure in which kingdom living is modeled and made livable in community. In other words, in a society in which the cultural tide no longer supports the Christian imagination, the formation of disciples requires a shared way of life in which kingdom virtues are practiced and nurtured together. More resources, podcasts, and books (such as this one!) simply won't cut it. Information alone—even good theology—cannot form us. What we need is a community marked by shared rhythms and visible love. Orthodoxy must be coupled with collective orthopraxy.

And if our formation in Christlikeness is to be missional and bear witness to the world, then the gospel must be embodied. This means there must be a focus on communal formation—the formation of a people (not just persons) to mediate God's presence in the world—and the communal practices that help bring this about. Ours is a late-modern, post-Christendom age where proclamation without embodiment falls flat. This is because in a time when words are many and trust is scarce, truth must be lived if it is to be believed. For the gospel to become credible to the world, it must take flesh among a people. Forming mature followers of Jesus through belonging to a

---

[10]Paul D. L. Avis, *The Church in the Theology of the Reformers* (John Knox, 1981), 13.

community of intentional praxis can be a primary way of engaging our culture redemptively.

Yet we must also raise critical questions about the idealism of such an ecclesial vision—namely, its strong confidence in the church's capacity to form people in Christlikeness—given the growing understanding of mission history, colonialism, and abuse scandals. How do we understand the genuine gifts manifested in Christian communities when those same communities have also brought such harm? In other words, how can we hold together the beauty and brokenness of churches in which God's grace is clearly at work, yet deep wounds remain? And what shape can formation take when the church must not only pursue its calling but also repent of how far it has fallen from it?[11] These tensions deserve honest reckoning, but they do not close the door on hope. If anything, they sharpen the need to reimagine what the church can be and its potential for transformation. The church must indeed grapple with them if it is to become a credible witness in our time.

If theology is clinical, then ecclesiology must be practical. It has to show up in real communities, in the lived rhythms and structures of congregations learning how to follow Jesus together. Willard's understanding of the church as a school of life, along with his proposal of discipleship evangelism as its primary outward ministry, holds real promise for this work. Taken seriously, it can reshape how local churches think about their purpose, organize themselves, and respond to the cultural moment we are in. His two deceptively simple questions—what is our plan for making disciples, and how is that going?—serve not merely as diagnostics but as catalysts. They invite

---

[11] I cannot provide a thorough response to these questions here, though I submit that the church's shadow side, if anything, proves Willard's thesis that if you do not have transformed people operating your systems (in this case, churches), then it is hard to transform the systems or make changes in the world. This does not, of course, solve the theological conundrum of how the church can be a sociality of divine presence yet also a creature fully infected with sinfulness. For substantive reflection on the destructive tendencies of an idealistic ecclesiology, see Daniël Drost, "Diaspora as Mission: John Howard Yoder, Jeremiah 29, and the Shape and Mission of the Church" (PhD diss., VU University Amsterdam, 2019).

us to envision what church could be if formation into Christlikeness were at the center.

In my own ecclesial imagination, the church is not isolated from society but set apart within it, marked by a different allegiance. It lives as a distinct community with its own values and rhythms, committed to a joyful unmaking of the world as it is—challenging injustice, offering grace, unsettling the patterns of power—through the quiet revolution of Jesus. It is in these academies of kingdom living that disciples are formed: shaped in Christ's character and strengthened by his Spirit to continue God's work in the world. In our day and age, the clearest glimpse of God's reign comes not through persuasive words alone but through a people learning how to worship, serve, forgive, and hope together. It is this way of life, practiced together, that makes the gospel not only plausible but visible. The journey is rigorous, to be sure, but it is not lonely. It is sustained by divine companionship, empowered by the Spirit, and undertaken alongside others who are likewise being drawn into the life of God.

PLOWING FROZEN GROUND: RESTORING MORAL KNOWLEDGE

As the conversation continues beyond this book, another question for future studies is how Willard's ecclesial vision might more fully inform his broader social theory explored in chapter eight. We can and should appreciate his conviction that the larger social level is too abstract for the general populace to engage with and transform directly; thus the role of competent leaders and the shape of their moral lives are indispensable for the good of society.[12] There is a strong continuity between this social architecture and the eschatological thrust of his theology. His "first/then" logic of individual before

---

[12]This becomes especially evident in moments of institutional fragility—such as during the civil rights movement, the post-Soviet transition in Eastern Europe, or the Covid-19 pandemic—when established systems struggle to adapt to disruptive change. In such times, it is often the moral character and discernment of deeply formed individuals that sustains faithful leadership.

societal change takes its cues from his framing of character transformation as training for co-reigning with God, and vice versa.

However, the place of communal formation within this social architecture remains underdeveloped. So, how might his ecclesiology complement and even augment the social theory embedded within his overall approach to spiritual formation? That said, we should take seriously Willard's insistence that personal transformation must by and large precede societal transformation. Some theologians and scholars may be skeptical of his conclusions, but they stem from, among other things, a deep-seated commitment to personalism: If reality is personal at its core, then we cannot *begin* with impersonal entities (institutions, social mechanisms, the Zeitgeist, etc.) to solve our most pressing social problems. At the very least, one can say societal transformation cannot happen if persons do not have a desire for such transformation. Jesus' summons to seek first God's kingdom and his righteousness (Mt 6:33) is a personal calling that also lays the groundwork for any true societal renewal. And, recalling Willard's idea of what constitutes true ecumenicity, perhaps it is precisely this personalist framing that could soften some of the doctrinal divisiveness within the church itself. For if we learn to see others within our broader Christian family—even those with whom we disagree—as persons genuinely seeking to obey Christ, it may help shift our posture from suspicion to solidarity.

Of course, this is no simple task. In a time when even basic moral knowledge and formation is in decline and when institutional trust is at historic lows, calling people into genuine transformation often feels like plowing frozen ground. The soil resists. The blade sticks. But the act of plowing itself is an act of faith—a commitment to preparing the ground for what only God can grow.

NUDI NUDUM CHRISTUM SEQUI: NAKEDLY FOLLOWING THE NAKED CHRIST

The theme of training for reigning is a salient one in Willard's approach to spiritual formation, and I have tried to show not only how he arrives at this understanding but how it is worked through the whole of his theology. It truly is the linchpin of his formational theology. But I admit that while researching and writing on this area of his thought, I wrestled with many issues concerning "ruling over," "domain of authority," and "the exercise of power." Willard is to be commended for not ignoring these motifs in Scripture but striving to integrate them into a robust theology of transformation in Christlikeness and participation in God's great agapeic work. Yet given the church's history—and in some places, the church's present—some will find his emphasis on co-reigning to be problematic at best and dangerous at worst. In an era informed by postcolonial studies and movements such as #MeToo and Black Lives Matter, which have heightened our awareness of power dynamics, injustice, and systemic harm, this emphasis certainly collides with exegetical sensibilities today. Such language also risks being confused with triumphalist or nationalistic forms of Christianity and so-called dominion theology. That is why I wish to add one final note to what I have already said about this theme.

Among the many items I came across in Willard's unpublished papers was his business card. It contains the expected details—his university position, contact information, and so on—but also one striking detail. On the left side of the card is an image of the haloed *Agnus Dei* (Lamb of God), carrying a cross, with blood pouring forth from its chest into a chalice. Beneath the image appears the Latin phrase *nudi nudum Christum sequi* ("nakedly following the naked Christ").

It is worth noting that Willard altered the Latin from the traditional singular ("naked one") to the plural ("naked ones"). Considering the singular form—used by the Franciscans, for instance—is far more common historically, this shift may have been a subtle but significant theological move on Willard's part: a way of expressing the communal nature of discipleship. We follow the naked Christ not as isolated individuals but as a community of apprentices.[13]

Figure 11.1. Willard's business card

I later discovered that both the image and the phrase also appear on his personal letterhead, dating back to at least the mid-1990s. According to his daughter Rebecca, Willard home-made the design by cutting the image from something, placing it where he wanted it, and then photocopying it into existence. Years later, when leaders at Westmont College were forming the Martin Institute (which would eventually lead to the creation of the Dallas Willard Center), they consulted with Dallas about a possible logo. He suggested the lamb image, though they ultimately went a different direction.

It is difficult to say exactly when Willard first encountered this particular image or from what he originally cut it.[14] The same is true for the Latin phrase.[15] What we do know is that he was especially fond of both.

---

[13]That said, Willard may have been echoing Wesley—one of the few historical figures to use the plural form—especially given that he underlined the phrase and dog-eared the page in his personal copy of Wesley's journals.

[14]The *Agnus Dei* has a long history in Christian art, but the specific image of a victorious lamb bearing a cross or banner gained prominence through the Moravians in the 1700s. The depiction of the lamb's blood pouring into a chalice was famously painted in the Ghent Altarpiece (fifteenth century) and holds strong associations with Lutheran eucharistic theology.

[15]*Nudus nudum Christum sequi* is an ancient phrase from ascetic Christianity, first attributed to Jerome in the fourth century. It was later popularized by Francis of Assisi and his followers in

This pairing of image and phrase is deeply significant for understanding Willard's formational theology in general and his vision of kingdom leadership in particular. Together, the image of the slain lamb and the call to nakedly follow the naked Christ evoke what it means to be formed in Christlike character and what it means to reign with *agapē* love—that is, sacrificial, self-giving love. The *Agnus Dei* and the Latin phrase thus serve as emblems of true authority in God's upside-down kingdom. To rule rightly is not to dominate but to serve, not to control but to entrust, not to grasp but to give (see Mt 20:25-28). In Willard's vision, reigning with Christ is ultimately not about bearing the sword but bearing the cross.

In Scripture we find a tension between the triumphant, reigning Christ and the suffering Christ who chooses to cede his power and endure the cross on behalf of others. This surely has implications for our apprenticeship, and I readily admit that Willard could have brought these two themes—kingdom reigning and cruciform following—into more direct theological conversation, asking how they ought to be integrated. Even so, when one considers his theology as a whole, it becomes clear that the symbols on his business card and letterhead are more than decorative—they are declarative. Christian formation is cruciform; to follow the Lamb is to be poured out with him for the sake of others. And placing the image and phrase so plainly next to his credentials and contact details—almost as a personal coat of arms—amounts to a quiet confession of a deeper identity than scholar or philosopher: an apprentice of Jesus, nakedly following his naked Lord.

All of this stands in stark contrast to many contemporary visions of Christian power, which so often borrow the posture of Caesar rather than Christ. As noted, Willard took aim at three false gospels: the gospels on the right (forgiveness only) and the left (entirely

---

the 1200s, who adopted it as a kind of motto for their order. Francis's conversion story—in which he stripped himself bare and forsook his family's wealth to follow Jesus—is a most vivid embodiment of the phrase.

social), and the gospel of churchmanship. Based on my reading of Willard, if he were still with us today, I believe he might name a fourth: the gospel of Christian nationalism, which reduces Christianity to a quest for political power and cultural dominance, dangerously conflating God's kingdom with national identity. This socioreligious phenomenon is not new in church history, and we might have expected it to emerge from the growing pluralism and secularization of the West. Yet it has intensified in America today, with more public leaders and citizens embracing an abrasive form of political engagement melded with religious convictions that resembles, I would contend, a more Nietzschean ethos than a Christian one. Willard was not shy about naming cultural distortions that were particularly relevant in his time—especially those masquerading as "good news." Returning to the present discussion about what he chose to communicate on something as ordinary as a business card, I can hardly imagine a set of symbols more at odds with these distorted visions of Christian power than the slain Lamb and *nudi nudum Christum sequi*.

Thus, when we imagine our eschatological reigning with Christ in the future—and our character training for that reign in the present—Willard invites us to do so through the lens of the crucified, naked Christ. We might say (with a nod to *Divine Conspiracy*) that Jesus is forever both Maestro and Meek.

EPILOGUE: TRANSFORMING FRIENDSHIP

One of the main claims of this book is that Dallas Willard's formational theology not only represents a lifetime of thinking deeply about the theological and phenomenological dynamics of human transformation, but it is also intrinsically missional. God is forming a community of persons with agapeic character to co-rule with him over the rest of creation and eventually the cosmos. This divine conspiracy therefore includes spiritual formation but also depends on it, for formation is the means by which his redemptive work goes forth.

And at the very center of this formational and missional process is friendship.

Because of the resurrection and Pentecost, Jesus is alive and accessible today. We can know the resurrected Christ through the Spirit, and the great invitation of the gospel, Willard insists, is to become his apprentices, learning from him in real time how to live deeply in God's kingdom. But we are not merely his apprentices. Just as Jesus called his first followers his friends (Jn 15:15), he now extends this friendship to us. This friendship, says Willard, forms the foundation of the Christian life, creating the relational context for our growth in godliness. At the heart of Willard's vision for Christian spiritual formation is not merely a set of practices or a theology of growth but a Person. Through Jesus we are invited to share in the life of Father, Son, and Spirit. This relationship with the Trinity is the main catalyst for moral and spiritual growth, enabling us to become people capable of sharing in God's loving reign.

Willard's original working title for *The Spirit of the Disciplines*, his second theological book, was *Exercise unto Godliness*—an intentional riff on 1 Timothy 4:7. His aim in writing that work was to present a compelling biblical vision of Christian spiritual formation that people could clearly grasp, enabling them to experience transformative grace through active apprenticeship to and friendship with Jesus. Formation and vocation are thus intertwined in his theology, and both are rooted in friendship. It is through walking with Christ, in the intimacy of divine friendship, that we are shaped into people whose agapeic character enables us to participate in God's redemptive mission. This union of formation and mission, animated by friendship, runs through Willard's project like a current—what we might call *exercise unto godliness . . . and godlikeness*. Such is the central drama of the Christian life: the slow, radiant work of becoming the kind of person to whom God can entrust the world.

ACKNOWLEDGMENTS

IF ONE WANTS TO UNDERSTAND that God created us to live in community, I suggest one write a tome. Undertaking such an endeavor reveals we need the help of others and quickly cures any illusions of self-sufficiency. To begin, I want to thank my mentor and friend Darrell Guder, whom I had the privilege of studying under at Princeton Theological Seminary many moons ago. His generosity and curiosity profoundly shaped my early theological imagination, and his encouragement over the years led me to research and write this book. Darrell also introduced me to Stefan Paas, whose missiological mind, incisive questions, and wise guidance helped refine this study and have sharpened my thinking in ways that will remain with me indefinitely.

Special thanks to three brave friends who read an earlier draft of this book in its entirety: Susan Schnieders, the late Henry Lederle, and Tiffani Boerio. I especially appreciate Susan, editor extraordinaire, for being an ongoing theological dialogue partner and for championing this work. My thanks as well to others who read parts of this study over the years and offered critical feedback, including colleagues and friends such as Trevor Hudson, Steve Porter, Ross Lockhart, Jeff Hoops, Murphy Alvis, Esther Meek, Aaron Preston, Vic Gordon, Emily Freeman, Walter Hopp, Lacey Mason, Bill Heatley, Jeremy Gallegos, Jacob Cook, Rein Den Hertog, Gert-Jan Roest, and Michael Stewart Robb. Michael also deserves appreciation for generously sharing with me many recordings of Willard that were not yet available to the public. Thanks as well to my dear friends, Keith Matthews and James Catford, and spiritual director, Bill Zuelke, for their encouragement and counsel over the years. Thanks also to Richard Foster, whose brief mention of "Dr. Dallas Willard" years ago sent me down a path I'm still walking.

Several other people and institutions contributed to my research in important ways. Thank you to Friends University for giving me the opportunity to direct and teach in the master's program in Christian Spiritual Formation and Leadership for the past ten years and for granting me the space to pursue scholarly work. I am grateful to be part of this unique university and its warm community. Thank you to my colleague and friend Jim Smith for bringing me to Friends in the first place; I'll never forget the words, "You had me at Balthasar." Thank you to my ride-or-die sisters, Carissa Bowers and Kristin Wilson, for their partnership in running the master's program and making the impossible possible. Thank you to the Martin Institute at Westmont College for giving me access to the Dallas Willard Collection, and especially to Diane Ziliotto for helping me locate certain unpublished papers and obscure notes. Thank you to Dallas Willard's family for their support, in particular Becky Willard Heatley for our many discussions about her father and his ideas and for her thoughtful comments on my manuscript, and John Willard for helping me decipher his father's handwriting in a few critical resources (which looks more like that of a medical doctor than one in the humanities).

A special note of thanks to my editors, Rachel Hastings and Noel Forlini Burt, and to the entire IVP Academic team. It has been a pleasure to work with such a fine publishing house—one I have long admired. Noel's insightful feedback spurred on my thinking and made the book better. Hats off to Rachel in particular; this is my first book, and yet somehow I landed with one of the best collaborators in the business.

I took the risk of sounding sentimental in the first chapter (don't worry, I do not expect readers to remember all my footnotes) and now do so again here at the end. Although Dallas Willard has become a close theological companion, I never had the privilege of meeting him in person. Nonetheless, I feel compelled to thank him, namely for exemplifying in many ways the virtuous character about which he so often taught. Along with reading his published and unpublished works and listening to countless hours of his recorded lectures over the course of my research, I interviewed and spoke to numerous people who knew him intimately. Willard practiced what he preached and was the real deal, as the saying goes. Considering the American church and our society are in a crisis of character, I do not take for granted this biographical detail about the main theological voice of my study.

Finally, I am most grateful for all that my family has done to support me in writing this book. It is in vogue today to think of oneself as a "self-made" man or woman. In my case, this could not be further from the truth. I am in large part the result of two amazing parents, Syd and Kathy Keasler, who raised and loved me into who I am. Thank you for always believing in and cheering me on. My wife, Sarah, deserves the deepest gratitude of all. Over the course of researching and writing this book (seven years, lest we forget!), we became the proud parents of three beautiful children, Theo, Norah, and Zoe. Yet this book has often felt like a fourth child with its demands and required attention. Sarah has sacrificed much while remaining my closest companion throughout this project, supporting me even though neither of us knew at the beginning what an arduous process it would be. Talk about a "long obedience in the same direction." I am blessed beyond belief to share a sacramental marriage with you, filled with grace and delight.

BIBLIOGRAPHY OF WORKS BY DALLAS WILLARD

WRITINGS

The Allure of Gentleness: Defending the Faith in the Manner of Jesus. Edited by Rebecca Willard Heatley. HarperOne, 2015. (Posthumous)

"The Bible, the University and the God Who Hides." In *The Bible and the University*, edited by David Lyle Jeffery and C. Stephen Evans, 17-39. Zondervan, 2007.

"C. S. Lewis and the Pursuit of Truth Today." *Sacred History* (December 2005): 69-73, 111-15.

"Can Wisdom Be Taught?" *Roundtable* (1971): 10-18.

"Christ-Centered Piety." In *Where Shall My Wond'ring Soul Begin? The Landscape of Evangelical Piety and Thought*, edited by Mark A. Noll and Ronald F. Thielmann, 27-35. Eerdmans, 2000.

"Comments on Articles by Nelson, Slife, Reber, and Richardson." *Journal of Psychology and Theology* 34, no. 3 (2006): 266-71.

"A Cup Running Over." In *The Art and Craft of Biblical Preaching*, edited by Haddon Robinson and Craig Brian Larson, 71-73. Zondervan, 2005.

The Disappearance of Moral Knowledge. Edited by Aaron Preston, Gregg Ten Elshof, and Steven L. Porter. Routledge, 2018. (Posthumous)

"Discipleship." In *The Oxford Handbook of Evangelical Theology*, edited by Gerald R. McDermott, 236-46. Oxford University Press, 2010.

"Discipleship: For Super-Christians Only?" *Christianity Today* 24, no. 17 (1980): 24-27.

The Divine Conspiracy: Rediscovering Our Hidden Life in God. HarperSanFrancisco, 1998.

The Divine Conspiracy Continued: Fulfilling God's Kingdom on Earth. With Gary Black Jr. HarperOne, 2014. (Posthumous)

"The Failure of Evangelical Political Involvement." In *God and Governing: Reflections on Ethics, Virtue, and Statesmanship*, edited by Roger N. Overton, 74-91. Pickwick, 2009.

Foreword to *Christianity in the Academy: Teaching at the Intersection of Faith and Learning*, by Harry Lee Poe, 9-11. Baker Academic, 2004.

Foreword to *How I Changed My Mind About Women in Leadership: Compelling Stories from Prominent Evangelicals*, by Alan F. Johnson, 9-11. Zondervan, 2010.

Foreword to *The Post-Evangelical*, by Dave Tomlinson, 11-12. Emergent, 2003.

"The Gospel of the Kingdom and Spiritual Formation." In *The Kingdom Life*, edited by Alan Andrews, 27-57. NavPress, 2010.

The Great Omission: Reclaiming Jesus' Essential Teachings on Discipleship. HarperSanFrancisco, 2006.

Hearing God: Developing a Conversational Relationship with God. 3rd ed. Revised and abbreviated. InterVarsity Press, 1999.

Hearing God: Developing a Conversational Relationship with God. 4th ed. Updated and expanded by Jan Johnson. InterVarsity Press, 2012.

"Hermeneutical Occasionalism." In *Discipling Hermeneutics: Interpretation in Christian Perspective*, edited by Roger Lundin, 167-72. Eerdmans, 1997.

"How Concepts Relate the Mind to Its Objects: The 'God's Eye View' Vindicated?" *Philosophia Christi* 1, no. 2 (1999): 5-20.

"How Reason Can Survive the Modern University: The Moral Foundations of Rationality." In *Faith, Scholarship, and Culture in the 21st Century*, edited by Alice Ramos and Marie I. George, 181-91. Catholic University of America Press, 2002.

In Search of Guidance: Developing a Conversational Relationship with God. Regal, 1984.

In Search of Guidance: Developing a Conversational Relationship with God. 2nd ed. Rev. with a new epilogue. HarperSanFrancisco, 1993.

"Intentionality and the Substance of the Self." *Philosophia Christi* 13, no. 1 (2011): 7-19.

"Intentionality Contra Physicalism: On the Mind's Independence from the Body." With Brandon Rickabaugh. *Philosophia Christi* 20, no. 2 (2018): 497-515. (Posthumous)

"Jesus." In *Dictionary of Christian Spirituality*, edited by Glen G. Scorgie, 58-63. Zondervan, 2011.

"Jesus the Logician." *Christian Scholar's Review* 28, no. 4 (1999): 605-14.

"The Kingdom of God, Law, and the Heart: Jesus and the Civil Law." With Robert F. Cochran Jr. In *Law and the Bible: Justice, Mercy, and Legal Institutions*, edited by Robert F. Cochran Jr. and David VanDrunen, 151-82. IVP Academic, 2013.

Knowing Christ Today: Why We Can Trust Spiritual Knowledge. HarperOne, 2009. British ed., *Personal Religion, Public Reality? Toward a Knowledge of Faith*. Hodder & Stoughton, 2009.

"Knowledge." In *The Cambridge Companion to Husserl*, edited by Barry Smith and David W. Smith, 138-67. Cambridge University Press, 1995.

"Knowledge and Naturalism." In *Naturalism: A Critical Analysis*, edited by William Lane Craig and J. P. Moreland, 24-48. Routledge, 2000.

Life Without Lack: Living in the Fullness of Psalm 23. Edited by Larry Burtoft and Rebecca Willard Heatley. Thomas Nelson, 2018. (Posthumous)

Living in Christ's Presence: Final Words on Heaven and the Kingdom of God. With John Ortberg and Gary W. Moon. InterVarsity Press, 2013. (Posthumous)

Logic and the Objectivity of Knowledge: Studies in Husserl's Early Philosophy. Ohio University Press, 1984.

"Looking Like Jesus." *Christianity Today* 34, no. 11 (1990): 29-31.

"Meaning and Universals in Husserl's Logische Untersuchungen." PhD diss., University of Wisconsin, 1964.

"Moral Rights, Moral Responsibility, and the Contemporary Failure of Moral Knowledge." In *Guantanamo Bay and the Judicial-Moral Treatment of the Other*, edited by Clark Butler, 161-78. Purdue University Press, 2007.

"My Personal Top 5." In *25 Books Every Christian Should Read*, edited by Julia L. Roller, 155. HarperOne, 2011.

"Naturalism's Incapacity to Capture the Good Will." *Philosophia Christi* 4, no. 1 (2002): 9-28.

"Nietzsche Versus Jesus Christ." In *A Place for Truth: Leading Thinkers Explore Life's Hardest Questions*, edited by Dallas Willard, 153-68. InterVarsity Press, 2010.

"The People of God in Individual Communion with God." In *The Renovaré Spiritual Formation Bible*, edited by Richard J. Foster, Gayle Beebe, Lynda L. Graybeal, Thomas C. Oden, and Dallas Willard, 1-5. HarperSanFrancisco, 2005.

"The People of God into Eternity." In *The Renovaré Spiritual Formation Bible*, edited by Richard J. Foster, Gayle Beebe, Lynda L. Graybeal, Thomas C. Oden, and Dallas Willard, 2259-63. HarperSanFrancisco, 2005.

"Personal Soul Care." In *The Pastor's Guide to Effective Ministry*, edited by William H. Willimon, 11-19. Beacon Hill, 2002.

"Predication as Originary Violence: A Phenomenological Critique of Derrida's View of Intentionality." In *Working Through Derrida*, edited by Gary B. Madison, 120-36. Northwestern University Press, 1993.

Renewing the Christian Mind: Essays, Interviews, and Talks. Edited by Gary Black Jr. HarperOne, 2016. (Posthumous)

Renovation of the Heart: Putting On the Character of Christ. NavPress, 2002.

Renovation of the Heart in Daily Practice: Experiments in Spiritual Transformation. With Jan Johnson. NavPress, 2006.

"Rethinking Evangelism." *Cutting Edge* (Winter 2001): 10-14.

Revolution of Character: Discovering Christ's Pattern for Spiritual Transformation. With Donald Simpson. NavPress, 2005.

The Scandal of the Kingdom: How the Parables of Jesus Revolutionize Life with God. Edited by Rebecca Willard Heatley and Jan Johnson. Zondervan, 2024. (Posthumous)

"The Spirit Is Willing: The Body as a Tool for Spiritual Growth." In *The Christian Educator's Handbook on Spiritual Formation*, edited by Kenneth O. Gangel and James C. Wilhoit, 225-33. The Christian Educator's Handbook Series. Baker, 1994.

The Spirit of the Disciplines: Understanding How God Changes Lives. Harper & Row, 1988.

"Spiritual and Emotional Maturity." In *Renovated: God, Dallas Willard and the Church That Transforms,* by Jim Wilder, 9-29. NavPress, 2020. (Posthumous)

"Spiritual Disciplines, Spiritual Formation, and the Restoration of the Soul." *Journal of Psychology and Theology* 26, no. 1 (1998): 101-9.

"Spiritual Formation and the Warfare Between the Flesh and the Human Spirit." *Journal of Spiritual Formation & Soul Care* 1, no. 1 (2008): 79-87.

"Spiritual Formation as a Natural Part of Salvation." In *Life in the Spirit: Spiritual Formation in Theological Perspective*, edited by Jeffrey P. Greenman and George Kalantzis, 45-60. IVP Academic, 2010.

"Spiritual Formation in Christ: A Perspective on What It Is and How It Might Be Done." *Journal of Psychology and Theology* 28, no. 4 (2000): 254-58.

"Spiritual Formation in Christ Is for the Whole Life and the Whole Person." In *For All the Saints: Evangelical Theology and Christian Spirituality*, edited by Timothy George and Alister McGrath, 39-53. Westminster John Knox, 2003.

"The Theory of Wholes and Parts and Husserl's Explication of the Possibility of Knowledge in the Logical Investigations." In *Husserl's Logical Investigations Reconsidered*, edited by Denis Fisette, 163-81. Kluwer Academic, 2003.

"Translator's Introduction." In *Philosophy of Arithmetic: Psychological and Logical Investigations—with Supplementary Texts from 1887–1902*, edited by Edmund Husserl, xiii-lxiv. Kluwer Academic, 2003.

"The World Well Won: Husserl's Epistemic Realism One Hundred Years Later." In *One Hundred Years of Phenomenology*, edited by D. Zahavi and F. Stjernfelt, 69-78. Kluwer Academic, 2002.

INTERVIEWS

"The Apprentices: What Is Spiritual Formation? And How Does a Church Do It? A Professor and Pastor Discuss the New Language of Making Disciples." With Dieter Zander. *Leadership Journal* 26, no. 3 (Summer 2005): 20-25.

"Authentic Disciples of Jesus." In *Subversive Interviews*, by Keith Giles, 15-25. Subversive Underground, 2011.

"A Conversation with Dallas Willard about *Renovation of the Heart*." By Lyle Smith-Graybeal. *Perspective* 12, no. 4 (2002): 3-5.

"Getting the Elephant Out of the Sanctuary: An Interview with Dallas Willard." By Gary W. Moon. *Conversations Journal* 8, no. 1 (2010): 10-19.

"Going Deeper." By Hope McPherson. *Response* (Winter 2000): 10-11.

"Gray Matter and the Soul." By David O'Conner. *Christianity Today* 46, no. 12 (2002): 74.

"The Making of the Christian: Richard J. Foster and Dallas Willard on the Difference Between Discipleship and Spiritual Formation." By Agnieszka Tennant. *Christianity Today* 49, no. 10 (2005): 42-44.

"The Man Behind the (Divine) Conspiracy: A Conversation with Dallas Willard." By Patricia Hanlon. *Stillpoint* (Spring 2009): 8-9.

"On the Gospel of the Kingdom." In *Subversive Interviews*, by Keith Giles, 67-82. Subversive Underground, 2011.

"Spiritual Disciplines and Means of Grace: Contrast or Continuum?" *Modern Reformation*, no. 4 (2002): 41-43.

"Spiritual Disciplines in a Postmodern World." By Luci Shaw. *Radix*, no. 3 (2000): 4-7, 26-31.

"Spirituality Made Hard." By Mike Yaconelli. *The Door*, no. 129 (1993): 14-17.

"What Makes Spirituality Christian? Dallas Willard Thinks It Is as Important to Live the Truth as It Is to Believe It." By John Ortberg. *Christianity Today* 39, no. 3 (1995): 16-17.

UNPUBLISHED PAPERS, PRESENTATIONS, HANDOUTS, AND OTHER MATERIALS

"Asceticism: An Essential but Neglected Element in the Christian Theory of the Moral Life." Paper presented at the meeting of the Society of Christian Philosophers, San Francisco, March 1985.

"Becoming a Disciple of Jesus." Unpublished paper, ca. 1990.

"The Craftiness of Christ." Unpublished draft chapter, 2004.

"Discipleship to Jesus and the Missional Church." Handwritten notes, 2009.

"Discipleship to Jesus vs. the Missional Church." Printed lecture, Crystal Cathedral, Garden Grove, CA, 2009.

"Engaging the Will in Personal Transformation." Paper presented at the Alumni Reunion of the Psychological Studies Institute, Atlanta, November 7, 2008.

"Faith, Hope and Love as Indispensable Foundations of Moral Realization." Paper presented at the meeting of the Society of Christian Philosophers, Loyola Marymount University, Los Angeles, March 25, 1987.

"Following Christ in Everyday Life, or Training for Reigning." Handwritten notes, South Africa, 1993.

"Getting Love Right." Paper presented at the conference of the American Association of Christian Counselors, September 15, 2007.

"God and the Problem of Evil." Unpublished paper, 1993.

"Historical and Philosophical Foundations of Phenomenology." Unpublished paper, 1988.

"How to Live One Day with Jesus." Handout, South Africa, 1993.

"Jesus' Good News of God's Kingdom." Handout, Woodlake Avenue Friends Church, Canoga, CA, June 18–September 10, 1972.

"Justification of Faith by Experience." Handout, St. Peter's by the Sea Presbyterian Church, Rancho Palos Verdes, CA, 1973.

Letter to Roy M. Carlisle of Harper & Row (concerning *The Spirit of the Disciplines*). November 15, 1981.

"Metaphysics," PHIL 460. Transcript, University of Southern California, fall 1993.

"Missional Church." Handwritten notes, 2009.

"My Journey to and Beyond Tenure in a Secular University." Transcript, C. S. Lewis Foundation Summer Conference, June 21, 2003.

"Non-Reductive and Non-Eliminative Physicalism?" Unpublished paper, 1995.

"On Apologetics." Handwritten notes, 2007.

"On the Mind's Independence from the Body." Unpublished paper, n.d.

"The Pastoral Responsibility of a Theologian." Handout, European Leadership Forum, Eger, Hungary, May 24, 2006.

"Professions and the Public Interest in American Life," PHIL 141g. Syllabus, University of Southern California, spring 2010.

"Proposed Project for Sabbatical Leave for Fall 1992." University of Southern California, ca. 1992.

"Seminars on Creative Ministry in Times of Crisis." Handout, South Africa, 1987.

"Sketch of Outline for *The Rage Against Identity.*" Unpublished manuscript fragment, ca. 1992.

"Spirituality and Ministry," GM720. Syllabus and notes, Fuller Theological Seminary, 1993–2012.

"Spirituality and Ministry," GM720. Transparencies, Fuller Theological Seminary, 1993–2012.

"Studies in the Book of Apostolic Acts." Handout, Woodlake Avenue Friends Church, Canoga, CA, November 28, 1971–January 30, 1972.

"Studies in the Gospel of Jesus Christ." Handout, Shepherd of the Valley Lutheran Church, Canoga, CA, 1975.

"Teaching the Teachers of the Nations." Printed lecture, Fellowship of Evangelical Seminary Presidents, Marco Island, FL, January 2004.

RECORDINGS

"The Acts of the Apostles and the Kingdom of God." *The Book of Acts*. Skyline Wesleyan Church, Lemon Grove, CA, July 22, 1974. MP3.

"Afternoon Session." *The Kingdom of God and Ministry Today*. Kempton Park Methodist Church/Bedfordview Methodist Church, Bedfordview, South Africa, August 4, 1987. MP3.

"Angels and Demons." *School of Pastoring: Studies in Timothy*. East Rand Methodist Churches, South Africa, August 19, 1987. MP3.

"April 2012 Interview." *Frank Pastore Show*. Radio interview, April 17, 2012. MP3.

"Attention to Christology and Atonement." *Denver Cohort—Session Two*. Renovaré Institute, Allenspark, CO, March 16, 2011. Video.

"Authentic Leaders for Christ." *Leadership in the Kingdom*. First Church of the Nazarene of Pasadena, Pasadena, CA, February 22, 1997. MP3.

"Baptisms." *Baptism*. Valley Vista Christian Community, Sepulveda, CA, 1987. MP3.

"Being Church." *Tree of Life Sermons*. Tree of Life Community, Garden Grove, CA, August 14, 2011. MP3.

"Being Kingdom People in the Character and Power of Jesus." *Ministering the Kingdom of God with Christ Today*. Association of Vineyard Churches, Cape Town, South Africa, August 2, 2000. MP3.

"The Best News You'll Ever Hear." *Essentials of Kingdom Living*. Valley Vista Christian Community, Sepulveda, CA, 1986. MP3.

"The Bible as Indispensable Source of Knowledge: The Best Knowledge on the Most Important Topics . . . on Earth." *The Knowledge of Christ in the Contemporary World*. Eidos Christian Center, June 27, 2003. MP3.

"Biblical and Theological Foundations for Spiritual Formation in Christ 3." *Atlanta Cohort—Session One*. Renovaré Institute, Atlanta, October 11, 2011. MP3.

"The Biblical Understanding of the Reality of God." *Reality and Spiritual Life*. North Park Theological Seminary, Chicago, April 24, 1990. MP3.

"The Biblical View of the *Imago Dei*." *Deliverance from the Law of Sin and Death*. Eastern Mennonite College, Harrisonburg, VA, January 15, 1985. MP3.

"The Blessed Hope." *Things That Accompany Salvation*. Rolling Hills Covenant Church, Rolling Estates, CA, October 19, 1986. MP3.

"Bringing the Kingdom into Our Life." *Training for Reigning*. Benoni Central Methodist Church, Benoni, South Africa, August 12, 1993. MP3.

"The Calling and Resources of the Pastor." *Kern Pastors Character Conference*. Kern Family Foundation, Green Lake, WI, July 6, 2010. MP3.

"Changing the Depth of the Heart." *Spiritual Formation*. NavPress/Theological and Cultural Thinkers, Colorado Springs, CO, April 1997. MP3.

"Christian Discipleship and the Mission to the World: Churches and World Leadership." *Spiritual Formation and Soul Care*. Denver Seminary, Monument, CO, January 8, 2010. Video.

"Church Communities." *The Divine Conspiracy*. e4, Hollywood, CA, July 15, 2004. Video.

"Considering the Whole Person: Heart, Soul, Mind, Strength and Neighbor." *Spiritual Formation and Soul Care*. Denver Seminary, Monument, CO, January 4, 2010. Video.

"The Current Captivity of the Church." *The Book of Acts*. Skyline Wesleyan Church, Lemon Grove, CA, July 26, 1974. MP3.

"The Desire of All Nations." *Spirituality and Mission*. African Enterprise, Pietermaritzburg, South Africa, May 1985. MP3.

"Developing a Theology and Models for the Church." *The Journey: Generations*. The Leadership Institute, Mountain Center, CA, May 5, 1998. MP3.

"Dialogue with Dallas Willard." *Scripture and Ministry*. Trinity Evangelical Divinity School, Deerfield, IL, October 26, 2010. MP3.

"Disciple or Christian?" *Themes on the Spiritual Life*. Faith Evangelical Church, Chatsworth, CA, September 18, 1977. MP3.

"Discipleship as Life in the Kingdom." *Denver Cohort—Session One*. Renovaré Institute, Colorado Springs, CO, October 13, 2010. Video.

"Evangelism." *Spirituality and Ministry*. Fuller Theological Seminary, Sierra Madre, CA, June 21, 2002. MP3.

"Faculty Q & A." *Spiritual Renewal Conference*. Bethel Seminary San Diego, San Diego, October 9, 2008. MP3.

"The Foundations of Confidence: Work." *Confidence to Be Leader Disciples*. Kempton Park Methodist Church/Bedfordview Methodist Church, Kempton Park, South Africa, August 15, 1987. MP3.

"From the Greeks to the Barbarians—Even to the Scythians." *The Book of Acts*. Skyline Wesleyan Church, Lemon Grove, CA, July 25, 1974. MP3.

"General Introduction to Acts." *Journey into the Spiritual Unknown*. Rolling Hills Covenant Church, Rolling Estates, CA, January 4, 1978. MP3.

"God in Himself—Part 2." *Life Without Lack*. Valley Vista Christian Community, Sepulveda, CA, February 12, 1989. MP3.

"The Good Life." *True Spirituality*. Christ Community Evangelical Free Church, Kansas City, MO, September 30, 2006. MP3.

"The Good Life and the Good Person Made Real by Jesus: Rethinking the 'Sermon on the Mount.'" *Spiritual Renewal Conference*. Bethel Seminary, San Diego, October 10, 2008. MP3.

"The Great Inversion of the Kingdom of God: Blessedness." *The Kingdom of God*. Faith Evangelical Church, Chatsworth, CA, April 9, 1978. MP3.

"The Heavens Were Opened." *Baptism*. Valley Vista Christian Community, Sepulveda, CA, 1987. MP3.

"How Kingdom Values Impact Leadership." *Leadership in the Kingdom*. First Church of the Nazarene of Pasadena, Pasadena, CA, February 22, 1997. MP3.

"How Spiritual Formation Empowers and Informs Kingdom Living." *The Church as a Community of the Kingdom of God*. Church of the Open Door, Maple Grove, MN, November 4, 2004. MP3.

"How to Establish and Lead a Community of Jesus' Disciples in a Congregation of Spiritual Formation in Christlikeness." *Spiritual Formation Track*. European Leadership Forum, Eger, Hungary, May 24, 2006. MP3.
"Human Effort, Human Character and Divine Grace: Why Grace Requires Effort 1." *Spiritual Formation and Soul Care*. Denver Seminary, Monument, CO, January 6, 2010. Video.
"Human Effort, Human Character and Divine Grace: Why Grace Requires Effort 2." *Spiritual Formation and Soul Care*. Denver Seminary, Monument, CO, January 6, 2010. Video.
"Interview with Dallas Willard." *Navigators International Council 2003*. May 5, 2003. MP3.
"Introduction to Spirituality." *Spirituality and Ministry*. Australian College of Ministries, Sydney, July 28, 2008. MP3.
"Jesus' Gospel and Ours." *Be Imitators of Christ*. Regent University, Virginia Beach, VA, May 29, 1992. MP3.
"Jesus: Master of the Arts and Sciences 1." *Westmont Chapel*. Westmont College, Santa Barbara, CA, April 22, 1998. MP3.
"Jewish Persecution Drives the New Community to the Gentiles." *Studies in the Book of Apostolic Acts: Journey in the Spiritual Unknown*. Woodlake Avenue Friends Church, Canoga Park, CA, December 19, 1971. MP3.
"The Kingdom and Its Instrumentalities." *Spirituality and Ministry*. Fuller Theological Seminary, Sierra Madre, CA, June 6, 2012. Video.
"The Kingdom Comes in Power." *Studies in the Book of Apostolic Acts: Journey in the Spiritual Unknown*. Woodlake Avenue Friends Church, Canoga Park, CA, November 28, 1971. MP3.
"Kingdom Living." *Leadership in the Kingdom*. First Church of the Nazarene of Pasadena, Pasadena, CA, February 21, 1997. MP3.
"The Kingdom of Evil on Earth." *Soul's Eternal Anchor*. Rolling Hills Covenant Church, Rolling Estates, CA, 1988. MP3.
"The Larger Self & the Disciplines for Spiritual Life." *Spiritual Formation Forum*. Biola University, La Mirada, CA, October 12, 1993. MP3.
"The Last Shall Be First." *Discipleship and the Kingdom of God*. Western District Conference, Ventura Missionary Church, Ventura, CA, May 15, 1984. MP3.
"Last Things." *Kingdom Living Today*. Kempton Park Methodist Church/Bedfordview Methodist Church, Kempton Park, South Africa, August 20, 1987. MP3.
"Leadership as Love of God and Neighbor." *Leadership & Spirituality*. Regent College, Vancouver, May 15, 2000. MP3.
"Life in the Kingdom 4/Understanding the Person 1." *Atlanta Cohort—Session One*. Renovaré Institute, Atlanta, October 13, 2011. MP3.
"Lifting Doubts About Living and Acting with God in the Kingdom of the Heavens." *Apologetics in the Manner of Jesus*. Grace Church, Los Alamitos, CA, May 13, 1990. MP3.
"Living in the Knowledge of Christ and His Kingdom." *National Gathering*. The Ecclesia Network, Chevy Chase, MD, February 16, 2010. MP3.
"Local Congregations as Schools of Discipleship." *Pastors Conference*. Hawaiian Islands Ministries, Honolulu, March 30, 2007. MP3.

"Man's Blindness to God." *Soul's Eternal Anchor*. Rolling Hills Covenant Church, Rolling Estates, CA, 1988. MP3.

"Many Mansions." *Things That Accompany Salvation*. Rolling Hills Covenant Church, Rolling Estates, CA, October 25, 1986. MP3.

"The Matrix of Mission 1." *Spirituality and Mission*. African Enterprise, Pietermaritzburg, South Africa, May 1985. MP3.

"The Moral Significance of the Academic Life." *Christian Leadership Ministries*. University of California, Irvine, Irvine, November 29, 1990. Video.

"The Morally Responsible Skeptic." *Veritas Forum*. Indiana University, Bloomington, IN, April 5, 1995. MP3.

"Morning Session." *The Kingdom of God and Ministry Today*. Kempton Park Methodist Church/Bedfordview Methodist Church, Bedfordview, South Africa, August 4, 1987. MP3.

"My Grace Is Sufficient." *Renovaré Regional Conference*. Renovaré/C. S. Lewis Institute, Fairfax, VA, May 2, 2003. MP3.

"Naming the Issues." With Linda Cannell. *The Unnecessary Leader*. Regent College, Vancouver, May 19, 2000. MP3.

"The New Community of God Reaches Out in Power to the Old Jewish Community." *Studies in the Book of Apostolic Acts: Journey in the Spiritual Unknown*. Woodlake Avenue Friends Church, Canoga Park, CA, December 5, 1971. MP3.

"The New Testament Theology of the Church." *The With-God Life: The Dynamics of Scripture for Christian Spiritual TransFormation*. Renovaré International Conference/Spiritual Formation Forum, Denver, June 19, 2005. Video.

"On Philosophy and Christianity." *Slipstream: Leaders in Formation*. Evangelical Alliance (UK), Sierra Madre, CA, June 2010. MP3.

"Our Current Situation and the Four Great Questions of Life." *Bringing Christ to the World of the 21st Century*. Northfield Methodist Church, Benoni, South Africa, July 25, 2000. MP3.

"The Pastor." *School of Pastoring: Studies in Timothy*. East Rand Methodist Churches, South Africa, August 5, 1987. MP3.

"Pastors as Teachers of the Nations." *Pastors Conference*. Hawaiian Islands Ministries, Honolulu, March 30, 2007. MP3.

"The Place of 'Disciplines' in Christian Discipleship and Spiritual Formation 2." *Spiritual Formation and Soul Care*. Denver Seminary, Monument, CO, January 7, 2010. Video.

"Postmodernism: Philosophical & Historical Roots 1." *Christian Critical Perspectives on Postmodernism*. Biola University, La Mirada, CA, August 19, 1992. MP3.

"Postmodernism: Philosophical & Historical Roots 3." *Christian Critical Perspectives on Postmodernism*. Biola University, La Mirada, CA, August 19, 1992. MP3.

"Postmodernism: Philosophical & Historical Roots 4." *Christian Critical Perspectives on Postmodernism*. Biola University, La Mirada, CA, August 19, 1992. MP3.

"Practicing the Presence of God." *Training for Reigning*. Benoni Central Methodist Church, Benoni, South Africa, August 11, 1993. MP3.

"The Purpose and Problems of the Church Today." *Lay Leadership in the Local Congregation*. Kempton Park Methodist Church, Kempton Park, South Africa, August 7, 1993. MP3.

Bibliography of Works by Dallas Willard

"Q & A." *Healing the Heart and Life by Walking with Jesus Christ Daily*. Valley Vineyards, Reseda, CA, Fall 2003. MP3.
"Q & A 1." *Leadership in the Kingdom*. First Church of the Nazarene of Pasadena, Pasadena, CA, February 22, 1997. MP3.
"Q & A: Prayer." *The Divine Conspiracy*. e4, Hollywood, CA, July 15, 2004. MP3.
"Q & A with Keith Matthews." *Atlanta Cohort—Session Two*. Renovaré Institute, Atlanta, March 16, 2012. MP3.
"Realism." *What Matters to Me and Why*. University of Southern California, Los Angeles, January 15, 2003. MP3.
"The Redemption of Reason and the University in the Next Millennium." *The Christian University for the Next Millennium: A Symposium Celebrating Biola's 90th Anniversary*. Biola University, La Mirada, CA, February 28, 1998. MP3.
"Regeneration and the Heart Jesus Wishes to Give Us." *Disciplines of Kingdom Life*. Church of the Open Door, Maple Grove, MN, August 25, 2000. MP3.
"The Saints Shall Judge the World." With A. Grace Wenger. *Deliverance from the Law of Sin and Death*. Eastern Mennonite College, Harrisonburg, VA, January 16, 1985. MP3.
"The Self/Spiritual Transformation and Discipline." *Leadership & Spirituality*. Regent College, Vancouver, May 17, 2000. MP3.
"Session 1—Part 2." *The Omission from the Great Commission—and How to Fix It*. National Pastors Convention/Youth Specialities, San Diego, CA, March 9, 2004. MP3.
"Session 1—Part 3." *The Omission from the Great Commission—and How to Fix It*. National Pastors Convention/Youth Specialities, San Diego, March 9, 2004. MP3.
"The Shape of the Church Visible: Today and Tomorrow." *Bringing Christ to the World of the 21st Century*. Northfield Methodist Church, Benoni, South Africa, July 26, 2000. MP3.
"The Soul as a Factor in Mental and Physical Health—the Revenge of the Soul That Was Lost." *Forum on Psychiatry and Christianity*. Loma Linda University Behavioral Medical Center, Loma Linda, CA, January 26, 1990. Video.
"The Spirit and the Heart." *Spiritual Formation Forum*. Biola University, La Mirada, CA, October 11, 1993. MP3.
"Spiritual Direction and How It Relates to Psychological Counseling." *School of Pastoring: Studies in Timothy*. East Rand Methodist Churches, South Africa, August 20, 1987. MP3.
"Spiritual Formation and the Disciplines." *Spirituality and Ministry*. Fuller Theological Seminary, Sierra Madre, CA, June 7, 2012. Video.
"Spiritual Formation as a Natural Part of Salvation." *Wheaton College Theology Conference*. Wheaton College, Wheaton, IL, April 17, 2009. MP3.
"Spiritual Formation as the Key Component of Leadership." *Formational and Missional: The Jesus Way for Church Life and Leadership*. Renovaré International Conference, San Antonio, TX, June 22, 2009. MP3.
"Spiritual Reality: God and the Human Soul." *Be Imitators of Christ*. Regent University, Virginia Beach, VA, May 30, 1992. MP3.
"Spiritual Transformation." *The Church as a Community of the Kingdom of God*. Church of the Open Door, Maple Grove, MN, November 5, 2004. MP3.

"Spirituality and the Churches." *Spirituality and Ministry*. Fuller Theological Seminary, Sierra Madre, CA, June 4, 2012. Video.

"Spirituality and Mission." *Spirituality and Mission*. African Enterprise, Pietermaritzburg, South Africa, May 1985. MP3.

"Starting from Community and Human Realities." *The Unnecessary Leader*. Regent College, Vancouver, May 19, 2000. MP3.

"Taking 1 Corinthians Seriously: Intending to Do It 1." *Spiritual Formation and Soul Care*. Denver Seminary, Monument, CO, January 5, 2010. Video.

"The Transformation of the Mind: Thoughts and Feelings 1." *Spiritual Formation and Soul Care*. Denver Seminary, Monument, CO, January 7, 2010. Video.

"Truth." *Feeding the Homeless Mind*. University of California, Los Angeles, Los Angeles, February 21, 1992. MP3.

"The Virtuous Life: The Substance of Holiness." *Personal Spiritual Renewal*. Renovaré, Wichita, KS, November 1989. MP3.

"Vision: The Cooperative Friends of Jesus." *The Church as a Community of the Kingdom of God*. Church of the Open Door, Maple Grove, MN, November 4, 2004. MP3.

"What Christ Did to Save Mankind." *Faith Evangelical Sunday School*. Faith Evangelical Church, Chatsworth, CA, 1979. MP3.

"What Does Holiness Look Like Shorn of Its Legalistic Expressions? 1." *Spiritual Formation and Soul Care*. Denver Seminary, Monument, CO, January 4, 2010. Video.

"What Does Holiness Look Like Shorn of Its Legalistic Expressions? 2." *Spiritual Formation and Soul Care*. Denver Seminary, Monument, CO, January 4, 2010. Video.

"What Is the Kingdom of God?" *Denver Cohort—Session One*. Renovaré Institute, Colorado Springs, CO, October 13, 2010. Video.

"What Is the Kingdom of God?" *Guidelines for Life in the Kingdom of God*. Rolling Hills Covenant Church, Rolling Estates, CA, January 13, 1985. MP3.

"What to Do 'In Church': Eternal Living Fostered by Church Activities." *Living With-God Today*. Northfield Methodist Church, Benoni, South Africa, August 5, 2010. MP3.

"Why Am I Here? The Four Great Questions in Life." *Denver Cohort – Session One*. Renovaré Institute, Colorado Springs, CO, October 12, 2010. Video.

"Why Such Lack and Evil?" *Life Without Lack*. Valley Vista Christian Community, Sepulveda, CA, February 26, 1989. MP3.

"Why There Are People on Earth." *Life Without Lack*. Valley Vista Christian Community, Sepulveda, CA, February 19, 1989. MP3.

"You Can't Have One Without the Other." *Discipleship and the Kingdom of God*. Western District Conference, Ventura Missionary Church, Ventura, CA, May 14, 1984. MP3.

BIBLIOGRAPHY OF OTHER WORKS

Alexander, Donald L., ed. *Christian Spirituality: Five Views of Sanctification.* IVP Academic, 1988.
Aquino, Frederick D. "Spiritual Formation, Authority, and Discernment." In *The Oxford Handbook of the Epistemology of Theology*, edited by William J. Abraham and Frederick D. Aquino, 157-72. Oxford University Press, 2017.
Augustine. *Confessions and Enchiridion.* Translated by Albert Cook Outler. Westminster John Knox, 2006.
Augustine. *The Trinity.* Translated by Stephen McKenna. Catholic University of America Press, 1963.
Avis, Paul D. L. *The Church in the Theology of the Reformers.* John Knox, 1981.
Baker, Lynne Rudder. *Persons and Bodies: A Constitution View.* Cambridge University Press, 2000.
Beaty, Katelyn. *Celebrities for Jesus: How Personas, Platforms, and Profits Are Hurting the Church.* Brazos, 2022.
Bellah, Robert N., Richard Madsen, William M. Sullivan, Ann Swidler, and Steven M. Tipton. *Habits of the Heart: Individualism and Commitment in American Life.* University of California Press, 1985.
Berger, Peter. *The Sacred Canopy: Elements of a Sociological Theory of Religion.* Doubleday, 1967.
Berkhof, Hendrik. *Christ and the Powers.* Herald, 1962.
Berry, Wendell. *Sex, Economy, Freedom and Community: Eight Essays.* Pantheon, 1992.
Billings, J. Todd. *Union with Christ: Reframing Theology and Ministry for the Church.* Baker Academic, 2011.
Black, Gary, Jr. *The Theology of Dallas Willard: Discovering Protoevangelical Faith.* Pickwick, 2013.
Bonhoeffer, Dietrich. *Sanctorum Communio: A Theological Study of the Sociology of the Church.* In *Dietrich Bonhoeffer Works*, vol. 1, edited by Clifford Green, translated by Reinhard Krauss and Nancy Lukens. Fortress, 1998.
"Books of the Century." *Christianity Today* 44, no. 5 (2000): 92-93.
Bosch, David J. "The Afrikaner and South Africa." *Theology Today* 43, no. 2 (1986): 203-16.
Bosch, David J. *Transforming Mission: Paradigm Shifts in Theology of Mission.* Orbis, 1991.
Brackney, William H. *A Genetic History of Baptist Thought: With Special Reference to Baptists in Britain and North America.* Mercer University Press, 2004.
Bridges, Jerry. *The Pursuit of Holiness.* NavPress, 1978.

Brooks, David. "How America Got Mean." *The Atlantic* (September 2023): 68-76.

Butler, Cuthbert. *Western Mysticism: The Teaching of Saints Augustine, Gregory and Bernard on Contemplation and the Contemplative Life*. Constable, 1922.

Calvin, John. *Commentaries on the Four Last Books of Moses*. Vol. 1. Translated by Charles William Bingham. Baker, 1989.

Calvin, John. *Institutes of the Christian Religion*. Edited by John T. McNeill. Translated by Ford Lewis Battles. 2 vols. Westminster John Knox, 1960.

Campbell, C. A. *On Selfhood and Godhood*. Allen & Unwin, 1957.

Canlis, Julie. "Sonship, Identity and Transformation." In *Sanctification: Explorations in Theology and Practice*, edited by Kelly M. Kapic, 232-50. IVP Academic, 2014.

Carpenter, Angela. *Responsive Becoming: Moral Formation in Theological, Evolutionary, and Developmental Perspective*. T&T Clark, 2019.

Cassian, John. *The Conferences*. Translated by Boniface Ramsey. Ancient Christian Writers 57. Paulist, 1997.

Chan, Simon. *Liturgical Theology: The Church as Worshiping Community*. IVP Academic, 2006.

Chan, Simon. *Spiritual Theology: A Systematic Study of the Christian Life*. IVP Academic, 1998.

Chandler, Diane J. *Christian Spiritual Formation: An Integrated Approach for Personal and Relational Wholeness*. InterVarsity Press, 2014.

Charry, Ellen T. *By the Renewing of Your Minds: The Pastoral Function of Christian Doctrine*. Oxford University Press, 1997.

Clark, Trey L. "Dallas Willard's Theology of Evangelism." *Witness: Journal of the Academy for Evangelism in Theological Education* 30, no. 1 (2016): 1-27.

Collicutt, Joanna. *The Psychology of Christian Character Formation*. SCM Press, 2014.

Comer, John Mark. *Practicing the Way: Be with Jesus, Become Like Him, Do as He Did*. WaterBrook, 2024.

Cosper, Mike. *The Church in Dark Times: Understanding and Resisting the Evil That Seduced the Evangelical Movement*. Brazos, 2024.

Covington, Jesse, Bryan T. McGraw, and Micah Watson. *Hopeful Realism: Evangelical Natural Law and Democratic Politics*. IVP Academic, 2025.

Cremer, Tobias. *The Godless Crusade: Religion, Populism, and Right-Wing Identity Politics in the West*. Cambridge University Press, 2023.

Davis, Ellen. *Scripture, Culture, and Agriculture: An Agrarian Reading of the Bible*. Cambridge University Press, 2008.

Dawn, Marva. *Powers, Weakness, and the Tabernacling of God*. Eerdmans, 2001.

Doriani, Daniel M. "Above Reproach? Moral Failure and Godly Character in Pastoral Leadership." *Westminster Theological Journal* 85, no. 1 (2023): 53-68.

Dorsett, Lyle W. *Seeking the Secret Place: The Spiritual Formation of C. S. Lewis*. Brazos, 2004.

Dreher, Rod. *The Benedict Option: A Strategy for Christians in a Post-Christian Nation*. Sentinel, 2017.

Drost, Daniël. "Diaspora as Mission: John Howard Yoder, Jeremiah 29, and the Shape and Mission of the Church." PhD diss., VU University Amsterdam, 2019.

Durant, Will. *Caesar and Christ*. In *The Story of Civilization*, vol. 3. Simon & Schuster, 1944.

Edwards, Jonathan. *Ethical Writings*. In *The Works of Jonathan Edwards*, vol. 8, edited by Paul Ramsey. Yale University Press, 1989.

Eims, LeRoy. *The Lost Art of Disciple-Making*. Zondervan, 1978.

Emerson, Michael O., and Christian Smith. *Divided by Faith: Evangelical Religion and the Problem of Race in America*. Oxford University Press, 2000.

Fitch, David E. *Faithful Presence: Seven Disciplines That Shape the Church for Mission*. InterVarsity Press, 2016.

FitzGerald, Frances. *The Evangelicals: The Struggle to Shape America*. Simon & Schuster, 2017.

Forde, Gerhard O. "The Lutheran Position." In *Christian Spirituality: Five Views of Sanctification*, edited by Donald L. Alexander, 13-32. IVP Academic, 1988.

Foster, Richard J. *Celebration of Discipline: The Path to Spiritual Growth*. Harper & Row, 1978.

Foster, Richard J., Gayle Beebe, Lynda L. Graybeal, Thomas C. Oden, and Dallas Willard. "A Panoramic View of God's Purpose in History." In *The Renovaré Spiritual Formation Bible*, edited by Richard J. Foster, Gayle Beebe, Lynda L. Graybeal, Thomas C. Oden, and Dallas Willard, xxxvii-xxxix. HarperSanFrancisco, 2005.

Foster, Richard J., Gayle Beebe, Lynda L. Graybeal, Thomas C. Oden, and Dallas Willard. "The People of God in Exodus." In *The Renovaré Spiritual Formation Bible*, edited by Richard J. Foster, Gayle Beebe, Lynda L. Graybeal, Thomas C. Oden, and Dallas Willard, 87-91. HarperSanFrancisco, 2005.

Foster, Richard J., Gayle Beebe, Lynda L. Graybeal, Thomas C. Oden, and Dallas Willard, eds. *The Renovaré Spiritual Formation Bible*. HarperSanFrancisco, 2005.

Friesen, Gary. *Decision Making and the Will of God: A Biblical Alternative to the Traditional View*. Rev. and expanded. Multnomah, 2004.

Giddens, Anthony. *The Consequences of Modernity*. Stanford University Press, 1990.

Goodall, Norman, ed. *Missions Under the Cross: Addresses Delivered at the Enlarged Meeting of the Committee of the International Missionary Council at Willingen, in Germany, 1952*. Edinburgh House Press, 1953.

Gorman, Michael J. *Abide and Go: Missional Theosis in the Gospel of John*. Cascade, 2018.

Gorman, Michael J. *Becoming the Gospel: Paul, Participation, and Mission*. Eerdmans, 2015.

Graham, Ruth. "Around Dallas, the Church Scandals Seem to Have No End." *New York Times*, October 3, 2024.

Green, Clifford J. *Bonhoeffer: A Theology of Sociality*. Rev. ed. Eerdmans, 1999.

Green, Joel B. *Body, Soul, and Human Life: The Nature of Humanity in the Bible*. Baker Academic, 2008.

Grenz, Stanley J. *Renewing the Center: Evangelical Theology in a Post-Theological Era*. Baker Academic, 2000.

Guder, Darrell L., ed. *Missional Church: A Vision for the Sending of the Church in North America*. Eerdmans, 1998.

Gushee, David P., and Glen H. Stassen. *Kingdom Ethics: Following Jesus in Contemporary Context*. 2nd ed. Eerdmans, 2016.

Hauerwas, Stanley. *A Community of Character: Toward a Constructive Christian Social Ethic*. University of Notre Dame Press, 1981.

Hauerwas, Stanley. "Nearing the End: A Conversation with Theologian Stanley Hauerwas." By Albert Mohler. *Thinking in Public*, April 28, 2014. https://albertmohler.com/2014/04/28/nearing-the-end-a-conversation-with-theologian-stanley-hauerwas.

Hauerwas, Stanley. *Sanctify Them in the Truth: Holiness Exemplified*. Abingdon, 1998.

Hauerwas, Stanley. "'Why Have You Forsaken Me?' Stanley Hauerwas on Atonement Theology, Mel Gibson's 'Passion,' and the 'Chilling' Meaning of Christ's Last Words." By Laura Sheahen. *Beliefnet*, March 2005. www.beliefnet.com/faiths/christianity/2005/03/why-have-you-forsaken-me.

Healy, Nicholas M. *Church, World and the Christian Life: Practical-Prophetic Ecclesiology*. Cambridge University Press, 2000.

Hector, Kevin W. *Christianity as a Way of Life: A Systematic Theology*. Yale University Press, 2023.

Herdt, Jennifer A. *Putting On Virtue: The Legacy of the Splendid Vices*. University of Chicago Press, 2008.

Hopkins, Burt C. "Dallas Willard's Contribution to Phenomenology." *Husserl Studies* 35 (2019): 117-30.

Hopp, Walter. "Dallas Willard on Knowledge and Its Role in Transformation." Paper presented at the Hildebrand Project Summer Seminar, Steubenville, OH, June 30, 2022.

Hopp, Walter. *Phenomenology: A Contemporary Introduction*. Routledge, 2020.

Howard, Evan B. *The Brazos Introduction to Christian Spirituality*. Brazos, 2008.

Hudson, Trevor. *Christ-Following: Ten Signposts to Spirituality*. Revell, 1996.

Hunter, James Davison. *To Change the World: The Irony, Tragedy, and Possibility of Christianity in the Late Modern World*. Oxford University Press, 2010.

Husserl, Edmund. *Logical Investigations*. Vol. 1. Translated by J. N. Findlay. Routledge, 1970.

Issler, Klaus. "An Orientation to Four Pervading Themes of the Christian Life from Dallas Willard." *Talbot School of Theology Faculty Blog*, March 9, 2015. www.biola.edu/blogs/good-book-blog/2015/an-orientation-to-four-pervading-themes-of-the-christian-life-from-dallas-willard.

James, William. *The Principles of Psychology*. 2 vols. Holt, 1890.

Jenson, Robert W. *Systematic Theology*. Vol. 1, *The Triune God*. Oxford University Press, 1997.

Jesson, Greg. "The Husserlian Roots of Dallas Willard's Philosophical and Religious Works: Knowledge of the Temporal and the Eternal." *Philosophia Christi* 16, no. 1 (2014): 7-36.

Jones, E. Stanley. *Is the Kingdom of God Realism?* Abingdon-Cokesbury, 1940.

Jones, E. Stanley. *The Way*. Abingdon-Cokesbury, 1946.

Kapic, Kelly M., ed. *Sanctification: Explorations in Theology and Practice*. IVP Academic, 2014.

Keasler, Keas. "Book Review: *The Kingdom Among Us: The Gospel According to Dallas Willard*." *Journal of Spiritual Formation & Soul Care* 16, no. 1 (2023): 167-76.

Kirk, J. Andrew, and Kevin J. Vanhoozer, eds. *To Stake a Claim: Mission and the Western Crisis of Knowledge*. Wipf & Stock, 1999.

Kruger, Michael J. *Bully Pulpit: Confronting the Problem of Spiritual Abuse in the Church*. Zondervan, 2022.

Langer, Rick. "Points of Unease with the Spiritual Formation Movement." *Journal of Spiritual Formation & Soul Care* 5, no. 2 (2012): 182-206.

Lovelace, Richard F. "The Sanctification Gap." *Theology Today* 29, no. 4 (1973): 363-69.

Luhrmann, T. M. *When God Talks Back: Understanding the American Relationship with God*. Knopf, 2012.

MacIntyre, Alasdair. *After Virtue*. 2nd ed. University of Notre Dame Press, 1984.

Maritain, Jacques. *The Person and the Common Good*. University of Notre Dame Press, 1972.

Mason, Mary Elizabeth. *Active Life and Contemplative Life: A Study of the Concepts from Plato to the Present*. Marquette University Press, 1961.

McGarry, Joseph M. "Christ Among a Band of People: Dietrich Bonhoeffer and Formation in Christ." PhD diss., University of Aberdeen, 2013.

McGrath, Alister. "Outside the 'Inner Ring': Lewis as a Theologian." In *The Intellectual World of C. S. Lewis*, 163-83. Wiley-Blackwell, 2014.

Meek, Esther Lightcap. *Longing to Know: The Philosophy of Knowledge for Ordinary People*. Brazos, 2003.

Meek, Esther Lightcap. *Loving to Know: Covenant Epistemology*. Cascade, 2011.

Middleton, J. Richard. *The Liberating Image: The Imago Dei in Genesis 1*. Brazos, 2005.

Milavec, Aaron. *To Empower as Jesus Did: Acquiring Spiritual Power Through Apprenticeship*. Edwin Mellen, 1982.

Miller-McLemore, Bonnie. "The Theory-Practice Distinction and the Complexity of Practical Knowledge." *HTS Theological Studies* 72, no. 4 (2016): 1-8.

Moon, Gary W. *Becoming Dallas Willard: The Formation of a Philosopher, Teacher, and Christ Follower*. InterVarsity Press, 2018.

Moreland, J. P. "Body and Soul: Tweaking Dallas Willard's Understanding of the Human Person." In *Until Christ Is Formed in You: Dallas Willard and Spiritual Formation*, edited by Steven L. Porter, Gary W. Moon, and J. P. Moreland. ACU Press, 2018.

Murphy, Nancey. *Beyond Liberalism and Fundamentalism: How Modern and Postmodern Philosophy Set the Theological Agenda*. Trinity Press International, 1996.

Murphy, Nancey. *Bodies and Souls, or Spirited Bodies?* Cambridge University Press, 2006.

Murray, John. *Redemption: Accomplished and Applied*. Eerdmans, 1955.

Newbigin, Lesslie. *A Faith for This One World*. SCM Press, 1961.

Newbigin, Lesslie. *The Gospel in a Pluralist Society*. Eerdmans, 1989.

Newbigin, Lesslie. *A Word in Season: Perspectives on Christian World Missions*. Eerdmans, 1994.

Nimmo, Paul T., and David A. S. Fergusson, eds. *The Cambridge Companion to Reformed Theology*. Cambridge University Press, 2016.

Oman, John. *Grace and Personality*. Cambridge University Press, 1917.

Peterson, Eugene H. *A Long Obedience in the Same Direction: Discipleship in an Instant Society*. InterVarsity Press, 1980.

Piper, John. *Let the Nations Be Glad! The Supremacy of God in Missions*. Baker, 1993.

Porter, Steven L. "On the Renewal of Interest in the Doctrine of Sanctification: A Methodological Reminder." *Journal of the Evangelical Theological Society* 45, no. 3 (2002): 415-26.

Porter, Steven L. "An Overview of Willard's Primary Writings: The Willardian Corpus." In *Until Christ Is Formed in You: Dallas Willard and Spiritual Formation*, edited by Steven L. Porter, Gary W. Moon, and J. P. Moreland, 19-52. ACU Press, 2018.

Porter, Steven L. "Will/Heart/Spirit: Discipleship That Forms the Christian Character." *Christian Education Journal* 16, no. 1 (2019): 69-94.

Porter, Steven L., and Brandon Rickabaugh. "The Sanctifying Work of the Holy Spirit in Christian Virtue Formation." In *Faith and Virtue Formation: Christian Philosophy in Aid of Becoming Good*, edited by Adam C. Pelser and W. Scott Cleveland, 123-45. Oxford University Press, 2021.

Porter, Steven L., Steven J. Sandage, David C. Wang, and Peter C. Hill. "Measuring the Spiritual, Character, and Moral Formation of Seminarians: In Search of a Meta-Theory of Spiritual Change." *Journal of Spiritual Formation & Soul Care* 12, no. 1 (2019): 5-24.

Riesen, Richard. "'Jesus the Logician': A (Very) Modest Proposal." *Christian Scholar's Review* 34, no. 3 (2005): 341-51.

Robb, Michael Stewart. "The Kingdom Among Us: Jesus, the Kingdom of God and the Gospel According to Dallas Willard." PhD diss., University of Aberdeen, 2016.

Robb, Michael Stewart. *The Kingdom Among Us: The Gospel According to Dallas Willard*. Fortress, 2022.

Saudreau, Auguste. *The Life of Union with God*. Translated by E. J. Strickland. Benziger Brothers, 1927.

Scheller, Christine A. "A Divine Conspirator." *Christianity Today* 50, no. 9 (2006): 44-48.

Schwanda, Tom. "Formation, Spiritual." In *Dictionary of Christian Spirituality*, edited by Glen G. Scorgie. Zondervan, 2011.

Shellnutt, Kate. "Above Reproach? Fewer Americans See Pastors as Ethical." *Christianity Today*, January 25, 2024.

Shoemaker, Samuel. *With the Holy Spirit and with Fire*. Harper & Row, 1960.

Smith, Gordon T. *Called to Be Saints: An Invitation to Christian Maturity*. IVP Academic, 2014.

Smith, Gordon T. *Wisdom From Babylon: Leadership for the Church in a Secular Age*. IVP Academic, 2020.

Smith, James Bryan. *The Good and Beautiful Community: Following the Spirit, Extending Grace, Demonstrating Love*. InterVarsity Press, 2010.

Smith, James Bryan. *The Good and Beautiful God: Falling in Love with the God Jesus Knows*. InterVarsity Press, 2009.

Smith, James K. A. *Desiring the Kingdom: Worship, Worldview, and Cultural Formation*. Baker Academic, 2009.

Smith, James K. A. *Imagining the Kingdom: How Worship Works*. Baker Academic, 2013.

Snow, Nancy E., ed. *The Oxford Handbook of Virtue*. Oxford University Press, 2018.

Soames, Scott. Foreword to *The Disappearance of Moral Knowledge*, by Dallas Willard, edited by Aaron Preston, Gregg Ten Elshof, and Steven L. Porter, viii-xi. Routledge, 2018.
Spohn, William C. *Go and Do Likewise: Jesus and Ethics*. Bloomsbury Academic, 2000.
Stassen, Glen Harold. *A Thicker Jesus: Incarnational Discipleship in a Secular Age*. Westminster John Knox, 2012.
Strong, Augustus H. *Systematic Theology*. 8th ed. Judson, 1993.
Taylor, Charles. *A Secular Age*. Harvard University Press, 2007.
Thomas Aquinas. *Summa Theologiae*. Translated by the Fathers of the English Dominican Province. Ave Maria Press, 1948.
Tillman, Micah D. "Dallas Willard: Reviving Realism on the West Coast." In *The Reception of Husserlian Phenomenology in North America*, edited by Michela Beatrice Ferri, 389-407. Springer, 2019.
Trueblood, D. Elton. *The People Called Quakers*. Harper & Row, 1966.
Van Kaam, Adrian. *Fundamental Formation*. Crossroad, 1989.
Volf, Miroslav, and Dorothy C. Bass, eds. *Practicing Theology: Beliefs and Practices in Christian Life*. Eerdmans, 2002.
Volf, Miroslav, and Matthew Croasmun. *For the Life of the World: Theology That Makes a Difference*. Brazos, 2019.
Wacker, Grant. *Augustus H. Strong and the Dilemma of Historical Consciousness*. Mercer University Press, 1985.
Walzer, Michael. *The Revolution of the Saints: A Study in the Origins of Radical Politics*. Harvard University Press, 1965.
Ward, Pete, ed. *Perspectives on Ecclesiology and Ethnography*. Eerdmans, 2012.
Wells, Samuel. *Improvisation: The Drama of Christian Ethics*. Brazos, 2004.
Whitney, Donald S. *Spiritual Disciplines for the Christian Life*. NavPress, 1991.
Wilder, Jim. *Renovated: God, Dallas Willard and the Church That Transforms*. NavPress, 2020.
Williams, Thomas D., and Jan Olof Bengtsson. "Personalism." In *The Stanford Encyclopedia of Philosophy*, edited by Edward N. Zalta, Summer 2022 ed. https://plato.stanford.edu/entries/personalism/.
Wink, Walter. *Naming the Powers*. Fortress, 1984.
Wolterstorff, Nicholas. *Justice: Rights and Wrongs*. Princeton University Press, 2008.
Woodward, JR. *The Scandal of Leadership: Unmasking the Powers of Domination in the Church*. 100 Movements, 2023.
Yoder, John Howard. *Preface to Theology: Christology and Theological Method*. Edited by Stanley Hauerwas and Alex Sider. Brazos, 2002.
Yount, Rick. "The Mind: Discipleship That Forms the Thoughts of Christians—Reflections on Dallas Willard's Thinking on the Mind (Thoughts)." *Christian Education Journal* 16, no. 1 (2019): 51-65.
Zahl, Simeon. *The Holy Spirit and Christian Experience*. Oxford University Press, 2020.

GENERAL INDEX

Abraham, 144
Adam, 49, 156, 165
agapē. *See* love
Agnus Dei, 280-83
Alexander, Donald, 141-42
"already and not yet," God's kingdom as, 53, 56
 Willardian twist on, 53
Anabaptist theology, 66, 205, 207-8
Ananias and Sapphira, 233
Anselm, 179
anthropology, 115-24, 131, 135-38, 194-96
 sanctification presupposes, 109-10
Antony of Egypt, 237
anxiety, 132-33
apologetics, 22, 263
 critique of bully-boy apologists, 263
 ultimate apologetic, 263
apprenticeship to Jesus, 20, 24, 41, 54, 58, 94-95, 159, 163, 213, 217, 236-39, 249-60, 263-66, 271-74, 281-83
 defined, 10-11
 See also church: as school of life; kingdom apprenticeship
Aquinas, Thomas, 19, 24, 66, 72, 93, 98, 111, 125, 144, 148, 179
Aristotle, 93, 98, 111, 114, 125, 136, 174, 200, 260
ascension. *See under* Jesus
ascetic pneumatology, 176-80, 181, 183
 defined, 177-78
 See also habit; Spirit, Holy; spiritual disciplines
asceticism, 174-76, 178
 critique of consuming, 178
Athanasius, 179, 237, 271
atonement, 144-45, 210, 251, 255
 See also soteriology
Augustine, 19, 26, 68, 71-72, 74, 93, 125, 137, 148, 158, 164-65, 179, 205, 207
baptism, 239
 as experiential union with Christ, 164-65
 as immersion into trinitarian presence, 229-30, 275
 water, 230

Baptist
 theology, 141, 158, 211, 228, 230
 Willard as, 14, 228, 230, 247-48
Barth, Karl, 143
Basil of Caesarea, 271
Bebbington's quadrilateral, 248
Bellah, Robert, 242
Benedict of Nursia, 221
Berger, Peter, 197
Berkhof, Hendrik, 223
Berry, Wendell, 223
Bible. *See* Scripture
Black, Gary, Jr., 21, 40, 42, 76-77
blueprint ecclesiologies, 243
body
 of Christ (*see* church)
 hatred of (*see* asceticism: critique of consuming)
 human, 50, 116-17, 121-22, 129-30, 135-36, 166, 173-76, 177-78, 194-96
 mind-body debate, 110-15, 117-19
 plasticity of human, 135, 174-75, 177
Bonhoeffer, Dietrich, 22, 81, 236, 275
 Sanctorum Communio, 233-36
born from above, 128, 143-46, 150, 177
 See also regeneration
Bosch, David, 67, 183, 211
bowels, 169, 173-74
 and squeamish editor, 173
Bright, John, 55, 57
Brooks, David, 270
cactus, hugging the, 79
Calvin, John, 19, 26, 66, 73, 90, 148, 158, 176, 179, 205, 207, 271
Calvinistic theology, 67, 147, 152, 158
Campbell, C. A., 148-49
Cassian, John, 72, 271
Chan, Simon, 140, 180, 244-45
Chandler, Diane, 76, 120
character, 51, 59-60, 148, 175-76, 204, 207, 217
 agapeic, 6, 49, 67-68, 77, 206, 271, 282-84
 crisis of, 2, 268-69, 279
 defined, 9-10, 171
 radiance of good, 262-63, 265

See also spiritual formation; will, human
Christ. *See* Christology; Jesus
Christ, real presence of, 60-61, 93, 240, 252, 258
 See also God: manifest presence of;
 phenomenology: of the Spirit's presence
Christian nationalism, 66-67, 282-83
 as false gospel, 283
Christlikeness. *See* spiritual formation
Christology, 4, 97, 143, 213, 247, 256-60, 265-66
 See also Jesus
church, 19-20, 54, 95-103, 219, 221-22, 227-46, 253-55, 260-66, 267-71, 273-79
 American, 2, 5, 14, 251, 263-65, 267-70, 283
 as continuing incarnation, 61, 235, 245
 as divine sociality, 229-36, 241-43, 245, 261, 274-75, 277
 gospel of churchmanship, 209, 241
 membership, 227, 263-66
 New Testament meanings of, 228
 no salvation outside of, 96, 245
 realism and idealism in vision of, 277
 as school of life, 229, 236-39, 241-43, 245, 260-61, 265, 274-75, 277-78
church fathers, 1, 71-72, 154, 179-80, 271
Clarke, William Newton, 158
Cochran, Robert, Jr., 190, 205-8
colonialism, 192, 277
Comer, John Mark, 184
commonsense hermeneutics. *See under* Scripture
community, 98-100, 184, 214-26, 231-35, 243-44, 252, 276-78, 281, 283-84
 all-inclusive with God at its center, 6, 69-71, 76, 190
 as missing piece in Willard's social architecture, 215-24, 274, 279

General Index

See also church
constructivism, social, 118-20, 126
contemplation. See *via contemplativa* and *via activa*
cruciformity, 128-30, 165-66, 282
Cullman, Oscar, 53, 56
curriculum for Christlikeness, 168-69, 175-76, 181
Dawn, Marva, 223
deism, Bible, 91
demonology, 191, 223-24, 275
depravity. *See* sin
desire
    divine and angelic, 127
    human, 127-28, 131, 137, 181, 267
discipleship. *See* apprenticeship to Jesus
dispensationalism, 211
Dodd, C. H., 55-57
dominion theology, 67-68, 280
Donatist controversy, 268
dualism, 110-15, 117-18, 123, 125
Durant, Will, 212
Eastern Orthodox, 239
ecclesiocentrism, 234, 239-41, 243, 246
    See also church: gospel of churchmanship
ecclesiology. *See* church
eclecticism, intellectual, 14, 21-23
ecumenism, 228, 238-39, 247, 279
Edwards, Jonathan, 8, 19, 48, 74, 92, 125, 249
effort, 2, 140, 144, 146, 149, 150-57, 159-60, 167, 179, 183, 272-74
    See also ascetic pneumatology; grace: relation to human effort
ekklēsia. See church
epistemology, 16, 22, 27-29, 31-32, 38, 41, 78-86, 97-104, 257-60, 272, 284
    epistemological therapy, 97, 100-103
eschatology, 47-48, 51, 53-77, 209, 270-71, 278-79, 283-84
    See also mission: of God in history; reigning with God
eternal life. *See* salvation: as a life
evangelicalism, 159, 244, 257
    history of, 248-52
    Willard's ambiguous relationship with, 247-48
evangelism, 232, 247-56
    conversion, 247, 250-51
    discipleship, 247, 251-52, 255-56, 277
    Willard as evangelist, 14, 22, 32
Eve, 49, 51, 134, 156
evil, structural, 53-54, 60, 190-92, 195-96, 213, 217, 219, 223-24

expert systems of modernity. *See* institutions
faith, 38, 95, 99-100, 102-3, 112, 142, 144-49, 249-51
    confidence that compels, 145
    relation to knowledge, 52, 145-46
faithful presence, 225-26
fasting, as off-the-spot training, 176
fellowship. *See* community
Finney, Charles, 142, 148, 158, 248-49
Forde, Gerhard, 142
Foster, Richard, 3, 16-19
    Celebration of Discipline, 18, 36, 89
Fox, George, 92, 158
Francis of Assisi, 158, 281-82
Franciscans, 280
friendship, divine, 24, 48, 179, 283-84
    See also God: communion with
Friesen, Garry, 35-36, 90
fundamentalism, 29, 210, 250, 256
Giddens, Anthony, 199-200
Gifford, O. P., 158
God
    communion with, 74, 92-93, 96-100, 170, 244
    as Father, 47, 90, 92-93, 100, 129-30, 148-49, 257
    gentleness of, 146-49
    manifest presence of, 232-33, 236, 241, 261, 274-75
    union with, 50, 72-76, 90, 164-65, 182-83
    See also relational sovereignty
Godet, Frederic Louis, 158
godliness. *See* spiritual formation
golden triangle of spiritual transformation, 162, 167-76, 181, 184-85, 273
Gorman, Michael, 183
gospel, 20, 41, 62, 91, 101-2, 163, 193, 212-13, 247, 249-56, 260, 263-67, 276, 284
    false versions. *See* Christian nationalism; church: gospel of churchmanship; gospels of sin management
    gospels on the left and right. *See* gospels of sin management
gospels of sin management, 37, 209-11, 241, 282-83
grace, 142-43, 144-52, 155-56, 163, 171, 180-82, 284
    common, 108, 167, 221
    as empowerment, 108, 141, 151-52, 166-67, 181, 272
    gratuity of, 144-46
    as presence, 144, 148-49, 179

prevenient, 147
    relation to human effort, 2, 140, 150-57, 159-60, 177, 272-74
    special, 107-8, 167
Graham, Billy, 193
Green, T. H., 125
Gregory the Great, 72
Grenz, Stanley, 112, 244-45
Grudem, Wayne, 158
Guder, Darrell, 98, 183
habit, 57, 94-95, 98, 122, 135-36, 166, 171, 173-76, 207, 252
    off-the-spot training, 175-76, 179, 184
    on-the-spot training, 175-76, 184
    See also character; spiritual disciplines; virtue
Hauerwas, Stanley, 93-96, 98-99, 205, 252
heart. *See* spirit: human
Hodge, Archibald Alexander, 158
Holy Spirit, 8, 12, 38, 88, 91-98, 107-8, 140-42, 146-47, 159, 169-84, 221, 249, 272-75, 278, 284
    walk by the/life in the, 51, 73, 85, 93, 129-30, 260, 273
    See also phenomenology: of the Spirit's presence
Hopp, Walter, 78
Howard, Evan, 76
Hudson, Trevor, 192, 217
Hunter, James Davison, 218, 225-26
Husserl, Edmund, 15, 29, 31-32, 81-84, 86-87, 104, 111, 121, 151
Ignatius of Loyola, 47, 92
imago Dei, 48-51, 57, 75
    as creative will, 49-50, 125, 131, 177
    human body as part of, 50, 113, 121
    relation to *imago Christi*, 62
inreach, ministry of. *See* mission: centripetal and centrifugal
institutions, 196-205, 218-19, 223-26, 279
intentionality, 28, 81, 111, 134
Israel, 28, 57-60, 65-66, 150, 163, 229-30, 254, 261
James, William, 81, 125, 127, 133-35, 147-48, 174
Jenson, Robert, 181
Jerome, 281
Jesus, 4, 10-11, 28, 37, 52, 81, 85, 89-97, 118, 150-51, 208-14, 219, 251-62, 266-67, 271, 279-84
    ascension of, 89, 92, 231
    death of, 129, 165, 210-11, 250-51, 257
    as face of God, 257

monothelitism and
    dyothelitism, 129
  naked, 280-83
  resurrection of, 89, 165,
    257-60, 284
  as revolutionist, 190, 205, 209,
    212-14, 278
  as smartest person who has
    ever lived, 4, 38, 41,
    256, 258-60
  spirituality of, 172, 175
  as teacher, 213, 237, 256-60
  See also Christology; mind:
    of Christ
Jones, E. Stanley, 55-57, 158
judges
  book of, 57, 59
  Old Testament system of,
    57-60, 65-68, 209
justice, 58, 65, 189-96, 205-12,
  209-11, 215, 222
justification. See
  atonement; soteriology
Kant, Immanuel, 80, 125, 260
Kierkegaard, Søren, 218
kingdom apprenticeship, 4, 163,
  239, 270-72
  See also apprenticeship to Jesus
kingdom of God, 27, 49-57, 61-63,
  66, 211-12, 251, 265, 283
  availability of, 52, 92, 253-56
  manifestations, 154-55
  ontology of, 52-53, 78, 86
  sources of Willard's theology
    of, 54-57
knowledge, 25-26, 38-39, 41, 78-79,
  82-87, 97-104, 137-39, 145-46,
  239, 251, 272
  loss of moral, 6, 115,
    215-16, 219-22
  moral, 38, 101, 191, 198,
    208-9, 278-79
  ontology of, 78
  spiritual (see
    mysticism, intelligent)
  See also faith: relation
    to knowledge
Kuyper, Abraham, 202
Ladd, George Eldon, 53, 55-57
  as "nuts," 57
law, civil, 205-9
Law, William, 158, 168
laying on of hands, 236, 268
Lewis, C. S., 21-23, 25-26, 158
liberalism, 158, 210, 256
liberation theology, 192-93
Lord's Supper, 233, 239
love, 50, 73-77, 115-16, 124, 137, 191,
  205-9, 237, 255, 275, 282-84
  center of moral reality, 206
  divine, 74-76, 108, 126, 232
  See also character: agapeic

Lovelace, Richard, 268
Luther, Martin, 19, 26, 112, 179, 205,
  207, 249-50, 276
Lutheran theology, 95, 141-42, 152,
  205, 281
MacIntyre, Alasdair, 93-94, 98-99,
  221, 252
manifest presence of God. See
  under God
materialism. See physicalism
Meek, Esther Lightcap, 99, 103
metaphysics, 16, 26-28, 36, 41,
  78-80, 97, 99, 102-4, 111, 120-21,
  177, 194, 232-33
millennialism, 60-65, 193
mind
  of Christ, 93, 169-70, 176
  human, 84, 89, 103, 109-18,
    120-21, 126-27, 131-38,
    145-46, 151, 168-69, 173-77,
    194-96, 225, 259, 273
  See also body:
    mind-body debate
missiology. See mission
mission, 32, 69-77, 97-104, 154-55,
  181-86, 195, 218-19, 247, 274
  centripetal and centrifugal,
    260-61, 266
  of God in history, 6, 69-71,
    76, 190
  missional Christianity, 5, 100,
    182-83, 255
  missional theosis, 183
  relation to spiritual formation,
    2-3, 5-6, 71-77, 184-86,
    252-56, 260-63, 271,
    276-77, 283-84
Moravians, 281
Moses, 57-59, 91, 229-30
monergism, 142, 157, 273
  as God dancing with a
    mannequin, 157
mortification of the flesh.
  See cruciformity
Mulholland, M. Robert, Jr., 76
mysticism, intelligent, 36, 86-93
Navigators, 250
Newbigin, Lesslie, 98, 100-101, 183
Niebuhr, Reinhold, 161-62
nondisciples, 250-51,
  264-66, 267-68
  as mark of contemporary
    church, 20, 267
nudi nudum Christum sequi. See
  Jesus: naked
Oman, John Wood, 148-49
ordinary life events (within the
  golden triangle), 169,
  171-73, 184-85
ordo salutis, 144-45
  See also soteriology
Origen, 71

outreach, ministry of, 251,
  253-54, 262
  See also mission: centripetal
    and centrifugal
parousia. See Second Coming
passivity, spiritual, 95, 142-43,
  150-53, 156-57
pastors, 59, 203, 236, 242-43,
  268-69, 273, 265
  as teachers of the nations, 239
  Willard as pastor, 14-15, 23,
    32, 114
Paul, 28, 51, 54, 73, 76, 83, 97,
  116, 128, 130, 135, 153, 159,
  164-66, 170, 223, 229, 233,
  240, 268
Pelagianism, 2, 149, 152, 156, 182
Pentecost, 230, 259, 284
Pentecostal theology, 53, 141-42
people of God. See church; Israel
perfectionism, 64-65
personalism, 80-81, 86-87, 97, 112,
  148, 190, 194-95, 219-20,
  234-35, 279
phenomenology, 17, 28, 80-84, 97,
  111, 201, 215
  of the Spirit's presence, 91-92
  theological, 140-41, 155-56,
    161-62, 180-83, 236
philosophy, 15-17, 78-86
  Willard's commitments in, 16,
    31-32, 80-86, 97
  See also personalism;
    phenomenology; Scripture:
    reading philosophically
philosophy of mind, 26-28, 111,
  118-19, 134-35
physicalism, 110-11, 113-15
  fictional brain-transplant
    scenario, 118-19
Piper, John, 72
planned discipline to put on new
  bowels. See bowels; spiritual
  disciplines: within the
  golden triangle
Plato, 93, 114, 118, 136, 200, 222
plausibility structure, 99-100,
  197-98, 216, 219, 223, 276
Porter, Steve, 18, 38, 129, 215
postcolonial theology, 49, 280
radiance, principle of. See
  character: radiance of good;
  mission: centripetal
  and centrifugal
rapture, 64
Rauschenbusch, Walter, 209-10
realism
  in moral
    transformation, 161-62
  philosophical, 31-32, 55, 79-81,
    83-84, 97
  sociopolitical, 65

General Index

in the spiritual life, 26, 38, 55, 86-93, 95-104
See also mysticism, intelligent; Scripture: commonsense hermeneutics of
redemption, psychology of, 19, 28, 133, 164
See also soteriology
Reformed theology, 66-67, 72-73, 90, 95, 141, 147, 152-53, 158-60
regeneration, 143-51, 165, 167, 177, 179, 181-82, 249-50
reigning with God, 49-51, 57-60, 65-68, 69-71, 73-77, 180-81, 271, 282-84
future dimension of, 48, 77
training for, 6, 48, 51, 67-68, 76-77, 184, 271, 279-80, 283-84
relational sovereignty, 146-49, 167, 177, 181
resurrection. *See under* Jesus
revivals, of First and Second Awakenings, 249-50
contrasted with twentieth-century crusades, 250
dark side of revivalism, 249
Riesen, Richard, 260
righteousness, 143-44, 159, 166, 205, 208
as rightness with God, 211
works, 2, 18, 182, 273
Robb, Michael Stewart, 19, 22, 35, 52, 84, 257
Roman Catholics, 93
bridging the divide with, 238-39
theology of, 8, 47, 66, 107, 241
Rousseau, Jean-Jacques, 191, 200
Rushdoony, R. J., 67
sacraments, 95, 163, 241
See also baptism; Lord's Supper
Sales, Francis de, 92
salvation
as a life, 35, 41, 143-44, 182, 249, 253-56
tripartite view of, 211-13
See also soteriology
sanctification
gap, 268-70
proper, 157-60
See also spiritual formation
Satan, 134, 191, 224, 240
Scripture, 15, 26-29, 250-51
commonsense hermeneutics, 26-29, 180
conceptual analysis method, 151
historical-critical interpretation, 28-29
reading philosophically, 33
Second Coming, 48, 60-65, 231

secularization, 14, 87, 99-103, 210, 267-68, 276, 283
sin, 50, 53, 57, 126-29, 147, 150, 164-66, 174, 209-11, 234-35, 277
management (*see* gospels of sin management)
Smith, James Bryan, 184
Smith, James K. A., 22, 98, 127, 136-37
social dimension of the person, 80, 117, 122, 126, 135, 194-96, 232-35, 245
societal transformation, 7, 60-61, 64-65, 201, 212-20, 222-26
importance of the professions in, 198, 200-203, 218, 223-24
relation to spiritual formation, 189-96, 203-17, 213-15, 262, 278-79
role of leaders in, 198, 200-203, 218, 223, 278
Sojourners, 210
soteriology, 19, 125-26, 143-52, 164-67, 177, 181-82, 247, 250-56, 265
soul, 14-15, 84, 86, 113-14, 116-24, 126, 136, 142, 195-96
spirit
God as, 111-13, 233
human, 107-8, 110-15, 116-17, 121, 122-24, 138, 146, 149-51
See also will, human
spiritual disciplines, 18, 36, 41, 92, 94, 184, 246
as bodily, 135
habit-forming power of, 132-33, 164, 166, 178-79
as means of grace, 174
most important discipline for pastors, 228
within the golden triangle, 169, 173-76, 184-85
spiritual formation
core theology of, 107-10, 125-38, 140-41, 143-60, 162-83
defined, 8-12, 107-8
as movement, 2, 5, 18-19, 20-21, 23, 71-72
relation to sanctification, 11, 159
as universal experience, 9, 11, 107-8
See also mission: relation to spiritual formation; phenomenology: theological; societal transformation: relation to spiritual formation
Spohn, William, 94
Stassen, Glen, 94, 211
Strong, Augustus Hopkins, 158-59

synergism, 152-57, 160, 177-79, 182-83
Taylor, Charles, 102, 137
teleology. *See* eschatology
Temple, William, 207
Teresa of Ávila, 271
theology, 23-24
clinical, 1, 24-26, 160, 180, 277
of discipleship, 251, 254-55, 271-72
perils when treated as "higher thought," 25-26
as roomy, 180-83
Willard as theologian of the Christian life, 1, 17, 21-23, 24-26, 28-29, 64-65, 160, 183, 193-94, 266, 271-72
theology of the "powers," 223-24
transformation, human. *See* spiritual formation
Trinity, 47, 74-75, 86, 90, 92-93, 100, 229-36, 242, 245, 261, 275, 284
See also baptism: as immersion into trinitarian presence; church: as divine sociality
union with God. *See under* God
vampire Christians, 267
See also nondisciples
via contemplativa and *via activa* 71-72, 74
virtue, 26, 57, 67, 74, 93-99, 107, 144, 179, 206-7, 219, 221-23, 237, 270, 276
ethics, 93-99, 252
See also character; habit; spiritual formation
Vision, Intention, Means (VIM) pattern, 137, 162-68, 177, 181, 273
vocation. *See* mission
Wallis, Jim, 210
Wesley, John, 8, 19, 26, 141-42, 158, 174, 176, 248, 249, 271, 281
Wesleyan theology, 141, 147, 151-52
Westminster Catechism, 47, 74
Whitefield, George, 249
will, human, 51, 125-38, 138, 147-49, 171, 177, 180, 182-83, 272-73
Willardian corpus, 16-17, 30-43
Wink, Walter, 223
Wolterstorff, Nicholas, 189-90
Woolman, John, 67
worship, 25, 72, 126, 175, 184, 275, 278
Wright, Christopher, 183
Wright, N. T., 27, 53, 57
awkward acceptance of award, 23
Yoder, John Howard, 66, 193, 208, 277
Zeitgeist, 198, 215-16, 218, 279

SCRIPTURE INDEX

OLD TESTAMENT

Genesis
1, *49*
1–2, *51*
15:6, *144*

Exodus
18, *58*
18:21, *66*
18:24, *58*

Numbers
11:16-17, *58*

Deuteronomy
1:9-18, *58*

Judges
21:25, *59*

Psalms
16:7-9, *118*
23, *42*
42:5, *114*
46:2, *62*
85:10, *209*
103:1-2, *114*
133, *71*

Jeremiah
29, *277*

NEW TESTAMENT

Matthew
3:2, *92*
4:17, *92*
6:25, *62*
6:33, *211, 279*
13, *264*
16:17, *89*
16:24, *28*
20:25, *208*
20:25-28, *282*
23:25, *212*
24, *63*
24:14, *62*
26:39, *128*
28:18-20, *251, 254*
28:19, *229, 275*
28:20, *92*

Luke
2:26-27, *90*
10:27, *117*
24, *89*

John
1:18, *257*
3:3, *144, 177*
4:34, *130*
8:28, *130*
14:9, *257*
15:15, *284*
17, *228*
17:3, *254*
17:23, *261*

Acts
1, *89*
17:28, *87, 159*

Romans
1, *126*
3:10, *147*
6–7, *164*
6:11, *165*
7:15, *128*
8:14, *93*
8:19, *54*
12:1-2, *135*
12:9-21, *83*
13:14, *170*

1 Corinthians
2:16, *93*
3:9, *155*
6:2, *51*
6:11, *153*
10:2, *229*
11:30, *233*
15:31, *28*

2 Corinthians
3:18, *97*
4:6-7, *240*

Galatians
4:4, *60*
5:24, *28*

Ephesians
2, *146*
2:1-3, *224*
2:19, *102*
2:21-22, *232*
2:22, *231*
4:12, *236*

5:26, *153*
6, *223*

Philippians
2:5, *170*
2:12, *249*
2:15, *261*
4:6-7, *62*

Colossians
1–2, *223*
2:3, *258*

1 Thessalonians
3:2, *155*

1 Timothy
4:7, *73, 166, 284*
5:22, *268*

Hebrews
13:8, *259*

1 Peter
3, *223*

2 Peter
1:4, *73*

Revelation
1:4, *56*
5:10, *51*
21–22, *51*
21:3, *231*
22:2, *76*
22:5, *51*